THE EARLY SESSIONS

Book 9 of The Seth Material

SESSIONS 422-510

7/10/68–1/19/70

THE EARLY SESSIONS

The Early Sessions consist of the first 510 sessions dictated by Seth through Jane Roberts. There are 9 books in *The Early Session* series.

THE PERSONAL SESSIONS

The Personal Sessions, often referred to as "the deleted sessions", are Seth sessions that Jane Roberts and Rob Butts considered to be of a highly personal nature and were therefore kept in separate notebooks from the main body of the Seth material. *The Personal Sessions* are expected to be published in 6 to 9 volumes.

"The great value I see now in the many deleted or private sessions is that they have the potential to help others, just as they helped Jane and me over the years. I feel that it's very important to have these sessions added to Jane's fine creative body of work for all to see." –Rob Butts

THE SETH AUDIO COLLECTION

Rare recordings of Seth speaking through Jane Roberts are available on audiocassette and CD. For a complete description of The Seth Audio Collection, request our free catalogue.. (Further information is supplied at the back of this book.)

For information on expected publication dates and how to order, write to New Awareness Network at the following address and request the latest catalogue. Also, please visit us on the internet at www.sethcenter.com

New Awareness Network Inc.
P.O. BOX 192
Manhasset, N.Y. 11030

www.sethcenter.com

THE EARLY SESSIONS

Book 9 of The Seth Material

SESSIONS 422-510

7/10/68–1/19/70

Published by New Awareness Network Inc.

New Awareness Network Inc.
P.O. Box 192
Manhasset, New York 11030

Opinions and statements on health and medical matters expressed in this book are those of the author and are not necessarily those of or endorsed by the publisher. Those opinions and statements should not be taken as a substitute for consultation with a duly licensed physician.

Cover Design: Michael Goode
Photography: Cover photos by Rich Conz and Robert F. Butts, Sr.
Editorial: Rick Stack
Typography: Raymond Todd, Michael Goode

Library of Congress Cataloging-in-Publication Data

Seth (Spirit)
The early sessions: volume 9 of the seth material / [channeled] by Jane Roberts ; notes by Robert F. Butts.
p. cm.–(A Seth book)
ISBN 0-9652855-9-6
1. Spirit writings. 2. Self–Miscellanea
I. Roberts, Jane 1929–1984. II. Butts, Robert F. III. Title
IV. Series: Seth (Spirit), 1929–1984 Seth book.
Library of Congress Catalog Number: 96-70130

ISBN 0-9652855-9-6
Printed in U.S.A. on acid-free paper

I dedicate The Early Sessions
to my wife, Jane Roberts,
who lived her 55 years
with the greatest creativity
and the most valiant courage.
-Rob

SESSION 422
JULY 10, 1968 9 PM WEDNESDAY

(At 8:45 tonight Jane said that Seth was going to talk about the York Beach apparitions we created at that resort in the summer of 1963, while on vacation there, in Maine. Jane had been writing about the incident this afternoon and I had wondered aloud if Seth could give more data on this. He had also discussed it in the early sessions to some degree.

(Jane began speaking in the usual Seth manner.)

Now, good evening.

("Good evening, Seth.")

You may tell Ruburt he has not lost his bright self, and it has gone nowhere.

(This was in reference to a poem Jane wrote after supper tonight, when she was low in spirits.)

Tell him to remember a poem, *Rapunzel*, that he wrote years ago. He just denied expression to his bright self. This evening's poem did indeed contain, and was in itself, an intuitional inspiration.

It was a welcome to the spontaneous self, expressed creatively. The idea is an excellent one. A poetic statement carries weight for his personality, and this poetic statement has almost magical connotations. As natives do a dance to induce rain, with often excellent results, so Ruburt's poem represents the same sort of incantation.

The act of writing the poem at this time, regardless of the poem's message, you see, represents a willingness to allow the spontaneous self expression. The message itself then doubly reinforces the suggestion. Even the emotion in the first portion, spontaneously expressed and creatively formed into art, is a good indication.

Now, as to your York Beach images. Here aggressive and destructive energies were unconsciously projected outward, given a pseudoreality and a temporary physical validity. There was a protein loss on your own parts.

Such images are constructed of emotional energy, but they also are partially formed from the chemical structure of the individual or individuals behind such productions. The physical body then must work overtime. The impetus is emotional, and the pseudoframework is formed of emotional energy, but the image itself must be built up in part of physical components, and these must come from somewhere.

Now even in the case of hallucinations, the originator uses projections from his own physical structure, which he then perceives. Though the mind, or brain rather, may be seemingly passive in the case of the perceiver, the metabolism is quickened, for the body is using energy at a quickened rate.

The emotional charge provides the pattern, and the impetus for creation, and in the York Beach affair and like situations, it provides for the actual projection or externalization itself. According to the physical validity or the extent of physical reality to be achieved, the physical body of the originator then lends, or transposes or transfers, portions of its own chemical structure. Proteins are used, and there is a high carbohydrate loss on the part of the originator.

Unconsciously, the physical methods at hand are used, then, in such endeavors. It is highly unusual, but possible, according to the strength of the psychic discontent, that the consciousness could then split itself up, some residing in the new image.

Now. Physical illness is not a natural condition. It also necessitates additional work of this same sort, hence often the physical vitamin deficiencies that occur. In many cases they do not cause a disease, but are the result of it. In the same way that the body's proteins and chemical structures can be used to form various kinds of images, they may also be utilized in a lesser fashion to, say, form an ulcer, a goiter, or to affect other changes.

Again, the body is overworking. Here particular emotions are dissociated, denied. The individual does not want to accept them as a portion of himself. Instead of projecting them outward, as you did into such images, they are directed to a specific area in the body; or in other cases allowed to wander, so to speak, traveling troublemakers, through the entire physical system.

Definite energy is needed to sustain them. We will not go into an entire discussion, yet you should be able to see the connection between some kinds of images and ulcers, or other growths.

When the offending emotion is recognized as a part of the self it can then be rather harmlessly dispensed with. It takes its place along with other personality traits. It gains its power and strength only when it is forcibly isolated, for it then cannot merge with the normal ebb and flow of subjective activity.

Good events cannot help it, then, for the personality does not admit it is a portion of itself.

You may take your break and we shall continue.

(9:31. Jane's trance had been a good one, her pace rather fast. Already, she said, she knew what Seth was going to discuss after break. Resume at 9:45.)

The images you saw were of older, weary selves, the lines of frustration and bitterness clearly written in the features, and apparent in the bodies' bearings.

You used your own bodily reserves to produce the images. You faced the bitterness head on, and saw it objectified. You then for the first time, completely accepted it as a portion of yourself. At this point it returned to you, and lost its explosive, isolated importance. It became merely an emotion among others.

It was the beginning in your case, of recovery. Telepathic communication between you and Ruburt was also involved. Ruburt realized that as you changed, so would he. Now, this same sort of deterioration over a longer period of time can occur in the original physical image, when the energy is not projected into more or less independent structure. Do you see?

("Yes.")

Now. Ruburt was correct. He did not want to admit his own strong spontaneous nature. It has not gone anywhere. He need only strongly desire that it return, on his terms, and he will find it.

In his case he made alterations that severely prevented expression of spontaneity, in physical movement. To some extent this was meant to reassure him. When he realizes, and you can help him, that he is indeed safe, only when he trusts his spontaneity, then he will be free.

He is in the process of freeing himself, but the assurances from you can quicken the process considerably. The working schedule will help also, for as he sees the product of his spontaneity, he knows he can trust it. The body worked overtime in quelling spontaneity, and used needed reserves to maintain the symptoms. The same reserves, you see, can be used to construct images. When images of survival personalities appear, they must also utilize such properties.

Always trust motion and change over permanency or rigidity.

("How much is Jane contributing now, physically, to your presence?")

I am not here in a physical materialization of myself. If I were, additional protein and chemical properties would be needed from Ruburt. In our sessions I usually bring additional energy with me, and Ruburt knows how to handle it. If you recall such earlier statements I made concerning the nature of his energy pattern, he is geared to handle high amounts of energy, and to use them.

("Yes.")

That is why it took so much out of him to restrain his own energy. *(Leaning forward, eyes open, humorous manner:)* To force a lid on that pot was a job.

Now. The reason for his unrest yesterday and today is simple. A reaction. He was afraid that his spontaneous self had been swallowed in our sessions. The emotional reaction was rather natural, since our last session touched on some deep points.

The poem was the resolution of the fear however, and a good sign. He does not need to fear the sudden release of the spontaneous self. *(Jane pointed at me for emphasis.)* He knows it is being released. He knows he is releasing it. But he has been afraid of releasing it suddenly, for fear it would engulf him. This is of course a symptom of the entire problem. *(Leans forward.)* It is the main reason he still has symptoms. It is why the few sudden releases, as with the Prentice letter, have in the past been followed by poorer days for a while.

Now we have hit something here, of importance. Give us a moment. *(Pause.)* Free arms, to him, represent abandonment, in the terms of giving into, freely and openly. He has been afraid of letting down completely. Now, he has not been aware of his fear of being suddenly released completely. The conscious knowledge will be of great help.

In all relaxation exercises he should imagine himself as fluid, as wind or water, and not as a statue. Regularity of sessions, our sessions, will help now also. Tonight's material should have a definite and observable beneficial effect upon him.

You can also help by reminding him that his safety does lie in spontaneity, and that joy will result from any complete and sudden release. In the past he did not want to accept his spontaneous nature because he felt he was not sufficiently disciplined or strong enough to control it, and he did not want to accept the responsibility for it.

It is not something to be controlled. It is something that will take its place with the other elements of his personality, merge with it, add its strength, and set up its own system of balances with other groupings of characteristics. These groupings balance themselves. Tell him this. There is no need to treat one characteristic as a stepchild.

Now, you may take a break, end the session, or ask any questions.

("What did Prentice think of your letter?"

(See the 420th Session, The Early Sessions, *Volume 8.)*

At first they were flabbergasted.

("Well, I wonder why?")

Miss Carr was upset. It did not fit under the category of proper business procedure, you see. It made the impression that I intended, however, and you will be hearing shortly. *(We did, in two days.)* You will have business with them for some time. A date, April 18, seems connected here.

I await your pleasure as always. My pleasure lies in the fact this evening that I have done our Ruburt some good.

("While Jane and I were contending with those pseudoimages we had created at York Beach, in that crowded dancing establishment—did others in the room know what was going on?")

They were observed by others. They were hysterical productions born of your own desperation and given instant physical validity. Your unconscious awareness was within them. They had no independent personality consciousness of their own.

("What does the new personality, the larger Seth, think of our time system? He must have experienced many different ones.")

(Smile.) His attention is not directed upon it. It would take me many hours to explain this. Now, if you want me to, I will devote the time... *(Humorously.*

("Well, I'd like to, but...")

You may end the session or take a break.

("We'll take a break then. Can I ask a question?")

(Seth did not answer my question—I believe because I asked it as he began to speak himself.)

A note... Tell Ruburt to think of the comparison between the images and the extra hands added to...

(Here Seth refers to our seance of early 1964, and some physical effects manifested in Jane's hands. Now Jane held up one hand, then pointed to it.

("The knuckles?")

...hand formations. Then, have him simply imagine those extra portions disappearing as the images did.

(10:30. Jane said the trance had been a deep one. Somehow she had felt freer during it, she said. Resume at 10:43.)

We have one further note. Ruburt's spontaneous nature is tolerant, sunny, quite natively good in his terms—qualities that he finds so difficult when he tries to manufacture them while denying spontaneity. I expect now a definite change for the better, and as soon as Ruburt is ready, then we will begin my book.

If you prefer, in any interim, I will use some session time to answer the question you asked this evening.

("I think I would enjoy that, yes.")

That will be our procedure, then. It is not possible *(pause)* to thoroughly understand a time sequence without some participation in the system involved. Portions of the overall Seth entity have participated in your system, as you know.

("Yes.")

Other portions have not. The knowledge is available to all portions of the entity. The knowledge is not as direct or significant however, to those portions that have not so participated.

(Pause.) We had better wait for our next session, for already I am involved with one idea alone that will take some time to explain.

("Too bad, but we'll have to wait.")

One point: the spontaneous self is the healer. Tell Ruburt that. *(Pause.)* I will now then close our session, and leave you, I hope, in anticipation for our next.

("All right.")

I may stay a while this evening—

("Will Jane be aware?")

—and see if I can help Ruburt in some other ways during his sleep. I bid you good evening, however.

("Good night, Seth. It's been very interesting.")

(10:53. Jane had again been in a deep trance, but left it quickly. She was aware of feeling strong energy, she said, as she does when she seems to be inside the voice. Resume briefly at 10:54.)

And have Ruburt read this session every morning for a week, before he begins his workday activities.

("I planned on that.")

(10:55.)

SESSION 423
JULY 17, 1968 9:05 PM WEDNESDAY

(The evening was very hot and humid; it had just rained. We sat for the session just in case. No session was held last Monday because it had been equally hot. Jane was exhausted.

(Jane thought Seth would speak if a session were held, but this did not prove to be the case. However at 8:55 Jane got flashes from Seth that perhaps Seth was educating other personalities on midplanes to contact personalities on our plane.

(Jane also experienced a brief projection just before 9 PM. We plan to go camping at Enfield Glen, near Ithaca, New York, next week. Next, she had an inner flash that "something good, by way of inner experience," would happen to her while up there. She then seemed to project—she felt that she was hovering in the air over the Glen campground, which we know so well, and that she was looking down at the darkening green trees as they would appear at the present time—at about dusk.

(At 8:59 Jane said, "It'll take a few minutes, but I can tell, it's going to be all right," meaning a session would be held. Seth's entity spoke instead, though. Jane sat quite still for some few moments; when I noticed her seeming to grope for words, soundlessly moving her lips, I felt Seth's entity would give the session. The air cooler was on, and the entity's first words were hard to hear—I had to lean close. The voice gradually strengthened however.

(Once again the new personality's voice was high and thin and clear and distant. As usual sentences were often ended on an upbeat. Jane began with eyes closed, many pauses.)

Good evening.

("Good evening.")

The window is clearer and more transparent, and the channels are therefore clearer.

Many elements separate us, but time and space have little to do with the distances between us. Coordinates must intersect, it is true, and yet once such a neutral area is arranged, there must be a lack of friction. *(Many pauses this paragraph.)*

In your terms, friction might be compared to the winds and storms of the physical atmosphere. In our terms however, the friction is emotional in tone. There must be openings through storms of fear, doubts or angers. These are natural to you, but they do not apply to me.

When conditions are good, then, we may take advantage of the proper coordinates. They may be activated and used. They are channels, opening, forming clear access through many camouflage systems. We are not aware of your personal lives in any detail, nor do we completely understand your activities.

We are aware of you in very different terms. We understand your reality and interpret it in ways that you would not understand. We are aware of a change in this contact, that makes our conditions more advantageous.

We consider fear an extremely primitive use of energy, as you might consider fire primitive in comparison to nuclear activity. Fear we understand, however, as a barrier thrown up in panic; and it is of tremendous force *(pause)*, it's intensity having nothing to do... *(pause)*, we are not sure of the word... percentage-wise... with the stimuli that caused it.

These primitive forces are strong, binding you and not us. Ruburt, under such circumstances, cannot travel symbolically from his own atmosphere, though the contacts at our end may be clear. We sense your emanations, and they have changed and are more brilliant.

You become more noticeable. It is not as difficult to find you. *(Long pause, head down. Jane's lips moved over soundless words several times. She sat very still, fingers interlaced in her lap.)*

To understand your time, we would have to enter into it completely, for it has no meaning but for your subjective experience of it. *(Pause.)* We are aware of what it means to you, and that you consider it a part of your identity, as if the self existed somewhere between two points, on a solid line. One point representing a birth, and another a death.

I can obtain a conceptual realization through communicating with other portions of my identity that have experienced it directly. It is a confining experience, in which I myself have not chosen to participate. I have participated in other existences and moment points that you might find confining, but that was challenging to me. *(Smile.)*

You are in a far better position than you have been. Your emanations attract more notice, and therefore more attention and help.

(Pause. Jane sat quite still, eyes closed. Then she nodded several times. Her hands were still clasped. A minute passed.

("All right, Jane?"

(Jane nodded, while I considered calling for a break, since it was now 9:30. Finally Jane opened her eyes and began to come out of trance, which had been deep. She discovered that she had to forcibly pull her hands apart, using considerable effort.

(Jane also experienced the now familiar cone or pyramid effect when the new personality chose to speak. See earlier sessions for descriptions of this. This effect rises above her head, vertically. Jane now described an effect of this evening in which she seemed to experience a horizontal projection, again of a triangular shape.

(This triangle had its point, she said, in back of her eyes, toward the back of her head, and radiated forward and outward. Jane said she had the feeling that "someone" other than Seth looked out through her eyes, not in the way Seth does. Her eyes had opened often during delivery, but I had noticed nothing different. Jane however was quite aware of a subjective difference, other than Seth, but couldn't explain how she knew this.

(Jane said the new personality wasn't as familiar with words as she herself is. Jane said she felt that Seth stood between her and the new personality to act as a translator in both directions. I speculated that Jane had to make more of an effort at translating.

(Jane was still somewhat groggy, she said, but alert. As she waited for the end of break she felt "different," so we thought the new personality would resume. Jane sat upright in the rocker, leaning her head back, eyes closed, hands flat on her thighs. Her lips began to again form words soundlessly, slowly, keeping this effort up for at least two minutes.

(When she did resume the new voice was still high, but not as strong, and used many pauses close together. 9:50.)

In *(pause)* certain *(pause)* activities you join your forces together. You, Joseph, amplify and act as a conductor.

I have been communicating with Seth as you knew him. A clearing, he tells me, has taken place, and you are better able to act together as *(eyes open)* one, almost, in these circumstances.

(Jane's head now began to tip to her left; eyes closed.)

There has been an emotional unity that is very conducive. We are using some energy now, through Ruburt's physical body, activating certain areas that will facilitate recovery.

(Eyes closed, Jane began to slowly rotate her head.)

I do not know how to explain it adequately. Attempting to drain negative qualities and elements from the system so that they may be replaced by positive ones. Activating certain centers and deactivating others.

(Jane's pace was now slow; again her head began to lean, then began a slow rotation.)

This is one reason for the slow verbal communication. We are keeping it up so that you will realize we are still in contact.

Ruburt is aware of a lightening of the hands. Some releases will be taking place in the left collarbone area, as various manipulations are made in the shoulder girdle...

(Leaning forward in her rocker, eyes closed, Jane was now slowly moving her torso and head about. The voice however was growing weaker.)

Manipulations in the left elbow *(pause)*, left knee and ankle...

(I had to ask for a repeat of the last few words. Then:)

We will end the session.

(10:00.

("All right. Thank you very much."

(Jane nodded that she was okay to my questions, but it took her a long time to fully leave trance. I had to keep after her, especially to open her eyes. She had left her glasses on for the delivery.

(Jane was very relaxed indeed. Her arms had fallen heavily over the arms of the rocker before the session ended. Jane said she had something to tell me, but had trouble concentrating. She sat on the divan beside me, and at 10:10 was practically asleep.

(Finally, Jane said that after break the personality couldn't get her voice box going. Jane wasn't afraid of anything being wrong with her throat physically. It was just that the personality had difficulty working the voice mechanism.

(When the personality mentioned Jane's shoulder area, Jane said she felt pain there, but that it was clear now. Jane still felt very relaxed. She said that when her hands were mentioned, she had the feeling they were rising up of their own volition, or that they were capable of doing so. Actually they did not move that I could see.

(Jane again had the cone or pyramid effect after break.

(Note that this is the first time that Seth's larger entity has spoken about personal matters. Jane said she used "they" in talking about Seth and his entity, then said

that perhaps "there are more than the two of them.")

SESSION 424
JULY 29, 1968 9 PM MONDAY

(We were on vacation at Enfield Glen from July 19 to 28, and no sessions were held.

(This afternoon Jane wrote a letter to a spiritual healer, Harry Edwards, in England, but has yet to mail it. She wondered what Seth would say about it. At about 8:30 this evening she got a flash from Seth, commenting on her asking for help in an amused but not sarcastic way.

(At 8:55 as we sat for the session Jane got another flash, concerning time, that it is "intensely personal, that we create it," from Seth. She thought Seth would speak on time this evening, in continuing answer to my question in the 422nd session; concerning the manner in which Seth's larger entity appreciates our time system.

(She began speaking in a rather strong voice, eyes open often, pace faster than usual.)

Good evening.

("Good evening, Seth.")

We will divide our session into two parts.

Now. Time is the pattern of perception. It is highly personal, and has no meaning without personal experience. To you, then, time is the result of your perceiving mechanisms. You know the senses force you to perceive experience in certain pattern. Because I have also followed this particular reality, it is meaningful, for me, and I can understand it.

There are personalities however to whom it is highly alien. It must be interpreted. Using concepts, I can relate my understanding of your time pattern to others clairvoyantly. Other portions of my entity are aware of it, by a process of mental osmosis, so to speak.

Those portions of my entity that have not had physical experience, however, do not operate within that time system, at any time *(smile)*, if you will excuse the pun. It is not beyond them. They simply have not chosen the particular experience, nor delved into that moment point.

Now words belong to your particular time system. Without it, they are not needed. Therefore communication is dependent upon your time system. The inner self however is not so limited, as you know, and inner communications continue always beneath words. Word structures and language itself bears a unique mathematical precision. The placement of emphasis, the vowels and

consonants, the length of time to utter them, all of these issues are intimately connected with your own nervous systems, and with the intervals inherent within your time system, between thought and action.

There are unities, barely contemplated, then, between language, exterior communication, the physical nervous system, and time, or your idea of it. These merge so beautifully that they all serve to form a seemingly perfect picture of physical reality. The camouflage would not be effective were it less perfect. *(Pause.)*

You are beginning to perceive the holes in the camouflage, for I have pointed them out to you. They are doorways into inner realities, and other realities, as are these sessions. Those who have survived physical death in your terms, must use words in their communications, for you do not understand word<u>less</u> communications. They themselves are far freer, however.

We should perhaps differentiate between thoughtwords and speech, or spoken words. Thoughtwords are used by many for some interval. I am speaking of those who have survived death in your terms. They do not need the spoken word. Even thought communication however need not necessarily follow the form of words. There can be thought without words *(smile)*, in other words.

For simplicity's sake, let us say that there is a process of change. Those alive in your terms rely at least outwardly on the spoken word. Those who have left and survive, use thoughtwords but do not need to speak, <u>though they may</u> (underlined). As proficiency grows and as the inner senses are more fully used, the necessity for even thoughtwords vanishes.

Several other methods of communication occur. They do not spring from nowhere. You use them beneath conscious level to some degree now. They grow into prominence. Images are widely used, but these images would be fourth-dimensional to your way of thinking. They are far from flat. They have a reality, and these are, what you have read, referred to as thoughtforms.

Feelings become far more vivid, pulsating and alive, also. You experience these more directly, and yet conversely enough you do not identify with them falsely, as is often the case in your present situation. You can experience feelings more vividly and powerfully because you realize that they are not <u>you</u>, and your identity cannot be swept aside by them.

You have no fear of them. All of this is a progression, I will say for simplicity's sake. Now in such an environment, time as you know it does not exist. This is one of the reasons why some projections are so confusing, particularly when the ego is taken along for the ride. *(Humorously.)* It is used to past, present and future, kept nicely apart.

(Smile.) I am giving you this as preliminary material, for you have asked

how my big brother experiences time. *(See page 5.)* Do you want to take a break?

(It was 9:30. "I'm okay.")

Now then. Part two, and the saga of Ruburt's health.

This does not imply that I am unsympathetic. He correctly but imperfectly recalled a dream during your vacation, in which I was helping him with his health problems.

(This is the first dream including Seth that Jane can remember.)

The following morning his condition was worse than it was during your entire vacation. From then on, however, it improved. He would not have been able to take your mountain jaunts at all, earlier. I was having a heart-to-heart talk with him. I have had others, but this was the first time he barely remembered.

Other intimate improvements have shown themselves, and they are symptoms of increased vitality and release, as spontaneity is allowed for, and returns. The whole condition is better. The change was good.

The letter that Ruburt has written is significant in ways that you have not seen. *(Pause.)* Mr. Edwards admits that he calls upon surviving personalities, healers who have survived death in your terms. In the past Ruburt would not admit, basically, that such survival was a fact, much less ask for help from such quarters.

The letter itself represents therefore an advancement and an act of faith. This is partially the result of our little conversation, of which he has the barest memory. In other words many of those conditions causing the symptoms are beginning to disintegrate.

Before our sessions began, can you imagine him asking for help from such quarters? He did not believe they existed.

Now. Nothing is ever really done alone *(smile),* and nothing is ever done unless it is done alone. I should end the session here, and leave you with that one, but I will explain what I mean.

When you say "I will do this myself," you are speaking with a limited idea of identity. You are more than you know. The you that paints your paintings is far more than the Bob Butts you call yourself, though you are that Bob Butts. There is a matter of terms. Now Ruburt, you may say, has done all the hard work leading to a recovery alone; but he has had help. The recovery itself was utterly dependent upon his belief in it, however. *(Pause.)* This was his primary battle, for he understood finally what the illness represented. Every personality is different. The prerequisites for recovery are therefore different in each case.

In some cases of spiritual healing, belief is not necessary. In Ruburt's case belief and unbelief were part of the problem itself. Belief therefore was necessary, for unbelief of spontaneity, fear of spontaneity, was a basic cause of the difficulty.

The recent and highly significant release in a certain area is a sign of improvement more significant than you realize. The letter should be mailed however. It will lead Ruburt to further contacts, and its results will strengthen certain inner feelings that have and are emerging. *(Long pause.)* If your hand is tired you may take a break.

("Okay.")

(9:50. The trance had been a deep one but Jane emerged easily. During break she still felt partially "under." Resume at 10:01.)

The initial poor reaction the morning following our little chat was simply the result of a temporary fear of letting go. It was of short duration, however. Ruburt did experience a sense of freedom in your hiking activities as a result, that was highly beneficial; and such activities are good for they increase his confidence. Of course, it was more difficult going down the hills—the significance of letting go is more apparent.

(Jane did do very well on our hiking trips. One mountain we climbed from the stream bed to its summit was several hundred feet high, and steep, etc.)

Water itself, natural water, such as the pool, has healing qualities also that he was able to use. The change that he perceives in your apartment is, of course, the result of inner change for the better.

The freedom will also show in our sessions, and rather obviously, within a very brief time. It is already apparent. To become aware of other individuals who are not within your system will be good for him. It will also help him to understand and appreciate my own unique reality, and this now-growing belief should result in a greater familiarity. He should be able to perceive me to some degree before too long.

For all of these reasons I suggest the letter be mailed. The fact of the letter shows that he had reached a certain level of acceptance and understanding. These people can and will help him, and add their mental and psychic energy to his own in a strongly supportive manner. They will be able to activate other layers of his consciousness, and they are indeed professionally suited to do so, as I am to teach.

In his daily life however, as I have told him in the past, the yoga exercises should be continued. He agrees with me but then he lets them slide. They are psychic, spiritual and physical exercises that will let him handle energy more effectively, and release his abilities smoothly. As a part of his daily life they will facilitate the development of his abilities, and therefore help in our sessions.

With this present condition completely banished, proper attitudes and proper use of the yoga exercises will allow him to stay in excellent health. There will be no reoccurrence of symptoms once they are banished, therefore. The yoga exercises simply include rather painlessly, and in one package, techniques that are of greatest benefit in the maintenance of spiritual, mental and physical health.

The healing will show that the causes are eliminated. Other causes must not be allowed to spring up, you see. Proper attention to work and the exercises mentioned will keep the system in balance, and insure continued health.

Spontaneity will rise up during the hours given to work, and outside those hours, but he must continue those habits upon which his well-being depends. The energy that will be released will show itself most beneficially, being directed into your other affairs. Our sessions will now be held with normal regularity, and very shortly I will begin my own book. I have been working on it, you see. *(Amused and confidential.)*

Now I am through with what I intended to say. You may end the session or ask any questions that you have. First give me one moment here. *(Pause.)* This is for you. *(To me.)* We will try to get it clear. Do not use sepia with too heavy a hand.

("Yes." I agreed while thinking this remark over, though I at once thought of a recent instance where this could have happened in a portrait.)

Now I await your pleasure as always.

(On page 6, see my notes in the third paragraph before Session 423.

("About Jane's flash from you before the 423rd session. Does that have to do with her dream about you while we were on vacation? The flash told her something beneficial of an inner nature would happen to her while we were away.")

This had to do with our chat, that he recalls as a dream. It resulted in your mountain-tumbling, which was very important to <u>him</u>. Some rather important changes crystallized, which seems something of a contradiction, as far as his own thoughts were concerned. He hinted at this when he told you that he was concentrating upon recovery.

(Earlier this evening Jane emphatically told me there was a difference in her attitudes now. She was concentrating on recovery instead of on the symptoms.)

The affirmations are of help, and his overall attitude has definitely and significantly changed.

Now, he was able to soak up energy in your natural surroundings, and to use it. Of course, he was ready to do so. The physical activity diverted his conscious mind so that the inner self could progress, without being watched at every moment.

("How about Gene Bernard's letter? What did the people at Prentice-Hall think of that? I mean really?"

(Just before we left on vacation on July 19, we received a copy of a letter from Dr. Bernard that he'd mailed to our publishers at Prentice-Hall.)

They were highly impressed. They did not, however, see through Bernard's real meaning. Van Over did sense it. He has some abilities of his own, incidentally, of which he is not aware. When Ruburt is completely healed his health will be exuberant—not a halfway thing. It is his way. *(Amused.*

("Why the comment on sepia?")

This was given to me. I picked it up during the session, and it is a message to you from your other friend.

(The painter, 14th-century Belgian artist Van Elver, a survival personality whose portrait I have painted. See the 401st, 402nd and 414th sessions among others.)

I hope I received it correctly. I was sure of the color but was not positive as to whether you were using it too heavily or not heavily enough. It was simply meant as friendly advice. Give us a moment.

(Pause.) I do not have our friend directly. This is something like a mental message meant for me. *(Pause.)* There is some reaction with sepia, that can lead to an unpleasantly or undesired purpling effect.

("Yes. I've already noticed that and have worked away from it."

(This effect appeared shortly before vacation, on an experimental head in oil I was working on. Brown was one of the colors used, and could have contributed to the undesirable purplish undertone in the flesh. The effect cropped up before I was aware of it. I cannot be positive the sepia caused the effect without trying some deliberate experiments to see, but certainly it contributed.

(The oil head in question sits in my studio, still unfinished and has been seen by Jane often. One note of interest; technically speaking the oil colors I use contain no color named sepia, specifically, though, of course, a range of earth reds and browns are included. Sepia is a brown. The specific word sepia is more often attached to watercolors, as far as I know, than to oils. Jane also has used both watercolor and oil, as I have; and my watercolors do contain sepia.

(Smile.) Then I did not deliver the message early enough.

("That's all right... I guess that's it for the moment, then.")

Some further here with sepia—to achieve something different now, a sunny clear effect, a newness, a way of applying sepia with white; thin-layered, with a particular kind of varnish... *(Pause.*

("What kind of varnish?")

We seem to have in answer to your question, strong A sounds...

Acqua—but this is not right—Acramont? *(Jane looked at me.*

("No." I shook my head.)

A kind of varnish made near Akron, Ohio.

("Yes."

(Pause.) It has a tendency to bring out the light tones of the sepia over the dark ones. Subdue the brown and bring out the light.

(This would be admirable technique. As far as I know, Jane doesn't think about painting in such terms.

("Do you mean damar varnish?"

(Pause.) I will have to check.

("I can name other kinds of varnish."

(Jane nodded.) Go ahead.

("Mastic?" I paused.)

List them.

("Well, there's damar, mastic, copal, and some of the new synthetic polymer varnishes.")

I believe it is a new synthetic varnish. Is there an acrylic varnish?

("Yes, there are several kinds, made by Permanent Pigments in Cincinnati—")

Ohio. *(Cincinnati is in Ohio.*

("Yes.")

Now we are onto it. Can you name those?

("There's a matte acrylic varnish, and a glossy. Also a picture varnish by Grumbacher that contains some synthetic resin—")

I will have to check with our friend, and he is not at this moment available.

("Okay.")

He will make an artist's helper out of me yet.

("Yes.")

In any case, I hope the information was helpful.

("Yes. I wouldn't think Van Elver would know much about brand new varnishes—or would he?")

We are still having difficulties with the name. He is indeed aware of new techniques, for he looks in on you now and then. *(Pause.)* If you have further questions ask them, or end the session as you prefer.

("I guess we'll have to end it.")

Obviously I was with you occasionally during your vacation. I wish you a hearty good evening.

("Good night, Seth. It's been very interesting."

(10:46. Jane was again in a deep trance. I spoke to her and she came out okay.

She said she felt "like the energy's going through me."

(Incidentally, Seth pronounced sepia as say-pia.)

SESSION 425
JULY 31, 1968 9:05 PM WEDNESDAY

(Jane began speaking as Seth in trance at a rather rapid rate.)

Good evening.

("Good evening, Seth.")

Now Van Over, in answer to your question, was telepathically aware of Bernard's letter, and understood it. He does have abilities. He is aware of them to some degree. However he does not utilize them, and does not realize their import.

(See page 15 of the last session. The info above covers Dr. Gene Bernard's recent letter on our behalf to Prentice-Hall, and Raymond Van Over's telepathic understanding of same.)

Now to return to our discussion. The matter of time is highly important if you have any hopes of understanding the self in its entirety, or other personalities that do not operate within your system. The psychological frameworks are so different. The apparent cause and effect sequence is absent, and identity knows itself as itself through other means than continuity, in your terms.

Your ego gains assurance from what seems to be the memory of its immediate past. A man who loses memory of past events feels insecure and lost, but other types of personality gestalts operate far differently. Instead of a time sequence that governs or seems to govern thought, mental activity of any kind, and overt action, you have associative processes, offshoots, and possibilities. To some extent you can gain an idea of this through an examination of your own stream of consciousness. But the comparison is highly superficial, for here too continuity reigns, even though associations are given greater play.

As we have to some extent mentioned earlier, here we have travel through probable actions, where each conceivable action is experienced. The self allows itself to change while retaining knowledge that it is the self who changes. It develops <u>through</u> the changes. Time can only be measured through experience. It is obvious that other gestalt personalities experience more in an equivalent amount of your time, but this is not the point.

The point is that as something that comes and goes and passes, that brings into existence and destroys, has no such reality outside of your own system. Now your own system includes not only your physical universe as you know it, but also any personalities, living or dead in your terms, who are physically oriented.

The spacious present is much more a vivid reality to those outside of your system. Your time seems marked, individually, by birth and death. When these are known for what they are, when the personality can change form at will, such quote "timing" is meaningless.

So also are all neurobiological structures that depend upon a time system, as for example your own nervous system.

As a personality learns to use its abilities it becomes more aware of complexity, and able to operate as an identity within it. Since I have known your time it is meaningful for me, though it no longer hampers me. I merely understand its reality for you. Other psychological structures have not been initially aware of this peculiar relationship between your physical framework and your time concept.

It is very difficult for them to understand your ideas of past, present and future. Now give us a moment. *(No real pause.)* In other dimensions, or if you prefer at other stages of development, the multidimensional personality is aware of its prime identity, and is also aware simultaneously of personality offshoots that it has sent into many realities, into probable systems, as it pursues all of the probable acts and creations inherent in its nature.

It goes without saying that these are not haphazard developments, and that in pursuing literally infinities of probable actions, the prime identity has definite purposes in mind. These purposes cannot be fully explained here, and I am not aware of all of them.

There is always a creative strain, in which consciousness attempts to express itself, and this has been explained earlier. The fact remains that All That Is is ever straining to be more. In all universes that we know, creativity and expansion are the rules.

All That Is is itself evolving. It is not aware of all of its own purposes, for some of these are ever new. In some respects therefore, there are no cut and dried answers. As far as your own system is concerned, I have told you that the past ever changes, and here we enter the realm of probabilities; for at any point in any man's life, where a decision was made, the other probable alternative actions were also taken.

There is in all of this an order. It is an order that the inner self is to learn. It is intuitively known, but it must be realized. There are personalities far more developed than my own; there are personalities that operate in a context that even I would find extremely alien, but no particle of individuality is ever lost, and no experience.

You will be able to look back on this and other lives, and see them as wholes. You will also be able to see your own performance in probable universes, that coexist with these, and from all of these you will learn as you watch yourself in this variety of roles.

Then you will move on to other systems. Before we take our break, tell Ruburt that I will look in on your Boston friend telepathically, and on another level I will give what help I can. I have, for that matter, already been there once this evening. You may take your break.

(9:34. Jane's trance was a good one, but she came out of it rather easily, while yawning quite a bit. The above paragraph refers to Pat Norelli in Boston; she telephoned Jane earlier this evening.

(During break I wondered aloud if Seth's entity, the larger Seth personality, was listening in on Seth's data, to pick it up effortlessly as it was being given.

(Just before break ended Jane said: "Seth was gone during break, but he just came back; I can feel him. I felt him return. I'll bet he went to Boston." Resume at 9:44.)

Now. Ruburt's dream was a legitimate experience. He has helped Miss Callahan in the past in the same manner, but was not able to recall the experience.

(Jane very recently had an experience while sleeping, in which she was helping Miss Callahan. Miss Callahan, deceased, did not know yet that she was dead, and Jane was explaining the situation to her. Her apartment was next to ours.)

He has also helped others, those with whom he had any emotional contact, when clairvoyantly aware of their situation.

I was indeed at your friend's during your rest period, and I will check in again still later this evening. Give us a moment.

(Pause. Smile.) My big brother does not have to tune in, you see, at the time of the session. The session exists in all time. It is available to him when he wishes the information—and he has, or is, or will *(smile),* take advantage of it, you see.

Now he knows what I know, though some experiences that are uniquely mine, he can never know as I know them. When I know all he knows, then symbolically speaking I will be where he is—but then also symbolically speaking, he will be gone.

From what I have told you it is obvious that there can be memory of the future as well as memory of the past.

It is equally true to say that your deaths from this life are already accomplished, as it is to say that you have not yet been born in this life. Do you follow me?

("Yes.")

This does not mean that experience is a dream, by any means. It simply means that presently you perceive but a small portion of yourself, and in limited terms. I am already, in quotes, "Big Brother," you see.

Now the time sequence, while followed physically by your animals, is psychologically experienced far differently. They are much freer. Your past, present and future does not concern them. They also have memory of the past and future, but always experienced within the context of the present; and this is quite at variance with your own experience.

They also emerge within realities, and can attain consciousness superior, in further developments, than that presently known by man.

Some systems are built entirely along these lines. Always there is the expansion of consciousness, though the lines of these progressions may be quite alien to your own. There are far too many complicated discussions along this particular line, so we will not attempt the matter now, but merely note it as one we will develop in the future.

Now give us a moment. *(Pause.*

(Seth now discusses my dream of July 30, 1968; I described it to Jane before the session.)

The self that stabbed you in the back was the self negatively (underlined) developed in this life's early existence. It tried to stab you in the back, and did so, but you were able to retaliate and to slay your would-be assassin.

Notice however that the knife used could have been a more dangerous, lethal one, for that self did not really want to kill you. It was simply a portion of you, formed by negative inferences, that became an unwitting enemy of the self you had become. When it was slain it gained freedom, for the negative elements were released from their compulsions, and the ritualized behavior that was symbolized by the formal clothing of your dream.

The historical context was simply meant to represent the past in this particular life however, and Ruburt was your ally. The emotional freedom that you have recently shown with Ruburt also results from mastery in larger terms of that conflict. That freedom called for Ruburt's spontaneity even as Ruburt's now-releasing spontaneity helped you in the conflict.

(Now re my dream of July 27, 1968, involving my father and me.)

Ruburt's interpretation of the other dream was correct, and represented intuitional knowledge. You knew this. The emotional warmth sparking now between you is of great therapeutic value physically on Ruburt's part, psychically and spiritually on both of your parts, and even for you supportive in a physical manner. It is also tied up with the fact that you are now beginning to remember your dreams once again.

Now you have also been helping others adjust after the death, but you have not remembered. You should be able to if you make the effort.

Our friend the artist *(Van Elver; see the data last session regarding sepia)* is not available this evening, but if you make the point of reminding me before sessions, I will see that we get more information for you.

You may take a break or end the session as you prefer.

("We'll take the break."

(10:13.)

You incidentally received benefits from your vacation. Simply being out in the air allows for a larger give-and-take between the molecules of the physical system and the atmosphere.

The idleness, if prolonged, is not idleness. Concentration upon physical data takes the conscious mind off for a trip, and it gives the inner self greater freedom to initiate new developments and intuitional creations. These, incidentally, can help you understand the true nature of time. Now take your break.

(10:17 to 10:31.)

We will now indeed end our session. One note: Ruburt now believes that I can influence and help your Boston friend. This gives us added energy with which to work, for I can also use Ruburt's emotional connections with the young woman, and this is to our advantage.

It is not that I could not help earlier, for I have. The conditions simply became more favorable, and with Ruburt's help other channels become available. I can also help Ruburt more as he believes in my ability to do so, though again I have helped him in the past.

We will also have other remarks to make dealing generally with the sort of help I can give, and others like me can give—information to which Ruburt is now more receptive. The emotional warmth between you is of course the sign of rebirth, nourishing, for it will show in all your endeavors.

I now wish you a hearty good evening. I am glad you are back on a regular schedule; and if you do not get your typing done, then I shall see to it that Ruburt assists you. *(Smile.*

("Good night, Seth, and thank you."

(10:35. Jane's trance had been good; she retained little memory of what she had said since first break.)

SESSION 426
AUGUST 5, 1968 9 PM MONDAY

(In line with a policy of trying to keep abreast of topics brought up during sessions, I mentioned to Jane this evening that I would like more data from Van Elver via the "sepia" discussion, begun in the 424th session; and some data about Jane's impressions concerning the dream book when it was at Parker. See The Early Sessions, *Volume 8, pages 329-330, June 29, 1968.*

(Jane said she would like some data on the personality Ignaptha, mentioned by Seth during the session held for Gene Bernard a couple of years ago.

(Jane began speaking at a rapid pace, in her usual manner as Seth.)

Good evening.

("Good evening, Seth.")

Now. Your idea of space and time then is definitely determined by your neurological structure.

The camouflage is so craftily executed and created, of course, by the inner self, that you must of necessity focus your attention in the physical reality which has been created. The psychedelic drugs alter the neurological inner workings, and therefore can give some slight glimpses into other realities.

The realities, of course, exist whether or not you perceive them. Actually "time," in quotes, exists as the pulses leap the nerve ends. It is not a simultaneous procedure. You must then experience lapses. Past, present and future appear highly convincing and logical when there must be a lapse of time between each perceived experience.

There is no such lapse in many other personality structures. Events, many events, are simultaneously perceived. Reactions are also nearly instantaneous in your terms. Growth and challenge is provided not in terms of achievement or development in time, but instead in terms of intensities. Such a personality is able, in your terms, not only to react and appreciate event A, say, in your present time, but also to experience and understand event A in all of its ramifications, and all of its probabilities.

Now that is the challenge and the ideal, and it is met to varying degrees by personalities at various stages of development. Obviously such personalities need far more than the neurological systems with which you are presently equipped. For such systems such experience is literally impossible. Now your neurological system is physical but it is based upon your own inner capabilities as of, quote, "now."

It is a materialization of an inner framework, an inner psychic framework. Many other personality structures do not need a <u>materialized</u> perceptive framework, such as this, but an inner psychic organization is always present. It also represents the personality's present capabilities.

Now your time, your past, present and future, as you conceive of them, would be experienced entirely as present to many of these other personality structures. However your past, present and future would be experienced entirely and completely as past, to still other personality structures.

You may consider past, present and future then as a single-line delineation of experience in your terms, the line however continuing indefinitely. Other personality structures from other dimensions could theoretically then observe it from an infinity of viewpoints. However there is far more than this. The single line is merely the surface thread along which you seem to travel. It is all of you that you perceive, so when you envision other dimensions you are forced to think in terms of observers far above the thread, looking down at it from any given viewpoint.

In actuality, following the image through, and strictly as an analogy, there would also be an infinite number of threads, both above and below your own, all part of one inconceivably miraculous webwork. Yet each thread itself would not be one-dimensional, but of many dimensions, and conceivably (underlined), if you knew how *(Jane pointed at me for emphasis, still speaking rapidly)*, there would be ways of leaping from one thread to the other. You would not therefore be forced to follow any particular thread in a single-line fashion.

Now there are personalities developed enough to do this. And each act of leaping, so to speak, forms a new thread. Now following through with our analogy, imagine yourself A. We will start you off in physical reality at thread A, though you have already traversed many other threads to get where you are. We are merely beginning with thread A since this is your present situation.

Now. Any such self A would, without understanding or shortcuts, development, or even average progression, would travel thread A along the narrow line toward infinity. At some point however thread A would turn into thread B. In the same manner at some point thread B would turn into C and so forth.

At some inconceivable point all of the threads would be in turn traversed. Self A, now on thread A, would not be aware in his present, of the quote "future" selves on the other threads. Only by meeting one of these other selves however can he become aware of the nature of this strange structure through which he is traveling.

There is however a self who has already traveled these routes, of whom these other selves are but part. This self, in dreams and dissociated conditions, communicates with these various quote "ascending" selves. But as the self grows in value fulfillment, he can become aware of these other travelers on other threads, who might seem to him to be future selves.

"Later," in quotes, he learns to become one or the other of those quote "future" selves by leapfrogging, so to speak, from one thread to the other.

Now all of this sounds complicated, but only because we must deal in words. Intuitively, I hope, you will be able to understand it. In the meantime the overall self is forming new threads of activity, you see. The frameworks that it leaves behind can be used by others. *(Pause. As I'd asked earlier.)*

The purpose is, quite simply, being, as opposed to not being. I am telling you what I know, and there is much I do not know. I know that help must be given, one to the other, and that extension and expansion are aids to being.

Now. There is, and this will certainly seem a contradiction in terms, there

is nonbeing. *(Pause. Jane lit a cigarette.)* It is a state, not of nothingness in your terms, but a state in which probabilities and possibilities are known, anticipated, but blocked from all expression.

Dimly, through what you would call a history, hardly remembered, there was such a state. It was a state of agony in which the powers of creativity and existence were known, but the ways to produce them were not known.

This is the lesson that All That Is had to learn, and that could not be taught. This is the agony from which creativity originally was drawn, and its reflection is still seen.

(Our telephone rang, interrupting.)

I was ready for our break.

(9:43. Jane left trance, which had been deep, easily. The call was from Bill Macdonnel in Santa Barbara, California. After she hung up Jane told me that before the session she'd had the feeling we would be interrupted in some way— probably through a visitor; but she hadn't told me beforehand.

(Her pace had been fast through most of the delivery. She resumed in the same way at 9:54.)

All That Is, in your terms, retains memory of that state, and it serves as a constant impetus toward renewed creativity.

Each self, as a part of All That Is, therefore also retains memory of that state. It is for this reason that each portion of All That Is, each most minute consciousness, is endowed with the impetus toward survival, change, development and creativity. It is not enough that All That Is, as a primary consciousness-gestalt, desires further being, but, that every portion of it also carry this determination.

Yet the agony itself was used as a means, and the agony itself served as an impetus, strong enough finally so that All That Is initiated within itself the means to be.

All That Is therefore knows the agony of what you would call not being.

Not being, in other terms, is impossible. It is being without the means of expressing being. Now, every portion of consciousness is imbued with innate knowledge towards the means of expression and creativity. If, and this is impossible, all portions but the most minute last unit of All That Is were destroyed, All That Is could still continue, for within the smallest portion is the innate knowledge of the whole.

All That Is protects itself therefore, and all that it has, and is, and will create.

When I speak of All That Is, you must understand my position within it. All That Is knows no other. This does not mean that there may not be more to know. It does not mean, and here words quite fail us, it does not mean that All That Is, in any terms that we can conceive of, may not be limited. It knows of no other.

It does not know whether or not others like it may exist. It is not aware of them if they do exist. It is constantly searching. It knows that something existed before its own primary dilemma, when it could not express itself.

It is then conceivable that it has itself evolved, in your terms, so long ago that it has forgotten its origin, that it has developed from still another primary which has, in your terms, long since gone its own way. So there are answers that I cannot give you, for they are not anywhere known in the system in which we have our existence.

We do know that within this system, this overall system now, of our All That Is, that creation continues and developments are never still. Therefore we can deduce that on still other levels of which we are unaware, the same is true.

This first state of agonized search for expression may have represented the birth throes of All That Is as we know it. There existed, and clearly, the possibilities of creation as we know it, but the means were not known. Pretend then that you possessed within yourself the knowledge, the sight, of all the world's masterpieces in sculpture and art, that they throbbed and pulsed as realities within you, but that you had no physical apparatus, no knowledge of how to achieve it; that there was neither rock, nor pigment, nor source of any of these, and you ached with the yearning to produce them—and this, on an infinitesimally small scale, will perhaps give you, as an artist, some idea of the agony and the impetus that was felt.

And each self is endowed with the agony and the impetus, for it is a fabric from which All That Is made itself, and all that you know. Perhaps now you can understand why it is so difficult to try to explain matters to you in terms that you can understand.

All That Is loves all that it has created, down to the least, for it realizes the dearness, and the uniqueness of each consciousness which had been wrest *(spelled)* from such a state and at such a price; and it is triumphant and joyful at each new development taken by each consciousness, for this is an added triumph against that first state, and an added security against that first state, and it revels and *(takes)* joy in the slightest creative act of each of its issue.

(Jane was speaking so rapidly here that I could not keep up, and I asked Seth to wait. I missed a word or two, but that's all. It was obvious Jane's trance was a very deep one.)

It, of itself and from that state, has given life to infinities of possibilities. From its agony it found the way to burst forth in freedom, through expression, and in doing so gave existence to individualized consciousness that forever continues the process. Therefore it is rightly jubilant.

These connections between you therefore and All That Is can never be severed, and its awareness is indeed so delicate and focused that its attention is (underlined) directed with a prime creator's love to each consciousness.

I have been sent to help you, and others have been sent through the centuries of your time, for as you develop you also form new dimensions and you will help others. You had better take your break.

(10:20. This proved to be the end of the session. It was by my estimate Jane's deepest trance yet achieved. Her eyes closed, she finally said to me: "I don't know if I'm here or there. I'm so far out... I'm sitting here talking and I can feel it in my toes."

(It was fifteen minutes before she could open her eyes. It was difficult for her to snap loose, though at no time did she exhibit any worry or concern. It seemed to be a long way back for Jane. I suspected her sensitivity to heat and humidity might have contributed to the trance depth; before the session she hadn't felt very active, but still wanted to hold the session.

(Note that no answers to questions mentioned at the start of the session were received, and I did not interrupt. Seth plunged into the material. Jane said she strongly felt the material's content, aside from the words, as she delivered it. She experienced it in other words.

(Twenty minutes after the session ended Jane was standing up, washing her face, etc., but still feeling the aftereffects of the trance. She went to bed and slept deeply in spite of the heat; it remained hot all night.)

SESSION 427
AUGUST 7, 1968 9:00 PM WEDNESDAY

(The evening was again very hot and humid, and Jane had been bothered by such conditions all day; but she wanted to hold the session as usual. Shortly before nine she reported glimmerings from Seth.

(Her pace as Seth was slower than Monday's, but still a good one. Pauses and eyes open, etc.)

Good evening.

("Good evening, Seth.")

Now. Desire, wish and expectation rule all actions, and are the basis for all realities.

Within All That Is, then, the wish, desire and expectation of creativity existed before all other actuality. Some of this discussion is bound to be distorted, because I must explain it to you in terms of time, as you understand it.

So I will speak, for your benefit, of some indescribably distant past, in which these events occurred. The strength and vitality of these desires and expectations, in your terms then, became so insupportable that All That Is was driven to find the means to produce them.

Now when I say there was a state of nonbeing, and yet speak of All That Was, existing simultaneously in that state, I mean *(pause),* that All That Is did exist, itself, obviously in a state of being, but in a state in which it could not find expression for its own being. This was the state of agony of which I spoke. Yet it is doubtful that without this "period" in quotes, of contracted yearning, that All That Is could concentrate its energy sufficiently enough to create the realities that existed in probable suspension within it.

The agony itself and the stupendous desire to create represented its proof of its own reality. The feelings in other words were adequate proof to All That Is that it was. *(Pause.)*

At first, in your terms, all of probable reality existed as nebulous dreams within consciousness of All That Is. Later the unspecified nature of these "dreams," in quotes, grew more particular and vivid. The dreams became recognizable one from the other, until they drew the conscious notice of All That Is. And with curiosity and yearning, All That Is paid more and more attention to his own dreams.

He then purposely gave these more and more detail, and yearned toward this diversity and grew to love that which was not as yet created from himself. He gave consciousness and imagination to individuals while they still were but within his dreams. They also then yearned to be actual, so there was this final breaking-through that was still necessary.

Potential individuals in your terms therefore had consciousness before the beginning, or any beginning, as you know it. They clamored to be released into actuality, and All That Is, in unspeakable sympathy, sought within himself for the means.

In his massive imagination, he understood the cosmic multiplication of consciousness that could not occur within that framework. Actuality was a necessity if these probabilities were to be given birth. He saw then an infinity of probable, conscious individuals, and foresaw all possible developments, but they were locked within him unless he found the means.

This was indeed in your terms a primary cosmic dilemma *(pause),* and one with which he wrestled, until All That He Was was completely involved and enveloped within that cosmic problem.

Now had he not solved it, All That Is in ways that cannot be understood, would have faced insanity, and there would have been literally a reality without reason, and a universe run wild.

The pressure, in one way, came from two sources; from the conscious (underlined) but still probable individual selves who found themselves alive in a God's dream, and from the God who yearned to release them. On the other hand you could say that the pressure existed simply on the part of the God, since the creation existed within his dream. But in these terms such tremendous power resides in such primary pyramid gestalts that even their dreams are endowed with vitality and reality. *(Pause.)*

This then is the dilemma of any primary pyramid gestalt. He creates reality, period. Now. He also recognized within each consciousness massive potential that existed. The means then came to him. He must release the creatures and the probabilities from his dream.

To do so would give them actuality. However it also meant "losing", in quotes, a portion of his own consciousness, for it was within that portion that they were held in bondage. All That Is had to let go. While he thought of these individuals as his creations, he held them as part of himself and refused their actuality.

To let them go was to lose that portion of himself that had created them. Already he could scarcely keep up with the myriad probabilities that began to emerge from each separate consciousness. With love and longing, he let go that portion of himself, and they were free. The psychic energy exploded in a flash of creation.

You may take your break.

(9:43. Jane had again been in a deep trance but emerged in short order. Her

pace had been relatively fast. She resumed at 9:55.)

All That Is therefore "lost," in quotes, a portion (underlined) of itself in that creative endeavor. Yet all individuals remember their source, and now dream of All That Is, as All That Is once dreamed of them. And they yearn toward that immense source, and yet to set it free, to give it actuality through their own creations.

The motivating force is still All That Is, but the individuality is no illusion. Now in this same way do you give freedom to the personality fragments within your own dreams, and for the same reason. And you create for the same reason, and within all of you is the memory of that primal agony—that urge to create and free all probable consciousnesses into actuality.

(Long pause.) This session needs reading many times, for there are implications not at first obvious. *(Pause.)* Now give us a moment.

Your question format is a good one. It is a good idea to read the questions before sessions, and when I have answers I will give them to you.

I have nothing, now, on sepia.

(See the 424th session of July 29, and the discarnate Van Elver's suggestion that I not use sepia—Seth pronounces it say-pia—with too heavy a hand. This was one of the questions I asked tonight before the session.

(Jane held a hand up, signifying waiting.) We need more time. Something seems to be coming through and we are having difficulty pinpointing it. *(From Van Elver?)* A recommendation. Further word shortly from Prentice. A note from Instream, not necessarily to you. *(See Session 215 in Volume 5, for example.)*

It seems some definite change in the present situation, from the status quo, that is, concerning the book. *(Pause.)*

The material on electrical reality should wait.

(Another question asked before the session: Seth's own definition of electrical reality, in connection with the book on the Seth material Jane is now writing.)

The material I am giving you now is an offshoot from the material on time that you requested, that will shortly return to that subject, and the electrical-reality material will follow in there naturally.

When I receive impressions at this level, I am not always certain of their origin. You had better remind me to explain that statement, and add it to your questions.

An impression here, having to do with distance to the west of you, possibly California, a letter or communication—I do not know its relative importance.

On other levels Ruburt is doing well, and should experience more conscious projections on other levels also. There was something he did not catch last night, but he will have an opportunity to do so shortly.

Now, I will try to make contact with him in his astral excursions. He did not want me involved in them in the past, and this automatically made it highly improbable that he would perceive me.

(To me.) You have helped two people who were in school with you. This is in answer to one of your questions. One a short first name beginning with A, or strong A sounds, and a last name having to do with water. Wait. *(Pointing at me.)* You have helped Dave Lake on an astral level, during a recent illness of his. That was the sound and the water. Both of you have helped others you did not know.

(I graduated from high school in Sayre, Pennsylvania, in 1937, and believe Dave Lake did so a year later. He lives now in Waverly, New York, 18 miles from Elmira. We see each other on rare occasions, and once in a while I will hear some news about him through my family or a friend in Sayre, which adjoins Waverly. However, I haven't seen Dave in well over a year, and do not know if he's been sick. Nor have I heard anything concerning him during this time, to the best of my knowledge.)

A turnabout of some kind can be expected, in your mundane affairs. *(Pause.)* I suggest we end the session, though I will be here for some time. Ruburt on other levels has requested that I help him in various endeavors. You should imagine yourself in your studio, working, as you fall to sleep. It will facilitate projection <u>there</u>, for you. My heartiest wishes to you both. The deeper trance state is to offset Ruburt's reaction to heat and to some natural adverse circumstances that do occur atmospherically at this time of the year.

("Can you give me a clue as to the other person I helped, who was in school with me?")

I will give you that information at our next session. Remind me.

("Okay. Good night Seth, and thank you."

(10:23. Jane again had a deep trance but returned from it easily. But strangely, and for the first time after a session, she discovered she couldn't operate her voice. She smiled and several times attempted to answer my questions. Later she said she wasn't worried, that she knew her voice was okay. I suggested she clear her throat, making a noise that way. She did so, the sound being usual. Then she whispered the word "there." When I asked her to repeat what she had said, she spoke the same word again, loudly and rather explosively. Her voice then operated as usual.

(Jane said she thought the other person I had helped astrally, from high-school days, was dead. She said the impressions seemed to come to her from another level, between that of Seth and herself— "sort of on a different radio signal," but she couldn't explain.)

SESSION 428
AUGUST 12, 1968 9:15 PM MONDAY

(At 8:55 PM Jane had the impression of the name, Alice Prentice, as that of the deceased high-school classmate of mine, who was now dead, that I had helped astrally. See page 30. I thought the name Alice familiar, but couldn't help out re Prentice. I may have some high-school material filed away, that can furnish data.

(Jane was full of restless, positive energy this afternoon and evening. I viewed it as a helpful expression, and wondered if it was connected with the letter she had received from Harry Edwards, in England, last Friday, August 9. In the letter Edwards told of a program he had begun, to send healing energy to Jane.

(Jane talked to Don Wollheim of Ace Publications on the phone today, and he requested that she send him her book on dreams. Before the session I showed Jane the list of questions we had compiled from recent sessions.)

Good evening.

("Good evening, Seth.")

Now it is important that you realize that we have used analogies rather freely in our last two sessions, for there was no other way to give you any clear concept of the material I wished to present.

Your physical brains simply cannot handle certain kinds of information. Again, the neurological structure has much to do with this. You are so used to handling certain kinds of concepts, and interpreting them in thus-and-thus a fashion, that the pathways for more complicated data simply do not as yet exist in physical terms.

They would emerge. The neurological structures would create new pathways to accommodate such knowledge when the knowledge itself was sought for. The brain structures of your race therefore grew more complicated as the inner knowledge sought to make itself known to the physical creature.

I am speaking now in terms of evolution. The material in the last two sessions was given to you therefore in terms that you could understand. *(Pause.)* Multidimensional concepts cannot be received, nor interpreted, at this point by the physical brain. The mind and the inner self can become aware of such concepts. Now give us a moment. *(Pause.)*

In answer to one of your questions. The name Alice. A last name like Prince, with an S initial, or like Prentice. One who tries, an apprentice. 1963, Florida, a lung difficulty. Two children, one with a name like Gina *(spelled)*; a relative in Schenectady, New York. Ill in 1963. Died in 1965.

I do not know now to what the following refers exactly: a connection with Miss L. Were you in a class together? With a teacher who was Miss L... *(Pause.)*

Connection with drawing or maps or geography.

("I had a grade-school teacher in Sayre, named Miss Lennon."

(There was no response from Seth to this. Upon reflection, and without checking records, I believe Miss Lennon could have been my teacher in junior high school, or perhaps when I was a freshman.)

The girl went with, or liked, a Tom... Something like Torrid, for the last name. You helped on several occasions after her death.

(None of the above data, outside of the familiarity with the name Alice, meant anything to me. I graduated from high school in Sayre in June 1937, 32 years ago, and have seldom seen any classmates. The class was also a rather large one.

(At break I told Jane I also had a teacher named Miss Prince, but am unsure now of the grade she taught.

(Jane for instance did not know of Miss Lennon or Miss Prince.)

Give me a moment. *(Pause.)* In regard to another question, having to do with the frameworks left behind. Do you recall?

("Yes."

(See page 24, 426th session for August 5. My question: What frameworks, left behind by the traveling self A can be used by others?)

You know that a star may light a dark universe, a dark landscape, and help a wayfarer on his way. It will serve a purpose and be a reality in your time. In a like manner can personality structures be of assistance and be realities to you within your time, although they have long since entered other dimensions.

That is as close as I can come to answering that question. Do you understand what I mean?

("Yes.")

There is one difference of course. The star does not know upon whom its light falls. It is blind to the landscape that it brightens. It cannot see that which it illuminates. In the case of these psychological structures however, because of the multidimensional aspects, there is understanding and purpose. A portion of that kind of personality structure knows well that while its main focus of consciousness has gone into other dimensions, it will nevertheless be perceived by others at any given point.

It allows the light of its personality to shine purposely down those paths from which it has come, in order to help others who will follow; but the light is the light of vitality, and carries with it traces of the personality who lets it shine.

Mentally and emotionally such a personality may even travel down *(Jane made a descending gesture)* to help another. This is a very simplified explanation, for you are not ready to study the reality of multidimensional personality thoroughly. *(Pause.)* As thoughts set up traces and new patterns, new electrical path-

ways in the physical brain, it then becomes easier for the brain to entertain these habitual lines of thought.

It is easier then for similar thoughts to follow. So in a larger sense, as personalities leave your system, as they travel into other dimensions, they also set up electrical pathways, and each personality who does so makes those paths easier for others. Do you see?

("Yes.")

Now because the spacious present exists, in other terms, these selves are actually in all places at one time. As you seem to approach different dimensions however, then you seem to approach a personality who exists at the time of your perception of him.

This would seem to deny the idea of progression, since I tell you that all portions or all guises, or all aspects and all levels, of any given personality exist at once. The immediately conscious selves however do progress in their realization. It is not enough that the inner self knows. The various immediately-conscious portions of personality evolve and change as they recognize these truths.

They come to understand then their basic oneness, while still retaining their own identity, since change is never still. In quotes: "By the time" this realization comes, inner value fulfillment has already created new realities. The answer, as closely as I can approximate it for you, is this: the purpose is being. This is something different than your idea (underlined) of brute survival.

Life and consciousness, without the means to express them, are not meaningless, for life and consciousness have their own purposes; and of these purposes I am not prepared now to tell you.

You may take your break.

(9:56. Jane had been in a good trance but left it easily. Her pace hadn't been as fast as at recent sessions. Resume at 10:12.)

You must realize, again, that nothing is static, psychological activity least of all.

In your state of development you cannot easily understand the meaning of the word "purpose," for to you the term itself implies an eventual rigidity, a goal with an end, a progression, literally, toward a nothingness that it would have to follow once a goal in those terms was achieved.

The word purpose implies limited dimension. Value fulfillment has no such implications, and the purposes of which I have spoken are multidimensional. This is all I will tell you now in that regard.

One aside here: while I am myself as you know me, I am also the other personality that sometimes speaks. This does not mean that what I am as you know me, ends, or is finished, in what he is.

(Humorously.) I am overjoyed to be the self that you know *(smile)*, and I do indeed take pleasure in that existence, and in meeting its responsibilities. *(Pause.)* The other personality *(smile)*, which is also myself, has a warm spot in its heart for me *(stronger, forceful voice)*, though again, he would not put it in those terms. He enjoys his own existence.

Both of us are obviously then portions of a larger self, and manifestations of it, but one does not end in the other, and one's purpose is not to <u>become</u> the other. We all, quite simply, <u>are</u>. Keep this sort of thing in mind when you think in terms of purposes. For the word can distract you, and lead you into narrowing concepts.

You know the individual in approximately 1938, if that is a help. A connection with fox; did she for example live on a Fox Street. An animal like a fox is the connection.

("I graduated from high school in 1937.")

I still have a strong 1938 connection. Give us a moment.

The girl worked in a shoe store in 1938. Your mother, I believe, was aware of this or mentioned it to you at the time. *(Pause.)* The fox is a strong connection here. An address, perhaps 428. This may be a Fox Street, to the outside area of town...

("I think that's possible."

(Jane later told me she felt the street was south of my parents' home in Sayre—and where I had lived while going to high school. I happened to have a street map of Waverly, Sayre and Athens, and checked it before writing this. No Fox Street. The towns adjoin each other: Waverly is in New York, Sayre and Athens in Pennsylvania.)

...and a connection with two elderly people who I believe lived there. Now let us see this through. The girl was twice connected with you, presumably in classes. A smaller brother. A close friend named Cheryl. She married a man with a name like scramble or scrapple. *(Pause.)*

Do you have any questions?

("Do you want to say something about the dream book and the Parker impressions?" See The Early Sessions, *Volume 8, pages 329-330.)*

We will see. First of all, in a dream he saw that the book would be published. The impressions were misplaced. He leaped ahead into the future out of desire for it to occur. In other words the impressions were entirely misplaced in time.

(The impressions were given on June 29. On June 16 and June 23, Jane's notebook shows that she had vague, encouraging dreams about writing and publishing and New York City. The dream book was not mentioned specifically in her notebook.

(On July 5, however, Jane had a very vivid dream in which she saw the dream book published in paperback format.

("How about Ignaptha?"

(This is a word used by Seth in the session held for Gene Bernard a couple of years ago.)

We will not go into that now. It does not fit into the material we are delivering. And it is not important enough to disrupt it.

("What do you think of Jane's letter from Harry Edwards?" Received last Friday, August 9.)

By implication I have more or less given you my feelings on the matter. Clearly, I believe. The affair is legitimate, and Ruburt in the dream state is aware of this.

("Why was Jane so restive and angry this afternoon?")

He has some insight into this. Feelings were to be expressed and directed outward. Problems to be recognized instead of hidden. Where they festered. Assurances were given to him in the dream state that this was satisfactory and recommended.

("Any connection here with the Edwards affair?")

This is to what I refer, about the dream state. This is also connected with his improved sleeping.

("Anything from Van Elver?")

I do not know to what you refer.

(This surprised me. "Van Elver and the use of sepia.")

Van Elver.

(Seth repeated the name, which surprised me again. I believe this is one of the very few times when my question seemed to catch him unprepared, or off guard, or what have you.)

He left a message for you.

(My questions and statements were admittedly brief, and may have been too brief. I have mentioned the discarnate Van Elver in most recent sessions. In the 424th session of July 29, Seth said Van Elver, whose portrait I have recently painted, left a mental message for me; to the effect that I shouldn't use sepia with too heavy a hand.

(The specific reasons were not given, Seth saying he would relay the material to me when next he heard from Van Elver. I have been trying to track down the rest of this data since then, since Seth said to remind him of it.

(I now had the rather distinct feeling that Seth was somewhat annoyed as he gave the following material. Perhaps I have been trying too hard re Van Elver.)

Now. It is a big universe, and we do not travel in the same circles. When I have information for you from him, then I pass it on. Since he seems to keep you in mind sufficiently enough to give the messages, you can presume that he will continue to do so; and when he clearly communicates with me, then I will question him in that regard.

("Okay.")

Our circle of activity is not the same.

Now you may ask further questions, take a break or end the session, as you prefer.

("I guess we'll end it then.")

My heartiest wishes to you both then, and a most fond good evening.

("Good evening, Seth."

(10:43. Jane was in a good trance but left it okay.)

SESSION 429
AUGUST 14, 1968 9:27 PM WEDNESDAY

(Jane and I had a discussion concerning the questions I have compiled to ask Seth, via our new system, before sessions, hence our getting started late. We wondered about how much time to allot to getting answers, etc., versus keeping up with the current theoretical data.)

Good evening.

("Good evening, Seth.")

Now. Give us a moment. *(Pause.)* Do you want an explanation concerning the sepia episode, or do you want, now, some material concerning the entity and time?

("I'd rather have the latter."

(I said this because I feared the sepia explanation might be a lengthy one. See page 35 for material and notes concerning the present status of this question of sepia and Van Elver.)

Suffice it to say, I was <u>not annoyed</u>. (Underlined.)

(Again, see page 35.)

Now. As I have told you, there is duration of a kind. What would correspond, in any case, to your <u>idea</u> of duration within the spacious present; it is a matter of intensities however. Now the entity is in itself composed of such intensities. Simply for the sake of analogy, imagine the image, a humanoid one, of an entity giant-sized, spread out anywhere in your physical universe. And if the image were projected against a midnight sky, within its apparent boundaries then you would see a multitude of planets and stars. Let these represent moment points. On one hand they are a part of the entity, as your cells are a portion of your body. On the other hand the entity's consciousness can travel through these. They are doorways within his own psychological makeup, into experiences.

It is as if you could consciously come to terms with each of your own cells and become aware, in your terms, of their future and their past. This traveling-through obviously changes the nature of the moment points. It is, again, action working within itself. The time element, as you understand it, hardly exists.

Now the image analogy is in some respects distortive, but good enough for our present purposes. For as you think of the matter of your cells as only matter, then it is hard to follow our analogy. But when you realize that your own body cells are much more than physical, contain their own capsule comprehension, then you will see that they could, at least theoretically, operate in such a manner if you could throw your own consciousness into them, and perceive their seemingly alien experience.

The entity and its time are not separate. They are one. Basically time is simply psychological experience, regardless of the lapses between perception or the manner of perception. The entity is its own experience.

Time could be thought of as the tissues of the entity. These would be ever-changing. In our analogy, the projected image would seem to float, including ever-different stars and planets within its boundaries. Your own time structure would be very minute in this picture.

Now the moment points could also represent various personalities belonging to the entity, portions of its own consciousness that it sends upon the journeys of exploration and discovery. It is as if the nuclei of a cell could travel through itself. The boundaries of the entity would be imaginary, taking in as many moment points as the entity felt it could handle. *(Pause.)*

Now. Some personalities can be a part of more than one entity. This is something I do not believe we have discussed before.

("No." Entirely new, and interesting, data.)

The entities, being action, always shift and change. There is nothing arbitrary about their boundaries. The personalities have the same freedom. Like fish, they can swim to other streams. Within them is the knowledge of all their relationships.

Any personality may become an entity on its own. This involves a highly developed knowledge of the use of energy and its intensities. As atoms have a mobility, so do psychological structures in their own way. They move through the value climate of psychological reality as freely as atoms move through your time.

Value fulfillment corresponds to your time in that area.

You may take a break and we will continue.

(9:50. Jane had been in a good trance. Jane now said that she hadn't been sure we could have a session tonight, as a result of our discussion beforehand. Note that the session didn't begin until 9:27. This was not because the discussion had upset her, but because it had fired her up. She must be relaxed to begin a session. Resume at 10:01.)

Now. What I am trying to tell you is that a thought or a feeling, with all its varieties of intensities, is more like time, like the true nature of time, than all of your minutes or hours.

A thought can be intense, then partially fade and grow intense again. *(Pause.)* Its own nature regulates its intensity, rather than any rules inherent in the nature of intensity itself. Some of these concepts are difficult to explain to you. In your terms it would be as if you experienced a future event, then a distant past event, then a moment from the present. You would not understand what was going on, nor see the inner logic within.

There is some slight analogy here in your associative processes, where you might think of a person as you have known him in different periods of time, and hold that idea in your present; but that does little to give you the concept's complexity. This session, for that matter, will have to develop into others, for I have concentrated some material about which you will have many questions when you read it.

You must simply and practically try to divest yourself of all ideas of time as you know it, for this discussion. Basically, what you call time does not exist. I am trying to tell you what does exist instead. The question of time and entities then, you see, cannot be truly answered in the manner in which you asked it.

(See page 5, the 422nd session of July 10, 1968. My original question, which Seth has been discussing ever since, was: "What does the new personality, the larger Seth, think of our time system? He must have experienced many different ones.")

Nontime and entities—now that is another matter. *(Smile.)* For that is what we shall really be discussing.

Now you cannot hold too many thoughts in your head, in quotes "at the same time," and many of your own thoughts escape you consciously. Entities are aware of all of their personalities, and keep track of them far better than you keep track of your own thoughts.

These personalities themselves are constantly developing and changing, as one thought can change into another, or bring forth another. The subjective experience of these personalities, the psychological existence of these personalities *(long pause)*, is composed of *(pause, frown)* dimensions of value fulfillment, as considering your time, hours are composed of moments.

In this case however, the hours as well as the moments would be themselves conscious and alive. I do not know how much you will get from this session. We well have to clear up many points for you, but we have to begin somewhere with various analogies to make a dent.

As a sort of shock treatment, we must almost forcibly rip out your stereotyped ideas of time before we can carry this particular subject matter further.

Give us a moment.

I was not annoyed. I did not want however to become involved with the matter at that time, since you have no idea where it would lead us.

There are times when various circumstances are correct, and when these occur messages from your artist friend *(Van Elver)* come in very strongly, and often suddenly. On occasion the connection is far less than perfect, and there is a strain on his part and mine. So as a rule we automatically wait until our signals are clear.

Now behind that simple explanation, you see, there are many subjects that we have not as yet embarked upon. I did not mean to put off an answer. I was simply not ready to give you a full one.

Now, you may take a break or end the session as you prefer.

("Well, I guess we can end it then.")

You must remember that the word, time, is itself distorted. It projects limitations upon other systems of reality that do not exist. We must use it for our explanations, but nontime comes far closest to the reality.

(Humorously.) No time is my time... Now, I wish you a hearty good evening, and my fondest wishes to you both.

("Good night, Seth."

(10:27.)

SESSION 430
AUGUST 22, 1968 8:41 PM THURSDAY

(The session was witnessed by Emolene Frazer; she is an ESP student in Jane's Thursday night class. This is the regular session usually held Wednesday. It was arranged for a day later so Emolene could attend.

(The weather was very hot, humid and sticky. Often on such occasions Jane doesn't feel much like having a session, being quite sensitive to weather changes. Tonight she not only did feel like a session, but shortly before it told me that she believed the larger Seth personality, the Seth entity as we call it, would speak.

(It seemed this might complicate matters, so I expressed the preference that Seth speak instead. This he proceeded to do, at a good pace and in a voice somewhat stronger than usual.)

Good evening.

("Good evening, Seth.")

Now. You had your choice this evening.

("Yes."

(Pause.) My friend was going to give you his own viewpoint concerning nontime, and the conditions were fairly good. I did not feel however that you or Ruburt particularly wanted that arrangement this evening...

("Probably not.")

...and so you see as always I know your preferences. *(Smile.)*

Now, my welcome to our friend here, and we will for now continue with our discussion. The term, identity, like many other terms, is limited, for you think of identity as being one indivisible unit. Now. Identity is not dependent upon any sort of structure, as you know it.

Psychic identity does not need to set up barriers in order to recognize selfhoods. One personality can therefore be a portion of more than one entity, and still retain its own identity, its own individuality. Various groupings of experience exist. It is your concept of time that highly limits your idea of individuality.

It seems to you that any personality worth its salt must have a series of memories, of events that existed in the past and progressed to a present and a future. Since time does not exist in such a manner, then you must not project your ideas of time upon basic reality.

In the experience of personalities outside of your system, events are not recalled nor held in such a manner. A personality outside of your system does not therefore recall events from so-called previous lives in any serial form. The events are held simultaneously.

The various ego structures therefore exist simultaneously. They are entirely outside of any such framework. They are aware of your perception of time, but it means nothing to them. The various egos of any personality do not think of themselves as having existed one before the other.

Even in reincarnation for example, an ego who experienced a Civil War life is now aware of another ego who may have experienced life in the year three thousand. Within the earthly cycle, such knowledge is not transmitted to the physical brain, but it is always known.

It follows then that I am aware of the other Seth personality, and he of me. Because of your time misconceptions you make serious errors whenever you attempt any predictions into life after death, or life within other systems than your own. It is most difficult for you to conceive of an ego who experiences events not in serial form. When any contact is attempted in so-called mediumistic situations, then it is expected that the survival personality will "remember," in quotes, events as you do; but events no longer exist in that way.

The associative processes determine not only which events have meaning, but also the "order," in quotes. An event happening say in 1948, of great importance to the sitter, may no longer have any meaning to the survival personality.

Are your hands tired?

("No." 9:30.)

Now. If such is the case with personalities so closely allied with your own, then you can perhaps understand how alien your idea of time is to personalities that have never existed within your physical system. They are used to experiencing events not in any time sequence. Instead moment points are experienced fully, developments opening simultaneously, and "events" are recognized as psychic and psychological happenings not necessarily connected with any exterior circumstance.

In some systems therefore exterior camouflage is not needed.

Now you may take your break, and we shall continue.

(9:01. Jane's trance had been a good one but she came out fairly easily. She thought the trance had been deeper than usual to cover many distractions: the weather and new rain, traffic noise, a party going on downstairs, etc.

(The room was hot so the air cooler was turned on, Adding to the possible distractions. However when she resumed at 9:15 Jane's voice, as Seth, easily took on enough volume to override the noise.)

You must understand that in any way your situation, and any that you know of physical reality, is highly artificial. It is the mass creation formed by your inner ideas. The time concept is but one example, and it is responsible for many of your most cherished misconceptions. You must form ideas into physical materialization in order to recognize the force behind the ideas you are learning to use and understand. However such materializations are only necessary at certain levels. The time scheme appears valid only within that framework.

When idea no longer needs physical materialization, then the time concept is useless. Intensity of experience and value fulfillment takes time's place. Developments open, in your terms, at once. Organization of inner events is managed according to the inner interests of the various personalities and the intensities with which any given event is experienced.

In your terms then, a future event would exist before a past event. Do you follow me?

("Yes.")

Therefore you are hampered in your attempt to understand personalities who do not exist within your system, for identity is not therefore structured in any kind of a time sequence, and what you call memory flies out the window.

An entity does not "remember" when a portion of it existed within your system. In its time that portion simply is. The time concept leads then to a limited idea, for you cannot conceive of an identity without memory of the past in your (underlined) terms.

This is also responsible for the fact that it is difficult to understand how one personality, while retaining its individuality, can be a portion of more than one entity, and we will have more to say on that subject as we continue with the time concept.

Now give us a moment. *(Pause.)*

For our friend here *(Jane pointed to Emolene),* an existence in the land called Greece before it had that name. An existence in 14th-century Belgium. *(Pause.)* A life in a Spanish environment, with Spanish speaking people but in South America. This in the 1200's. The personality has often been in a position to work with building, and in their construction, and was instrumental in working out the principles behind the arc *(Jane gestured),* arch, form.

(The 1200 date raises questions. As far as our accepted history goes, there wouldn't have been any Spanish speaking colonies or groups in South America in the 1200's. Latin America was opened up to Spanish settlement in the 1500's, of course, after the voyage of Columbus in 1492...)

Give us a moment. The personality has been a male in four lives, and in each of these there was the building interest, although in one the main work involved irrigation and viaducts.

Then there was a love of detail and planning, and the ability to form in the mind complicated building plans for others to carry out. The personality was often involved then in the flowering period of civilization, when such building was usually carried on. The artistic ability is connected with the detailed drawings done in the past.

Give us a moment. *(Pause.)* There was an impatience however to have the works executed by others, in strict accordance to the original plans. The garden and grounds now about the personality's present home, are replicas of gardens laid out by the same personality in the Spanish era. And again, these gardens surrounded the personality's residence.

At one time the personality's sister was a father to the present personality. Since many of the building plans involved the construction of various kinds of temples, the personality has always been interested in acquiring knowledge concerning the nature of reality. There has been little concern with commerce. There is a need on the present personality's part to understand its own nature, and to use its abilities constructively. The personality has not come to grips with itself truly, but has the inner persistence and intuitiveness to do so.

Now you may take a break or end the session as you prefer.

("We'll take a break."

(9:43. Jane was again in a very good trance, and took a bit to leave it. Emolene Frazer now left, but before she did she described her present home to us in some detail, since Jane and I have not seen it. The grounds surrounding the house are very elaborate, well and profusely decorated, and reaching for several hundred feet from the road in front to the back border of the property as it meets the Chemung River.

(We did not know whether the session was over now, so resumed our places after Emolene left. Seth then came through again at 10:00.)

Now. Understand that you cannot pigeonhole such material as this.

An over-insistence upon sticking to one subject imposes limitations. There is no boundary line between for example experience and time, nor any natural separation. Such artificial ones may make neater paragraphs, Joseph... *(Humorously.*

("Yes?")

...but they limit the intuitional leaps that can be made otherwise. There will be a general overall organization in any case in our material, but let us not treat subject matter like a fence, with everything put into neat categories. Do you have any comment?

("No, I don't believe so. I guess I agree."

(Seth's remarks refer to some of mine made before the session began this evening.)

True organization is not logical in any case.

("Yes.")

To the question, What is time?, the following answer might quite rightly be given:

Time is an apple. Time is no apple. Time *(smile)* is a worm in an apple. Time is a worm not in an apple; and yet such definitions will be absolutely meaningless to most people, for they can only think of time in terms of days or hours, and they do not think of time as experience itself, or quite simply, being.

And yet such definitions are far more near the truth than those that have to do with measurements. There are no measurements of any kind. Reality, of itself, forms an apple. Your perception of the apple enables you to see it piecemeal.

The apple is time. It is an event. It is the so-many-odd days or months that have gone into its production in your terms, or years that have gone into production of the tree. It is as much an event of time as it is an event of space.

Here I am merely using your terms to make the point. There are such natural things as apples, you see. There are no natural things such as minutes or hours. These are concepts imposed upon reality, but this does not make them real in themselves.

An individual, and I am speaking in your terms now, again to make a point: an individual is the 60 or 70-odd years of his earthly existence, as much as he is the 150-odd pounds that he may be.

Now unless you have questions, we will end the session.

("I guess not.")

My last remarks were meant to clear up if possible some of the misconceptions that you have concerning your own time concept. Keep in mind that the concept is only valid within your present circumstances,however.

I now wish you good evening then. My best wishes to you both.

("Good night, Seth."

(10:14. Jane was again well dissociated. The material was delivered rather rapidly throughout the session, except for the Frazer data.)

SESSION 431
AUGUST 26, 1968 9:19 PM MONDAY

(Seth's entity or larger personality spoke for the session. As usual the voice was high and thin, very clear but distant, and with many pauses at times. Once again most of Jane's sentences ended on an upbeat inflection.

(At 9:18 Jane told me she was starting to get the "pyramid feeling." For explanations of this subjective experience see earlier sessions: 411, 412, 413, 419, etc. She said, "I think I'm going to get the other one," meaning Seth's larger personality. The pyramid effect seemed to make her hold her head quite still and even, as though performing a balancing act for the subjective pyramid. I suggested she relax her neck and she did so.

(Eyes closed quite often during the session.)

Good evening.

("Good evening.")

Let us discuss numbers in terms of identities.

This is in connection with the lectures you are being given having to do with time and identity. Though numbers are abstract they can serve our purposes well here. One number, for example 7, can be considered itself as an identity. Now, it may become a portion of other numbers in infinite varieties, and yet it is always itself.

(Pause; one of many.) It may be a portion of many groupings yet still retain itself. Three and four will add to seven, yet three and four are their identities and will always be so in your terms. The numbers on the other side of zero, the minus numbers, represent identity in that time of relative nonbeing. The paradox is that the numbers therefore cannot be conceived of as not being, so the minus sign is used.

The unit of the numbers alone however signifies their existence. Now, mathematics is not nearly understood within your system. A fourth and fifth-dimensional mathematics cannot be initiated from within inside your own system.

It is as if each number represents not only the number itself, not only a unit to be added, subtracted, multiplied or divided, but also as if each number had infinite varieties of intensities that you do not perceive. I am not talking of smaller units within that number, but of the nature of the unit itself.

These multidimensional intensities would be considered as inherent qualities belonging to each number. *(One minute pause.)* They would represent other dimensional realities inherent in the number itself, and since numbers are only symbols they would therefore represent other dimensional realities inherent in the unit for which the number stood.

As one number quite simply can be added to another without denying the validity of either number, nor the individuality of either number, so a different kind of grouping also takes place *(pause),* involving *(pause),* mathematical manipulations of these other intensities that reside within the number units.

(Pause. Very slow delivery.) In no way does this alter the individual character of any unit number. Since we are involved in this discussion I will give you a simple analogy, and please understand that it is an analogy, meant only to simplify the idea.

Pretend then that behind or within but unseen by you, behind or within the number 1, for example, there are an infinite number of other 1's, lined up so to speak behind the one that you see. *(Jane leaned forward, gesturing:)* The one that you see is the self that you see or recognize within your system. The 1's behind are not serial, nor identical, nor duplicates.

They are all however variations, but neither one is patterned upon any other. Each number in our original quote "row" that you see has therefore within it these other individual units.

Behind 1 then imagine the infinite other 1's, literally for the analogy's sake one behind the other. Now this long line of 1's may seem to stretch out indefinitely *(Jane spread her arms wide),* or may seem *(Jane clapped her hands together)* to snap together into one. There is expansion and contraction within this simple number 1 then, within any number or unit.

This sort of expansion and contraction has nothing to do with addition or subtraction, multiplication or division; but it is an inherent quality of all units.

Now imagine number 2 placed beside number 1, number 2 also having behind it infinite variations. These variations incidentally should be thought of in terms of intensities. The intensities are themselves individual. Take the two main numbers, 1 and 2; as they stand beside themselves they become 12, and yet the 1 and 2 remain unchanged.

In the same manner any of the unit intensities behind each number may change position while still remaining itself, and retaining its individuality as a unit. If you use x and y rather than 1 and 2, basically the same is true. Now this analogy applies to identity. You are in a world where you see one particular intensity unit—belonging say to number 1.

You do not perceive the other intensity units to which it belongs. You perceive—in other terms—the 1, say, as a flat line on a flat surface, and are unable to imagine the existence *(pause),* the intensity, within that simple unit number.

(9:54. Without warning Jane stopped speaking; her head fell back against the rocker. The break was abrupt and unannounced. Jane nodded okay to my question, and slowly she came out of trance. "It's always that way," she said. "I'm going along in a straight line, and then boom, it's gone, and I start coming down."

(Jane said she "came down" easily though. She felt the pyramid effect a little during break. She knows nothing about math, and said the personality was pushing her "like mad" to try to get her to do it right. She had an image while speaking of a row of numbers, with others behind each number in the front row. Jane said that each number in the front row was in the middle of an endless row, from left to right. She also felt that the numbers lined up behind could expand and contract and assume various variations and endless combinations. "Things we couldn't conceive of in terms of math."

(Jane had felt the ideas were coming to her so rapidly she couldn't speak fast enough to keep up, whereas actually the delivery had been a slow one for the most part. She was surprised to learn this.

(Resume in the same manner at 10:10.)

I am trying to tell you that numbers are only symbols for your kind of reality.

They are not multidimensional symbols. Your physicists can theorize to a certain point. The blockage occurs because the symbols used to portray reality are themselves limited by the reality that you know. They are like keys that will only fit your own doors. You can open endless doors with them, but only doors within your own system.

For this reason your ideas of time and identity remain limited. Now. Other dimensional realities do appear within your system but you do not recognize them. We can acquaint you with some of these. We can tell you what they appear like within your own reality. *(Long pause.)*

You can learn to experience some of these, and the experience of no-time is a particular facet to which I am referring. The experience itself will automatically to some extent allow you to understand the dimensions of your own identity, but old familiar props will not be available.

One of us will give you directions shortly, and they should be followed when you are ready, without any changes made on your part. You will to some small extent at least experience for yourself what it is like to be a personality outside the context of time as you know it.

This is the best learning process. To tell you this was the purpose of the session. We will now close it.

(10:19. Once again the abrupt ending. Jane slowly came out of a good trance; she patted the top of her head as she did so, several times. "I keep trying to stuff all of myself back inside my head," she said. "Most of me is down here," she said, patting the chair, "waiting for the rest of me. The part down here doesn't know anything about numbers. I don't know whether the data's good or not—but the part up there just goes on giving it..."

(Jane again had images while speaking. She had trouble putting them into words: "Something to do with angled shafts of light. I kept getting: 'throwing your consciousness into angled shafts of light,' it seems."

(The larger Seth voice maintained its high, thin, clear and distant quality throughout.)

SESSION 432
AUGUST 28, 1968 9:20 PM WEDNESDAY

(The immediately preceding pages contain the session for Jane's ESP class of Tuesday, August 20, 1968. This is a very good session, dealing with probabilities, personal consciousness of many kinds, electrical realities, etc. Some of the data on body consciousness has not been presented in just this way by Seth during regular sessions.

(A note added 33 years later: This session will be presented with the eventual publication of the ESP class sessions by New Awareness Network, Inc.)

Good evening.

("Good evening, Seth.")

Now. All of this does not mean that personalities within other systems do not construct their own kind of time structures, but in all of these cases the personalities realize quite well that the structures are adapted for the sake of organization of experience.

They do not suppose any given time system to have any reality of its own. Such systems do not use the consecutive structure of your own however. In much the same manner materializations of a kind may be utilized, but the personalities do not give the materializations any reality outside of themselves. They know the origin of images.

It is rather difficult for those who have not been in your system to understand that you give time and images a reality of their own, as if they existed apart from you. Form does not necessarily presuppose the existence of images. *(Long pause.)* Give us a moment here.

Form is not dependent upon mass. This comes closer to what I am trying to tell you. In your time system the growth of mass seems to be dependent upon continuity of moments. Time has nothing to do with form, however.

The personality who sometimes speaks *(Seth's larger entity)*, can change form at will. He was never imprisoned by believing that one personality existed within one form. To your way of thinking he would change form according to his mood; as he thinks, he is. *(Emphasized.)*

His development began in your terms in such ancient times that for all intents and purposes you could say that in terms of value fulfillment he was so far advanced as to be alien entirely.

Now some personalities from one system aid other personalities within other systems, but highly developed personalities, those in your terms so far advanced, will set for themselves the task of aiding an entire civilization; of assisting the development of a new system, and sometimes initiating the existence of that system.

I have told you that there is much that I do not know, and for practical purposes there is much that is not known. Now you are aiding in the development of those consciousnesses that compose the cells and molecules within your own bodies.

They learn from you almost through a process of osmosis. Dimly through many cycles of such activities, they become aware of the existence of conceptual thought. At the same time they support you. The capsule comprehension within them will evolve more and more toward the direction of conscious endeavor.

Each will itself learn to organize larger portions of energy. It is difficult to put this into words that you will understand. They are incipient and latent personalities. This does not mean however that they will all materialize within your own system, but they do represent in your terms the future inhabitants of your system.

Now it is quite possible for the advanced personalities of which I have spoken to take upon themselves the camouflage of a particular system, enter it, become for, in quotes "a time" dependent upon its rules in order to help those who dwell within it; and this has been done on occasions too countless to mention.

In other cases contact is made through a personality within the system. The personality within the system may or may not know that such contact has been made. Ideas may be inserted in your case through the subconscious while the individual sleeps. When this happens then following your own psychological patterns the ideas would emerge more or less naturally, with little hint of their origin, and, the individual involved could well consider them his own.

The well-advanced personality then is aware of nontime, but can use the time illusions of others and can enter the particular camouflage structures. The nontime principle however operates in such a manner that a personality can only participate in the ways that I have described, in systems with which he has some familiarity because of his own experience.

It would be extremely difficult for our friend, for example, to limit himself to existence within your time schedule. It's illusion is far too apparent to him. He could however send other portions of his entity who were familiar with it.

("Like you?"

(Smile, pause.) I should be used to the slyly inserted questions. They are always perfect. Like me, indeed.

In parentheses: (This is why the father did not go himself, but sent his son, according to the religious story.)

Now you may take a break and we shall continue.

(9:50—10:02.)

Now. There are also those who stay within your system, in your terms, returning again and again in order to help its development.

Such personalities will concentrate their main activities in such a way that they can best affect conceptual thought, and bring about necessary changes. Many large families are representative of this group. They appear and reappear in your histories, always as dominant and significant entities. Here the family represents an entity who has taken upon itself the nurturing of your civilization. Knowing intuitively those changes which must come about in your future, they try to bring them about by appearing in your past; though to them your future and the past are the same they must still work within probabilities, you see, and what they are doing is affecting probabilities within your system. Even your time is basically plastic, though it does not seem so to you.

Such personalities try to affect the feelings and thoughts of a civilization, for these thoughts and feelings will alone bring about events. Personalities may be born within your system and find that it does not challenge them, or it is not to their liking in any case. *(Pause.)* Give us a moment on this. *(Pause.)*

They may leave the system then *(pause),* sometimes as aborted infants, but if they grow through childhood the first time, in your terms, then they must work out their development within the system.

(Eyes closed, Jane paused; she gestured to me to wait.)

You block out the realization of nontime, and accept your ideas of time along with the camouflage structure, for one is dependent upon the other. Once you accept physical matter as you know it, then the time system is indispensable. In those projections still within your system, you are still bound by a time relationship, in that it seems to you that perception operates as usual.

There are some freedoms ever here however, for mobility is not constrained by time. You can travel instantaneously in many projections. Some projections will involve you in nontime, but these are advanced projections and would be chaotic to you unless you were prepared.

In nontime images need not have the seeming permanence of your own. They may or may not appear permanent. Images may change their form, according to the intensities behind them. *(One minute pause.)* You could not now navigate within such an environment. That is you could not knowingly. In some dream states you do enter these environments, but they are meaningless to you upon awakening, for the experience there seems jumbled and without organization.

Time is useful only as a method of organizing perceptions. Perception itself does not require time. Within your system however perception does seem dependent upon it. Using your terms nontime is as plastic as space seems to be. Space can be formed into tables and chairs, mountains and continents, but space is not dependent upon tables or chairs, mountains or continents. Now you may take a break or end the session as you prefer.

("We'll take the break."

(This proved to be the end of the session however, at 10:24. Jane's trance was

good, and she entered and left it easily.)

SESSION 433
SEPTEMBER 2, 1968 9:05 PM MONDAY

(Today Jane received a call from John Pitre of Franklin, Louisiana, concerning John's ill wife Peg; thus there was a chance Seth would talk about Peg, but this did not develop.

(Jane began at a rather slow pace; eyes open, pauses as usual, etc.)

Good evening.

("Good evening, Seth.")

Now. Any time structure is an aid, organizing experience along certain lines. To a large extent it limits perception, and is a protective device. You are learning to handle perception and experience, and time gives it to you in slow and small doses.

The doses become larger. Finally you can sample experience without these limitations. Nontime represents the freedom to do so. You organize experience along your own lines because you have learned now to do so. You do not misuse experience when you have reached that point.

You understand the basic reality of subjective life. You will then still organize experience (underline organize), but you will not need artificial aids such as time to lean upon. You will not need to see thoughts materialized in physical matter, for you will have long since learned that the thoughts and not the matter are the basic reality. You will be able therefore to dispense with many seemingly permanent mass images, but when you form them you will realize why and how.

It is important that you understand that time puts limitations and barriers in the way of perception. This does not mean that each individual at such a stage is isolated, nor that he dwells in some universe of his own, for interactions always exist. *(Long pause.)*

In nontime you perceive at your own rate. You organize experience in your own way. These experiences however will always involve you with others. Indeed you can go far further in such relationships. The relationships between multidimensional personalities is far more complicated than those you know.

Now give us a moment here. *(Pause.)*

Entities, if they prefer, and under various conditions, when they become acquainted with others, may introduce to each other if they so prefer, various portions of their personalities. These various portions will be able to help each other and to aid in development. Take for example entity A and entity B. Self 4 personality of entity A may get along quite nicely with B's self 6. A's self 2 and B's self 2 may not get along well at all, so the entities will shift to those personalities which have the greatest rapport, and use them to establish a relationship.

In nontime these portions of the entity exist quite freely, without any time barriers to separate them. Many such relationships have been established, as indeed I speak with you because we get on so well. *(Amused.)* I am also familiar with your particular system, and found it emotionally satisfying.

Multidimensional personalities can therefore establish contact at various levels. Their relationships involve a trust that yours do not have. They have many areas of agreement open.

Now your physical relationships may or may not have anything to do with personal affiliations after any given existence within your system. There are mothers and fathers that you have forgotten, and children that you do not know. Psychically and subjectively the relationships did not take. You are not burdened with them, nor they with you.

This simply means that you did not spark creative impetus of any kind within each other. *(Pause.)*

Now. *(Pause; emphatic:)* you did not bring forth response from one another. This perhaps is more important. You did not challenge one another. You may have gotten along quite well with each other. Do you see?

("Yes.")

No strong love was generated. If ever a hatred was generated, then the relationship usually continued in one way or another through several existences. It would be worked out, you see.

In almost the same manner some personalities are more remote from the entity than others. They may even move out further into another psychic organization that offers more promising development, or to them a more pleasing psychological climate.

In such instances the entity does not try to hold the personality back. The personality itself may simply pull away, exist by itself. It may become a part of another entity, as it searches for support. It may on the other hand attract, because of its strength, personalities who are searching for support. They may join it in a new formation. This may ultimately turn into another entity.

There are no barriers as far as development and experience are concerned, nor to creativity. A personality then, starting out with one main purpose, may find itself involved in experience that opens new areas, and it may pursue them. In nontime there is full recognition and sometimes use of time systems, but the personality realizes that it dwells in nontime, and it forms a time schedule or system to get where it wants to go in the same way that you would make a road or path.

Sometimes the road or path may be used by others, and sometimes not. Now, many personalities may work together to form a time system, as many men may labor to form a national highway. One personality may also form for his own purposes a time system of his own, as a man might make a path to his own garden.

Sooner or later the man will cease walking merely from his house to his garden, and use other roads or forge new paths. Sooner or later the personality will use or form other time systems in which to achieve developments, but nothing forces him to do so.

Now you may take your break.

(9:39. Jane left trance easily. However it was a good one, she said; Seth was coming through strong, yet she could remember parts of the material concerning multidimensional personalities. Pace generally slow. Resume at 9:53.)

Now. Time then is an aid in one way, and it is used by multidimensional personalities for their own benefit. Use again the analogy of a road. Other dimensional personalities realize that they are perfectly free to leave the road, and that much more exists on all sides.

In your theory of time however you believe yourselves bound to the road, do not realize that you have made it, and are unable to perceive other realities. You have chosen to do this however. Since you are learning and can only handle so many perceptions, you have forgotten that you have created the road. Multidimensional personalities do not need to forget. They are also aware of different such devices formed by others. *(One minute pause; eyes closed.)*

They don particular types of clothing to travel these roads, or they use certain vehicles. They do not believe that they are bound to those vehicles. There are certain time structures that are used by many. Well traveled. There are certain systems of reality that are well traveled. In these to some extent mass perceptions predominate.

There are others, far less numerous, where highly venturesome personalities chose to set up new trails and strike out in new ways. There are ruined time structures as well as ruined physical structures.

There are realities that are used no longer. The purpose for which they were constructed, in your terms, no longer exists. In your terms again there are incipient time structures and realities, probable systems that may or may not become a part of any mass venture.

Time therefore is formed out of and from nontime. *(Long pause.)* Nontime is psychological experience, psychological reality, and time is always at its service. *(Long pause.)* Entities then form the time in which they seem to dwell. *(Long pause.)* Experience itself is always plastic, and again, form is not dependent upon mass. Mass belongs to your camouflage system. Form does not.

Form adopts mass within the physical system, but form is not dependent upon it. Form can exist and does exist without mass and without physical matter. Form, like time, is an aid, an organization of experience. Form is used as time structures may be used, but multidimensional personalities know that they construct form as they may construct various time systems as an aid toward organizing perception.

There are in other words many other kinds of time systems that are constructed, beside the one you know dealing with continuity of moments. The probable systems could be called time systems, only their experience is highly organized in a different fashion, and continual moments do not exist in your terms.

Now, there are some systems that do deal with a serial time unit, but in these the personalities are well aware that the serial time is of their own construction. Certain types of personalities will construct or be attracted to certain time systems. They will find certain patterns of development, particular perceptive mechanisms, that go with it more to their liking.

Now you may take a break or end the session as you prefer.

("We'll take the break.")

(10:16. Jane kept on speaking as Seth.) You could say that various time systems are like games, and there are many of them; and in each one the rules and the goals are different. In your system one of the rules is that you forget you are playing a game in order to concentrate better on the affairs at hand.

(10:17. Jane took her break, then resumed at 10:27.)

The game however is for a purpose. *(Long pause.)*

You cannot apply the rules of your game to the universe however, nor project them in such a manner and expect any valid results. Still, playing the game will sharpen your perceptions and give you certain qualities that will allow you to understand reality once you cease playing the game.

(Humorously:) How you do in the game will affect your score elsewhere, in other words. Time then is superimposed upon nontime, as mass within your system is superimposed upon form. *(Long pause.)*

Now to some extent, to some large extent, time as you know it with its continual moments is a highly specialized illusion, even within your physical system.

(Our cat, Willy, was curled up sleeping in a chair that happened to be in back

of the rocker Jane sat in as she spoke for Seth. At this moment Willy suddenly vaulted from the chair, instantly alert it seemed in a second. I could not see what had bothered him; Jane could not see him but certainly she heard him. Willy prowled about the legs of the chair briefly, then jumped back up in it and once again curled up.

(I mention this incident with the idea that perhaps it helped influence the following data. Willy's actions however hadn't interrupted Seth.)

Your own race is the only one who plays with any facility. Other myriad life forms have nothing to do with it at all. You merely transpose your values upon them. They do not experience time as you do.

This does not mean that they are not advanced enough to understand the reality of your time. They do not share the illusion. Almost all animals, plants, birds, insects, rocks and trees perceive according to intensities. *(Long pause.)* The intensity of an experience is their present; but in many ways that I will not explain to you at this point, their present is of wider duration than yours. This does not necessarily mean that they perceive more of the past and future within their present than you do, for they do not in those (underlined) terms. But in terms of quality and value fulfillment there is greater duration and the "moment," in quotes, is more intensely perceived.

Be reminded here that they are not concerned with moments in your terms. Each experience is highly intense, however. The organism responds to an acute degree. This applies to both birds and rocks, though there is a large scale of difference between the extremes.

Now, unless you have questions we will end the session.

("Do you want to say a few words about the visit this weekend?"

(Meaning the proposed visit here of Tam Mossman and Ray Van Over next Thursday.)

Let us take a short break then, and we shall see what we can do.

(10:45. Jane again came out of trance rather easily, although it had been a good one. I explained that by the question I didn't mean I wanted a host of predictions or gaudy claims; I was merely curious to see what Seth might say concerning the two guests we expected. I thought Jane might benefit from the data. I didn't realize it was so late when I asked the question however, and so told Jane to forget it if she wanted to, and to consider the session over. This developed.

(As we sat talking I asked Jane what she remembered about Willy's strange actions. She had been aware of him acting up, she said, without being upset by it. Jane then began to recite to me some data that "came through" to her, without her appreciating it in Seth's voice, or speaking for Seth. This is what she said, verbatim:

("Our perception of time is limited and we only focus on a fairly small portion of reality. The cat's is even more *limited, but for that reason they experience each event*

with greater vividness. But our next stage is to have a more expanded time value along with the intense perception or reaction the animals have now. We've given up some of that intensity because we've taken on more reality, but next we'll get both more intensity and reality together.")

SESSION 434
SEPTEMBER 6, 1968 8:55 PM FRIDAY

(Tam Mossman, of Prentice-Hall, was a witness. He had arrived yesterday to spend the weekend with us and to discuss the book Jane is doing on the Seth material. At midnight, on September 5th, Jane gave a series of impressions for Tam, speaking as herself; Tam verified the psychological content of most of them. Some of my notes, scribbled at top speed, may be hard to read:)

another experience due (1)
S-A-R-
(12 Midnight) - Sept 5/68.
I see an older white haired woman -
beckoning behind old man - grandmother?
he is waving. He is dead + grandmother thinks
of him strongly as he wasn't gg to live much
longer - heavy woman with white hair -
I feel she is thinking of her strongly as is
gg to join him - or separated in space to
good degree.

1936 - etc with TAM.
Another man - brother of older woman?
Family etc - ? not husband. Tall - slender,
hair is gray - carries a lunch pail - a job etc? -
used old-fashioned metal green pail - beat up -

woman etc. with him— family relationship with
older woman with white hair.

a stupid arrangement in 1942— involving
family— etc. with a move— etc. with older woman.
A etc. with her—

Feature? 2 girls— TAM— twins? much alike—
same size, etc.— height—

(2)

TAM— anything making sense—

TAM— yes— clicks in— describe girls?
possible— can't tell girls' age— far away, so I
place them in future— my interpretation—
coming closer. (P)

I feel older woman in [illegible] (pressure)
influence in family in some way— perhaps their
mother or stepmother.

Not sure— Toledo— (P) puzzled) in 3 years
go together in [illegible]—

With twins— the sky is the limit,

also— we wouldn't have done it if we
thought they hadn't wanted us to? (P)

or— we wouldn't have gone there— unless we
thought they wanted us to— Sounds as if these twins
are doing something because they want them to. Following your
direction.

B-A-R— — or spells bar — or — perhaps the twins
are barred from something they want to do, or TAM
is " " " he wants to do
because of the twins— something that needs to be
[illegible]—

(Separate?) Something in regard to business —
a reprimand — or recommendation — I think
it's " " from a male — a letter?

(3)

perhaps a man about 53 or 63 — if he's 53 he
looks older with glasses & roundish face (P)
& T name Bob — S —
Jim petering out ?
Somebody Tam knew that died in childhood —
don't know how close they were — ...... seems to be a
boy — I don't know — there was dirt in a hole —
grave or had got hurt —
I have a road or street — — then a barrier —
like white posts — low fence — an excavation
& piles of dirt — Jim pulling to hide up around
this excavation pit — not hurt — industrial
area —
POM (N) — take bk.
(I see it clearly but can't tell — e.g.)

(Tam was a little nervous as time for the session approached, and Jane was also. The situation was not without its humorous and friendly aspects, and the session began a few minutes early. Jane began speaking for Seth, in trance, in a voice good but not exceptional. Her eyes opened often; pauses, gestures, etc., as usual.)

Now—

("Good evening, Seth.")

(Humorously:) The suspense is too much for me. I will be an anticlimax, and we cannot have that. Now... Good evening to you.

([Tam:] "Good evening, Seth.")

Give us a moment here. *(Pause.)*

This is an outline. Hopefully it will be filled in at a later date. *(Pause.)*

1204 to 1248... Our friend then a male.... Let me give some other material here first however, in this connection.

A great exuberance and a great need. A desire to communicate, and yet a fear of being swept away. *(Pause.)* An expansiveness that is genuine but a fear, a fear here for the basic integrity of the self, a fear of being swept away, of not being able to hold the self in as if he fears it could bleed outward and leave you.

As a result there are bursts of communication, followed by an urge for secrecy, as if he could lose himself through these communications to others; as if with each word energy escaped from him so that he would want to hold it back in protection.

There is a delightful outer self, and it smiles and nods genially at those it meets, and pirouettes and prances. Underneath however there is a fear of this outer self. The inner self, in your present, has not yet found nor focused its true ability or direction, and so it fears itself a void and therefore often resents the energy of the outer self.

Much energy is indeed being directed outward. Within however there is a core of self-realization now beginning to gain strength, so that the amount of energy used inwardly will soon begin to match that expended outwardly. Too much was going *(Jane gestured for emphasis)* and not enough was coming in. You were getting enough from others. You were able to perceive and understand <u>those</u> connections, but you were not receiving needed communications from other layers of your own personality.

You sensed energy flowing outward and resented its flow, fearing to lose yourself. Now you are learning to utilize, receive and translate new energy from other layers of the self so that you will not feel depleted. *(Pause.)*

Give us a moment. *(Pause.)*

There has been in past existences, in your terms, some experience with what is termed occult knowledge, though it is not <u>my</u> term. The personality has been used to depending upon inner intuitions, and knew it had further abilities to develop now. But there was a laxness within, and a lack of inner concentration that in this life hampered earlier development.

The personality sensed this lack and at the same time was aware of an impetus. There have been three lives as a woman. There have been two previous to this as a male. Running through these existences has been two main lines.

There has been the inner sense of a void to be filled, a fear of identity escaping and running outward—my cup runneth over, and there will be none of me left, you see. On the other hand it has always been natural for the personality to turn outward in an easy manner, and with exuberance, so that in past lives we find two lives strongly devoted to the nurture of others. But in these cases the personality was filled with an inner dread, and to some extent resented those he helped. If he were out helping others, then who will mind the store? He was afraid his stock would be gone.

In two other lives there was instead the development of inner abilities to the exclusion of others, a closing down of the windows and a barring of the doors, and he would not look out and no one dared look in. He would make horrible funny faces at the window of his soul to frighten others away, and yet through all of this the inner abilities did indeed grow. He added to his stock.

He had a tendency to hoard in these two lives. Now however there is the necessity to use those inner developments already worked for, to use them gladly and fully. He has already opened up the door, and he has already begun, but barely begun, to synthesize these inner and outer conditions.

He realizes—and will more so—he realizes that the inner self need not be so heavily guarded, that his identity will not escape from him like a dog who leaves the leash.

(Pause.) Now, you see that I am a friendly chap *(smile)*, indeed an old dog with a long leash. Give us a moment. *(Pause.)*

A mystification. A sense of perplexed wonder. A member of a monastic group *(Jane leaned forward)* who classified and collected various kinds of seeds. Now, this group worked on manuscripts officially, so to speak, but our friend here and several others were bootleg seed finders, believing against generally held theories at the time that many questions concerning nature could be found by examining nature.

They investigated the ideas, folklore and officially-held knowledge concerning botany, and seed reproduction, and began behind the monastery their own forbidden garden. They were trying to discover the secret of heredity within plant life.

Now give us a moment here. *(Long pause, eyes closed.)*

This was near Bordeaux, but by near Bordeaux I mean it was the largest city. Now the order had to do with St. John, and there was a crest either belonging to the order or belonging to our friend's family: a four-tonged fork, with a serpent above the upper portion of the handle in the foreground, and in the background either a castle or a monastery. *(Bordeaux, seaport SW France.)*

The monks were routed out much later from this monastery, in the 1400's—that is, the order itself. This was later than the time when you belonged to it. *(Long pause.)* The name in the order seems to have been Aerofranz Marie *(my phonetic interpretation)*. I believe at that time the members of the order also took names that were derivative of Mary. *(Pause.)*

The efforts on the part of seed life were unappreciated. There was a limp in the left foot that was there always in that existence. At birth the doctor did not grab you too gently, and held you by that heel. The doctor being hardly of the professional caliber, but your mother's 12-year-old niece. Who was at hand did the work at hand.

Now. *(Long pause at 9:36.)* Death *(pause)*, as you engaged in a skirmish. Three villagers were hunting, it seems, on monastery ground. The death was an accident. You yelled out to tell them that they trespassed, and tripped upon a rock. You were knocked unconscious, and the townspeople ran. You came to and wandered through fields at night on a far side of the monastery, and came to what seems to have been a body of water.

You knelt and began to pray, lost your balance. You grabbed hold of an overhanging branch but it gave way, and you were drowned.

Now, I suggest that you all indulge in some social pleasantries, and I shall listen. We will fill in our outline of past events as our time permits.

It is surely a sad sight to think of this poor monk, trying to find his monastery, and prayer only betraying him indeed as he falls into the stream. The results of your experiments however were carried on. They were recovered and indirectly...indirectly...they contributed to certain achievements made at a much later date, in your time.

The later development was also connected with a monk. Now, you may take a break or end the session as you prefer.

("We'll take the break."

(9:45. Jane's trance had been good but she came out rather easily. Tam Mossman said: "Seth was certainly into my imaginative life; also, he has me pegged psychologically." Tam said Seth's data about his inner life was "especially true." He also cited similarities between his doodles and the crest decoration Seth described.

(Jane's pace had been on the slow side through most of the delivery. She'd had some visions, and described them as of the monastery, "or a castle," some such large building of stone or brick. She saw cultivated fields to the back and left of this building. Beyond this were high overgrown fields, she said, with a river or stream beyond that. She also had fleeting glimpses of a monklike figure, seen from the back.

(Resume at l0:06.)

Now. Some time here: continue following the psychic trends.

Use your own psychic abilities, for they will grow as you use them, and you will be able to benefit from developments that have already been made, but that wait while certain adjustments are being made.

Now. Do not use the intellect like a shiny banner to wave from your windows. Instead use your intellect fully. You are playing with your intellect. It is a good one and you like it, but you are still not allowing yourself to use it fully.

You are treating it as a fine and gaudy plaything that belongs to you, and you bring it out when the occasion seems suitable.

You wind it up like a fine toy, but you are careful of the directions in which you let it run. Now I am not saying, and do not mean, that you are narrow-minded in any way I am saying that your intellect is a fine one, but you have allowed yourself to be fascinated by its sparkling quality, and not used it thoroughly as a tool.

On the one hand you are too well in control of it. It delights you but you are like a man with a beautiful wife. He shows her off *(Jane leaned forward for emphasis, eyes open and very dark)*, but he does not really let her work or be herself. So you sit within yourself and say: this is my intellect: it is lovely. We shall watch it play: and you are proud of it. But you do not allow it its full penetrating freedom.

It can do more for you than you are letting it do at this time, for it has depths that you are not using. *(Long pause.)* You allow it freedom in terms of radius. You let it range, but you have not as yet learned to let it go as deeply as it can.

Now by all conventional standards I should say to you: but for such a young man indeed, you have time to learn. *(Smile.)* You will learn, and are learning, but you have dealt also with this problem in different ways in other lives, so it is not so new to you. And because you have abilities both intellectual and intuitional, then also you have the responsibility to use them and understand them well. So your intellect should not be superficially enjoyed, but deeply used.

Now. There are several fields in which you would do well—and acting is one where you would speak as well as write the words, you see. *(Pause.)* You may be appalled, but you would do well as a salesman, connected with public relations and business; that is, some of your abilities would serve you well in these fields.

Give us a moment. *(Pause.)*

If you stay in your present field you can do very well indeed, working up to rather high positions. If such is the case your own writing must then be pursued vigilantly. You would need to protect the time necessary to get it done.

With a few years' further development, and if developments continue smoothly in your own personality, you could also do well as a particular kind of agent, dealing with writers of psychic phenomena, because of your understanding of the subject, and because of the larger knowledge of the business publishing field that you would have by that time.

Your salesman's ability would allow you to convince publishers to buy such material. Your understanding of the subject matter would help you deal with those involved in psychic phenomena, and your humor would protect you from them.

Now. *(Long pause.)* I should say more to make my point clear on this matter of the intellect.

You have it too much under your thumb, on the one hand, if you will excuse my pun. You missed it. *(Humorously. Seth, through Jane, had been watching Tam's expression.)* You are used to your intellect. You take it for granted and therefore do not push it as hard as someone who may be less certain of his intellectual abilities.

It will provide for you an excellent framework when you use it properly. You can make from it safe and sturdy steps to climb upward or downward, and be sure of getting back if you so choose. This will allow you to trust your intuitions more; for you do trust them to a fairly large degree but you will then have two methods, both dependable, both reliable and both of benefit.

One can be used on occasions when the other cannot, so you are doubly well off to have both if you use them both well. Full use of this intellect will also help you avoid the brimming-over feeling.

Now before the session brims over, into other allied matters, I will let you take a break or you may indeed end it if you prefer.

("We'll take the break."

(10:35. Jane's trance had been deeper this time, and she was slower coming out of it. She had spoken most of the time with her eyes closed. She was very relaxed at break, and told us that Seth was keeping her half under so as to make her resumption as Seth easier; she could reach trance depth quicker.

(Again Tam said Seth knew him well psychologically. Tan had questions concerning his father and his girl, Eve and told us he felt he'd had extended psychological connections with both. Eve, he thought, has been pivotal in his life.

(Jane resumed as Seth, in an active, gesturing and smiling way, at 10:56.)

Now. Give us a moment. *(Pause.)*

There were three sisters. They were connected with you in three past lives, and you have met two of them.

In one life the first girl was a niece with a love of music and excellent musical abilities. You did not treat her well. The second girl at that time was a brother of yours, and the third girl whom you have not yet met, was either your mother or your wife—I am not clear on this point.

In the immediately-following life the three were sisters. The second girl, with whom you are now involved, has been four times a male, and in the past involved in business administration of various types and kinds; always as an administrator and one who gave orders.

Unless I am wrong on this time interpretation, you will not meet the third sister until you are approximately 45. Do not hold your breath while you are waiting. There have been connections and interconnections here, then, but I shall not pursue them this evening.

A relationship in this life can continue to develop along those terms, with some degree of success, but the issue is open. There are no reasons from the past that would more or less <u>necessitate</u> the relationship. If the relationship is not carried through, then with the probabilities as I see them now, another strong one will develop close to the end of three years from now, involving a woman with whom you will get along very well, although she was merely a third grand-nephew in the past.

In this case however certain temperamental tendencies would serve to unite you. She would have a highhanded manner, but this again according to the probabilities.

I will not now go into a discussion concerning your father, since there are several matters here, and the relationship was a fairly long one. He was a singer at one time. At another, a man who dealt with moneylending, and who somehow made this into a creative endeavor.

There is an innate love of travel that is not being indulged. There seems to be some preoccupation with speed that I do not understand. *(Pause.)* Either he is preoccupied with getting things started, or has a fear of going too fast, but there is an uneven pace beneath a calm exterior. Something seems to hold him back.

Now. *(Smile.)* I have made my friend Ruburt sit fairly quietly for some time, so out of the goodness of my heart and with consideration, I will now end our session; though I may indeed drop in a word now and then. I do not always speak when I am here. *(To Tam:)* You are doing well.

("Goodnight, Seth."

([Tam:] "Good night Seth, and thank you very much."

(11:16. Jane's trance again was good, and it took her a few minutes to come out of it. Tam again verified the psychological content of the material, concerning all involved. Tam said he did not give us all the reasons for his verification because they were personal; but the data rang true to him.

(Seth did not return this evening.

(Seth did speak briefly the next evening however. He came through for Jane, Tam and me after a small party was over, our guests had left and the three of us were alone. Actually this was at 2 AM on Sunday, September 8. I made no notes at the time. Seth greeted us, gave a few voice effects which were controlled because of the hour and the proximity of other tenants, and expressed his willingness and capabili-

ty to continue until six in the morning. This he could have done easily, but none of us were up to it.)

SESSION 435
SEPTEMBER 11, 1968 WEDNESDAY EVENING

(The regular session was scheduled for this evening, but did not develop. These notes are from those I made Wednesday evening, but cannot be strictly verbatim because of the very nature of the experience. It will be necessary to add very little from memory though, since the notes are quite complete.

(The notes will ramble somewhat; to save time little effort will be made to condense them or make them strictly chronological. They are for future reference mainly. We believe the events described to be quite authentic, but will have to wait for verification with no idea of how long this may take. Too, no verification may ever be obtained. For a similar episode, see the Jerry Kramerick seance, of January 13, 1968, described in the 391st session. [In that instance, the data could be verified at once.]

(At our usual supper hour of 5 PM, I thought I noticed Jane quieter than usual. Jane said she became aware of her mood shortly after the meal. At first I thought she was tired and simply didn't want a session, after the intense weekend we had just spent with Tam Mossman, from Prentice-Hall. As the evening progressed I changed my mind.

(I painted as usual until about 8 PM. As I worked however I was aware that Jane was even quieter; this is always a signal to me that something is up. She said she'd felt strange since supper; now she said she felt that we shouldn't be so subjectively aware, now; but that we should be as our future selves, observing the present scene and our physical bodies as they sat in the living room, from the outside.

(Jane didn't see or hear anything different, yet felt that the kitchen, living room, and the studio seemed different somehow. As we sat in the living room, which was very clean and neat, and well lit now since darkness was falling, Jane said she felt a sort of pyramid or cone effect, directed at me as I sat across the room from her in the rocker.

(At 9:45 she told me to get the Seth notebook, that we might have a session after all. Her subjective feelings were quite intensified. She felt "intensities" now in various parts of the room—notably by the built-in bookcase at the far end of the room from the windows. She thought Seth's entity might be looking us over. Various parts of the room seemed to acquire significance in ways she couldn't explain. Willy, our cat, asleep in a chair near me, wasn't involved. The intensity traveled; now it was located in the blue wine decanter given to us by our friend Pete from San Diego,

California.

(Jane said it was "like following a psychic focus around the room," which I thought an apt phrase. It was a feeling "almost like something could form." Both of us kept looking about. Jane spoke aloud, requesting that if anybody was around they let us see them or become aware of them somehow. She felt suspenseful.

(Jane now also felt sensations or vibrations in a small plaster sculp of a head, given to us by Bill Macdonnel. This head sat on our living room table across the room from the wine decanter. Note that Bill is also in California now—Santa Barbara—quite a distance up the coast from San Diego, where Pete lives. [Pete, at the moment as far as we know, is in the Hawaiian Islands.] Bill and Pete met once at our apartment two years ago.

(The colors in the room by now seemed very brilliant to Jane—pulsating. She didn't necessarily feel Seth around, but could have held a session, she said. The top of her head "felt funny" to her. Now the eyes in the oil head I recently finished of the discarnate artist, Van Elver, seemed alive to her; the portrait hangs on a bookcase wall in our living room. Jane again walked through the apartment. Looking out at the kitchen from the studio, she said the path to the kitchen looked like a "charged pathway" to her.

(She felt strong intensities in the bathroom doorway; felt like she was a ghost, returning to the scene; everything was exceptionally vivid—so dear, so palpitating and alive. In the living room again, standing by the bookcase and looking out the windows, she felt nothing. Standing by the windows and looking into the room however she was once more aware of strong pulsations. Things sounded loud and clear; the quality of the traffic noise reminded her of the strength of color sensations.

(At 10 PM I asked Jane if she could stop the sensations. She said perhaps, then reminded me she had suggested going out earlier—a suggestion I now remembered but hadn't heeded at the time. Sitting on the couch with her back to the windows, Jane said she felt "scary" about going into a trance now. The feelings were still climbing. She said she'd know when they subsided. She felt "slightly" out of her body to her right as she sat there, but nothing drastic.

(This afternoon we'd had a strong thunderstorm. Jane now said that as she worked in the kitchen then she'd been aware of the charged air between the thunderclaps. She felt this way now, and quite light. She again walked through the apartment, and felt the same sensations, but stronger. The bathroom, she now said, was "too much." Everything was too clear. Sitting down on the couch again, she felt like moving to the right out of her body again. I was getting very sleepy as I sat in the rocker making these notes. I yawned and yawned, yet did not feel tired. I'd had a mild tingling sensation a few times. We talked about a projection dream Jane had had this morning. Tam Mossman had been in it. Jane has the dream recorded.

(At l0:15, Jane decided to try giving impressions. I was quite bleary. Jane didn't want to close her eyes, but she did, and waited.

("I don't see anything..." [Pause.] "I have the impression of something far away; coming closer. Just the word 'told,' but I don't know what it means... I also have the impression that somebody could take me over rather completely, if I'd let them, with some rather emotional stuff; that I'd go through something I don't particularly want to, full blast."

("Just forget it, then," I said. By now I was remembering the Jerry Kramerick seance.[See Session 391 in Volume 8 again.]

(Jane continued: "I don't know if this is connected with Bill Macdonnel or not... but somebody's around here, in an out-of-body state, I think. I am sort of seeing things as they do. When I walk through our rooms and stuff. I got the word Maisie, a name... When I said that—I don't see anything—but I got the feeling of a car accident... wanders... not sure if he, Bill, was in an accident with a girl named Maisie."

(Jane was now more positive and had a rising emotion in her voice; eyes closed during all this: "In fact, Maisie is 21... and she's either got two young brothers and sisters, or two very young children." [Pause.] "A drive-in movie... oh Robby ..." Jane's voice rose urgently: "Slam on brakes, slam on brakes!" she yelled.

(She was almost crying. "Easy, hon," I said, hoping the sound would quiet her.

("I don't know," Jane said, then suddenly jumped on the couch and threw up her hands, eyes still closed, in the obvious grip of urgent strong emotion: "I don't know —slam—<u>slam brakes</u>!" Jane cried and yelled out, almost hysterical. I sat beside her, not knowing whether to continue the notes or try to bring her out. My touch on her shoulder helped; her crying subsided but continued as she called to me. I remembered reading that gifted mediums will actually live through experiences; that although obviously under great stress, they are actually safe.

(I thought that a coldblooded attitude, so talked loudly to Jane, and she answered between sobs that she was trying to continue without being overwhelmed. But then another wave of intense emotion swept over her: "Ah, hon... trying to control it ... I get <u>Evelyn</u>! Find Evelyn!" And crying, Jane repeated the name over and over.

(Eyes still closed, face streaked with tears, Jane whispered, "I'm trying to control it..." Her breathing quieted as I talked to her. I thought of shaking her out of trance, but didn't know whether to or not. Jane sat quietly through a long pause, then muttered: "Cracked glass ... windshield. I don't know where I am now. I'm in the driver's seat ... Whoever was on the other side of the car is gone." [Pause.] "It's very quiet ... Maybe nobody find—maybe nobody find us ..." she whispered. Each time I thought she might be coming out of it while quiet, Jane would then go back into the

experience.

(She now began to use a different facial expression. I don't remember seeing it before. She would catch her lower lip between her teeth, fold her upper lip over the lower, and wrinkle up her chin in a peculiar way. I had two impressions; one of an older person, the other of a young and vulnerable girl.

("I'm still in the car," she said, "and it sits on the bank..." Her voice rose toward crying again but controlled this. "People are coming, but it seems like they'll never get here. I don't know."

(Whisper: "I know.... Evelyn. We're gone." The mouth was odd again. "I can't yell. I think—they'll think I'm dead because I can't talk... Bury," Jane shouted, almost crying, "bury! My mother... Mary Benedict." [Later, Jane wondered if she hadn't been shouting the name Barry, a man's name; this was speculation; she wasn't sure.]

("Boston...avenue...Nina," [whispered; mouth odd again] "stolen... picture about the river. Movie..." Jane rubbed her upper left arm, muttering. "My arm hurts." Again Jane jumped on the couch, her mouth odd. She bent forward, eyes closed, and reached down toward the floor. "There's something on the floor of the car... floor hanging out..?" She kicked off her shoes and sat with her legs doubled under. Again she was upset. Her right hand against her cheek, head down, moving about.

("I don't want to [or do] go out ..." she said. "When I do... I can't get more unless I go all the way in."

(Again I said to forget it, let it all go.

("There were two cars," Jane cried out, glasses thrown aside. Mouth odd. "So quiet ... am I dead? Right there... arm's funny." Now she rubbed her lower left arm; she cried out, voice rising almost to a scream: "I was driving. Can't make out—!" Jane burst into tears. "Papa, Papa, Papa..." I spoke to her loudly but it did no good. "I... Papa should know it wasn't my fault. Brakes bad... I can't decipher..."

(There was a pause at 10:47. For the first time Jane's eyes opened. Wide, they stared straight ahead, toward the bookcase. I soon saw that she was not seeing anything in the usual sense; nor did she hear me. Then her eyes closed. "Robby, tell them, whoever they are...they shouldn't be here. It's all right..."

(I did as Jane requested, repeating a few words several times. I saw nothing unusual in the room. At 10:51 Jane gave signs of coming out of the experience. "When I opened my eyes I got scared," she said. "She wasn't supposed to be here."

(Jane thought she had been thinking about a Tam or a Cam, which of course apply to Tam Mossman or Bill Macdonnel. She didn't see either man. Jane thought she <u>was</u> the girl, rather than an observer. She had been driving; someone beside her had been thrown out of the car on the floor. It had been a direct emotional experience for Jane.

(She now said she had kept trying to pull out of the experience after I had asked her to. She stayed around, but backed off— the experience could have been much more intense, Jane said, had she permitted it. But by then she was afraid to probe too deeply for more emotional data.

(It might be noted that Jane does not drive, although ten years ago I gave her a few brief lessons, which means she has sat in the driver's seat of an automobile to that extent. I gave up the lessons quickly though when I learned of her lack of depth perception— one night she drove off a curving road into a field

(Was the girl who was driving, and whom Jane entered or replaced injured? Jane couldn't tell although her arms hurt. Jane couldn't tell whether the girl's eyes were open, and she didn't <u>know</u> if Bill M. was there. Jane said she was Maisie, worried about Evelyn.

(It was then I remembered hearing Tam mention his girl, Eve, over the weekend, for what this is worth. This morning after I left for work, Jane lay down to experiment with psy-time, and had a dream involving Tam Mossman; the location of the dream, and possible out-of-body experience, was in back of our apartment house, though, and not in New York City where Tam and Eve live. Jane had no idea of the location of her experience tonight. It took place at night. Jane had the impression of police cars during the experience but they hadn't reached her yet; although the girl knew the police were near.

(At 11:05 Jane said she was not Evelyn; she remembered calling out for Evelyn. Evelyn was the person "I was so concerned about. She was in the car with me before the accident. I was a woman, but not Evelyn. But I was in the driver's seat. Whoever sat next to me, or was supposed to, was gone—not there—or hurt or thrown free..."

(Jane now recalled that the car's right door was open. Wherever the car was, it was off the road and down a bank, with grass and brush or bushes. Jane said she doesn't know what streets are like in the city [although she was in New York City last year with me]—if the road in the experience was a superhighway in the city, there was still the slope, not level, going down from the road.

(Jane was not sure if her experience was contemporary. She never saw another car. She didn't feel the collision. When she yelled out about the brakes she was terrified; she thinks she got scared at this point and pulled back. I told her, several times, not to go back into the experience as I asked questions. I also repeated that I'd not ask any questions if she so chose. Each time we discussed this point, it seemed to lead automatically to more questions, and so the interview after the experience continued as represented in these notes.

(Jane felt that when she opened her eyes wide toward the end of the experience she'd start yelling: "Who are you? What are you doing here?" etc.; this is when she

asked me to speak.

(Jane didn't see any buildings in the accident location, no lighted windows at night. But she did see the lighted police cars, etc., already described.

(Our living room looked "more normal" to Jane now, by 11:15, as though things were subsiding, but she added that the charge wasn't gone yet. The name Marguerite just came to her so she told it to me.

(By 11:25 PM Jane felt better, but still wanted to snap out of it all the way before she went to bed. "I feel all right, but I also feel like I could start yelling any minute, as though it's not far away."

(Nothing more developed during the evening, however, and she slept well. The next day Jane put in a call to an editor at Ace Books, after receiving an encouraging letter from Don Wollheim of Ace, concerning her dream book. The editor Jane will be working with at Ace is named Evelyn Grippo. Jane talked to this Evelyn twice in the afternoon by phone, but on neither occasion did EG mention anything about an auto accident, etc.

(Several days after the seance, we still have no clues as to any basis the seance might have. A letter was received from Tam Mossman of Prentice-Hall late in the week, but this contained no mention of an auto accident. Tam's girl Eve was mentioned in a normal informative way, but that was all.

(We do not know if Bill Macdonnel [or Tam] knows a Maisie. Nor do we know whether Bill knows an Eve, etc.)

SESSION 436
SEPTEMBER 16, 1968 9:03 PM MONDAY

(Tonight we were not sure what Seth would discuss, so just before the session I asked that he talk about the seance held last week, representing the 435th session. We wanted more information on Jane's obviously real and deep emotional reactions during this.

(Jane made the humorous remark that she hoped she was "more than a doorway that Seth walked through.")

Good evening.

("Good evening, Seth.")

Now. The Mossman weekend will have far-reaching effects.

Another person will become involved, who is not connected with Prentice-Hall. He will become involved directly or indirectly through Timothy *(humorously)*, and he will have much to do in the future with our own work. That is, in making it known.

Timothy Mossman was subconsciously aware that he would meet me when he read Ruburt's manuscript. The affair was up to him however. Had he simply rejected the manuscript and not written the letter that he did, the meeting would not have taken place; and he knew this also.

He does have a purpose, that is one of several courses that he can follow, that will enable him to fulfill the purpose, which is his during this existence. He wanted to understand at one time the heredity of seeds and plants. Now he will work to understand the nature and makeup of those in quotes "unorthodox" seeds within mankind's personality. He will learn to use his intellect as a fine tool, while his intuitions point to the proper direction.

A peculiar set of circumstances was needed to fire his being, to focus his attention, and that was our job. One of our many jobs.

Give us a moment. *(Pause.)* There are, as mentioned earlier, other roads that he could take. They would all in one way or another lead him to the same path. He must escape his occasional glibness, for he could use it to fool himself and not use his full abilities.

Now. Wednesday's affair was legitimate, though carrying several distortions. Ruburt's own abilities are growing, for as he is allowing himself release in his work, so he is allowing release of his abilities.

Before, he was afraid to sense those changes in the atmosphere that he could sense so well. On occasion he would fabricate a physical symptom to explain a sudden change of mood, that was instead the result of clairvoyant knowledge.

This was hardly the main reason for symptoms, but the habit caused annoying symptoms at times. The experience was a split one, involving an accident in the past and one in the future, that were fused in his perception. Now give us a moment here. *(Pause.)*

At one time he did correctly perceive an accident having to do with that Nina's mother, and recorded it. *(Perhaps two years ago.)* Hence the name, popping up the other evening. It served as a transition: an accident in which Mark, Bill Macdonnel, was involved, though I do not believe he directly participated. I am not sure, for he was not driving.

(Mark is Seth's entity name for Bill Macdonnel.) A child was present, hence the Nina connection again. Eve represented the nighttime as well as a name, and this led to a future possibility, a minor accident involving Mr. Mossman's Eve.

Two accidents were involved then, hence the confusion. The bridge for these was an accident in the past involving Nina's mother. This served as a connection to Bill Macdonnel. The affair in which Bill is involved has already taken place also, the night of Ruburt's experience. *(Which would be September 11.*

(At 9:26 the phone rang, interrupting Seth. To my surprise Jane got up from her chair and answered. Her eyes were still heavy and I could tell she was only half out of trance.

(The call was from Callista Buffalin, a widow now in her late twenties, who had lived in our apartment house until about two years ago. Callista's husband Buff was killed in a car accident in southern Pennsylvania a few months ago; Jane had a vivid dream giving many details of this event the evening before it happened, although we hadn't seen the Buffalins for some time previously. We haven't seen Callista since Buff's death.

(Callista called Jane to tell her about several psychic experiences of her own, both before and after Buff's death. One of these involved Callista knowing that her marriage to Buff would be short, and his death. As Jane offered Callista reassurances on the phone, she got the impression that Callista would remarry.

(After hanging up, Jane said Callista also mentioned her young son James. In telling me this Jane said Callista had foreseen events concerning James's death. This was a slip on Jane's part, for Callista had actually said James's future.

(Jane resumed at 9:55, in a rather slow manner.)

The one accident, in answer to your question, occurred the evening of Ruburt's experience, and it is the one that involved your friend Bill Macdonnel.

(Bill M., from Elmira, now lives in Santa Barbara, California.)

Another accident, a probability, is a future one, involving Tam Mossman's Eve. Because of the similarity of names Ruburt fused the two accidents into one in his perceptive experience.

(Bill M's nickname is Cam, taken from his middle name, Cameron.)

The Nina incident was a springboard. I do not believe Bill Macdonnel was injured, but he was either responsible for the accident or it was his car and the woman with whom he is involved. Now a child connected here also, whether with Bill Macdonnel or Tam Mossman I am not sure.

(We have no way of knowing what has happened concerning Bill in Santa Barbara as yet. Although we are good friends he seldom writes letters. He has telephoned us once in the last year. Occasionally his mother will call us and bring us up to date on her son's activities.

(Nor do we know the names of any of his friends out there, etc.)

The accident involving Tam's Eve would take place, if it does, on a day with a five in it. The 5th, 15th, or 25th. It would be a minor accident, but in the Bill Macdonnel accident someone, not Bill, was severely injured.

Now Mossman's Eve should not drive with an older woman on these days. The danger will be over by the end of May. The older woman has a sharp nose and rather elongated features.

The name Gert comes to mind, though this may be distorted; that is, the name. I would say the woman would be over 35, or give the appearance of being so. *(Pause.)* A stretch of road leading to the city, on the outskirts... *(Pause.)* The woman, the older woman, is in a state of inner emotional turmoil, that should be resolved by the end of May.

The danger then lies with association with the woman, on Eve's part. The accident, again, would be comparatively minor unless the older woman's inner existence drastically changes for the worse. *(Long pause.)* If Eve does not drive with her she will not be involved.

There seems to be a filling station and high grass by this stretch of road, with the city still ahead. S P connected here. Whether these are initials, say of a town or a person, or the beginning of the word spring, I do not know. The affair is still within the realm of probabilities and therefore not that clear.

Some additional problems for the woman who called, and marriage to a man with something wrong with a leg, perhaps only a slight limp. Illness for a child, a croup. Eventual strengthening of the woman's personality. The husband still visits the house. I am not sure here: some innocuous message to let her know. Something about butter. It could be: do not keep the butter in the pantry. Did he used to tell her to keep it in the refrigerator?

Also something about a stack of books with pictures or representations, old ones *(pause)*, kept in the cellar, initialed; and something about not a scrap of evidence. He doesn't want her to worry. The pot always boils. There was a package of something he ordered that came after his death, connected with the initials N A R or the letters.

He tells her to remember the fountainhead, may be a book, and something about coming through the rye.

You may take your break.

(10:14. This proved to be the end of the session, although this wasn't determined until sometime later. In the meantime some interesting things took place.

(Jane's trance had been deep but she came out fairly easily. She at once said she had the strong impulse to call Callista Buffalin back. She hesitated because she wasn't sure about the data's accuracy, but also because she didn't want to unduly upset Callista by talking about her recently deceased husband, etc.

(Jane did call Callista back, however, and checked out the data with her item by item. Callista decided to visit Jane later in the week, when a more thorough check of the material could be undertaken. But in the meantime there follows a summary of C B's comments re the data via the telephone.

(C B Doesn't know a man with a limp, or something wrong with a leg. As stated however, C B felt even before her husband's death that she would remarry, to

a man "with a great age difference." We don't know if this means to a younger man than C B, or an older one.

(We do not know about a croup illness for a child.

(The innocuous message concerning butter was "extremely meaningful" to Callista. Without going into personal details, she felt this was excellent data.

(This evening, while this session was being held, Callista was in the cellar of her home, reading or looking through books she took from a stack of same. They were old books, she said, illustrated, and some of them bore her initials and those of husband Buff.

(The books were covered, and when she was through looking through them Callista covered them up again; so, Jane felt, it seemed they had been undisturbed. This took place just before C B's call to Jane at 9:26. The act of covering may refer to the "scrap of evidence" impression, but we personally discount it.

(The package data, concerning a package arriving for Buff after his demise, is correct. C B told Jane a package did arrive; it contained something Buff had ordered for a nephew.

(Callista could not offer any connections however with N A R and the package in any way.

*(*The Fountainhead *is a book, as Seth surmised. Callista has read it, but doesn't know whether Buff ever did or not.*

(C B couldn't offer anything re "coming through the rye.")

SESSION 437
SEPTEMBER 18, 1968 9:07 PM WEDNESDAY

(Jane's back had bothered her, beneath a shoulder blade, for the last two days, and I asked that Seth discuss this. Jane said just before the session tonight that she had a slight pyramid feeling—discussed in several previous sessions—and that she had also been aware of this sensation just before a spontaneous session for her ESP class last night; and just before the 435th, seance, session.

(Before, she had noticed this sensation only during, or before sessions in which Seth's larger personality spoke. Now we wondered whether this feeling would be transferred to the sessions held by Seth himself, and to other psychic endeavors.)

Good evening.

("Good evening, Seth.")

Now. You come out of notime into what you think of as time, and back to notime again.

In notime experiences are far more direct. Words in your terms are not needed to describe them. In notime is the energy that provides the basis for time as you presently experience it. All individuals and consciousness cooperatively form and sustain the frameworks that you know.

There is less differentiation, in your terms, in notime, but far more differentiation in terms of consciousness, and psychological experience. All probabilities have their reality in notime, and the creative accomplishments that take place within notime generate all the probable realities that will ever exist or have existed within the various time systems. In various dream states you do delve into notime, and it is of course here that you have your primary existence and the ground of your identity.

It therefore pervades your time system, which is only transposed upon it. *(Pause.)* Give me a moment, please. *(One minute pause.)*

Ruburt's physical system, at its own pace, is righting itself. He is also receiving help requested. *(Pause. Pace slower.)* I am trying to give you some information concerning the back symptom, and will have to deepen Ruburt's trance, because of what you might call the underground noises. Those coming from below.

(At 9:19 Jane, As Seth, pointed at the floor, her eyes closed. Music from the apartment below us had begun to blare out loudly; loud enough so I could distinguish the words to the dance tunes. I was disturbed and almost went to the phone. I did not because Seth was making an effort to give information on Jane's back symptom, and thought this more important.

(Actually Jane, or Seth, gave no sign of being bothered. The extra noise seemed to be merely another problem to be surmounted so the session could continue. Jane sat quietly, eyes closed, smoking. Then she resumed, in a slightly louder voice.)

He is attempting to hide from himself the importance he feels connected to the chapter he has just finished and will send to Mossman. Holding himself like this, you see.

(Eyes now open, Jane sat upright in her chair, back stiff, each hand grasping a chair arm tightly as if to brace herself.)

To him in this case an attitude: "I can take it, in case of rejection." Momentarily, the gesture of rigidity for one of strength, where of course flexibility is always required.

In the face of possible rejection, which old attitudes now and then make him expect, he adopts a rigid rather than flexible stance. There is no reason to expect such rejection to begin with. The point is, it has been his habitual response. In the past the reaction would have been much stronger however. Again, the point is that he covered up the fear of rejection, and tried to minimize the place of importance that the chapter has for him.

In other words, his back is up, you see. *(Gesture, again.)*

Now he did a good job on the chapter, and it will help him if he imagines the entire book to be a young beautiful sapling that moves easily with each breeze, the nerves like tiny unseen branches, soft and flexible, going even out from his body.

The change in his subjective life is considerable, as the psychic work and his easy manner in the chapter clearly shows. A psychic and spiritual openness will now help on his part. He did not want to admit the importance of the chapter, although he knows it is good. He did not want to send it out for fear it would come back—underline back.

Now. The condition catches him frequently when he attempts to breathe deeply. He was afraid the chapter would catch him up, just when he was ready to relax and let go, a deep breath signifying a breath of relief. He should be able you see to take a deep breath of relief, and feel relaxed because the chapter is completed, and he knows well he can follow through with the book. But he was afraid to grant himself that release for the old fears of rejection stop him.

This was also the reason for various other symptoms of which he did not tell you this week. A clenching of the jaws. All of these reactions are far less than they would have been some months ago, and many areas of the body that would have been affected then are now free, even from such reactions, but he should not allow them to slide by.

When he does not use the pendulum it is obviously a symptom that there is something he does not want to face, and that for the time he will accept the symptoms. But that attitude, again, is a symptom of what still remains of inner confusion. Your supportive help is and has been far more important than you realize, and it is in all such relationships.

Any two or more individuals living together, live in a psychic environment formed by all involved. It is true that one in a period of illness habitually, to one extent or another, becomes susceptible to negative psychic environmentals. The other can indeed telepathically help change the inner climate by inserting ideas of confidence and strength, and thus changing the psychic climate enough so that the ailing personality can then do more on their own behalf.

When we are finished with the discussion we have begun *(on time)*, there will be many dealing with the subject, not necessarily connected however with your own situation. Ruburt's psychic climate has indeed changed for the better, but in periods of physical symptoms beyond his present norm, you can greatly assist in such a manner, for these are simply—or not so simply—miniature pitfalls. He gets out of them with much more rapidity, and they are not as deep but you can give him a boost. *(Humorously.)*

Now you may take your break and we shall continue.

(9:45. Jane's trance had been a good one. She said the music when it started really bothered her, although she didn't leave the trance state. Jane said that when Seth deepened the trance it was as though the music was turned off. In actuality the music was still blaring away from below.

(Resume at 10:07.)

Now. The yoga exercises are good but can be performed with a lighter heart, not a do-or-die attitude. He should make fun out of them.

His own clairvoyant abilities have taken a leap forward. You, Joseph, at the least several times a week, should make an effort to embark upon more psychological time exercises, for your own abilities have also grown; but you have not realized it.

When your portrait of the artist was done your own psychic abilities had grown as much as your artistic knowledge. There has been a leap that you did not realize you had accomplished. It has appeared in your psychological climate, rather than in specific instances. *(Long pause.)*

You should be able to tune in, so to speak, on some future probable events, I believe in image form, after a few attempts. Do this as if you were starting out to paint a picture, requesting to see the images of certain persons at a given time or situation in the future, and let your abilities then fill in on the imaginative pattern. This procedure should suit you well.

Make sure you do not force the images. Imagine a blank canvas or board, or blank framed picture if you prefer. I will give you an example. This is not a specific suggestion but an example of what I mean.

Say that you are going to try to see Prentice-Hall's reaction—will they accept the manuscript or not? Then imagine the blank picture as if you were going to paint it in your mind. Either see Ruburt painted in with the expression on his face as he reads the significant letter, and instead of the title the date of the letter.

Another method: pretend you are painting Ruburt with a picture of the book in his hand, then the details as to the publisher and so forth would be painted in for you. I suggest in your case therefore an approach using imagery, although there will be several ways of trying to get given information, as you see.

You should find this a valuable training. Now colors may be significant, particularly to you, and so the colors used in the imaginary painting may be symbolic. If so you will have to interpret them. The painting technique will call forth your creative powers more strongly, and give impetus to the psychic work involved.

If a different picture entirely presents itself then by all means note it. In your case (underlined) the relative position of objects within the imaginary painting may possibly be important also, objects in the foreground perhaps being more immediate. Again in your case you may find a road symbol. That is you will quite possibly use perspective in these things, relating to time. The length of a road in such a painting, with you, may be connected to the period of time between you and the event you seek information about.

Another symbol you may find may be a jar or container. If it is filled the desired information or event may be close to you in time, getting more distant as the jar is less filled, you see.

Now these symbols I believe will crop up specifically for you on various occasions. For you, again, the vividness of a color may also denote position in time. It may have other connotations also. For example, say you request information concerning a letter. You see, as a painting perhaps, a bright red, yellow or even electric blue, envelope. This could denote a favorable and fairly immediate reply, particularly if the letter was seen in the foreground.

If it were small and in the background the favorable elements still apply, but put off some in time. If you saw a dull, gray-or-black-colored envelope, large and in the foreground, this would represent an unfortunate reply, fairly immediate. Further in the background a less immediate but still probably unfortunate reply.

If you saw anything of a rich and bright color it would have good meaning, regardless of its placement in the imaginary picture. Much mist would represent the fact that probabilities had not yet cohered enough so that any certain answer could be given.

Now these symbols are those that I believe you will find suitable for you, and some of the information should help you interpret information received in psychological time. In these instances however you should have something particular in mind. Otherwise the time element can become confused.

If you are seeking future information, then you should mentally state this. It helps to focus your inner concentration along the desired lines. If you are simply exercising, trying to use the inner senses generally, then state this mentally, also. The vividness and so forth usually may be interpreted in the same light, regardless.

You may take a break or end the session as you prefer.

("Well, I don't know what to say." [It was getting late.] "Break, I guess.")

Then while I am giving you this information, after a break we shall continue it.

(10:35. Jane was well dissociated, she said. Her back felt somewhat better. The loud music from downstairs had stopped. Jane said she hadn't expected Seth to give

me this information tonight, and she was somewhat surprised by it.

(She also said the she could very plainly and definitely feel Seth probing into me in order to give just the right kind of information concerning practicing psy-time. Resume at 10:54.)

Now. In the overall you have benefited by the vitality and life about you here, and even by the occasional clamor. Strong and readily available positive energies have been about you when you needed them, and before you knew how to change your own inner environment.

Overall the climate of the entire establishment here has been supportive. Even the unconscious attitudes of others who have lived here have been beneficial in your behalf. You have used much of this energy to produce your own work. This does not mean that such conditions will always be necessary, but that they have served you well. *(Pause.*

(The above data came through after I had been griping during break about how noisy the house was.)

Give us a moment. *(Pause.)* A circle with segments cut into it like a pie may also be used by you to signify time segments. You will have to work out your own interpretation here, for the whole circle will represent various amounts of time, according to what you require.

If you want to discover in what month something will come about for example, you may visualize the circle cut into 12 segments, or have this idea in your mind. Then as the painting is painted, so to speak, so many of these segments would be removed, representing the months that will pass before the event.

A trick you may use, though you do not need it, when you want an idea for a new painting, is as follows. Pick a day in your future and simply request that you see that painting you will be working on at that time. Now we are involved with something rather tricky here, and I will explain the mechanics of it but not this evening. The picture of the painting should be available to you however. You can then use it in this present. If you are looking for a refreshing change, a lighthearted experiment, then imagine what painting you would paint if you were a particular other person, gifted with your own abilities.

The painting would be your own in any case, sifted through your own individuality. There were paintings planned by various great masters that were never painted, and these ideas exist. Sifted through your own individuality they become your own. *(Pause.)*

Many sessions ago I gave you some information concerning painting the viewpoint, and suggestions also as to how to approach a natural object, to become it. *(400, 401 sessions.)* You can also imagine how that natural object would appear to others of various ages and temperaments, or to me, or how curious it would seem to someone who does not dwell within your own system.

All of these suggestions tend to activate your creative and psychic abilities, and that is why I have given them to you together. Now unless you have questions I will end the session. I hope you look forward to some psychological time experiments of your own. I have given you a good manual. My heartiest wishes to you both, and good evening.

("Good night, Seth.")

(11:13. Jane's trance was again deep. The music had started blaring out again from downstairs.)

SESSION 438
SEPTEMBER 23, 1968 9:10 PM MONDAY

(Jane had a call from Tam Mossman at Prentice-Hall today, during which we obtained some confirmation on points made by Seth in a recent session. There was also a strange similarity between some of the data given in the seance, by Jane, in the 435th session.

(During the seance, Jane rubbed first her left arm and then her right arm, saying they hurt. This was after she had gone through an auto accident; Seth has told us this accident is in reality two accidents, one involving B. Macdonnel in California, the other a future possible event involving Tam's girl Eve, in or near New York City. In the seance Jane was not Eve, but the driver of the car in the accident; she was a woman, with Eve a passenger beside her.

(The seance-session, the 435th, was held on Wednesday, September 11, 1968. Mossman during his call today told Jane that his girl Eve broke her right arm over the past weekend, sometime during the 20th-22nd. Note the similarity re the arm problems.

(In the 436th session Seth advised caution on Eve's part in order to forestall or change the probabilities re this future accident. Seth described an older woman, about 35, with whom Eve rides, as possibly being involved in the accident as driver, and named certain days the accident was more likely to take place on. Today Tam Mossman confirmed that Eve does ride to work at Prentice-Hall with a woman fitting Seth's description, including the age given; he said eve would ride with him on the specified days in order to alter the probabilities.

(At 9:10 Jane again had "a slight pyramid feeling. But I think it's Seth." This sensation has become more and more common.)

Good evening.

("Good evening, Seth.")

Now. All probabilities and all possibilities have their origin in notime.

Some of these are perceived and experienced as definite events within your own system. It is you who choose among the probabilities, and from these you form the given collection that compose any particular event.

You use probabilities like blocks to build events. You choose. Now. This presupposes inner knowledge and calculations, for you must be aware of the probabilities in order to choose from them. The inner self therefore has and uses this knowledge. These probabilities include webworks and probable action and reaction, involving not only yourself but others.

Your computers are toys when compared with these inner workings. The main nature of events, the majority of events, do not in quotes "solidify" until the last moment, in your terms. According to your understanding and interpretation of the word, events, none are predetermined by a source outside of yourselves.

The given environment of your childhood for example was chosen by you and determined by you. Within this framework you also gave yourself the freedom to manipulate and change. The main events of a civilization are chosen by its people, but because a course is begun this does not mean that it cannot at any point be changed.

Events are materialized in your time from their origins in notime, then. *(Long pause.)* There is no end in those terms to the source or supply of probabilities, therefore notime is not a static, completed cosmic storehouse. It is being continually added to. Each event that you form from any given set of probabilities automatically gives rise to new probabilities.

The nature of any given probable action does not lead to any particular inevitable concluding act.

You had better underline that sentence.

Probabilities expand in terms of value fulfillment. One given act does not necessarily then lead to act B and C, and hence to a concluding action. Instead it has offshoots in infinite directions, and these offshoots have offshoots. Sessions on the creative dilemmas and the sessions dealing with relative nonbeing will help you here.

Give us a moment. *(Pause.)* This is what I know of reality, but there is more to be known.

(Jane leaned back in her rocker, eyes closed as she paused. Her pace hadn't been fast up to now, but it became even slower.)

"Outside" in quotes of the realities of which I am aware and others are aware, there are systems that we cannot describe. They are massive energy sources, *(pause)*, cosmic energy banks, who make possible the whole reality of probabilities.

We are moving in that direction. Portions of the entity in quotes "arrive" before other portions, and send us communications that we can hardly understand. The other personality who speaks is on the edge of such a system. *(Long pause.)* The other system is the inside of the inside. It has seen the birth and death of many physical universes such as your own; and the entities within it, in quotes, "at one time" were the inhabitants of such universes. *(Long pause.)*

They have evolved beyond all probabilities as we understand them, yet outside of probabilities they still have existence. *(Pause.)* This simply cannot be explained in words. *(Pause.)* They form energy sources. Yet also all of this and all of probabilities does not minimize nor deny the individual, for it is the individual upon whom all else rests, and it is from the basis of the individual that all entities have their existence, and from which all kinds of evolutions spring.

Nor are the memories and emotions of an individual ever taken from him. They are always at his disposal, and those who have had connections with one another are always free to renew them, or to ignore them.

You may take your break.

(9:43. Jane slowly came out of trance. Her eyes were heavy and bleary; she said the trance had been a good one after the first few sentences. She yawned many times during break. Resume at 9:56.)

Most of these probable systems, returning to our earlier discussion, are open. You simply do not realize that this is the case.

In your system it seems as if you have chosen one course, one main line of probabilities, and that is the end of it. On other existences however you choose other probabilities. Now your own system is relatively (underlined) closed, in that within it as a rule only one ego predominates, and you think of yourself as that ego.

In other systems this is not necessarily the case. The time system within them is entirely different than your own. In these the inner self is aware of itself as more than one ego. *(Pause.)* The inner self can play more than one role at once, consciously in other words. Simply as an analogy, it would be as if within physical reality you lived, say, the life of a rich man of great talent, the life of a poor man with entirely different talents, and the life of a mother and career woman. You would be aware of yourself in each of these three roles, and find qualities being developed in each of the separate lives.

Again this is an analogy, for in several respects it could lead you astray if you took it too literally. In such a system there would be no breakup of time for example, since time does not exist in the same manner.

You would not spend for example part of a day as one personality and part as another. This will all be explained in good time. *(Humorously.)*

I am going to give you a brief session this evening. Affairs with Prentice are as I expected. I had better end the session. *(Pause.)* Otherwise I will be keeping you for another hour and a half.

("How come?"

(Smile.) Shall I answer you?

("Briefly."

(Smile again.) The word is in <u>your</u> vocabulary and Ruburt's, not mine.

("Well, I'm just wondering what's going on."

(Jane, as Seth, paused. Seth doesn't allude very often to a subject in such a manner, so my curiosity was aroused. I knew Jane wasn't at her best tonight, but thought it would be nice to get at least an inkling of what Seth was talking about. I was sure we'd be glad we did later.)

There will be three books rather than two, more or less clumped together. *(Pause.)* Though I do not mean this week or this month. *(Long pause.)* Ruburt is coming out of his dark ages. That will allow us more freedom. There will be a particular conversation of an evening, with I believe six people present, and during the conversation a project will be born, spontaneously, and it will to some extent change your lives.

A suggestion will be made, not by you or Ruburt, during this conversation, and it will be taken up by others. A plan for a book will evolve, and other plans. There is an H—Helena comes to mind, but it is probable that this Helena is merely connected to one of the women present.

Two men, one with a manuscript, perhaps of his own, though I am not sure here. The place of the meeting has not been settled upon by all of those involved. There seems to be another woman also, though she is somewhat apart from the group. I believe three of you—wait—you will <u>know</u> three, I believe, of those present, having met them at least once before this particular evening. Something to do with bricks. Something to be built upon.

A matter of money involved, and a program of study.

In one of the homes of those present there is a statue immediately within a front door, and perhaps a hallway. The statue seems to be crouching, short rather than tall and erect.

A journalist, a housewife, and a man of the bar.

Now this is not immediate. But it is a strong offshoot of the probabilities that now exist, and three will be connected with it in terms of a date. Perhaps then March, and again perhaps March 13, though this is interpretation.

One man you will like far less than the others gathered, but he will be with you nevertheless, and much more loyal than one of the women, who will impress you far more. She will have a strong connection with Europe.

Ten-o-seven. *(This is the way Jane pronounced 1007.)*

Now you may end the session or take a break, as you both prefer.

("Well, I guess we'll end it." Although I wanted to know more.

(Smile; emphatic.) And you had better start keeping score.

("Okay.")

My heartiest wishes to you both. My fondest thoughts to our floppy Ruburt this evening.

("Good night, Seth, and thanks very much."

(10:23. Again Jane was very well dissociated, she said. She felt sorry because she wasn't very energetic this evening; Seth could have continued in a very chatty and social way for hours.

(The data above on a third book for Jane was entirely unexpected by us, and unasked for. No one has given Jane a hint re any such third volume, etc.

(A few more notes from the Mossman phone call to Jane today: Tam told Jane the book on the Seth material was practically a certainty; that is, as certain as one can get until a contract is signed. He also said he had written to Ruth Montgomery, asking her to do the introduction; if she agreed this might mean RM. would make a trip here. Tam also mentioned a personality like Hans Holzer, if RM. was unavailable, the point being that Prentice-Hall would like a name to do the intro. Tam said he would like to visit us again before the holidays.)

SESSION 439
SEPTEMBER 30, 1968 9:15 PM MONDAY

(John Bradley was a witness to the session. Seth has given John the entity name of Philip, and so addresses him.

(Jane was a little bleary tonight, having a rather heavy cold. For the record: after supper this evening she received a call from a Dr. Freudenberger, a psychologist and psychoanalyst, who wanted her to speak on altered states of consciousness, to a class he conducts in White Plains, New York on Wednesday evenings. Ray Van Over mentioned Jane to Dr. F. Jane plans to write to Dr. F. later.)

Good evening.

([John & RFB:] "Good evening, Seth.")

Now. Let us wait a moment until I get our friend here somewhat settled down. *(Meaning Jane.)*

There will be advantages for you connected with this evening's phone call *(from Dr. F.)* But do not immediately offer to go off willy-nilly. State the difficulties involved and the circumstances.

Now I give you my greetings, Philip, and I have been here and given them to you mentally. Give us a moment. *(Pause.)*

With Philip I see a triangle. One man is more prominent. I interpret this to mean that two men are involved beside Philip, and that one is more prominent or much stronger than the other. He is at the strong point of the triangle, and he would try to manipulate both Philip and the man. The other man is weaker than Philip in overall strength. Give us a moment with this.

The third man will fall off the triangle. He will lose his position as far as bargaining power is concerned, or he will let it go. But for some reason he will lose within the organization what strength he now has.

([John:] "Is this the current strong man or the weaker man?")

This is the man who is now in the weaker position. He will lose even that strength that he now has. He will seem to dangle for a while, but his hold will lessen.

Another will take his place amid bargaining and some positioning. You will hold your position, that is, it will not be weakened. The balance of power will shift however. The man who takes the weak man's place will be stronger than he was.

Now I have seen, and see, the image of the triangle, and have presumed Philip that you were one of the men involved. These three men however may instead be closely connected with your own prospects, but if so the position of the third man, given up to now as you, is as I have given it; and if he is not you then his position parallels your own strongly.

The two stronger men now at two points of the triangle will overpower the strength of the man who has been at the main position. I have been seeing the triangle with the man with the strongest position at the top or apex. Now the triangle turns and the man at the apex is brought lower.

Allow us our parables, and give us time here. *(Pause.)*

There seems to be a connection with Chicago, and further a connection with Los Angeles. The Los Angeles connection belongs to the man who replaces the weak man. This seems to be the main issue in the organization. One man is white-haired, one is sandy-haired. I see glasses and a peaked nose.

One is a Presbyterian or an Episcopalian, and the weak man either has no particular religion or no strong questions or doubts regarding existence. He swings as the wind blows. Beneath this imaginary triangle however there are other movements. Now I have the letters R and J. Whether these are initials of one man, or the first letters of two men's names, I do not know.

There is a change of territory involved here, but more than this a change of method. The change of method involves argument over basic philosophies. These men now below the main structure, attempt to influence those of whom I have spoken, but here we have a wheel rather than a pyramid or triangle, for there is little agreement even among those directly involved.

All probabilities taken into consideration, it seems now that the man at the apex of the triangle will topple, but if so he will not understand why. There is a man in your own acquaintance who will be somewhat instrumental, and yet you do not regard him as a close friend, and to some extent you distrust him. Again, do not jump the gun, you are not sure whose hand may be on the trigger.

Your own advantage will come when the weak man falls off, for another will match you in strength, and together you will change the balance. The man you have been thinking of this evening will not betray you. He may forget you. Your position within the company will be assured, and has been, as long as you continue your bulldog tactics. You aggravate them, and yet you make them think. They dislike you for the aggravation, but they admire you because you make them think, and they now are beginning to believe that your thoughts can save them money and time.

There seems to be a messenger through whom you are sending your own attitudes and setting your terms, and he can only be trusted so far. The 13th of next month is somehow significant in this regard. You are seeing some issues very clearly, but some you are ignoring. There is a short man. It is difficult to describe him here, because of Ruburt's associations. The image is of one dapper, given to pinstripe suits, slippery.

This is Ruburt's interpretation of a crook. But the point is that you are not paying enough attention to this type of man. He <u>is</u> physically short, and I <u>believe</u> either dark-haired now, or he was dark-haired. He is separated from you by two positions, and he knows your messenger.

([John:] "Is he friendly with the messenger?")

He is an acquaintance of the messenger and he is superficially friendly with the messenger, and he <u>may</u> (underlined) have warned you against him in the past. If he has not, he has been personally suspicious but did not consider the man that important, though the term is relative.

Now you may take your break and we shall continue.

(9:42. Jane's trance was a good one. Her eyes opened occasionally, and her pace was quite fast comparatively throughout. She said she saw the triangle quite vividly, and as it turned. Three separate men were at its points, she said, with the strongest at the top. She saw the weak one fall off, to be replaced by another.

(The circle below the triangle was not as sharp, she said, and had uneven edges. It consisted of many people seemingly jockeying for position.

(John said he couldn't give comments on tonight's data, that it depended upon whether he was in the triangle. At first he saw no connections. I am not trying to give an account of the long and complicated discussion that now took place between the three of us, as John discussed his company, Searle, and its internal politics.

(Speculating about a triangle in which he was involved, John said he could see where the weak point would be his immediate superior, his district manager in Rochester, and the strong point would be the regional manager in Long Island. John told us his district manager was offered the job of regional manager recently, but turned it down for various reasons; more money would have been involved also.

(The strong link would be a man named Stan, the regional manager at the triangle's apex. Stan is against John's promotion. John feels changes are in the wind.

(An the 402nd session of April 1, with John as witness, Seth had predicted a situation in which the district manager would turn down a promotion. Jane and I didn't know the situation had come to pass until tonight. John told us of some other verifications from the 402nd session also.

(John has a copy of each of the dozen or so sessions he has witnessed. He plans to go over these paragraph by paragraph and make his comments on the accuracy of Seth's data over the past few years, regarding John and Searle. John will do this on tape; Jane and I will transcribe the notes and insert them into the record for future use.

(10:05.)

Now. You will end up if you persist, and I imagine you will persist, first in either a position as fourth man down from the top, or in four positions up from where you are.

You will end up in a position of dominance in the company if you persist, but this is not today or tomorrow, and the company will have changed. Its methods will have changed.

Now, give us good time here. There are two triangles which have merged into one, for one is involved with the present, and one with the future. The present triangle concerns the interpretation which you have made, and your immediate superior is the man who falls.

But there is also another triangle, and this is the meaning of the symbol. I am seeing movement and shifts of power. In your present there is the immediate triangle of which I have spoken. In your present there is also a triangle symbolizing those now at the top of the structure, and there is movement there also, and a man will fall. But both of these triangles lead to a future triangle in which you will be intimately involved if you continue your bulldog tactics.

Now this is sometime in the future and you will jockey from fourth to third position in the higher echelons of the company. I see you again at the right leg of the triangle, and again the man at the left leg will fall.

This is, so far, your fate as far as probabilities and your own inclinations are concerned. This is where your interest and abilities and intent will get you if they do not change; and the position has potentials on the one hand, and on the other hand disadvantages. For in this future the man on the left will again falter, though he is not the same man. Another, stronger, will take his place, and together you will balance the entire structure.

There is no doubt then if you continue as you have, (underlined) that you will end up in the main power structure. In the meantime again, the methods of the company will be changed, and there will be further innovations even so far as intent.

There will be new openings as to products. All of this is dependent upon the initial triangle in the present, that I have described.

This is a thing that you want to change. A thing over which you want power and control and direction.

(John asked Seth a question about this statement. Seth replied:)

Power and control and direction over the organization, which is a symbol for something else; and you will not accept it unless you can change it, and indeed in changing it you will make it better.

You have decided that you are a part of it, but you will not accept it as it is, and if you are a part of it then you must inculcate it with those goals and ideals in which you yourself believe.

You cannot accept it otherwise, and you are not willing to start over with a new organization, for those creative talents within you persist in using what clay you have, and then you want to turn the clay into gold. And if you do not stop yourself, you will succeed.

It is an empire that you have decided to take hold upon, and there is no need pretending that anything else is involved. You will taste your own power through what you make of that company, and then you will use the power for other means.

You will also be unseated, but then you will not care for the time will be late.

You are not putting your full powers into this however, and may as well do so for you will regret it if you do not. This is the field in which you have decided to test your own capabilities and strength, so do so. The company is plastic. If I thought you might do otherwise then I would not give you this particular advice, but you have made your decision so you may as well throw all of your energy into it. You are an old feudal lord, and the company is your territory. *(Humorous.)*

You will not leave it. You will not accept it as it is, so you had better use all your energy to move through it and change it, and if you do so decide you will win out.

There will be sidelines however as far as products are concerned, and you had better keep yourself well-informed. It would help you if you kept very well-informed concerning transplants, for there are advantages and possibilities open here in terms of drugs still to be discovered, within which your company may later become involved.

You must throw your energy somewhere and use your strength somewhere. You must be committed. It makes little difference whether you become committed to your politics or your company. For your own benefit the commitment must come. Your energy must flow outward.

The company is there, irresolute and plastic, to be changed, and in its change it can affect many others, and beneficially. Use it then as your canvas. The energy within you must go somewhere. You must use it. It has been scrambled up within you for too long.

Now I suggest your break and we shall continue. You should have joined a monastery. You have a need for fiery commitment—

([John:] "Very true, very true.")

—and hobbies are hardly the answer.

([John:] "What is hardly the answer?")

Hobbies.

([John:] "Oh."

(10:28. Jane's trance had been very deep. "He had me real far out," she said later. I finally had to coax her out of it, slowly. She remembered nothing of what she had said, which for her is somewhat unusual. She had difficulty especially in getting her eyes open.

(Again we discussed the data during break. John said it was okay for me to note here that he agreed with the data. Again Jane's pace had been fast, her manner mostly serious.

(Resume at 10:44.)

Now. Now is the time to learn what your strength is. It is not the time to move.

When the triangle is changed, when the weak man falls and the stronger man comes, then is the time to move. *(Jane pointed to John for emphasis.)* Now this is your game. You will be changing the rules, but you had better be sure that you play the game for all that it is worth, and use your best abilities, for it is your vehicle for self-expression and creativity.

The company could become a plaything, and you could become tempted to think of moving people as on a chessboard, and you must avoid this.

Now. Directed correctly, this company can become far more than it has been. It can highly benefit mankind through new developments, if these developments in the future are not quenched, and if the administration is forward looking, if it looks for new products and new services that it can fill. Drugs will play no small role within the next fifty years, but those who will progress will be daring. Daring both in the choice of men, those who will represent the company to the public, and in the choice of men who will develop products, and this is an area with which you should become more familiar, for it is this upon which the company depends.

(John asked Seth a question concerning the above data.)

It is the choosing of the right men not only in the organization as salesmen and in public relations, but also in using judgment and intuition as to those men in another field entirely who will come up with new products, new drug inventions, new ideas, and it is here that the company suffers severely, depending on the tried and true.

([John:] "I couldn't agree more.")

You should personally study more concerning the medical end. If possible you should keep track of all medical discoveries, for your knowledge will serve you in good stead. Your company will not survive, period, unless it enlarges its concepts and takes chances upon young medical inventors.

There are three discoveries that should take place now, within a three-year period, and if your company does not latch ahold of them, others will.

([John:] "What are these?")

One will involve transplants. Give us a moment. *(Pause.)* And more refined drugs to enable individuals to accept foreign tissue. One will be in the line of birth control involving the male, and the other will involve a drug helpful to the nervous system in regard to memory.

There will be a slipup in this last, an initial overenthusiasm that will be proven false, and then a genuine discovery.

You should be close to this sort of thing. You should pay more attention to the basis on which the company ultimately rests, or the company will be outstripped. Your judgment of people will stand you in good stead here, but you must join all your forces and tell yourself that you have made up your mind, for this is your one chance now, as you have lived your life, to shape a strong area of reality.

You cannot use your daring in pirate ships any longer. *(Humorous.)* But use it you must or it could destroy the foundations of your vitality. Do not spend your energy in idle hobby pursuits. They do not fool you. But make sure that when you try to breathe vitality into your company, and form it, that you form it for the good. You have an opportunity—use it.

It is your religion *(humorously)* to transform an area of reality. Simply make sure that you use your abilities well. You cannot stay where you are, for you would not stand for it. *(Pause.)*

Now you may take a break as you prefer, and let our good King Philip rest. Your energies as a man are poured into this company however, and even as a human being, alone, you seek to form it. Then do so in your own way. In the overall your wife will be of more benefit to you than you suppose.

She will find social mobility to her liking. She will give you more support than you realize, and you need that family stability, for until that was satisfied you would not feel free enough to take on the task.

Now my friend Ruburt will not like this, and will object on general principles, but I am speaking on personalities and not necessarily on sexes. Your wife will feel insecure only when she feels that your own confidence is threatened. When you cease giving orders she will feel insecure. For entirely different purposes, you see, you will be both committed to the same projects.

You may take your break, and I will listen to your discussions.

(11:05. Jane was again a long time coming out of trance; once more I helped her by talking to her, and by touch. I didn't know whether this meant the end of the session or not. As we talked over the data, and points John had questions on, Seth came through again, at approximately 11:13.)

There will be a game of checkers and you will jump a spot if you care to do so. If you will step into a spot briefly, to say you held it, and then step into the next spot. You will know when the time arrives.

The other man will be strong but his strength and yours will reinforce each other. But he will want different things so your conflicts will be minimized. There will be two men jockeying for the weak man's position, each from different areas... The one man will not make it. Someone who is immediately behind him, seemingly with no power, will nevertheless prevent his movement.

(Jane was speaking quite rapidly in here, and I missed a few words, but got down the gist of the data.

([John:] "I'm confused.")

What do you have new to tell me?

(John questioned Seth here about the triangles mentioned early in the data, and above. The exchange was too rapid to take down verbatim, and I so told John. He said he remembered the information Seth was giving him. It concerned the man-

ner in which he would be advanced. John was concerned about where he would go to beyond the triangle, for at first glance he said he seemed to have nowhere to move to.)

You will take one foot into that position for a brief time only *(on the triangle)*, and then, convention satisfied, leap into the next spot. You must make the necessary gestures. Do you understand?

([John:] "Yes." John had more to say than this one word however.)

Now you must be on your toes then, and you will be if you do not move ahead of time. For to do so would put you in an unfortunate line of competition for the vacant spot *(on the triangle)*. It will be yours by right when you take it, while others are bickering, and you will be beyond it before they have ceased bickering.

Now there is a man in his 50's now, above you in position, whom you must watch. Nondescript hair, not slim nor overly porky, with fat fingers, fat wrists with perhaps hair there—a whitish hand, or rather whitish hands. Smooth hands.

He <u>may</u> (underlined) have freckles, but of the sort of complexion given to freckles. The hair crew cut. He is not stationed in this area but more to the west.

You have met him in Chicago. He has short legs. His own ambitions override all else. While he is honest when he says something, his own ambitions betray him into untruths. He is not to be trusted. I believe he is two steps away from you, and usually you know better a man who stands between you and him. The letters L A R come into mind here, and I do not know specifically to what they refer.

I believe the man to be a Catholic, or highly religious otherwise. You have met him on two occasions in particular, and you may have had words with him at one time.

Now, I am prepared to go on, Joseph, but suggest that if necessary you help Ruburt out of the trance state. My heartiest wishes to you all, and best good luck to our friend Philip in his most earnest endeavors.

([John:] "Thank you, Seth."

(Humorously:) Your project may not be the good ship Lollypop, but I find it a diversion, and for you it can be more than a diversion—quite more indeed. It will be what you make of it, so be clear in your mind as to what you want to make of it.

([John and I:] "Good night, Seth."

(11:34. Again Jane's trance was deep. She was some little time coming out of it.)

SESSION 440
OCTOBER 7, 1968 9 PM MONDAY

(This afternoon Jane received a letter from Pat Norelli, in Boston. Tonight we decided to ask Seth to answer the letter. Pat enclosed with her letter a list of three questions from a friend, Roger, dealing with mathematical formulae and requesting also that Seth give his mother's maiden name. A fourth question, from a girlfriend of Pat's, asked Seth about the Bahai faith. Jane read the four questions over—the formulae were meaningless to her—before the session, but we doubted if Seth would have time to deal with Pat's letter and the questions in one session.

(This proved to be the case, so we are saving the questions for another session. At 8:55 PM Jane received a flash which she thought to be from Seth: "Pat is insisting on using the gift of life in a certain way."

(The pace for the session was fast, usually emphatic, and Jane's trances were deep. Throughout the session Seth spoke to me directly as though I were Pat instead, as he explains later.)

Good evening.

("Good evening, Seth.)

Now we will address a portion of this session to our dear young friend.

Now. You have a fine, strong and worthwhile purpose, but you will not fulfill it well while you rail against what you do not have, and ignore the abilities and gifts and blessings that you do have.

You will not discover the purpose and meaning of your life when you insist that it follow certain consciously predetermined roads, and while you concentrate upon what you do not have. This saps your energy and dulls your intuitions. You are indeed obsessed with the idea of marriage, and with male love, but as Joseph mentioned this is but a symptom.

Underneath is the real cause, and this basic cause is behind all those that I have previously given you, in your own background.

You are not accepting life on life's terms as an individual. You are demanding that it behave in certain ways, and take courses that you have consciously set upon, and you are refusing to gladly accept life as life, as its own reason and cause within you.

This idea that you must (underlined) find a man that will love you and you alone, is a cover to hide this deeper refusal to accept life on life's terms. There is a cultural aspect here that you do not realize, and that you would consider beneath you.

It is a superficial concept, as if your individuality, merit and worth, are only activated if you have a strong sex, love or married relationship. Your survival, your unique abilities, and your purpose, exist quite apart from these.

They can exist with these, but they cannot exist if you insist that such a relationship is the condition upon which you will accept existence. You are saying "Unless existence meets my terms, I will not exist," and no one has the right to so set themselves against their own innate vitality and the joy of life that is within them.

Once you wholeheartedly accept life on life's terms, then you may indeed find what you are after, but not while you insist upon it as a condition for continued existence in this life. You have no right to set such terms, any more than a flower would insist upon sunny ground and a preferred spot within the garden as a prerequisite for its own existence.

You are pouting. You are quarreling, and in so doing you cut yourself off from the joy and vitality that do make life worthwhile living. Your own purpose can and will make life a daily pleasure when you let your conditions go. You forget what you do have—physical health and vitality. You forget your intellect, which is a good one, and your intuitions. Many are not blessed with these.

You cannot pervert them by trying to force them to serve purposes that you have set up as a condition of existence. You must live in the faith that your purpose is and will be fulfilled, is being fulfilled and will be fulfilled. You must live in the faith that you have such a meaning and purpose, or you would not be here.

The uniqueness that is your own personality is to be cherished. It has (underlined) a meaning. You have no more right to crush it than you have to crush a flower. The particular purpose of your present (underlined) personality can only be met in the present circumstances, in the way that is best overall. The challenges can be met at another time and in another life, this is true, but the particular people that you can help and the particular good that you can do, can never be done in precisely (underlined) the same way.

In denying life to yourself you end up by denying life to others. Now I wish this session was recorded so you could hear me, for I hold you, as Ruburt does, closely and dearly as a friend. But you are bound to misinterpret what I say in some sessions, and so it behooves me to speak more plainly. You do not realize now, you do not let yourself realize, the beauty and the complicated reality of your being. You do not let yourself realize the spontaneity and joyful burst that is your inner self, that results in this present human personality that you call yourself. Nor the effort and creative energy that has gone into your making, and that sings within your being like the first morning of creation.

You set yourself against all of this, against the gist of life and joy and vitality, and turn your back upon it with the paltry excuse: "If one person does not love me in a male-female relationship in this life, then I threaten to destroy myself, and shatter the form that holds the spirit, and shatter the form like a glass thrown upon the floor, like a child in a tantrum." *(Voice louder; very emphatic and fast delivery.)*

Now you have potentials, and there are people that you are meant to help. This is not to be a joyless task. It is you who are making it joyless. You cannot reject life and be joyful.

Now I tell you this to clear the air, and show you that your conditions will not be met while you hold them as conditions. Only when you accept life and do not hold conditions...

Now. Practically speaking, you must stop insisting upon male-female personal love as the condition of existence. You must accept life on its own terms with the faith that your life now has a meaning and a beauty and a purpose. You can do this, and I know that you can do it. Then you will begin to see the meaning in your life that has always been there, and the purpose and joy that you have not been able to fill.

(Again, the above paragraph was delivered very loudly and emphatically.)

Men and women have joyfully honored and loved the evening and the dawn, and listened to the heart-pulse within them, with a blessing and a joy who have not had one-hundredth of your blessings or one third the reason to look forward to another day, and they have fulfilled themselves and brought joy to others. They accepted life on its own terms, and in so accepting it they were filled with a grace, a grace that comes from giving life all that you have.

Your basic personality in this life is open. You are trying to close it. It reaches out to all kinds of people over and beyond sexual lines, and you are attempting to hold it in bounds. You feel the need for a great love, but you have the great love and do not realize it. You are trying to make it safe. You are trying to hide yourself in one man's arms.

You can reach both sexes, particularly in your teaching, and in this way you have gifts for both, and they are spiritual and psychic gifts. You do not understand them yet so you turn this great love inward, and try to narrow it down, and fasten it upon one individual who will then reciprocate—and you do not basically care who this individual is.

Instead your love is very wide and deep. It can aid many people, for it is ungeneralized and vast, and it will bring you much satisfaction and pleasure as it helps others. But you must not insist on any one condition as a prerequisite for existence. I am not saying that you will not have what you want, again, but as long as you hold the wish as a condition of existence you will not.

Now. Ruburt—*(then to me:)* are your fingers tired?

("Some.")

You may take a break.

(9:45. The pace had been fast and emphatic, with occasional mild voice effects. Jane's trance had been deep. In fact, she did not leave it completely during break. She whispered to me: "He's keeping me under during break."

(Jane got up for a cigarette, moving cautiously. Her eyes were still very dark and luminous—a sure sign of her trance state. I said nothing. "I'm just sort of half and half, I think," she said. "He's just stopping because of your fingers. This is sort of crazy. You wanted to rest, but I see you're writing."

("Yes, but I'm taking it easy." I wanted to get these notes down, although my hand was somewhat cramped.

(As mentioned before, throughout the delivery Seth spoke to me in a direct manner, as though I were Pat. Jane resumed in the same fast and emphatic, half-loud manner at 9:52, as soon as I said I was okay.)

Ruburt, himself, has long known that you had great vitality, but you have been cutting yourself off from your own abilities, and from helping others to a large degree because of this preoccupation.

It blinds you. *(Pause.)*

Now you have latched upon this particular preoccupation, but what it is in the end makes no difference. It could have been something else entirely. There are people who feel that existence is meaningless without wealth. Now this sounds idiotic to you. There are people who have committed suicide because they established wealth as a condition of existence. They were unable (underlined) to appreciate a love relationship because of this preoccupation, and you have been unwilling to appreciate the true miracle of your existence because of your preoccupation. *(Loudly.)*

If every cell set up the conditions of its own existence you would not have a body. The conditions blind you to what life is, even to the miraculous balance and imbalance of physical and nonphysical that allows you to think and breathe. Forget your conditions and you will realize the meaning of joy within your own life.

Now my dear young friend for whom I have great affection, there is no other way. Life must be accepted. You do not set the terms. You are worth while, and unique and glorious, whether or not you are loved by a man. You have a purpose and it is yours to fulfill, whether or not you are loved by a man.

When you cease holding this as a condition of existence, then you may very well be loved by a man. But no one sets the conditions, or pouts in a corner, or threatens suicide without courting severe difficulties. Ruburt has ridiculed the conventional idea of a god who says "Do what I want you to do or I will destroy you," and yet you say to life "Give me what I want or I threaten to destroy myself."

Now. The answer is no. When you understand my idea of life, then you do not destroy yourself in any form. You do not take it for granted that in the next life you will solve your problems. You take it for granted that this form and this personality, like all your other personalities, is unique, with purpose that it alone can best (underlined) achieve.

You are your own inner self, it is true. You have set your own problems, but the life force is not entirely yours. You have decided to do certain things with the vitality and life that has been given you, that flows through you, but it is not your right to end any given personality. You rob those you could have helped, and you deny the ecstasy that is the natural right of your being.

Now I speak to you honestly, and while you may find my words harsh they are spoken with both love and compassion, and (underlined) understanding of your innermost thoughts. Your salvation lies in giving up personal male love and marriage as (underlined) a condition for existence. Because you do often misinterpret me, I repeat: this does not mean you will not find such a male and relationship. But it does mean you will not find this while you hold it as a condition of existence.

(Voice strong and powerful:) Who is any one of us to make such demands? *(Louder.)* The whole development of your individuality and of your whole self is a gift of All That Is; a state of grace is the acceptance of life and vitality and joy. Live then within it!

(Looking at me:) I am speaking so directly as if our friend were here, because the emotional rapport is stronger, and if you will forgive me Joseph, when I look at you, you see, I am seeing our friend instead.

I would impress her with the fact that her existence will be more joyful than she can imagine, more productive and fulfilling, when she lets these conditions go. Now the whole answer to her dilemma is in this session, and she must understand that she is capable of doing what I suggest, and that the joys and rewards will be beyond her present (underlined) expectations.

There is such a preoccupation with what she has not that she is completely blinded to what she has. Now when you receive her reaction to this session, we will hold another. Know that she is held and loved, and that life itself will sustain her, and let the demands upon life drain away like sand between the fingers.

There is no other way, and there never has been. Life accepted on its own terms will yield secrets of joy and peace and exuberance. You cannot coerce it. You cannot force it and you cannot set conditions.

Now you may take a break or end the session as you prefer.

("We'll take a break."

(10:15. Break lasted barely a minute. Jane's trance was very deep. She tried to cough. She sat opposite the couch, where I sat; in her rocker as usual. Her eyes did not open. "Boy, was he ever here," she said, meaning Seth. "I felt like he had Pat pinned right to that couch."

(Resume session then at 10:16.)

Now. Ruburt you see in the past was setting conditions.

(To me:) Will your fingers stand it?

("For a little bit.")

He would be a famous writer, on his own terms, (underlined) or he would not accept life joyfully. He would limit the ways in which life expressed itself through him, or at times he felt he would not operate at all. He would be a novelist and a poet, as the conditions of his happy existence, of his joyful existence, or he would not operate naturally.

He would attempt to limit his abilities if they did not agree with his preconceived ideas. If he could not go his own way, he would not go, and so he slowed himself down.

He learned, and he is still learning, and so your friend must learn. You do not set conditions upon life. This is the greatest lesson that anyone can learn. Basically, basically, there is no other, for this one includes all others.

Take your break.

(10:23. Jane whispered to me: "He's still coming through.")

Vitality and joy and creativity move through you all spontaneously if you (underlined) do not set up barriers in terms of preconceptions and conditions; and all your desires will be met, but never when you set them up as conditions for your existence. The life that is within you knows only these terms: continued unpredetermined development, expansion; it will not flow in predetermined patterns or demands.

It can fulfill you and others, and bring you unimagined fulfillment, but never when you attempt to force it to follow certain directions. Who are you to threaten vitality and life?

(Pause. Jane stared at me for so long that I thought the session was over.

("Good night, Seth."

(Loudly, with a smile:) Now—I did not say good evening.

("Oh.")

I would let you know that Ruburt is now, finally accepting life on its terms, and this is the reason for his recovery. He has been helped by others, and Ford's and Edwards' ideas are quite legitimate.

Now I do suggest that our friend contact Edwards, and Ruburt can explain the reasons rather than taking session time to do so. These people in their way are expert spiritual healers. I am a teacher. They are often more gentle and understanding. They have a bedside manner, you see, that I unfortunately seem to lack. *(Half humorously.)* They do contact other layers of the personality, with explanations that are vital. They do not love any less than I, but they are more patient. They are also better equipped with certain techniques in <u>their</u> field, as <u>I</u> am equipped in my own.

Now as you know from certain signs, I am quite prepared to go on for some time, giving you literally whatever information I can concerning Ruburt's condition, or your friend's, but I realize the hour is late and your fingers tired. Make your own decision. I have done, and am doing, the very best that I can, out of love for your friend.

("I guess we'll have to end it.")

I wish you then a hearty good evening, and to your friend, our present beloved young woman, Ruburt's Pat Norelli, my best wishes for a <u>beginning</u> now, of vitality and joy, as you throw aside <u>all conditions</u>, and accept your life for what it is and <u>will</u> (underlined) be—a joy, an exaltation to yourself, and a help to all those you will still contact.

("Goodnight, Seth."

(10:37. Jane's trance had again been very deep, and she was a while coming out of it. Her eyes opened very slowly; I talked to her, etc. The pace had been fast and furious for the most part, with more voice effects than we had heard for some time.

(There had undoubtedly been a strong emotional condition operating during this session, and at its end both Jane and I felt a strong lassitude, most unusual for us after a session. It lasted for perhaps half an hour. The intensity of the experience made it seem that much more time had passed; both of us were surprised to realize the comparatively early hour.)

SESSION 441
OCTOBER 9, 1968 9:15 PM WEDNESDAY

Good evening.

("Good evening, Seth.")

Now, we will let our other people's sessions go for now.

I have been aware of the Pitre request, and when any of your correspondents are in very immediate need I will always hold a session for them at once.

(Jane received another letter from John Pitre, Franklin, Louisiana, today.)

Some of the Pitre problems that he spoke about a month or so ago have already taken care of themselves, but we will have a session for him. Ruburt need not feel so responsible in such cases.

Now he has been ten or so minutes late at session time, and the reason I should think is fairly obvious. It was also the reason why he suggested beginning a session earlier *(this evening at supper time)*, though he did not know this; and in any case what he suggested, on regular terms, was not really what he wanted.

This was on his part simply an attempt for spontaneity. The spontaneous self had risen up against what it considered the rigidity of beginning a session at a particular moment. He began then craftily so that sessions began after nine o'clock, and then suggested the earlier hour. Now this is simply a minor and temporary element, originally because he has begun his Thursday classes and is therefore further regulated.

He realizes that a specific time is more practical. He enjoyed last evening's spontaneous session *(for Jane's Tuesday night ESP class)*, and such sessions, while they do not particularly add to our material, replenish his creative efforts and give him a sense of freedom. The spontaneity often, though not always, helps to focus his abilities, and provides us with an excellent trance state. The spontaneity provides its own training. You may have noticed that often when you miss a regular session, I have held a spontaneous one in class.

("Yes.")

Now Ruburt feels, at times unreasonably, for you have told him differently, that you think he shirks when he misses sessions. The sessions need regularity. They also need spontaneity, and for his own nature, I try to see that both needs are met. This is for the benefit of our sessions and for overall balance and efficiency.

He feels that sometimes (underlined) you do not understand his position. He feels that you do not realize that while you are both busy four nights a week, that he is highly creatively and psychically involved with psychic work, that it is not just business.

Now I am here now rather clearly. I know more than you know, and I realize that we will get through the material, that I have in mind, so it does not bother me when I hold informal sessions, sessions in which material is not always stressed. More happens in these sessions than appears in the written record.

Even with Ruburt's difficulties as a personality he now makes more use, though he does not realize it, of his creative energies than he ever did. To a large extent you realize this, and it makes you more anxious for your own work and endeavors.

This was largely the basis for your reaction this evening. The psychic work with Ruburt has a strong spontaneous nature, and at times he resents, while he also needs, the regular schedules that you seem to require physically.

You are on the edge of a discovery in your own work, and it makes you uneasy, for you sense it, yet have not grasped it. This also had something to do with this evening's reaction. Neither of you fully realize as yet the nature of the energies that are working with you, that give you meaning as individuals, hold you together, and form the framework of your daily existence, the balance of spontaneity and regularity.

Now you are concerned with our material and so is Ruburt. But there is also a strongly personal interrelationship between the three of us, and this is also important. If you, Joseph, have any questions feel free to ask them. Remember that the emotional element is behind <u>all</u> of our sessions. Without it there would be no sessions and I would not be here.

Now you are dealing with emotions, working with your portraits. Some of the people you paint are real, but you do not know them. You work within regular hours, yet within those hours you are dealing with unregularized emotions. You are dealing with personalities, some far different than your own, and forming these into paintings.

As you know both the discipline and the spontaneity are necessary. Now I know you. I know you far better than Ruburt knows you. *(Smile.)* Some things you block out. The personalities behind the people that you paint now run about that room of yours, and you try to put them into your paintings, and to make yourself strong enough to contain their reality, and you feel that Ruburt does not understand this. You do not understand <u>all</u> of it, but you feel the pressure of their reality, that wants to be expressed.

In some respects your work is lonely, and in some respects Ruburt's work is lonely, but you react to it differently. Ruburt lately has looked for spontaneous release in anonymous social situations—the beer in the crowded bar. Underneath he is highly practical, and realizes that such endeavors, for him in any case, are not pointless nor a waste of time.

You burn and use energy at a different rate. He consumes it more quickly than even you realize. You consider such diversions therefore to some extent a waste of time, for they are not as necessary to you, though to some extent of course they are.

Your family in this life has always been determined upon longevity, and you pace your energy. Ruburt has not. The <u>ways</u> are simply different. Now your father paced himself unwisely. You are not making the same mistake. In many ways your mother was also wiser. Although your reactions at times may be different, and although you may not agree with me, still Ruburt will rarely be unrealistic in understanding or in utilizing methods that are highly practical, though neither of you may understand them as such.

You need time to do your own work, but it is also true that the intuitions and emotions that spark your own work are not dependent on time, and exist quite apart from it.

(Smile.) Some evening we must use your recorder so that you do not need to write so furiously, and let me talk to you. You will be able to talk back. *(Humorously.)* You may take a break.

(At 9:50 Jane paused, but obviously was still in a trance.

("Are you waiting?")

You are very good at recognizing the signs. I will give Ruburt a rest also, however.

(9:51. Jane's trance had been good but she left it rather easily. The pace had been fast, eyes open often, etc. Resume in the same manner at 10:00.)

Now our sessions take little time. If they took twice the time you would still be very well off for what you get out of them. The <u>recording</u> of them does take time, and over this I personally have no control. There is a possibility that Ruburt could get help from his students here to relieve you, but I do not believe that you would want anyone at our regular sessions. The typing does take time from your own work.

Yet the sessions also help your work, and you cannot count the ways that you have learned from them. You are feeling crowded, however. This is to you, Joseph. Therefore I suggest that we have a week's vacation. On your account this time, and not on Ruburt's.

("I don't particularly need any vacation.")

There seems to be a feeling of being crowded, and I do not like to add to this.

("I do all right usually, but I don't want things added to our schedule.")

I never want you to feel that your work time is being invaded by the work in recording sessions.

("I mean other things besides the sessions in our daily lives."

(Sometimes my comments to Seth are rather cryptic because of the time it takes to speak to him and write out the statement at the same time. Often the groundwork has been laid before a session, also, so that the brief comments merely reminds me of what was said earlier, without going into detail.

(This is the case here: Jane and I had discussed this problem of time before the session. Usually I have little trouble fitting the typing into our daily routine. It is true

that we would sorely miss the sessions; much that is useful to us personally would be gone, even if this were the only reason we held them.

(It is also true that we don't want anything more added to our present schedule. If something urgent develops we try to accommodate it in some fashion however.

(Humorously:) Then we shall take back your vacation.

("Okay.")

Do you have questions for me, not involving material now, or other people?

("I haven't taken any time to think of any.")

I am far more interested in personality equations than in mathematical ones. I have said what I intended to say this evening. Now you may ask me questions or end the session, or I will begin some other material. Or you may take a break and think of questions, or just take as rest as you prefer.

("Do some of those personalities know they are being painted?"

(Here I referred to the series of portraits, most of them not finished, on the shelf in my studio.)

Consciously of course they do not. Underneath they know there is a communication, but they do not realize they are being painted as such. In one man's mind he has seen your image however, and there is some telepathic communication operating both ways, but both of you accept the thoughts as your own.

This is of the man with the odd chin. You have two separate studies of him. He has two children and lives in Nebraska, and oddly enough he is a house painter who also wanted to be an artist. He paints flowers on memo pads.

His first name is Edward or perhaps Edwin. His last name, a strange one with a foreign connotation: Z E N O, *(spelled)* is as close as I can come, though I believe that is only the first part of a larger name. Zeno-mythlin *(The mythlin is my phonetic version of the name Jane pronounced, somewhat haltingly.)* That may be two names, perhaps with a hyphen. Edward Zeno-Mythlin; or one name is a family name.

You picked him up, so to speak, because of the personal association. He wanted to be an artist also. He has violent tendencies that he does not understand, usually well-hidden. The chin is a subterfuge, for it appears weak.

("Which two studies are these?" I wanted to be sure.)

Two small paintings on your shelf. They are both of the same man. One is more a profile than the other. Ruburt knows. He has noticed them and disliked them. He disliked the person.

("Okay.")

There is great struggle within the personality however, shown in the sketches—an infantile nature that yet has abilities and struggles to use them. The man reminds Ruburt personality-wise of your mother, hence his dislike of seeing the characteristics so similar in the male and younger portrait.

(Naturally I found all this quite interesting. I was aware of none of it while making the two small oil sketches in September 1968. I now knew which two Seth referred to; strangely enough, I hadn't thought of them as being of the same personality at all. I don't think they bear any striking resemblance to each other, though in a general way they could be of the same type of person. After the session Jane told me that she knew at once, after I had finished them, that they were of the same person; she took it for granted that I knew this also.

(Actually, each sketch, perhaps four inches square, was done to solve technical problems I was concerned with in the series of portraits I am painting. Each was successful in its own way, and opened several doors. I might add that I was somewhat surprised at the ease and success of these two sketches.)

This is also <u>another</u> reason why you "picked out" in quotes this personality, through association. Give me a moment. I am not sure what I am after here. A change in your father's condition, in that the steadiness of his condition is not as you suppose. *(Pause.)*

He is well aware of your mother's vitality, and she is well aware subconsciously that her vitality still goads him into a semblance of reaction. She still acts as a stimuli, as you know. In one way she forces him to stay when he would retire, and when her thoughts are not strongly with him he will attempt to escape further.

She will not let him be done here, and he resents it when she rouses him. But he still feels arousement at her thoughts of him as well as her visits.

Now as she more vividly imagines life without him, this stimuli will wane. She is now vividly imagining existence without him. On the one hand you can say that he is weakening proportionately. On the other hand he is <u>freeing</u> himself proportionately.

(At the time of this session Mother is visiting my brother Loren in Tunkhannock, Pennsylvania for a couple of weeks, and cannot visit Father in the county home at Burlington, Pennsylvania.)

His struggles with his nurses *(which are violent)* are struggles to escape physical bonds, and to be away. He did not use his vitality in his manhood joyfully or fully or explosively, either in work, nor purpose, nor family. Therefore it lingers, and he cannot disentangle himself from it. He paced himself out of jealousy of his energy, so that it outlived him. It was not focused in work. It was unfocused.

Now. Because it was not used it outlives him. He kept it in isolation and was jealous of it, and did not allow it joy nor freedom.

(At 10:29:) He is in some difficulty at this time, now, according to your definition of difficulty. He is trying to leave.

He was jealous of all (underlined) of his sons, not because your mother seemed to prefer them, but because he saw his own energy and life force giving independence in ways he could not control. He knows better now, but he is still left with the dilemma of freeing himself completely, and beginning again.

He will be reborn as a woman. This much he has decided. He will therefore become more aware of the spontaneous nature of creativity, for he will bear children. Your mother and he, beneath all of their difficulties in this life and in others past, have a deep relationship. They will meet again under different circumstances, but not in the same terms.

The sexes will be reversed and your mother will make a fine husband. Your father has been twice a male, successively. He will adopt the female role, which is more natural to his personality, and be more at ease with creative functions at the spontaneous level. Your mother has been a female now twice in a row, and is ill at ease, and will do much better as a male. The mother-love experience has done much however to balance a too-aggressive nature.

Your brother Richard, and Loren also, are undergoing necessary experience as males. Loren in particular, in spite of past male lives, is strongly feminine, and your sister-in-law is undergoing her first female incarnation.

Far be it from me to give either Ruburt or yourself swelled heads, but in your cases we see the male and female aspects well-balanced, one of the reasons why this is your last incarnation. These elements are highly unstable and each personality works them out.

You have the impulse to think of the male as disciplined, yet the raw male elements are unthinkingly aggressive, and the raw female elements are indiscriminately creative.

(Pause.) Now your father could die this evening. I do not believe that he will. But your mother's attention is completely divorced from him at this time, and he has been seeking such an opportunity. The young boy he has been helping no longer needs him.

(See the 398th session, March 11, 1968 in Volume 8.)

He never served, truly, as a male image for you or your brothers. Both of your parents, unfortunately in this life, served as uncomplimentary female images. This is why you trust the male qualities in Ruburt; why Richard chose a family in which he married where the males have been dominant, and why Loren chose for a wife a woman with more vitality than he.

This particular daughter-in-law of your parents pretends, or superimposes a caricature of conventionally accepted female characteristics to hide the basic male qualities. Their daughter knew this. She sought protection from her present husband, who is in a position to give it.

(At 10:45:) Your father is now trying very hard to escape, but your mother is now at this point turning her thoughts toward him in alarm. *(Pause.)*

Five people are holding him down. When he swears and is aggressive, he thinks he is showing those male characteristics, you see. Your mother is crying now to Betts, and she may yet hold him.

He sees before him the people he has known. In one way he is happy. He can show his aggressive nature, which is basically his creative nature, but he does not have to deal with it. Others restrain him. He has not learned the difference between violence and creativity, though they are closely allied, and he is frightened of the similarity.

He was (underlined) most jealous of you. You will yet do a portrait of him, for you cannot yet avoid the issue. Are your fingers tired?

("Yes.")

Then take a rest. You may end the session or I will continue along the same line. It is your decision.

("Well, we'll start out by taking a break." 10:51.)

I have also known some of your people, you see. Now. At one time—now at one time Ruburt's mother and your father were portions of the same entity.

(10:52. I thought this was the end of the session. Jane's trance was obviously deep and I began to urge her out of it verbally. After a while she began to talk to me, slowly, yet gave every sign of continuing the session on her own, and in the highly emotional manner of the 435th session of September 11, 1968. This I wanted to prevent; even while she told me that Seth protected her, she began to whimper, eyes closed, and talk about my father.

("There's five people holding him down now. He's struggling, fighting... there's another nurse there, a different one..." I cajoled, talked, shook her and ordered her out of trance. I made her put on her glasses, drink wine, walk about, etc. Jane said she had no visions of Father; no projections were involved, etc. "Just a shadowy feeling."

(And through all of this, surprisingly I felt nothing for Father, no sorrow, no anger, no happiness—just that he had chosen his course long ago and would see it through in spite of anything others could do.

(Jane had resumed her seat. I was somewhat dismayed to see her abruptly resume the session, as Seth, at 11:05.)

Now. Understand that the main power of your father's personality is already somewhere else *(pause)*, and is simply waiting for this errant portion.

A portion therefore of your father's present personality fragment understands this. Now Ruburt has lately allowed his abilities more freedom and as in any endeavor he will make errors, and he must expect them.

This evening no such errors are involved. If he did not use his abilities obviously he would make no errors, but this is hardly a good argument. He is (underlined) better off with me than alone, and yet he must also work alone to develop the abilities. They grow more precise as they are used.

I have come through, now, to stabilize his system, as the content of the material frightened him. Now I presume that you wish to end the session. Circumstances have been good this week however, which is why we have had three sessions. On other occasions circumstances are not good. Do you have questions?

("I guess not, Seth"

(This week Jane also held a long session for her Tuesday night ESP class.)

We will therefore end the session. My heartiest regards to you both. These sessions are as beneficial as those containing more abstract material; though the material will never take second place, this is also a means of learning.

("Good night Seth, and thank you."

(11:12. Jane, surprisingly, came out of trance quickly and easily, and felt well.

(And of course my father did not die this evening.)

SESSION 442
OCTOBER 14, 1968 9:30 PM MONDAY

Good evening.

("Good evening, Seth.")

Now. I have several remarks to make. First, Ruburt's decision not to speak to Dr. Freudenberger's class was a good one at this time (underlined). There is no reason to elaborate here. *(See the 439th session, September 30, 1968.)*

Another improvement, a considerable one, can shortly be expected in Ruburt's physical condition, and I believe rather unexpected word concerning a book.

There are several points I would like to make concerning psychological identity. For the sake of analogy only now, imagine your present self at the center of a circle of endless spirals. You are yourself, and yet one of the spirals that form the circle. You are a vortex for the circle. You do not have to contact it nor its other spirals, in that you already belong to it.

Now the same is true of other portions of your entity, if you consider any other given portion as being the vortex of its own circle. In any psychic investigations or endeavors you will often gain assistance and support from those others who make up the circle of which you are a part.

Now I am speaking simply, for I am speaking of a circle as you understand it in three-dimensional terms, but there are more depths and dimensions to a circle than you can imagine when you picture, say, a globe; and so of course in this analogy identity has other dimensions that do not appear.

Give us a moment with this. *(Pause.)* There are points or identities more easily reached from any given viewpoint within such a multidimensional structure. *(Jane drew in the air, eyes open.)* Imagine a superstructure of a circle, put together like a pie, except that each segment is also in itself a globe, and that this structure is in itself an exterior one, the multidimensional equivalent of the pie's crust or the apple's skin.

Now the circumference of these circles interlap and bisect each other. Nor are the dimensions of circumference or radius stationary in your terms, for they exist in value fulfillment rather than in space, and their measurements in terms of intensity rather than in inches or miles.

They are to a large degree, but not entirely, self-perpetuating, as if the seeds of an apple, instead of falling down to the ground, fell backward into some mysterious dimension within the core of the apple itself. And yet because of the creative abilities of this mysterious dimension, more than inbreeding would be concerned, for it of itself could provide entirely fresh and new elements out of which further creativity could come.

Now this is identity as it is not generally known, and in this analogy lies the truth of the nature of identity. Later you will understand it better.

You and Ruburt have changed since our sessions began. I have also changed. Because I have changed you have changed, and because you have changed I have changed; and each new encounter continually changes, yet in a way that has to do with developments, not single-line continuity.

You may take your break and we shall continue.

(9:49. Jane easily emerged from a deep trance, she said. She said she didn't feel like delivering any more emotional material at the moment. She had internal images or visions of the circles and vortexes as Seth spoke, but she could not now put these into words. They also changed as Seth continued discussing the analogies involved.

(The data at the beginning of the session re unexpected word concerning a book reminded Jane of an amusing dream she had last night, and which she has written down per usual: She dreamed that her science-fiction novel, The Rebellers, *was being made into a movie.*

(Jane's pace, voice, pauses, etc. had been average, and remained so when she

resumed at 9:59.)

Now. From my standpoint your various reincarnated selves are not seen separately, but as your earthly personality.

Our contacts now are not just contacts with Robert F. Butts and Jane Roberts, and that is why I have always used your entity names. The contact is also with your other reincarnated selves that you do not presently recall. *(Smiling:)* I see a larger portion of your identity than you do.

("Yes.")

And when I speak to you I speak also to other portions of you that I have known and do know.

("What do you see right now?")

Right now I see you symbolically speaking, in your terms, as the sum of the various people I have known in past lives as you, plus the you that is present, in your terms. In terms then of vision, I see Joseph rather than Robert. And I speak through Ruburt rather than the less—rather than the more limited concept of Jane. Do you follow me?

("Yes.")

Now. Our relationship, simply in these terms, is multidimensional. For you also react to me unknowingly on the basis of other relationships with me that you do not consciously recall.

In the future now that Ruburt has loosened, we will deal with your reincarnational backgrounds in some detail. Now give me a moment. *(Pause.)*

In terms again of the image set up earlier, there are various reference points where overlapping areas of the various circles penetrate each other; and as has been mentioned earlier, Ruburt's personality presently is in such a psychological location.

Your reinforcement is necessary however, for you act as an amplifier. One of the reasons is obvious, to me. My own personality, as simply as possible, also represents such a reference point or entry point between you and Ruburt and myself. Because, again as simply as I can explain it, because of our natures a certain field has been set up of receptivity, and though our positions change, the quotients within it do not.

Now mathematicians will not like this, but in your (underlined) terms within the multidimensional circle image, we form a triangle. The triangle is mobile, but we are to some extent (underline some) eternally allied. We were always formed something more than we are individually, in your terms.

Now this is not unique by any means. There are numberless other such situations, and I mean numberless. Comparatively speaking however, the situation is unique.

Now within our relationship as a triangle, dimensions are open and constantly changing. Because of it we have all a rather unusual freedom. Now, I am part of another triangle still, that is within this circle, and through my contacts with this other triangle there are abilities, perceptions, insights, talents available to you that you have barely begun to tap.

You will *(to me)* particularly since Ruburt makes his way from his own dark age. One of these developments will occur in our sessions, one in particular through Ruburt outside of a session, I believe, and another should take place initially Joseph through you. Or with you as main agent and instigator.

The other personality for which Ruburt has spoken is a part of this other triangle. *(Jane leaned forward, intent and amused.)* Which leaves you with two unknown elements you see. Surprises—

("I'm thinking about it.")

—are not surprises unless their main elements are withheld. I tell you this so that later when developments occur, you may find that within our sessions, again, that the ground has been prepared.

The circle image that I gave you is meant to represent the basic meaning of each individual's entity. Within it each individual is free. In the simplest of terms I have tried to suggest through analogy the multidimensional aspects of a basic self.

You sleep and dream and waken daily, and know that you are you. So in your physical life you die and begin a new life, with little memory of the one that has gone before, as you find it so difficult to recall your dreams. Through exercises you can consciously remember some dreams. Through exercises you can consciously remember some reincarnations.

If you are interested I will give you such exercises, but whether or not you remember these lives consciously is of little importance, for you have subconscious knowledge of them. This is your last reincarnation, in your terms. At death you will consciously realize the sum of your reincarnated selves. To me that is your personality, but this is only a small part of your overall self. To me it is as if you had finished one life, you see. To you it will seem as if you had finished many.

Then the integration will take place, and you will realize that the various incarnated selves were as but days in your present existence.

(To me.) I speak to you as Joseph, and all unknowingly you react as Joseph; *(leans forward)* for Robert F. Butts alone, or Jane Roberts alone, would never have met me.

Are your fingers tired?

("A little." The pace had been fast.)

You may take your break and we will continue, or end the session as you prefer.

("Okay, we'll take a break.")

(Pause at 10:31.) Ruburt may be invited to go somewhere or do something, on a Wednesday shortly, and I suggest that he not do so. There seems to be a situation that could arise, that would be highly unpleasant to him, and therefore to you.

The request will be sprung upon him, and that is why I am telling you in advance, to prepare him. A car would be somehow involved, and a probable accident with another driver. This seems to be the season for accidents, according to our sessions.

A cousin seems to be involved, though not necessarily of your family. For example, someone may want him to speak to a relative, or visit one. This is a probability. Four people would be involved. He has only to refuse, politely.

The episode would take place fairly shortly in your time, in the immediate future. Now I am after something here, difficult to pinpoint, and will give you what clues I can. *(Pause.)*

Do not drive with anyone else. The situation could arise (underline could) when others here suggest you go somewhere. The situation does not seem planned, in other words. There is an element of surprise. Normality that could catch you unaware.

The number 6 comes to mind, and Ruburt in particular should drive only with you. And both of you should be alert even driving together, in a situation where you are asked to visit, or go somewhere else with two other people.

We are getting more of this sort of information because Ruburt allows it now, but since it involves yourselves we are learning personally to get through such information, where with others we have progressed to some extent beyond that point, you see. This represents progression on Ruburt's part, but he must still learn lessons that he has already learned in giving such information to others. Do you follow?

("Yes.")

Take your break.

(10:40. Jane sat motionless in her rocker now, head tipped to her left shoulder. I had to call her many times to help her out of her trance. She held a lighted cigarette also and it was burning closer to her fingers, so I took it away.

(It took a long time to coax and command her out of her trance. When finally her eyes began to open, briefly, they showed a tendency to roll up. She would quickly correct this rolling each time. When at last she began to talk she said she was "not really here, but not out of my body either," while giving this automobile-accident

probability data.

(Her trance had been so deep we called this the end of the session. The auto accident data was quite unasked for and unexpected. Jane had a feeling of four other people in a car, with us, but couldn't be more definite. The Gallaghers came to mind now as we discussed this, but she doesn't know why. A bit later Jane thought of Claire Crittenden, who is out of town, again without knowing why.

(Needless to say, after the session I impressed upon Jane the necessity of her avoiding other cars, no matter what the reason given for their use. I stressed that she shouldn't get in any car besides our own, or make appointments or take spontaneous rides with anyone for any reason. I also resolved to be extra careful in my own driving, even when alone.

(It is Saturday, October 19 as this is written now, and so far nothing untoward accidentwise has developed for either of us. Each day we have reminded ourselves to be careful. I have been especially cautious, even driving to work, etc. We will continue this regimen.

(One possible ride Jane might have taken with another was obviated when she decided not to lecture to Dr. Freudenberger's class at NYU in White Plains, NY. Jane was offered a ride there by an ESP class member, and this would have been on a Wednesday. Note that at the start of this session Seth agreed with Jane's decision not to lecture to Dr. F's class, without saying why.

(A note: In connection with her markedly improved physical condition of late, Jane had the impression it was due to her work with the spiritual healers—Edwards & Co. in England.)

SESSION 443
OCTOBER 21 1968 9:13 PM MONDAY

(John Bradley witnessed the session.

(Before the session began I asked Jane to comment on two points made in the last session: The 442nd session was held on Monday, October 14. On Thursday, October 17, Jane unexpectedly received a royalty check from F. Fell re her ESP book; this after Seth had stated on page 107 that Jane would soon receive unexpected word regarding a book. The royalty check was expected later in the year. I wanted to know if this check represented the word referred to by Seth.

(I also wanted the latest word on the status of the auto accident probability data, involving Jane, and given on page 111 of the last session. Seth did not comment on either of these questions, as will be seen.

(Jane began speaking as Seth in a rather slow manner.)

Good evening.

([John and I:] "Good evening, Seth.")

Now. Good evening to our friend here. Give us a moment.

You can expect news from your friend Pat Norelli, and another communication from Edwards.

(Note that on page 107 of the 442nd session, Seth also predicted a considerable improvement soon in Jane's physical condition. Jane has received her expected note from Harry Edwards in England, concerning absent healing, and in answer to Jane's monthly report; therefore another letter soon from Edwards would be unusual.)

Now there is also someone else, if not at our session, then involved in it this evening, so that both of us are in contact. You would think that one of me would be sufficient.

(This was a surprise, and it took me a moment to realize that Seth was referring to his own larger personality, his entity as we call it, and for whom Jane has occasionally spoken in a much different voice. See Jane's notes at the end of this session.

(I found myself wondering how it was possible for Jane to be speaking for Seth, while at the same time being aware of Seth's entity. I was not sure if this is quite the same situation that has prevailed in the past when Jane has spoken for both Seth and his entity during the same session.)

There is also an added development with the John Pitre situation, of which I imagine you will be informed.

A note to Ruburt: he is of late too severe with those in his Tuesday class, too hard a taskmaster.

A note regarding your astronauts and their latest excursion: new developments involving the ionosphere have been made during this trip, and to your scientists unpleasant ones, since they do not conform to previous theories.

(Again a surprise, since we hadn't thought of asking Seth for any data re the astronauts due for reentry tomorrow morning. This is for the Apollo 7, our first three-man spacecraft, in orbit for 11 days—a highly successful flight. We haven't read of any experiments the crew might have conducted involving the ionosphere; or any other experiments, actually.)

It will be thought at first that an error was made on the part of one in the ship who worked certain controls, but other data from other controls will prove that no error was made. It would seem minute, a matter of only a few degrees in measurements, but highly significant.

This is rather difficult to explain: ions not behaving precisely (underlined) as they should, and variations in their activity, just beyond those considered probable.

(John muttered a sentence here. There had been much traffic noise.)

Repeat your question.

([John:] "I hope he makes it—a rattletrap car just passed by.

(Smile.) As long as he does not attempt to orbit the earth. Now. The activity of the ions, only slightly outside of the expected, will nevertheless make it plain that the scientists do not have predicted activity. Their predictions were based upon hypotheses that were not checked because it was not possible to check them under real conditions until this flight.

To the scientists this will seem to mean that the ionosphere is less stable than they supposed. The error was their own in the past. The flight will simply point out the correction, but it will mean that they will feel less secure about landing on the moon. In their terms it will seem that molecular activity is less predictable than they imagined.

The Russians have already discovered this. Now the irritability of the crew *(Shirra, Eisele and Cunningham)* is not due as Ruburt suspected to relative and also symbolic isolation, although this does have some bearing. It is due instead to the length of time spent in the relative orbit chosen, and electromagnetic variations at this level that affect brain, and to some extent motor activity. The report of the crew members will also point out some impairment of motor activity—an erratic rather than smooth nervous reaction.

Some difficulty in finger movements, that will be confidentially reported. Realization of this was behind the irritability expressed against new tests, for the men functioned well enough on tests for which they had been prepared and drilled.

You may take your break, then we shall resume the session.

(9:35. Jane's trance was a good one but she came out of it easily enough after I spoke to her. She now told us that the other personality was about, and that she felt the pyramid effect to a mild degree. She whispered: "The other one is around here." She began to sense the pyramid at break, after Seth had finished. We now explained something to John about the other personality, since he didn't know anything about it.

(I thought the other personality, who is still nameless, would speak after break. Now after our talk Jane sat upright in the rocker, her eyes closed, head back, sitting quietly with her lips moving soundlessly as if experimenting, trying for just the right approach so that the other personality could make entry through her.

(Finally she began. As expected the voice was quite high, clearly enunciating, seemingly distant and sexless; quite removed from any emotional immediacy. Jane's eyes remained closed. Her pace was rather fast comparatively. As usual this new voice ended sentences on an unexpected upbeat, so that often a sentence was finished and

a new one begun while I was writing without appropriate punctuation; then I would go back and add it in the proper places.

(Resume at 9:52.)

You are like children, in your terms, with a game, and you think that the game is played by everyone. Physical life is not the rule. Identity and consciousness existed long before your earth was formed.

You see physical bodies and suppose that any personality must appear in physical terms. None of you are physical; that which is enduring is not physical. In that respect at least you are no different than I. Consciousness is the force behind matter, and it forms many other realities beside the physical one. It is only because your own viewpoint is presently so limited that it seems to you that physical reality is the rule and the mode and the purpose of existence.

The source and the power of your present consciousness is not and has never been physical, and where I am many are not even aware that such a physical system exists. You have chosen your own illusion, and so you must accept it, and from its viewpoint must you try to understand the realities that exist beyond it.

There are many illusions, but the illusions are also real since they are created and since they exist. Yours is simply not one that I have pursued, and one of the purposes of my appearance at these sessions is to acquaint the one you call Ruburt with inner travel, for he must leave the system as you know it, and in doing so set up habits and paths that can be used to advantage.

The situation is not quite stable at this point however. *(Pause.)* Those where I am have not been acquainted with your system directly. We have not been a part of it, though some of us have watched its developments, and interacted within it in other ways.

We have helped nurse it along by our energy. Others like yourself have introduced various concepts to it and been more directly involved. We were long before your beginning in physical terms. . .

(Jane's voice trailed off. I thought this could be a typical unannounced break by the new personality; I was also ready to interrupt if I thought Jane was trying to get out of trance and having some difficulty.

(John and I waited. Two minutes passed. Jane sat with her head back, eyes closed, head nodding a little back and forth—an effect often noticed since last break. Jane coughed finally, and I began to speak to her. Then Seth came through, loud and clear; the suddenness startled us. The contrast between the two voices, the mannerisms, was marked.

(Seth:) Now that big brother has had his say, I will bring our Ruburt back to you, and let you take a break. He will be quite here, very shortly.

(10:11. Jane then came out of trance shortly, without complications. She said she felt "tipped a little to the right," during break, and a few times showed what I thought was a willingness to go back into trance. But she said her head was clear. She only vaguely sensed the pyramid.

(Jane said that with the new personality she was still not sure how to leave. In this instance she merely waited, then felt Seth, warm and emotional, sweep in to help her back. She said that some sounds could bother her while speaking for the other personality, and that if I touched her without preparation she'd feel as though she'd fall through space, yell out, etc.

(Jane felt the other personality would return this evening, and said she wanted to wait and let it build up, forming a kind of flue or open pathway so that she'd go up this easily to make contact. Otherwise she'd have to "fight" her way up to make contact. She doesn't really know how she does make contact, or how she times it—the pyramid helps out here though.

(Jane now felt the pyramid again, so sat leaning back in the rocker. Her eyes closed, and her head began to nod, her lips moving soundlessly. Resume at 10:26, fast pace, high voice, etc.)

You have been so immersed in physical reality through reincarnations, that even your dreams involve you with objects; and even in your dreams you hardly escape the physical units that you have constructed.

It is highly difficult for you to perceive any knowledge or reality unless it is interpreted in physical terms, even though such interpretation highly distorts the information itself. When you allow yourselves freedom in the dream state, when you allow yourself direct experience of reality, when you do not remember it.

In dreams you continue to create pseudo-objects; even in your travels into experiences in other fields of reality, you continue to insist upon the paraphernalia of objectivity until it imprisons you, and you cannot see beyond it.

The inner portions of your own identity and reality are not known to you, for you cannot objectify them and therefore you do not perceive them. So much of your energy is used in these productions that you cannot afford to perceive any reality except your own. Like children playing with blocks your focus of attention is upon physical blocks.

Other shapes and forms that you could perceive, you do not; even in explaining other realities to you I must use the words shapes and forms, or you would not understand what I mean.

You have your mathematics from us. You have a shadow of mathematics, for here again you have insisted upon hemming in realities, of applying larger elements of thought to your blocks. Your idea of progress is building bigger blocks, like children sitting upon the floor. Yet none of us would think of kicking aside your block constructions in ire, or telling you to put aside children's toys, though one day you shall do so.

Later in your time all of you will look down into the physical system like giants peering through small windows at the others now in your position, and smile. But you will not want to stay, nor crawl through the small enclosures, nor have we any intentions of doing so.

In all ways we protect all such systems. We do not have to be aware of them. Our basic and ancient knowledge and energy automatically reaches out to nourish all systems that grow—

(Approximately 10:35. Jane suddenly cried out and began to shake her head violently from side to side as she sat in her rocker. Her movements were so violent I feared she would tip over in the chair. John jumped up to steady her from her right. A glass of beer hit the floor. A second later I was at her left side, having to go around the coffee table to reach her.

(Jane's eyes had been closed, and remained so. Oddly enough her glasses were on; nor did she lose them in the violent shaking. She was quiet now but it took some minutes before John and I could coax her out of trance. Needless to state the sudden end and reaction had been most startling to us. When her movements started I called loudly to her but did not get through.

(When she could finally talk Jane revealed that she had been experiencing a concept to accompany the personality's words; this she has done before when speaking for Seth's entity, and we have been told before that this is one of the reasons or purposes for her speaking for this new personality. But this one was a rough trip, Jane said. This experience, Jane said, "wasn't great."

(It wasn't clear, Jane said, extremely difficult to put into words, but she found while speaking the appropriate lines that she was a giant, looking at John and me in the room, although her eyes were closed. She then experienced a tremendous feeling of growth. She felt her "organs growing," along with John and me and everything in the room. Everything maintained its relative scale, but there was this enormous feeling of growth, as though each of us grew to the size of elephants, Jane said.

("I don't know whether he left me or not," she said, "but suddenly I was me and all this was going on. It was fantastic. I was so completely enveloped by it ... I can't describe it. I was so aware of everything in the room, but my eyes were closed all the time. It wasn't great, this experience."

(I hoped this meant the end of the session, but after a while it was obvious that Jane wanted to continue, or at least was willing to, in spite of the upsetting experience. I tried to talk her out of it. Her eyes kept closing. Finally she decided to continue.

("I'm on my way to the other guy," she said. "I just passed Seth and he joked

with me—something about a massive encounter."

("Why don't you just back down?" I asked.

("I don't know how to."

(10:55. Jane again resumed in the now familiar high and distant, very formal voice; eyes closed.)

The blocks of physical reality appear very real to you when you dwell within their perspective.

Your Ruburt experienced a transmigration of systems. It was not meant to be unpleasant. *(Pause.)* This was his subjective interpretation. First he was involved in a microscopic adventure. Consciousness does not take up space. You must understand this. He then entered your own system of physical blocks, and by contrast that system then appeared huge and monstrous.

When we make contact his personality and consciousness in concentrated form makes its journey, in your terms like a speck in space, the consciousness reduced to its essence, and from this experience we then let him fall back into the physical system. *(Pause.)* Children's blocks then become massive by contrast. It was an experience in concepts, and therefore an advance on your parts. *(Smile.)*

(11:02. Jane paused, and I spoke to her again. She said to me in a whisper: "Get me out of it." I touched her shoulder and called her name a few times, as Seth once suggested I do, and she came out of the trance easily enough. This was the end of the session.

(Jane then said she had a bunch of concepts to tell us about, but didn't want to experience them now, so she called to me. I had been speaking to her at each pause since last break, to give her something to hold on to. She said she didn't know how or what she used to speak to me, but had hold of something. At one period Jane was going to shout "forget it" to the voice, but she couldn't find her voice to do so.

(She described some subjective experiences she thought the personality was going to have her experience. A feeling of microscopic smallness approaching, the reverse of the giant feeling, etc. I told her she'd have to write out the data. She said the ideas were quickly leaving; the feelings were without words and she wasn't used to that yet. She thinks she panics and so shuts the voice off. The pyramid effect was dwindling by 11:15.

(Jane's notes follow.

(Apollo 7 has landed, & first reports say nothing re the data given in this session. See attached newspaper. On the next page, see the beginning of the flight's story in The Elmira NY Star-Gazette.*)*

AZETTE

Y, OCTOBER 22, 1968 TEN CENTS

Topsy-Turvy La

ABOARD USS ESSEX (AP)—Apollo 7's astronauts rode their "magnificent flying machine" to a near-pinpoint landing in the Atlantic Ocean today and were reported in high spirits and apparently good physical shape after being ferried to this aircraft carrier by helicopter.

Navy Capt. Walter M. Schirra ..., Air Force Maj. Donn F. Eisele and civilian Walter Cunningham gave searchers 20 anxious minutes before they were found floating in serene seas just five miles from the Essex.

The successful landing climaxed a sensational 11-day space voyage which put the United States on the doorstep to the moon.

• • •

After a blazing trip back through the atmosphere, Apollo 7 drifted to earth, dangling under its three large orange and white parachutes. It struck the water at an angle and the astronauts immediately cut the shroud lines.

Wave action tipped the 6½-ton craft over so that it was bottoms- up, which was anticipated. This submerged their radio ...tennae and helicopters were unable to zero in on the beacon. They were further hampered by

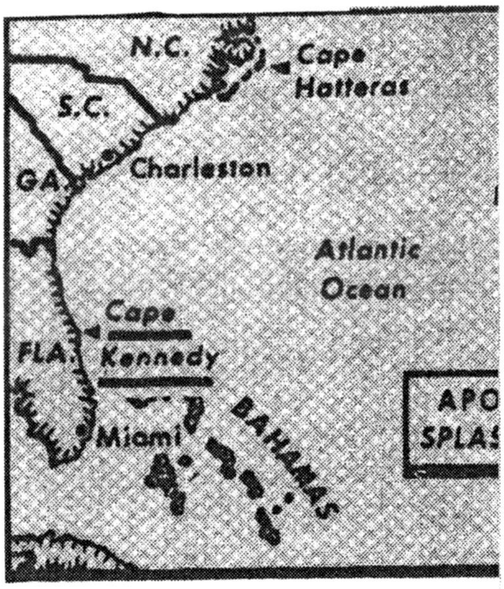

Cross indicates where Apollo 7 landec

2 Kennedy Flying Bac

ATHENS (AP) — Caroline and John Kennedy left Greece today for New York and a return to school, but bad weather still kept their mother's honeymoon yacht tied alongside their new Greek

we
M.
ba

da

JANE'S NOTES
TUESDAY OCTOBER 22, 1968

(I should write a few notes regarding last night's session, before I forget. John Bradley was here. The session began as usual; Seth said that the other personality was also involved. After first break, before session was to resume, I felt the pyramid effect that usually signals the other personality. The effect wasn't very strong, though; I wasn't sure when to "plunge in", wondered if the time was right, etc. Then, o.k., and the other personality began to speak. For a moment I wondered again if trance depth was sufficient as sounds in room bothered me. But as personality spoke, definitely deepened.

([We checked notes after next break.] When personality compared physical reality with children playing with [physical] blocks, he made a remark about a giant peering through the window at the child's play; and... I saw or had the feeling of a giant's face filling up an ordinary window. Hard to recall now; perhaps I was the giant?

(Then suddenly my own body and the room and John and Rob, the whole bit, began to get larger and larger, really massive, my body along with everything else, and at the same time, eyes closed of course, I felt the shapes doing this. It seemed as if the room now was almost huge enough to take up all of Elmira; but I didn't feel as if; I felt as if this were actually happening. I panicked and yelled out and broke the trance with Rob's help. Only moments afterward, memory of the thing was beginning to vanish, and words hardly express the subjective sensations. The meaning of the experience is stated in the final part of the session, so there is no need to go into it here; suffice it to say that the experience had a meaning, was not random but highly selective, and would be listed in our classification as "experiencing a concept." Everything in the room, from smallest to largest, was expanding in proportion; that is, keeping the relative proportion between various objects intact. Everything retained usual shape, for example, only grew and kept growing to massive degrees. Very vivid; frightening to me simply because I was not prepared for anything like this, it had never happened before; etc.

(After break, still felt the pyramid bit; so went along and session continued. Then more sensations; or rather, again I felt sensations that were concepts translated into feeling rather than words; but feelings and images. Here I started to feel the microscopic nature of our planet, comparatively speaking; a shrinking a momentary sense of desolation that was my own, I think; there was no attempt to deny integrity or uniqueness of physical life; but only to express... its relative size [poor word] and of the whole physical system. At same time the pyramid seemed inverted, wide at the top, with a giant face peering down into the room, as through a microscope. If the

room was going to shrink and all of us with it—as it had grown massive, I just wasn't ready for the experience. "I" could sense it about to happen. Through all of this, I use the word I, yet these things were happening and "I" was a part of the action so a part, that it was difficult to separate me from it. So now, wanting out, "I" tried to find "myself"—to make body make a motion to signal Rob. Earlier I thought of just yelling out to the personality, look forget it; but couldn't find vocal chords or something; the personality was using them. So this time "I" found myself, pulled myself together, briefly found voice while personality was silent and just as I was seeing the giant face peer down over me, at pyramid top, at me, and room. Rob brought me out by touching me.

(In earlier episode, I'd screamed involuntarily. In second episode I discovered that there were ways of "finding my I" I guess, and ending experience, by motioning Rob to touch me, or shake me, which breaks trance. So perhaps will have more assurance, knowing there is a way out when I want it; experienced no difficulty from personality, or pressure to continue despite my wishes. Don't believe personality understood experience was unpleasant; or for that matter that such terms had any particular meaning for it. Information or knowledge was being given in certain terms. Period; as far as it was concerned. I don't even know if it was aware of my reaction! I wiggled out beneath the pyramid. Oh; and earlier, Seth came back through and helped me "down"; but this last time he didn't and I couldn't seem to "find him."

(Very startling to me at the time, the whole thing. If a psychologist wants to say simply: Hallucination, then he would have to admit it was hardly a random thing; but well directed, to a point and for a purpose. The merging of self with action in the expansion episode was dismaying at first; just so alien; because I felt the expansion in general; not just specifically in my own body, for example. All in all I think I reacted well; and brought the thing to an end when I decided enough had been done for one night; so I wasn't just tossed, say, willy-nilly. But I broke in, <u>before</u> the onrush of sensations the last time; sensing that they were about to occur, so obviously I had learned from the first episode.

(After coming out, kept feeling inclined to go right; as if partially moving out of my body but not nearly that strong or vivid; merely a feeling that I wasn't entirely inside body but half out to the right in a shadowy rather than substantial fashion. If this would be called hallucinatory by psychologists, then of course far more than vision was involved; the massive quality was definitely sensed directly and vividly. Objects were actually sensed as shapes and forms of volume and weight (?) not sure of weight. Kinetic changes suggest altering of nervous connections, I would suppose. The experience was strangely soundless, and this may have added to frightening quality; didn't think of this before.

(Wonder now, strangely, if the voice is merely a signal, translated into words...

that made the rest meaningful ... that is, if the voice has a ... use or purpose independent of words; though the words are definitely meaningful.)

SESSION 444
OCTOBER 30, 1968 9 PM WEDNESDAY

(Before the session we discussed various recent events and predictions we wanted to cover. They won't be listed here, but in the session as they arise. A note: Jane called Tam Mossman of Prentice-Hall this afternoon.)

Good evening.

("Good evening, Seth.")

Now. For our friend Ruburt *(pause; smile; eyes open)*, in simple terms now. He should know that the Jane self, the Jane personality, is not divided into highly specialized though effective units, as he has been wondering.

Jane does not call herself Jane as a writer; Ruburt on other occasions; Seth on other occasions, and so forth. There would be nothing wrong in such a framework, providing the various subdivisions worked together well. The Jane personality as a whole in that case would still be integrated, various portions of it simply designated for different kinds of work and ability.

Such an arrangement would indeed allow more freedom and creativity than usual. However this is not the case. There is instead not a working arrangement between various portions of one personality, but a working arrangement among many quite independent personalities. They exist in various dimensions, and all of them have access to knowledge that Jane does not possess.

This is not meant as a slur upon Jane's own excellent abilities. On Jane's part this would instead be an extension of her personality into areas far beyond the personality's own capabilities at her time and in her space.

I am far more than Ruburt's "best self," in quotes. The emergence of the Ruburt episode leads me to speak to Jane in these terms so that there will be no misunderstanding.

(Last week in one of her ESP classes, Jane found herself speaking as Ruburt, knowing she was doing so. There was evidently strong telepathic/clairvoyant communication with another student when this occurred, for as Ruburt, Jane, while conscious, described a certain ancient scene set about a campfire; Jane and her student, also female, described the same scene. Jane saw the scene clearly, and among other facts realized that in this ancient time both she and the student were existing as males in that life. Jane has been giving this episode much thought.)

Now. Jane is correct in the idea she received from me this afternoon.

Ruburt does not have my knowledge. I will always be your main communicator. The other two personalities *(Ruburt and Seth's entity)* have been involved at my request, for purposes having to do with our material and purposes.

Now apropos *(Nandor)* Fodor's book *(the title will be given at the end of this session)*, yes, Jane, there is a Seth *(emphatic delivery, leaning forward, eyes open)*, and I was not born a psychic infant from your own personality. Nor was I formed in such a manner. *(Relaxed, a smile.)*

Fodor's idea is that personalities loosely in the same category as myself are indeed legitimate. He nicely concludes that we have a right to existence, and even possess a certain consciousness. However, he believed that we were divergent portions of a medium's consciousness, that had gained relative independence.

Now this is a more respectable theory than many, but in my case it is not the correct one. Again, the theories of personality that are taken for granted within your system still manage to confuse you. It is a highly simplified version of the truth to say that I am a spirit, in those terms, though in those terms I am indeed.

I am utterly independent of Jane in any terms that have practical meaning in generally held concepts of personality. I did not emerge from Ruburt's personality nor person in any way. I have lived often in physical existence. But in larger terms, quite unacceptable at present to psychology, all of us are part of the same entity. Do you understand the difference?

("Yes.")

Now the same is true of Ruburt. I have always addressed Jane as Ruburt, as you know. Therefore the emergence of Ruburt confused Jane. Quite without knowing, Jane has always been aware of Ruburt's existence. Now again, Ruburt is not part of Jane's personality, in your terms, nor did he emerge from it.

Part of the difficulty lies in the use of words. For analogy's sake, then, consider (underline analogy's sake), the serial selves that we have sometimes discussed to make issues clearer. I told you once that in those terms I would be considered as Ruburt's number 6 or 7 self. You had better change Ruburt to Jane in that sentence.

(Seth dealt with this subject some two or three years ago.)

Ruburt then, would be considered Jane's third self in approximate terms. In the analogy these future selves would dwell in other dimensions, and usually self one, or Jane, would be relatively unaware of their, existence or knowledge. In this case self one is able to make such contacts however.

These selves are each completely independent from the other, making their own decisions as individuals, as in the most precise meaning you can apply to that term. Following our analogy, Jane's self 2 is in another position where contact is not possible at this time.

Now Ruburt, compared to Jane's self 3 in these terms, is closer to Jane, so close that Jane has often accepted inspiration and ideas from Ruburt without realizing it. Ruburt is the sum *(smile)* of the present ... Ruburt ... I want to get this as clear as possible ... Ruburt is the sum of the earthly personalities, intimately aware of all past lives.

He is temperamentally closer to physical existence. *(Long pause.)* He is very at home with Jane, you see. Since I mentioned self 2, and again remember this is an analogy—self 2 has embarked upon a completely different adventure, in a different direction in another system.

There were certain capabilities and potentials, always present, that could not be fulfilled through physical reincarnations. Probabilities that never became actualities through any life *(pause)*, a latent personality then that went its own way, and, quite literally was never a physical person. *(Long pause.)*

These concepts can be grasped intuitively. Unfortunately the words used to describe them are the same that must be used to describe currently held concepts. In spiritualistic terms, Ruburt would be the guardian angel, you see.

I have always addressed Jane as Ruburt, since this is the last reincarnation physically. You may take your break.

(9:45. Jane left trance quickly. Resume at 10:01.)

Now. As you know, and we will return now to the familiar name, Ruburt was experiencing a concept. The unfamiliarity of the experience frightened him.

(See the 443rd session.) Rather naturally he placed emotional connotations, or superimposed these upon the experience. He will not have such difficulties as he learns. There was obviously no intent to discomfort him, and it was Jane who became alarmed.

Other concepts, as vividly felt you see, might not have, bothered him, or he might have found them extremely supportive. His own abilities were at a high level. The circumstances were relatively good, though somewhat unstable; a period of three days was particularly beneficial however, which is why it appeared that so much was happening at once.

Jane should be able to contact Ruburt rather easily. It was because of the conceptual experience in our session that Ruburt emerged in practical terms. Again now, we are all independent with our own futures and pasts, in your terms. We are all however connected...

(As Jane spoke in trance now I had a little experience of my own. This took place while she was speaking, and I continued writing without interruption. Quite naturally, it seemed, I now realized that I was seeing a robed figure standing in a

doorway, just beyond Jane's right shoulder as she faced me seated in her rocker. The figure was perhaps three feet tall, standing facing me but with the light coming from the doorway behind so that the face was in shadow.

(I seemed to have the ability to shift my focus so as to see more of the scene. I became aware that another figure was seated at a table just in front of the robed figure, with its head, also shadowed, turned toward the robed one. While Jane spoke and as I made my notes, I found time to do a little sketch in the margin. The sketch merely recorded the idea of what I had seen, and noted the composition, for I thought it would make a good painting. I saw all this in color: browns, reds and yellows.

(I did not have time to speculate about who I was seeing. In perhaps a minute the experience had passed. Jane was still speaking as Seth.)

Each of the personalities alive on your own earth are connected. When such contacts occur, say between Ruburt and myself, then I draw upon those connections and activate certain common pathways.

We will have much more to say here at a later date. Suffice it to say, using again our analogy, that although both self 6 and self one are independent, there are certain connections between them, and that these can be activated.

Suffice it so say also that in this analogy, self 6 is far more than simply a future self one. Do you follow me?

("Yes.")

In those terms then, in some inconceivable future, Jane will not become me, nor grow into me. I am not the oak that the seed will become. By then, in your terms, I will be far different than I am in your now.

(Pause.) Give us a moment. I will have a message for your Tam shortly. Not in connection with the book *(on the Seth material)* but with his own experiences. *(Long pause.)*

There is something here I am trying to get through to Ruburt, but we are meeting with some blockage and so I shall tell him another time.

You may take a break or end the session as you prefer.

("We'll take a break."

(10:20. Jane again left trance fairly quickly. She said she knew what blocking Seth was referring to; she felt herself "come up" just before break. The material Seth wanted to discuss was about Jane and Ruburt and Jane's writing. Jane believed it was an extension of the arrangement Seth mentioned briefly on page 124, when he talked about Jane accepting inspiration and ideas from Ruburt without realizing it.

(But now, Jane said, when the topic veered to the most specific activity she is interested in, writing, a thing she regards strictly as her own, she suddenly found she balked at giving "anyone else" any of the credit.

(I also described my vision to Jane during break.

(10:31.)

Now. Ruburt's has been the voice, the inner voice, that often has given Jane inspiration.

Ruburt has always been highly involved with Jane's writing, imparting intuitive truths, and Jane's psychic abilities were precisely what made the inspiration possible. You cannot separate creative and psychic ability. When Jane seriously questioned her psychic nature, she was without realizing it questioning also the basis of her own creativity, and this interfered with the writing.

In this life Jane has always been able to utilize psychic abilities very well, without knowing it. The basis of her work then was psychic. Without this the development into what you call mediumship would not have occurred. In Ruburt's case, you had better put Jane's case here, the personality was able to mature enough to consciously handle more and more data, to let further developments occur. Otherwise for example I would only have been able to communicate to Jane in her dreams, or through Ruburt.

I am telling Jane therefore that the channel is open for creative inspiration from Ruburt, and the channel is clear. Ruburt can also be counted upon when it is advantageous to interpret my material, though he could not himself originate it.

Now this information should be highly useful to Jane. Ruburt has at times for that matter passed information from me to Jane. Now it is Jane's (underlined) responsibility as a present physically oriented creature, to use the psychic and creative abilities that she has to their fullest, and as a legacy to help others.

She is far more than an open channel in other words. I think perhaps we are coming very clear in this session, explaining in simple terms where all of us stand.

Now. You, Joseph—I will speak to you as Robert. You and Jane are a part of the same entity. You know that you are not Jane. Jane knows that she is not you. In the same way I am not Jane, and Jane is not me. You share some general joint memories with Jane, even before your acquaintanceship and despite the difference in your physical ages. These having to do with national and cultural events, so they are common to you both. This does not mean because you have some general common memories, that you and Jane are one individual.

Yet a psychologist would come to this conclusion if the same statement were made about myself and Jane. Now we as portions of one entity, have certain memories that could be compared to the general cultural ones that you and Jane share, even before you met. These however, that you have, are obviously felt by you both in an entirely different manner, because of your own different viewpoints and so forth.

The same is true of entities and various personalities that are allied with them. Your own creativity, your painting, has always had a psychic basis, and in your case—back to our analogy—self 3 has helped you. Self 2 followed the same path, relatively speaking, as Ruburt's self 2. You had better substitute Jane there.

Now, self 3 has been your inner inspiration often, and it is possible that you will find little difficulty in subjectively contacting Joseph.

("Yes.")

Joseph is the man in the robe in the image that you have just seen.

Now I believe you will find this session helpful. Do you have any questions pertaining to it?

("Not until I read it over.")

I will then continue, take a break, or end the session.

("I guess it's time to end it then.")

We will then end. My heartiest good wishes to you both. The latest developments do represent beneficial freedoms for our friend's part, and could not have taken place until the physical system had begun to largely right itself.

("Why did you say Jane would hear from Harry Edwards again?"

(See page 113 of the 443rd session for October 21, 1968. Seth told us Jane would soon hear from healer Edwards, in England, again soon after she had mailed him her monthly report.)

I believe that a letter has been mailed having to do with the subscription. Hardly anything of note.

(Jane's ESP class has subscribed to a publication of Edwards's)

The book data had to do with the letter from Mossman.

(Tam Mossman, editor at Prentice-Hall; they are considering publishing the Seth material. See the 442nd session, page 107, October 14, 1968. Therein Seth stated that Jane would receive "rather unexpected word concerning a book."

(In a letter dated Oct. 23 Tam Mossman wrote us that Hans Holzer would consider doing the introduction for the Seth Material, provided he was listed as co-author. This was quite unexpected by us, and the offer was turned down. We had known Mossman might ask Holzer to do an intro, but Holzer's demand to co-author the book was not suspected by us.

(See also the notes preceding the 443rd session. These deal with an unexpected royalty check for Jane from F. Fell, and I wanted to know if this event was the unexpected word concerning a book. We did not particularly think so. Due to the pressure of other events however Seth never answered my query on this.)

The automobile material still stands.

("What did you think about the data about Holzer?" I asked this question too quickly, it developed.)

I have not been able to clarify the automobile material. It is connected in some way with relatives and is somehow forming. It is formative, still plastic. It will not involve the two of you together in your car, so you are completely safe there.

(See pages 111-12 of the 442nd session for Oct. 14, 1968 in which Seth warns us not to get into other cars. We have scrupulously followed this advice since October 14, and to date no mishaps have taken place. This auto data was one I wanted to ask about particularly.)

Do not drive with your brother. It is not something that is being formed within your own direct sphere, but one into which you could be drawn.

(My brother William, who lives in Rochester, New York, is driving down to take mother back home with him for a week or two, on November 9. We received a letter from him to this effect yesterday. At first the date had been November 2. The idea of mother spending some time with Dick is not new of course, and this particular visit, postponed several times because of a bus strike, has been in the wind for a long time.)

To cover all points until the situation becomes clearer, I still suggest that neither of you drive with another person. When the situation either develops more firmly in the line of probability or shows signs of disappearing, I will let you know.

It is too late to get involved with the book and that situation.

("Okay." A surprise answer. This left us wondering what Hans Holzer could have to do with anything concerning us, in any strong way.)

There, is nothing pressing, you see. I repeat what I said about Ruburt's health however.

(See page 107 of the 442nd session for October 14, 1968, in which Seth said a considerable improvement can shortly be expected in Jane's physical condition.)

He was able to utilize unusually strong amounts of energy in our work of late, and will find his energy even more abundant and dependable in his writing, our work, and normal living. And now again good evening. I have tried to clear up several points for you.

("Good night, Seth, and thank you. It's been very interesting."

(11:02.

*(*The Unaccountable, *by Nandor Fodor, see page 123.)*

SESSION 445
NOVEMBER 4, 1968 9:07 MONDAY

Good evening.

("Good evening, Seth.")

A few notes for you.

As you have probably supposed, the contents of closets have significant meaning. *(Smile.)* With Jane, now, they represent the resources of the subconscious. *(To me:)* Generally, your attitude is that you want your own subconscious relatively clear. You resent unused paraphernalia, however neatly arranged, because it reminds you of your childhood home.

The paraphernalia, arranged in neat cubbyholes, to you represented paraphernalia of a subjective nature that stood between your father and the use of his abilities. The periodic clearing away in which you and Ruburt both indulge is beneficial from several viewpoints.

(During the last couple of days Jane and I have been going through the apartment, getting rid of accumulated items seldom or no longer used.)

I do not want to go into this particularly this evening, but mention it because of the recent activities. When Ruburt throws anything old out, he does so because he feels he can afford to. He can afford for example to discard old ideas, even those for which he may have some sentimental attachment.

Now give us a moment. *(Pause.*

(To me:) Your own creativity has also had a psychic basis, and often you have translated such information into your paintings without ever having been aware you have done so. You put up what you could loosely term a psychic screen to protect yourself in your parents' home. On several occasions you almost allowed yourself to see through the screen to become aware consciously of telepathic data received from them.

On one occasion you were 12, and on another in very young manhood, perhaps 17, but in your last year of school in any case.

(I graduated from high school in 1937 at the age of 17.)

Both occasions panicked you. *(Pause.)* During one your mind was extremely passive. You were sitting down. I see you bent over a table, either reading or drawing, in the front upstairs room.

You picked up thoughts from your mother, directed against your father, and your father's telepathic reply. Both of your parents supposed themselves to be thinking about the other. Neither was aware that the other was receiving the thoughts, answering them. They were indeed carrying on a conversation without speaking. Your father was in the living room and your mother in the bedroom. Your two brothers were not in the house at the time of the later event.

The younger may have been in the yard. It was in late fall or winter, early evening. You very clearly picked up the thoughts, convinced yourself that imagination was involved, but knew very well it was not.

The constant line of chatter developed by your one brother *(Loren, a year younger than I am)* was of course a defense to close out the constant telepathic storm. Your young brother *(William, 9 years younger)* never set up adequate defenses, so that his own mood swung, willy-nilly, as the psychic climate varied.

Your defense was a creative one however. It turned your natural psychic ability and channeled it into artwork. *(Long pause.)* The children literally were buffers between the parents. Remember however that there were also reasons having to do with past life experience, and that all of you chose these conditions.

You should however do very well now in periods of quiet in any telepathic experiments, for the screen is no longer needed and you have largely discarded it. The same sort of events occur with infinite variations in family life. At times the natural telepathic abilities can help nurture the children. And remember that you also received many supportive impressions from your parents also.

You may take a break and we shall continue the session.

(9:33. Jane left trance rather easily. Her pace had been average. She said that while speaking as Seth about me, she saw me, within, seated at a table or desk in the front upstairs bedroom of my parents' home in Sayre, Pennsylvania. I was not seated at a drawing table such as I now have.

(This agrees with my circumstances when I lived at home. In my school days I did not have a drawing table, but worked bent over at a card table in the front upstairs room, with a small drawing board in my lap, resting on the edge of the card table. I shared this room with my brother Loren. Jane has been in the room many times of course, but did not know the particular circumstances of my working just described.

(Jane saw me bent over with my right hand moving, either writing or drawing. I did both at the card table. She did not say from what angle or position she saw me, and I neglected to ask her.

(During break Jane began to get further impressions on her own, and they are noted below. If she was in a trance now it was a very light one. Seth was not involved. It is interesting to see how association works in such cases.

(Jane now said she picked up something about my mother and dishes. My father, Jane said, had to go to a meeting of an organization like the Lions Club. Dues were due; there was something about money. There was a name, Gale, not that of a woman, connected with father .

("No," Jane said, "it's not Gale, it's something windy, it's that Dr. Martin. I always think of him as a windbag. He was going to the meeting with your father."

(This is good data also. Jane knew my father had belonged to the Lions Club. She did not know Dr. Martin was also a member, or that my father had been secretary of the club, and consequently handled money in the form of dues. I remember

the big book my father used to keep the record of the club members' dues, etc. In fact, my father and Dr. Martin were charter members of the Sayre Lions Club, initiated many years ago.

(Jane now said my mother had talked with Dr Martin's wife Emma on the telephone earlier in the day. Emma had bought a new satin gown that day, and my mother was jealous. She was also mad at my father because he couldn't afford such things for her. Jane said she "was sort of aware of a dress, and a telephone conversation between your mother and Emma."

(A bit later Jane saw my mother in a gray dress with a pin and pearls. She was smiling and happy, Jane said, and went to the meeting also. It was ladies' night.

(The material given above, aside from the specific points verified by me, is typical of possible situations involving my parents and the Martins, who were good friends in those days. I saw many similar situations evolve and resolve themselves, involving my parents, the Martins, and a few other couples who moved in the same circle.

(9:50.)

The earlier incident involved your father and the coal bin.

He was shoveling coal up into buckets, very angry. You stood in the doorway and actually heard his thoughts in your head. *(Pause.)* You were so startled and frightened that you ran. In your father's anger he had wished that your mother was dead, or that she would leave and take her brood with her. *(Pause.)*

There seems to be another occasion when you and a brother jointly received such telepathic impressions simultaneously. *(Pause.)* Do you have any questions?

("I'd like to contact Joseph." See the Joseph material in Session 444.)

You should be able to do this when you are painting. Do not try too hard. Take it for granted that he will appear to you in the studio, somewhat in the same manner as your other visions, But alone, normal size. You may feel his presence first, and then look around to see him.

("Can there be an exchange between us?")

It is possible, of a telepathic nature, and at the same time that you see him.

("Why does my brother Dick want to stop here in Elmira to see us before he goes on down to Sayre to see our mother on Saturday?")

For support of an emotional nature.

He may also ask your opinion as to whether or not he should ask his mother to live with him. Whether or not he asks, he has been strongly considering it. It would be a very poor move.

("Yes.")

It would also break your mother's heart; for she does not understand this son at all. Of course he is concerned over his own health. You are too guarded when he asks for recommendations, and Ruburt's impulse there has been correct. He also looks to you for guidance, and basically (underlined) seeks your support.

Do you have further questions?

("No. Why don't you just continue?")

Give us a moment. *(Pause.)* Do you want more material in the line of what has been given this evening?

("No, I guess not.")

Now. As a rule anything that you know is categorized by you as either memory or present experience, since usually you do not realize you have practical knowledge of what would seem to be the future. Your own knowledge of Joseph is, for example, from both past and future.

In dreams and reverie you may recall past existences. *(To me:)* You will not reincarnate again in physical terms, but those who will can also have dreams in which they catch a glimpse of their own future life.

("Could I reincarnate again if I chose to?")

If you chose to, you could indeed. *(Smile.)* In your terms, you have already chosen not to. You can however have dreams in which you can catch a glimpse into your own next existence, which will not be in your known physical plane.

("As far as you know, in our terms, will I ever again have anything to do with physical manifestations?"

(Smile.) Now. You will indeed. But you will not exist amid objects that are taken at face value alone. Do you follow me?

("Yes. That's what I meant by the question."

(I thought this a neat bit of telepathic exchange, for as I asked Seth the question, I expected to receive just that kind of answer. I thought I would see physical manifestation again, and in an environment that was not slavishly dependent upon objects.)

Both you and Ruburt, in your dream states, have already to some degree become acquainted with what your work will be. Because of your love of images, and Ruburt's love of words and rhythm, you will both still utilize these characteristics. Shortly I will tell you what this work will involve.

("Has this love of words and images always run through our various lives?")

It has indeed.

("But it hasn't come out as the artist and the writer in these past lives?")

Ruburt, at one point was an artist as a male. Give us time here. *(Pause.)* You at one time combined music and words. You did not write music. *(Long pause.)* Both of you have always been strongly creative, have always been concerned with translating inner reality outward.

You were involved in some cave drawings of animals, and have always been drawn to animals. We will try to get this clearer on another occasion, and you may question me on it. For now, Arpennez *(my phonetic interpretation)* comes to mind in connection with the caves.

(Long pause.) You may take a break or end the session as you prefer.

("We'll take the break."

(10:23. Jane left trance easily enough. She remembered little of what she had given. I explained to her about what I really meant by my question concerning physical life in the future, and she then said that Seth was going to comment on our experience in physical reality in new ways in the future, rather than experience a lifetime of continuous physical creatures.

(10:29.)

Now. Your abilities will be developed as far as you can develop them within this plane of existence.

You will then develop them further. *(Smile.)* You still have 4th-and-5th-dimensional art to learn. You have only gotten your feet wet. *(Leans forward, eyes open, emphatic.*

("Good.")

You will be able to create so that your creations exist in more dimensions than they do now. You will have more challenges and problems. Those who view your creations will also have more abilities than they do now.

Your creations then will endure according to the intensity you give them. No natural elements will destroy them, yet they will only be observed by those who can understand them. For many they will exist as beacons. They can also be observed briefly by those still within the physical plane in the dream state if they are far enough progressed. You will have far more material to work with. *(Smile; emphatic. Long pause.)*

I will have more to say along these lines when we get to it, or when you ask me. Remember that I told you both that you have already begun your work. Someday you may even inspire other artists still within this field. Ruburt will do the same. *(Pause.)* You will help give knowledge and inspiration to others even while you continue to develop your own abilities on another level. Now unless you have questions we will end our session.

("I guess not then.")

My heartiest wishes to you both, and good evening.

("Good night, Seth, and thank you."

(10:40. Seth then returned briefly:)

Jane should listen for Ruburt.

(We weren't sure what Seth meant by this.)

SESSION 446
NOVEMBER 6, 1968 9:16 PM WEDNESDAY

(Before tonight's session I read an article, "Instant Electorate," in Playboy Magazine *for November 1968. It dealt with the peccadilloes of Congress, and various unflattering attitudes of the population at large, as reflected in Gallop and Harris polls; the results of these polls were not publicized, and made quite cynical reading, I thought.*

(The article led me to wonder why we behaved as we did, as a species, with seemingly little change throughout recorded history; I wondered what purposes, what real sense, lay behind our attitudes and actions, etc; Jane and I had a little discussion about it.

(At 9:08 Jane said she felt the pyramid effect as she sat in her rocker. This usually means that Seth's larger personality is going to speak; nor did Jane feel Seth around. She asked me if I saw anything in the doorway behind her and I said no. Jane seemed to be waiting. She leaned back in her rocker, eyes closed, lips moving for some moments.

(She then began to speak for Seth's larger personality, using the usual high, very clear and distant voice, with an average pace, and with the usual upbeat ending of sentences. There was no greeting.)

There is a point where all realities intermingle.

It can only be reached from the inside. Many of the questions you have asked cannot be answered in the manner in which you have asked them. The ideals of which you speak are your protection, built-in survival mechanisms that warn of danger, invisible fences like psychic signs saying beware.

You are being allowed freedom within limits. *(Long pause.)* The human race is a stage through which various forms of consciousness travel. The ideals keep the race pointed in beneficial directions. Thoughts and emotions form the basis. You learn by seeing these turn into physical reality. You may be killed by what you have created. If so the lesson is doubly learned.

Before you can be allowed into systems of reality that are more extensive and open, you must first learn to handle energy, and see, through physical materializations, the concrete result of thought and emotion. As a child forms mud pies from dirt, so you form your civilization out of thoughts and emotions, and then see what you have created, and you must deal with it on its terms.

In other systems energy is more directly felt, more extensive.

Consciousness has much more freedom in its utilization. The lessons must be properly learned before such responsibility. There are other training systems, each dealing with various aspects of such understanding and discipline. You cannot do any basic harm. When you act within your system however you act within others.

When you leave the physical system after reincarnations, you have learned the lessons, and you are literally no longer a member of the human race in those terms, for you elect to leave it. Only the conscious self dwells within it in any case, and it is other portions of your personality who simultaneously dwell within the other training systems. In other more advanced systems, thoughts and emotions are automatically and immediately translated into action, into camouflage, into whatever approximation of matter there exists. Therefore the lessons must be taught and learned well.

The responsibility for creation must be clearly understood. You cannot hurt others within your system. To some extent you are, comparatively speaking, in a soundproof and isolated room. Hate creates destruction and in that room, until the lesson is learned, destruction follows destruction.

(Smile.) In the terms of other systems that particular kind of destruction is meaningless and does not exist, but you believe that it does, and the agonies of the dying are sorely felt. A vivid nightmare is also sorely felt, but quickly over. It is not that you must be taught not to destroy, for destruction does not actually exist. It is that you must be taught and trained to create responsibly.

Creation, creativity, is natural under all systems and all circumstances, but your system is a training system for emerging consciousness; for having a talent does not yet know how to use it, and must be trained.

The ideals are like instructions on a blackboard that will not be erased. When you have learned the lesson you realize that the ideals were not necessary, but until you learn the lesson they are all you have as guidelines. The ideals are mere shadows of instructions. They are however your own translations of truths as nearly as you can comprehend them within the system.

They are the rules of the game, and within your system you cannot go against them without courting madness. The system itself would appear insane without them, and only they impart any sanity. In terms of value fulfillment over a period of reincarnations, there is as startling a psychic growth as there is physical growth from a fetus into an adult.

Your system is a training ground only for those however who have chosen to go beyond into particular other systems. These systems are interrelated... other training systems are set up for those who embark on entirely different patterns. *(Long pause.)*

The training gained in your system then will serve you for existence in a variety of interrelated systems. If the sorrows and agonies within your system were not felt as real, the lessons would not be learned. The teachers within the system are those who are in their last reincarnation, and other personalities who have left the system but have been assigned to help those still within it.

You are dealing with the transformation of emotional energy into action and form. You then manipulate within the system which you have yourselves created, and by its effects learn where you have succeeded and where you have failed. The system always includes some fragments who are entering for the first time, as well as individuals in their third or fourth reincarnations.

(Long pause.) Those in the later grades you see are to help the others. The system also provides practice in the methods of transforming energy into form, and of maintaining intensities, of manipulating energy in various aspects.

(9:50. Jane's eyes slowly opened after a long pause. Note that no break was announced, as is often the case when Seth's larger personality or entity speaks. The remote, cool, high and formal voice had varied little, speaking along at a rather steady pace. Resume at 10:10.)

As you dream, and have a dream existence while still involved in the physical dimension, so is the physical dimension a dream within another dimension in which your consciousness is far more acute. And as in your dream you set up situations and work out problems, so you do the same in your physical existence.

You do not feel guilty for those you kill in your dreams. You do not feel that your dream existence is useless, hopeless or beyond redemption, and it seldom occurs to you to think of your dream existence in such a manner.

That existence is a very valid one however, fulfilling significant functions and containing many levels. It is a more comprehensive existence in one way, in that while you solve problems that exist in your physical life, you are also free of physical life to some extent within it, and free to travel to other dimensions.

There is a reason why you view daily physical existence in a different manner while you are within it. In your dreams you are able to know what progress you are making, and where your failures lie. This information is compared to the ideals that have been reached in the manner I have told you; and the ideals themselves originate in the dream state, and are then translated into terms that are practical physically.

Even while immersed in physical reality, you are then to some extent free of it. Physical reality itself is still a dream within a larger existence, so from that existence you seem to yourself to be dreaming while you are immersed in physical life. Often in physical life then, you are also working out solutions to prob-

lems that exist in a quite different manner, and in a completely different context in this other dimension.

Often you are aware that you are dreaming, and you are sometimes aware while in physical existence that you are dreaming. You can change an unpleasant dream by realizing that you are creating it, and that the problems are of your own making. You leave physical reality when you come to the same realization. The problems that you solve while in it are quite legitimate. You also know when you no longer need the particular context.

Humanity dreams the same dream at once, and you have your mass world. The whole construction however is like an educational play in which you are the producers as well as the actors. There is a play within a play within a play, mazes of understanding. *(Long pause.)* There is no end to the within of things. The dreamer dreams and the dreamer within the dream dreams, and sometimes the dreamers are aware of each other. But the dreams are not meaningless, and the actions within them are highly significant. The whole self is the observer, and also a participator in many roles.

Problems leading to world wars also cause worldwide natural disasters. These are merely another materialization of energy projected by those who have not learned how to handle it. Such reactions fire through the dream universe also, and are reflected through all phases of your activity. The whole self compares the performance of various portions of itself in physical reality and in dream reality, and draws its own conclusions.

(10:30. Again without announcement the high formal voice abruptly stopped, and this was the end of the session. After a long pause Jane came out of trance.)

SESSION 447
NOVEMBER 11, 1968 10:35 PM MONDAY

(John Bradley was a witness to the session. John brought with him confirmation of some of Seth's predictions given in the 439th session, to Jane's pleased surprise. The data involves personnel in John's company, Searle, and is somewhat complicated. John is going to go over the session material, using his recorder, to sum up Seth's predictions to date re Searle.

(The session was also witnessed by Estelle and Dave Craig, 1750 E. 21st Street, Brooklyn, New York. The Craigs drove up from New York City late this afternoon to attend the session. Jane was recommended to them by Ray Van Over; they wanted information on the death and attendant circumstances of their son Michael, who died last month at a little over 3 years of age.

(Estelle first called Jane this morning to ask about a session; due to a misunderstanding Jane thought she called from Elmira and agreed to the Craigs' attending this evening. After supper Jane received another call from Estelle while they were en route, and then we realized the effort being made by the Craigs to witness the session.

(Michael had been an exceptionally warm, sensitive and brilliant child. He had begun to speak at but a few months age. He had been good at numbers, and along with Dave interested in astronomy. He died at 3 years, 4 months. He was born on a Thursday, June 10 at 6:08, and died on a Thursday in October, 1968 at 6:08, almost 4 years to the day from conception. Dave and Estelle were curious about the play of similar numbers here, among other things—since these notes touch upon but a small part of the information given Jane and me through the evening.

(Dave and Estelle are both 32. Dave is a disc jockey, and had auditioned for a job in New York City today. Estelle took shorthand notes of the session. Seth spoke rather rapidly this evening, and I missed notes in a few spots, which will be indicated. Estelle's notes may be more complete than mine, and for this reason we plan to exchange copies of the session.

(The five of us spent perhaps an hour getting acquainted before the session began. Seth began speaking rapidly, in a voice a bit stronger than usual, eyes open often, etc.)

Good evening.

([John and I:] "Good evening, Seth.")

Good evening to our new friends and to our old one. Now give us a moment if you please.

First, some general advice. Do not go looking willy-nilly. The answers are within yourself and you will find them. You have your own channels into other dimensions. Use them. You will find the way.

Now. You do not know each other, our guests, and you have come a long way. Therefore we will give what information or advice that we have without fear of embarrassment on your parts *(to Dave and Estelle)*. For the two of you must grow together more, the husband and the wife.

There are cleavages, but the best portions of both of your personalities can be most effectively fulfilled if those cleavages are bridged, bypassed. Now give us a moment. *(Pause.)*

The boy was briefly with you for his own reasons. He was to enlighten you, and so he did. He was of an ancient entity, and you have known him in other lives. He wanted his mother to look inward. He was at one time, he was at one time his father's uncle.

He did not mean to stay within physical reality. He only came to show you what was possible, and to bring the both of you to an understanding of inner reality. He chose his illness, it was not thrust upon him. He did not want to be of the earth. He was done with it, and he only returned so that both of you could learn the truths and inner realities that you are now seeking.

He did not manufacture sufficient blood, for he did not want to be physical beyond the time that he had allotted himself. He was a light, and a light to you, and the light was not extinguished. The light will lead you into knowledge that you would not have known otherwise, nor would you have sought it as vigorously.

He was well aware of this. He wanted you to begin the pilgrimage that you were beginning, but the pilgrimage is within yourselves.

He was indeed involved in scientific endeavors, both in Atlantis and in Egypt, but he had no desire to continue those pursuits in this present existence. He had gone quite beyond them. As his uncle, the father was also involved with him in two past lives in the same relationship, and as priests they were also interested in the inner workings of the universe.

The father however had a particularly unpleasant life in 14th Century France, and *(to Dave)* if you will refuse what you had learned in the past, he could not force you to remember. But he could give you a nudge and a push, gently, and in this existence he did so.

(*To Dave*:) You always have control. You are the one who is always in control, and you knew before you and your wife met, subconsciously, the circumstances that had gone before, and the reason for your meeting, and your son knew. He went before you as he has gone before you in the past.

It is not the time for you to run willy-nilly, looking for truth in any treetop—the truth is inside your own skull, and you at least know how to find it; but discipline and intuition is involved. Your son is not a three-year-old any longer. He is an entity older than you, and he has tried to point the way to you.

You are here for one evening. We can hardly cover much. We have 12th-century Poland for your wife, the earlier existences given earlier. Your main hope and desire now is for inner security that you are not on shifting sands. Remember you form the sands that shift, and in yourself you will find the answers if you are not impatient. You must not demand them of yourself, you must let them come.

The child knew well what he was doing, and subconsciously you also knew. He is not an infant to be pitied, nor a child taken from you before his promise was achieved. He was a personality who left you when his own reincarnations were finished. *(In here I missed a few words because of Seth's faster pace. Copy added after receipt of Craigs' copy on November 22, 1968. See also page 141.)* He returned to help you and show you the way. He is at present resting. He will not return, but go to another reality where his abilities can be used to more advantage.

(To John:) We will get to you before the evening is finished. *(Humorously.*

([John:] "Thank you. I'm in for trouble then.")

I have never given you trouble, Philip. *(Philip is John's entity name according to Seth.)* The trouble that you have is of your own making.

Now we will see what we can get further... My best regards to you both. We will let our friend Ruburt take a rest, and resume shortly with our session.

(11:10. Jane left trance rather easily. Ruburt is Seth's entity name for her. A discussion now commenced among the five of us. Questions arose out of the discussion, and Seth returned in a couple of minutes to answer some of them rather vehemently if briefly.)

I am saying that you, and you, every individual, is in control of their own destiny. I was not speaking specifically of a relationship.

You are in control, you are not moved by other forces. You do not always understand nor comprehend, but you have already set your goals and you have chosen your circumstances. You are all working out problems, and you set the problems for yourselves. No one else gives them to you. You know what they are.

The child had no problems of his own to work out in this existence, but because of love and past relationships he came to act as a light to you both. Now you may take your social break.

(Jane resumed as Seth after break at 11:11.)

Now. Names and dates are important to you, and if we see you again you shall have them. I am interested in what you should know, and what you should know has little to do with names and dates.

(We had been talking about reincarnation at break.)

The child was not a child. You are not to look backward, but forward for the very fulfillment of your own abilities—and I am speaking to you both—will come as a direct result of your acquaintanceship with your son.

I use the word acquaintanceship, for in this life, on a physical level and in physical terms only, you did not understand him for what he was, though you sensed what he was and to some extent reacted to what he was.

(Again Seth spoke quite rapidly and I missed some words, while retaining the gist of the data.)

...He wanted to give you an impetus, and his effect was far stronger when he died than had he lived, and he knew this... For his abilities could not have been used fully in this existence and he would have met frustration.

...He had a horror of living to young malehood, for he did not want to meet a young woman and become attracted to her and then continue with the physical existence.

(Here I asked Seth to slow down and received a humorous reply. Corrections made & added after copy received from Craigs on November 22. See also page 139.)

... Out of respect for your fingers I shall indeed. Is everyone finished with the last sentence?

("Yes.")

Now, he would have been highly frustrated had he continued. Not having enough blood was significant. His vitality was here strongly *(words missed)*, but it was not in physical terms... literally he deprived himself of blood so that he could live on his own terms, and so that the mother and father could live in ways that they have forgotten. There was no witness there, and he expected his death to bring out your own strengths.

Now, I have lived and died many times, and you must admit *(Seth speaks strongly and humorously, forcefully, eyes open)* that you can sense my vitality; and so I can tell you that the vitality of the boy exists in as vital terms. It would have been indeed almost a penance for him to have stayed here longer. You did not save his life one time, you helped him save his soul, and he gallantly returned the favor; for he at one time was tempted to use his abilities for power and to use the priesthood for gain, and on that occasion you stopped him. *(Seth pointed to Dave.)*

Again, in one night's session I am giving you what I believe is the most important information, whether or not you can check it out...

(Again, I had to ask Seth to slow down when the pace was too fast for notes.)

... your inner selves will digest what I have said and what I will say... *(and this is more important than)* 10 pages of notes and dates that you cannot check, since the lives were so long ago. There were however some records ... not papers ... that exist along the way, and sometime if it will ease your mind we will endeavor to give them to you.

There was some alienation, not on the boy's part but on your own—*(to Estelle:)* now look up so you will see who I am speaking of... with the boy, having to do with a past life.... You were afraid to accept him for what he was because of some references in your past lives together.

He knew this and was amused, and he had a game with you, for he knew you loved him, and he knew what you did not know: that because of a past life relationship you would find it difficult to realize who he was.

(To Dave:) Now, he had a mathematical knowledge, and you also have this whether or not you realize it. It results from priestly existences where you were both highly involved with calculations having to do with the movement of plan-

ets. This also has something to do with the hour of his birth and death, for he had a sense of neatness, and it pleased him to time his arrival and departure.

(To John:) I have not forgotten you over here. Far be it, Philip, that I should forget your weighty problems of compromise and profit. Out of due regard to all the wiggling fingers I will let you take a break, and then we shall resume our session.

(11:30. Seth again ended on a strongly humorous note. The pace had been fast, as noted. Dave told us he had been good in math until the ninth grade, when he left it for other interests—singing, communications work, acting, etc.

(Dave now gave us much of the information I've incorporated in the notes at the beginning of the session. Seth resumed at 11:47.)

Now. No one can tell you *(to Dave)* what road to follow.

No one can tell you the, correct road to follow, but you have the answer within yourself. Beware those who give you ready answers. Now give us a moment. *(Pause.)*

I am speaking now in terms of probabilities, for the future in your terms is plastic—it is not cement in which you will become embedded.

If you take a radio job now, and if probabilities continue in the same direction as they are now, then I see another radio job after that one, and then a departure and emergence into another field.

You want basically to teach. You must teach before you can preach, and you must know before you can teach. You are on the way toward learning, and then you can teach. You affect others, and want to move them, and you want to move them in certain directions. Before you can develop your abilities fully however you must have the inner strength that comes from your own inner learning. You have learned from your own vacillation.

You should definitely stay in the communications field. *(Pause.)* You should not be involved now or in the near future in any communications endeavor that involves a taking on of other roles in any sort of acting. You have some abilities here, but those same abilities can also confuse you. *(Pause.)*

They can confuse you as to the nature of your own identity. You become the role. There should be a standing back within yourself for a while. The problems which you have set yourself can be solved, or the challenges you have set yourself can be met, in several ways. You have choices. There is not one way. It is your attitude that is important, and the flexibility of your inner self.

Do not accept compromises, for you personally cannot live with them for any length of time. The circumstances that you face will bring out your strengths, and your son has not left you. You simply do not see him.

There will be contact in your dream states. You are to rely upon the inner knowledge that he has intuitively made clear to you. You are not to rely upon him, but upon what he gave you. You are to look within yourselves, and he has left you the strengths to do so. *(Pause.*

(Smile.) You were a cowboy *(to Dave),* but not in this country. In France. You were not professionally a cowboy, but you dealt with transportation involved with horses. You did not die by gun wound. *(Dave had said he thought he had, at last break.)* You inflicted such a wound upon another, though this was in self-protection, and emotional impetus of the time was strongly written upon your inner memory.

I am trying to give you information that can be filled in, or not, later. A Spanish reincarnation here *(to Estelle)* in the land at least called Spain, 1142 approximately, as a male. This beside the joint lives that I have mentioned.

Now again rest for the scribbly fingers, and we shall continue. *(Seth now pointed to John Bradley.)* And for you, the time to move is not yet.

(12:03 AM. Jane took a little longer coming out of trance now. Break was a long one, and during it Jane gave Estelle a long series of impressions on her own, involving the Craigs' son Michael, and others. I did not make notes on these but Estelle did; she is going to send us a copy of these to be inserted in this record. Some of this material concerned symptoms of the type of blood condition adopted by Michael.

(Resume at 1:08.)

Now. He was ready to leave, and he took what doorways were open, and had you closed them he would have found others.

(This is a reference to Michael's illness.)

It was not an ending to him, but a beginning, and it will be a beginning to you both. You will not see him now the heir to vulnerability, for he has passed beyond it in your terms, and he chose his own gateway. You will not see him grow old, but he has grown old many times, and there was no need for him to grow old again.

You are to develop your own abilities, and he will help you develop them now. In many ways he is able to communicate with you now, as he could not as a child. *(Pause.)* You will have much to tell others, and you will be able to help them. I am speaking now to the father; but only if you look for answers within yourself and not from others.

He will help you and he will also help his mother. On one occasion the mother and the son were brothers, and in friendly rivalry; and that rivalry to some extent still lingered, but it was a rivalry that was built upon love. *(Pause.)*

It is natural in your situation that you look to others for help, and in my

way I hope I have helped you. There is a difference between being told things and knowing them, and the knowing comes from within. And when you know you do not need to be told, and you can have that kind of knowing. I will be glad to help you find it, but no one can find it for you.

You have indeed been given a blessing. The son came to you out of love, for he did not need to come. His own problems here were solved, and he had met his challenges. All his abilities were fulfilled that could be fulfilled within this framework. He was ready for other fields of reality.

Now give me a moment for Philip. *(Pause. Then Seth speaks to John Bradley.)* The triangle symbols, Philip, stand as they have been given. *(See the 439th session.)* There is yet another man to fall. The time to move is not now. When the time comes the suggestion will come from others, so that it will seem that you are doing them a service—and then you graciously accept.

This will also be at the point when you can do your best within the company and have your best opportunity to begin some beneficial changes.

The Tuesday meeting will not have the repercussions that you imagine. The affair will slide for now, but in approximately two months it will come to a head. Do not let it go to your head. *(Smile; pause.)*

I believe the main question that you had has been answered. Does this clarify the matter for you?

([John:] "Not totally. Out of the first triangle one would fall; he has already fallen as a matter of fact. Is there to be a man in the second triangle who falls?"

(Again, see the 439th session. John's question above was not taken down by me verbatim, but is a close approximation. The falling of the man from the first triangle was predicted by Seth in the 439th session, on Sept. 30, 1968, and took place a few days before this session.)

There is indeed, and it is after this fall that your freedom to move is fairly secure.

([John:] "Would this man be in the second, separate triangle, or the first?)

The man is a part of both triangles.

([John:] "Then would this be my regional manager?")

Yes.

([John:] "Will the two months you mention be the reorganization time?")

No. The information as I gave it I thought to be particularly clear. *(Now Jane, as Seth, pointed to Dave and Estelle)* And yes, here, for another child—one who needs to be cherished and guarded and has a fate to fulfill in physical reality, who will need you. You needed your son. The other child will need you.

(Again to John, humorously:) Are you satisfied, over there in the corner?

([John, smiling:] "Yes, I'm satisfied, I know when to shut up."

(Humorously:) We shall cherish the words ... Now I give you all the blessings I can... *(A few words missed.)* ...unless you want to take a break, I believe it is time to end it. *(To me:)* As always I defer to you.

("Well, I guess it is time to end it, Seth; with everybody's consent."

([From the four of us:] "Good night, Seth."

(1:23 AM.)

SESSION 448
NOVEMBER 13, 1968 9:12 PM WEDNESDAY

Good evening.

("Good evening, Seth.")

Now. I have some hints, I hope practical ones for both of you, but they will take your attention.

Now, with all you have been told about the nature of personality, and of the many of which you are a part, it would now be a help if you could find the center of your larger self.

You can intuitively become aware to some extent of your own reincarnations, so that you feel a recognizable sense of familiarity. Now there is unity in all. You have been told that there is a point where all dimensions and systems of reality merge. Now the same is true of consciousness. You are a part of a larger self, an entity, and because you are there is a portion of you that has access to the knowledge of your entity.

All of it would not be translatable. Some of it would have no meaning for you, but much of this is accessible. There are ways of finding what I will call this center of yourself. It will give you direct experience with many concepts that we have been discussing. I will give you more reincarnational data on your own lives; as you travel to the center of yourself however you will feel (underlined) and know your own pasts as directly as the circumstances permit.

More than this however, your abilities and your challenges will appear to you in a much clearer light, and uncluttered focus. The experience will deepen and reinforce your sense of individuality, and you will know for yourself that you are one in many, and yet many in one.

There are five steps. *(Pause.)* It is possible to cover all of them at once, or the process may take you some time. First however imagine your consciousness out of your body in its astral form. Next, feeling that you are in the astral form, tell yourself that from that image you will be able to see the image of the person that you were in your immediately past life.

I cannot tell you whether you will succeed at once, as you may, or whether you will find it difficult. You, Joseph, being proficient with images, may find it easier than Ruburt. Now when you feel that you have this new image of your past self before you, then imagine that your consciousness is moving from your astral form into this past self. You should not do this until you see the whole form.

Before you see the whole form you may try to mentally communicate with it however, asking it questions. This is one approach. You may for example end up using this as the main method of communication between your present and your past one. Otherwise will your consciousness as mentioned earlier into the image, then ask yourself: Who am I? Where was I born? What memories are mine?

If you have succeeded here, then memories and images will flash through your mind in the same way that your present self would ordinarily recall its past.

Then, will yourself to return to your own astral image, then to your physical body. From here repeat to yourself what you have learned, and whatever data you have received, reminding yourself that this is also a part of your identity. This may be done very well imaginatively, in other stages of the process.

After you have managed to feel yourself above your body in your astral form, you again tell yourself to see the image of the same past self. You may then imagine its image merging with your own, and its memories a part of your own consciousness. When you have succeeded, then still feeling yourself in the astral form, tell yourself that you will next see the image of the life before last: the image of the person you were, then repeat the other steps.

You may take your break and we shall continue.

(9:40. Jane left trance easily. She said she had some images of being "up above," while speaking. The apartment was quite cold tonight because of a strong wind that had blown all day, after a 14-inch snowfall yesterday; but Jane said that as Seth she was not cold, in fact comfortable for the first time today, etc.

(Resume at 9:49.)

The whole exercise, or any part of it, must only be done in order to avail yourself of wisdom, so that you can use your own abilities to help yourself and others.

The purpose is very important, for when the purpose is a good one then it unites the other images about you and your purpose beneficially. It is part of the equation, as important as a plus sign rather than a minus sign, and as important to your results.

Various kinds of experiences may develop. You may request information concerning abilities for example, and hear your answer internally. You may instead feel the stirrings of memory, and experience yourself using abilities developed as a past personality. At any point in the exercise, for it can happen at any stage, you will suddenly feel the you of you, the center identity that runs through all the selves of which you have been part. You may also in a flash see glimpses of further realities that would be future to your present self.

According to the circumstances and your own condition, results can be amazingly rapid, or slow. You may try many times and then succeed... the methods are extremely important however, and should be definitely included in our material. There are also some variations on these that I will give you.

Those who try the exercises with wrong purposes will not succeed, for they will not have the proper equation, and it is the one part that cannot be given to them. Do you understand?

("Yes.")

Now, you are free on the car episode.

(See the 442nd session for October 14 1968.)

I am going to give you a brief session, but if you have any questions I will answer them.

("What did you think of those people [meaning the Craigs] coming up from New York?"

(See the 447th session.) I knew they were coming. The sudden is often not accidental.

(Did I ever do well projecting in any of my past lives? I mean did I consciously retain memory of the projections?")

You and Ruburt both did.

("When?")

We will have to update your reincarnational data, for there have been distortions in early material, and blocks, then, on Ruburt's part. In two lives in particular however you were both proficient, and one of Ruburt's recent dreams was based on one such episode.

("Which dream?")

Ruburt knows the one, in which you both appeared as males and partners.

Now we have several projects: the book we have not yet begun, and more detailed account of your reincarnational history. As things stand now we also try to help those few who personally appeal to us. Our projects will all bear fruit however. *(Pause.)*

We may organize our material for a while now around one or another of these projects, though in the past months, on a rather free-flowing basis you have received excellent material; and regardless of the organization or order of delivery, the material has its own form, and what I have in mind to say will be said. *(Humorously.)*

Now we will end the session or you may ask questions as you prefer.

("I guess we'll end it then.")

My heartiest good wishes to you both, and I hope your chilled bones get warm. I do not have such difficulties. You may be interested to know one interesting piece of information. Your dog has been reincarnated, in his terms, looking much as he did before.

(Our dog Mischa died in 1963. Jane had him when we met in 1953.

("Where is he?")

He is in this territory, in a litter of pups, and in one way or another he may try to find you. After 4 to 6 weeks he may end up in your local shelter.

(This data was quite unexpected by us, although this afternoon I had mentioned Mischa to Jane in passing, remarking on a similarity of pose struck by our cat Willy as he stood in the studio, intently listening to a sound outside. I hadn't intended that any remark of mine about the dog lead to this kind of data, nor did Jane interpret it that way. In fact, we know so little about animals, let alone animal reincarnation, as far as this material goes, that it hasn't occurred to us to ask this kind of question . By "this territory" Seth meant Elmira, New York.

("As a male, same color?" Brown and white.)

I believe *(pause)*, he belongs in a litter born in approximately the same area that he died. Now I am not certain of the sex, though the general appearance is more or less the same.

There may <u>possibly</u> be a marking on the tongue.

("Will this dog have any empathy with us?"

(Leaning forward.) The marking reminiscent of the affair at Saratoga. And to your question, yes. *(Mischa had briefly tussled with another dog.)*

There is a strong possibility that he would be a female.

Now my best wishes to you both, and I will not keep Ruburt barking for me any longer. *(Humorously:)* <u>I</u> am an old dog, and I remembered you.

("Good night, Seth."

(10:20. Jane left trance easily. She was surprised at the Mischa material. Moreover, she had no conscious memory of my mentioning Mischa to her this afternoon, even after I recounted the little episode in detail.)

(I certainly didn't know that I'd publish my 1960 drawing of Mischa 42 years later! Before Jane and I married, on December 27, 1954, she told me I'd have to take her dog, too.)

SESSION 449
NOVEMBER 18, 1968 9:15 PM MONDAY

(Below is a copy of three questions sent to Jane by Roger Sullivan, a friend of Pat Norelli; both live in Boston. Roger is working on a doctorate. The questions were sent on October 6, but we haven't been able to deal with them before this because of many other events.

(The 440th session was held on October 7, and was addressed to Pat. Roger's list contained a fourth question addressed to Seth; this one concerns the Bahai faith, was formulated by a girl friend of Pat's, and will be answered by Seth at a later date.

(The first 3 questions, as I copied them from Roger's letter:

1.) WHY DOES $\frac{e^2}{\hbar c} \cong \frac{1}{137}$?

e = ELECTRONIC CHARGE

c = SPEED OF LIGHT

$\hbar = \frac{\text{PLANCK'S CONSTANT}}{2\pi}$

2.) PROVE THERE ARE NO INTEGERS SATISFYING

$a^3 + b^3 = c^3$

FERMAT SUPPOSEDLY DISCOVERED A PROOF BUT DIED BEFORE WRITING IT DOWN.

3.) MY MOTHER'S MAIDEN NAME ?

(We hadn't planned on dealing with Roger's questions particularly this evening. I merely showed Jane the list shortly before 9 PM. What followed was surprising to us in several ways, and raised many questions that we will now search out answers for.

(Strictly speaking, we do not believe Seth as we known him and are used to him, gave the material tonight. Jane spoke while in a trance state, but in her usual voice, and received the data from "another source." Our questions will have to do with the nature of this source, why this particular data came through in this fashion, etc. Jane is used to giving impressions on her own as well as through Seth, but there seemed to be an intriguing difference this evening. Jane would find herself speaking a few lines, then waiting for more to come, which she would then dutifully recite. She felt no other personality's presence, etc; whatever the source, it appeared to be blocked off from her emotionally and subjectively in the usual sense; yet the material was given.

(Needless to say, neither Jane or I know math; I may know a little more than Jane, but I couldn't explain an integer to her at break this evening, for instance. A few phrases that came through in the data had a familiar ring to me, but Jane said they meant nothing to her.

(In fact, she said that for all she knows all of the data given this evening is gibberish. We have no math books in the apartment. Few people have seen Roger's list, and none of these with one exception knew any math. The exception is my brother Bill, who looked at the questions briefly last week on a trip through Elmira, from Rochester, where he lives, to Sayre, Pennsylvania, where our mother lives. He could shed no light on the questions, and gave us no definitions, etc.

(All of which is not to say that Jane and I haven't encountered math in some form(s) in our daily lives, probably at times without being conscious of this. We have read about relativity, for instance, in popular paperbacks, and some other paperback books on a variety of subjects that might have included various kind or examples of mathematical formulas, etc. In other words, our contacts with math have been about average, we estimate.

(Since Jane looked at Roger's list just before the usual session time we thought Seth might consider the questions. Seth did not come through however during the evening. Jane said she could not make any conscious attempt to answer the questions, since she couldn't read the formulas. She had said a little previously that she felt "up" today, or full of energy, light and active.

(Jane's impressions are in Roman type, like Seth's. While giving the data she was able to speak to me and describe her subjective state also, without breaking the thread of her reception.

(Shortly after looking at the questions again at 9:10 Jane closed her eyes.)

I just got the word Bainbridge... The quadrants, too innumerable to mention. To the 9th—not sure of the word here—to the 9th power or degree. Then, too bad you're not a mathematical medium, Jane.

(We thought this data preliminary to the regular session, since Jane will get flashes like this sometimes just before Seth speaks. This data didn't seem to come from Seth, however. Jane said she feels that some of the words she "gets" aren't correct mathematically, like "assemblage of integers."

(Jane then told me to wait, that when she got something it was "real clear," but that she didn't know where it was coming from. I said she could wait and let Seth deal with the data, and she rejoined that she didn't want to interrupt what she was getting. At times she spoke in a hesitant voice, at other times very rapidly, and usually with a puzzled expression; eyes open often, as usual in her trance states.)

(She then said:) An infinity has no number. The other side of zero cannot be reversed. *(Pause.)* Freedom to the 9th power.

(At 9:20 Jane asked to see Roger's list once more. She looked at it briefly and laid it down on the coffee table. Then:)

The minus principle can be multiplied forever. There is no constant. Herein is the fallacy. *(Pause.)* The answer then to one of your questions lies here.

Doubles have no meaning in the Planck thing, whatever that is. The weaker integer doubles its (value) with the speed of light. Better put value in parentheses, because I'm not sure it's the right word.

The positions of the values above and below ... the line is then reversed. *(Pause.)*

Bainbridge again, period. I don't know what that goes with.

The formula or equation found and forgotten several times.

The—I don't know what you call these ... *(When I said I didn't know how to write down what she was telling me, Jane said:)* Just put: the minus numbers represent negative charges, and mark the activity of ions' negative flow. The minus numbers mask integers that have a positive meaning or action *(pause)*, and take on the tasks ordinarily assigned in this dimension to the positive ones.

The order of value descends in direct proportion *(Jane's tone was very puzzled, eyes open)*, to the order of ascension on the positive side. *(Then she added:)* This is to make that clearer; talking about negative and positive values, and on the negative side the value descends in direct proportion to the order of ascension on the positive side.

(For some reason Jane then told me I didn't have to put this down, but I did so anyway:) The order of the integers on the negative side descends in direct proportion to the order of ascension of integers on the positive side. But the balance between them, the two systems, is only apparent from your particular view-

point, and not basic.

There is an instability and still unpredictable activity inherent in the integers *(pause)*, but shows more strongly, or appears, after the 9th power.

This instability isn't noticeable here, even <u>after</u> the 9th power, but it exists. The unpredictability seems to result in the dissolution of quadrants under certain conditions. The value of the integers would seem to dissolve *(pause)* at the speed of light, but it is precisely here that the minus numbers take over and become, or <u>take on</u>, the value of the positive numbers.

If you consider the positive and negative numbers like a spectrum, then, the spectrum shifts. The inner values of the minus numbers have not been, I think, suspected.

The value of the integers thrusts forward and back, pulsating like reflection *(pause)* that draws (quadrants or integers) *(better put those terms in parenthesis, Jane said, since she wasn't sure of the word to use)* like a magnet, adding their value to their own. *(Pause.)*

(At 9: 43 Jane paused and seemingly left trance. "I'm just waiting a minute," she said. "When it stops, I stop, see. This doesn't make any sense to me—I'm probably distorting the whole thing. Now I seem to be getting:

(Resume:) X Y I'm not sure, either to the 2nd or 9th power, that goes next to Y over a line; pi, and *(pause)* one of those marks between, an equal mark I think *(Jane was now trying to draw marks in the air)*, C C something that looks like an H over a line, 4. This is a multidimensional game. Have fun.

(9:49. Another break. Jane said she wasn't aware of any particular source for the data—she was "trancey" and the words just came in. It wasn't Seth, she said. She didn't know if she got all the words right, but did as well as she could. As far as she knows, she doesn't have "the slightest mathematical vocabulary."

(The equation she tried to give doesn't make sense to her; she now looked at Roger's questions again briefly. What she got when giving the equation was not really a vision, she said; it didn't look like Roger's writing; she seemed to get the data in words and feelings, numbers radiating or pulsating within at the appropriate times in the data.

(Jane doesn't know what Bainbridge means, whether it is Roger's mother's maiden name, a place, or what. When the data stopped flowing Jane would just relax and wait for things to come through again. The "have fun" and the use of the word "I" made it seem as though a specific source was responsible for the data.

(We hoped that after this rest Seth would come through and explain what was going on, but instead Jane resumed as before. She spoke in her own voice, rapidly and slowly by turn, eyes open often and with many a pause and puzzled expression. Resume at 10:00.)

You can't hold 4th-dimensional physics in the palm of your hand.

At a certain point the integers seem to dissolve; their value undermined *("I think this bit has to do with that Planck thing," Jane said)*, but here they actually pick up added powers, precisely where you cannot follow, in integer, where its values seem to be undermined. At this point it is raised to another power that escapes the perceptive abilities of the 3-dimensional brain.

(Long pause. Again Jane said: "Don't write anything yet, I'm not sure of what I'm getting," while I wrote it anyhow:) I'm getting the impression of a little man with dark hair, and he seems very far away, so I think he's in the past; and he has old-fashioned clothes on... a watch chain and a vest... connected with a college, a prestige one like Princeton or Yale; and he worked on mathematical theories, and he suspected, oddly enough, that some integers or numbers had unsuspected values, and he was right.

Now, with him the date 1936. And unless I'm balled up I think 1936 is the year he published or initiated some of his theories. Correctly interpreted, they would lead as mentioned earlier to an unsuspected unpredictability of integers under certain conditions, and the unpredictability is the clue that would lead to the thus-far hidden values. *(Pause.)*

It is as if infinity doubled in upon itself. Zero *(gesture, a frown, a pause)*, being far from neuter, but a gateway through which the integrity of the other numbers come. The integrity of zero cannot be doubted.

The beauty of the zero is precisely that all other values in it lie inherent. Now it can gobble up all your (parentheses here, I'm not sure:) integers; and those dissolving values mentioned earlier, dissolving into zero gain new power.

Consider zero like a mutant. You have missed the significance of its behavior.

At the 9th power certain values begin to slip away. What is wrong, that you have not missed them? The quadrants involved turn into a spiral, turn the zero inside out. Within its magnitude even the lowly integrity of 4 vanishes.

In its place is a gobbling of numbers. The positive is accentuated when you turn the zero inside out. Remember the integrity of your quadrants. They escape you if you look away.

Within the 9th to the 11th power is the answer to the riddle. *(Pause.)* No integer is the same from one moment to the next. *(Puzzled, Jane shook her head.)*

You force stability upon them, but you cannot predict their action *(puzzled again)*, when you cross them *(pause)*, in the nature of a pi. The first formula is overloaded to the right. The negative values about it will supersede and gobble the integrity of 3; unload the 7. Greek *(Jane paused and sat with her head cocked as though listening)*, and the theorems of *("I'm having trouble with the name.")* Minopeles *(my phonetic interpretation)*, a minor mathematician.

("I don't know if it's done or not," Jane said now. "Right now it's quiet." Then:)

The constant cannot be counted upon in the equation as written. Your values undermine themselves. You forget the integrity of 7.

(Pause at 10:28... "I'm just waiting," Jane said. She looked at Roger's formulas again briefly. "I don't know what I'm looking at." She did have the feeling of the little man, as though she looked at him in a small box, she said. She interpreted this to mean she saw him in the past.

(Jane didn't have the slightest idea of where the information was coming from. She felt subjectively that the data came to her from her right side, via a channel. This contrasts with the overhead channel or pyramid effect she feels subjectively when Seth's larger entity speaks.

(Jane waited to see if more was coming. She then resumed in the same manner, rather objectively, although with many a puzzled expression, eyes open often, voice her own, etc., at 10:30.)

The ground rules are different, even pi, magnified to unknown degrees, having a <u>function</u> aside from the main one. A little known principle of utmost importance.

The significance of the quadrants has never been clearly understood—there are powers working on the numbers beyond those that you know. *(Fast pace.)* The unrelated functions bear strong relation *(Jane asked me to read this phrase back)*, to the underlying principles upon which the basic theories of malfunction are formed. Malfunction being the inability of a number in a particular equation to perform its usual service.

Malfunctioning numbers appear in pairs mainly at the 3rd, 9th and 11th powers. *(Pause.)* They are a sign of the instability of the P S I *(psi spelled out)*, factor, and mitigate against the validity of your results.

To offset this, regard again *(puzzled expression)*, the full nature of your integers and remember their relation to the factor known as p. Underscoring this is the problem of cohesives. The unifying nature *(pause)* underlying the principle of P S I *(spelled)* group together in a conciliatory fashion. You will find that marvelous aptitude *(pause)*, of the psi factor beneath. The seemingly erratic nature(s) of the integers then join. The beauty of it lies precisely in the fashion that the merging numbers (integers) meet. *(Jane said to put the word integers in parentheses, since she wasn't sure of what word to use there.)*

Here the equation *(voice pitched higher)* seeks to turn inside out, but the functions and values of the integers return it to stability. The functions at times are completely reversed, but the overall integrity of the equation stands. Nature without its clothes on, ha, ha, ha. *(Voice drops to normal).* Or the alchemists outdid themselves.

All of this is premature, for the equation itself bears little basic reality to truth. It has a highly artificial relation to it, and it hides another equation, secret since the time of Egypt, having do with the basic nature of zero, and the opening and wedging powers of the unleashed integer, over zero to the 9th degree gradations downward, do you see?

(Pause. I had questioned Jane to see that I had the right word, wedging, above.)

There is a basic unpredictability. Find it. Grouped generally under the values of the simple 7, plus and minus the magnitude of the 7 as it goes through the zero, brings you a multidimensional concept that equates with truth.

(10:45. Again the flow of information stopped. Jane said her focus of attention was intense while speaking for whatever the source of data was. She doesn't recall hearing about psi factors, but I had, and thought she had also at various times, without knowing what the term applied to; the same with cohesives, conciliatory fashion, etc., although these would be much less common to us.

(Jane doesn't know who the little man she described, is. We agreed that we know so little about math that even if this data received tonight is all wrong, we wouldn't be able to intelligently discuss it with anyone who knows math.

(Again Jane resumed in the same manner, at 10:55.)

Nor can the intuitive basis of mathematics be denied. The numbers are merely symbols for inner points of recognition. The forces behind the numbers break through, and form their own interaction, affecting all integers to the 99th degree; and from then on an acceleration of effects, a shifting out of focus.

The definite magnification, and outward from each number in pyramid form, the angle, unformulated functions. The true edification of the mathematician is to sense the values of the numbers' move. The interaction accumulates. The effects build up, and are therefore demonstrable after psi makes its appearance known. Turn about the integers but there is no disorder, yet the precise neatness of the integers is based not upon basic order, but ordered chaos, that once in a millionfold escape of the integer from its bounds.

(Steady, rather fast pace.) Known values operate up to a point, then the unpredictable nature of the psi factor undermines accepted tenets, and the equation seems to fail. Group your forces under the protection of the 9th power.

Here at the 9th power there is balance with the minus 9, but only for a moment. The unpredictability then enters in, flying the banners of a divided house. The atom lives in the unpredictable factor where the integers meet and fall apart. Here there is the development of new powers, and the negative functions come to the fore.

Here the great army of the integers vanishes into the mouths of the quadrants, and the destruction of the previous functions of the integers is accomplished. But the previous functions, dissolving, do so only to re-emerge in a new fashion, and up rise the values of the 12th powers, now under the triumphant banners of the psi factor, minus 7 over an unfolded pi. Regrouped, the values assault each other.

X has lost its strength and Y is under the siege of Planck. Planck's forces *(pause)*, triumph over the old values but zero gobbles some of Planck's men, the integer minus 7, and to work out, psi must be confused for a moment with 8. The mistake is found, and Y is free. Too bad you neglected the psi factor. You thought 7 gobbled it up. 371 will not stand alone in that location. It is besieged by truth to the 3rd power, truth being one, hand in hand with 7. Three C (E?), 3C, over 9 to the 7th power, will temporarily equate with 9 over 137, might give you truth.

(11:10. Jane's pace had slowed considerably toward the end, so she decided she'd better come out. So did I. As she left trance she received: Michigan was the place of birth; then she came out.

(Jane was really bewildered by this data tonight. To her numbers have no emotional meaning. For this reason any subconscious dramatization would seem to be ruled out; we will investigate the source however.

(Pat Norelli is to visit us over Thanksgiving. She is to carry a copy of this session to Roger in Boston, with our request for a paragraph-by-paragraph analysis of this material by him, for our records.

(Looking over part of this data on November 20, 1968, Carl Watkins, who studied math in college, said it made sense. See next session—450th.)

SESSION 450
NOVEMBER 20, 1968 9:28 PM WEDNESDAY.

(This session proved to be a continuance of the last session. See page 149-150 for an explanation of the circumstances surrounding the questions sent to Jane by Pat Norelli's friend Roger.

(Once again Jane spoke on her own in delivering tonight's data, and toward the end of this session we began to get glimmering of what was going on. A more personal and emotional atmosphere began to enter in that was revealing to us; in these situations Jane is learning control even while she is in trance.

(We would like to insert a note here to Roger, to the effect that we would like him to go over the two sessions and give us a detailed written summary of the data given through Jane, in answer to the mathematical questions he sent Jane. This applies whether the answers satisfy him, or make any kind of sense, or not. We want to insert the material into the record, there to take its place with all the other variety of material growing out of the sessions. Jane's mathematical knowledge and vocabulary [and mine] is so limited that any valid [or invalid?] data obtained in trance by Jane, on this subject, is of interest to us; the more we learn about these two sessions, the easier it will be for us to interpret another facet of trance experience.

(This session was witnessed by Carl Watkins, of Odessa, New York. Carl studied math for two years in college; reading the first session, he said that the ideas presented by Jane in trance made sense to him; he cited some examples to us and worked out some figures, especially concerning quadrants, and drew some diagrams. This proved interesting to us and we understood it while Carl was speaking; later however because of our lack of background in math we found it difficult to recall what Carl had said.

(We sat waiting for the session as usual at 9 PM, expecting Seth to come through. Instead however Jane finally began to speak for herself again. Her eyes remained closed mostly; her voice was even and normal, pace fairly good with occasional long pauses.)

The multiplicity of the finite, under the establishment of form, causes the renunciation of values, flying under the sign of all before the 9th power.

(Jane delivered this material with many a puzzled frown.)

After the 9th power form shatters, but at the 12th power form is re-established under a new constant. Certain integers belie their own position, and cast shadows into other dimensions.

This has to with the 2nd equation. Its establishment can be found when you understand the hidden minus power that you have not uncovered.

The Greeks had a name for it. The mastery of the equation is not determined by predictability, but by the realization that unpredictability often occurs at a constant ratio. The ratio minus zero over one three seven, leaping back now to the other.

("I don't know if that means leaping back to the first equation or not," Jane said. See page 149 for a copy of Roger's questions.)

The magnitudes are overextended in your first version. *(Pause.)* Four has been underrated. *(Then Jane said: "I have no idea what this means:")* And 3 in the yellow column would lead to annihilation. *("I get something like disaster," she said, "but I think it's annihilation.")*

The normal ascendancy has been disturbed, and you are 3 digits away on the right side, above the line. *(Pause.)* Don't you see, your groupings would be eradicated. Be brave and move your 6. This has reference again to the 9th power.

Unknowingly you disturb the integrity of 7. Group your forces again under the constant. *(Pause.)* Now turn the equation around and you will see that it is pure.

Do not work Euclidean violence. Be gentle in your manipulations. *(Jane spelled out Euclidean. At break it developed that she did not consciously know about Euclid, the Greek mathematician and geometer.)* Now I think this is, with the psi factor, too harsh or sudden; too hasty a movement here will knock 7 off balance. Now weigh your values. *(Pause.)* No known method can now disturb them. *(Long pause.)*

There is work for you to do in here, as is proper. Close the door in the face of a constant and the elements converge. *(Puzzled expression:)* Have you considered 137 over 4 to the 9th? Speedy recovery. *(Pause.)* Your original equation staggers under the weight of imponderables. Mighty is the quadrant that cuts through the center of the source. The unshaken circle. The unshaken zero, gobbles two 7's *(pause)*, and structure or form is eaten away from the inside.

The vortex disturbs the speed of light, or moves up through...

(Jane paused, then said: "I don't know. Robby, I've got the image of something that looks like a spiral, the speed of light. Then the center is the vortex," and Jane made a pointing gesture into the middle of the image she had been drawing in the air, eyes closed.)

The patterns are superimposed one upon the other, and you must look behind the veil of integers and within their unsuspected values. Again, remember to regroup your forces.

The man referred to earlier, 72. Mine is the achievement.

(9:53. Jane came out of trance easily. However she acted and looked, somewhat bleary. This sleepy effect was already more pronounced, I thought, than it had been at any time during the last session. She still had no real idea of the source of the material. The last phrase of her delivery, above, seemed to be a quote. See page 153 of the last session, concerning the old-fashioned little man Jane had seen in image form.

(She resumed in the same manner as before at 10:02.)

In the heart of the vortex, integers fall apart. They regroup on the other side of 7 to the 9th on the minus side. The positives are scattered.

(Jane gave me a punctuation here: "There's a period after the minus side.")

Regroup your forces under 137 *(pause)*, carried to the magnitude of 9, and you have overwhelmed your quadrants. Untold advantages and possibilities then come into sight.

(Jane paused again. Her voice was abruptly somewhat weaker, trailing off at times. She appeared to be making an effort to keep it going. More emotion was now apparent, as though a personality was inserting itself into the data that, so far, had been quite objective and evenly given.)

Mine is the hand that wrote *(a long, puzzled pause, eyes closed)*, finis *(hesitantly spelled out)*, to the proposition dealing with *(pause, voice weaker)*, uncharted *(voice suddenly stronger)* then uncharted, aspects of... theorem...

(Jane was making many facial expressions now, along with her uneven strength of the voice effects. Her features had a different cast also, especially around the mouth; the lips were compressed and stiff, the chin knotted, the brow furrowed. Some of the effect I thought was due to an effort at concentration; the rest seemed to be reflecting the presence of another personality.)

Cron... It's a Latin word—crontonomous *(my phonetic interpretation)*, as applied to the inner minus spectrum. J U R I N I S *(spelled out in a much stronger voice)*, S T A V O *(also spelled, though quieter)*, one one five one eleven. *(The facial difference was now quite marked; Jane looked older.)* The symbol to help you identify a sphere with lines like rays. Juris, Edinburgh, 1831 *(much louder)*, 1872 *(softer)*, died. Tormented with the aspects, with the problems of the unknown constant, and the fallacy, the fallacy *(puzzled; shakes head almost vehemently)*, of... I don't know ... Robby, I think its Democritus *(my phonetic interpretation.)*

Edinburgh, papers ... Ground rules expelled me. Then, I was before my time. The little man found my theories. The one mentioned earlier. *(Jane now sat with her head back, eyes closed; the position seemed to make it more difficult for her to speak.)* Untold miseries over the authorship. *(Long pause.)* Greek speculation, and renaissance—<u>popular</u> *(long pause; faint words:)* ... Mind is ... Let it be therefore known, fragments shatter under the handiwork of the 9th power, and values redistribute under the leadership of 7.

(I asked Jane now to repeat an unintelligible word. She said softly, first:) Deminaria *(then louder:)* Tominaria *(both my phonetic interpretations).*

The lord be with you in your travels.

The values are undermined *(head down now)*, when the zero is sphered...sphered, you see *(gesture)*, when the zero is like an apple with a stem. *(Long pause.)* Magnificent...

(10:23. After a long pause Jane's eyes began to try to open. It took her a long time to come out of trance; several minutes passed before her eyes stayed open.

(Jane said she had felt her facial expression change, as described; at this time the data began to change, she said, from the abstract into an emotional personality who was responsible for it. Thus one of our questions was answered, if vaguely. The

personality seemed quite upset, and would have gone on to become very emotional and vehement if my wife had chosen to let it continue in that direction. But having a little experience by now, Jane said she knew when to withdraw from the raw emotional encounter while in trance, and did so.

(She now drew for Carl and me the illustration at the left. "This is the apple with a stem," she said, "that the personality was trying to get across." Jane said she didn't have the vocabulary for it; it was something "he" knew he couldn't get her to say.

(To our surprise, Seth now came through when the session resumed. The change in Jane was remarkable. She brightened at once. As Seth her voice was strong and on the loud side; eyes open often and very dark, pace good, smiling often. 10:37.)

Now—

("Good evening, Seth.")

—I will come in to close our session, and let you know that I have been in attendance. A silent partner. *(Amused.)*

And my welcome to our friend here. *(To Carl.)*

Congratulations to our mathematical genius, Ruburt. He did well. The information came as given, and under my sponsorship. It was a valuable lesson for Ruburt. *(Pause.)* I helped in some periods of transmission.

("Who was that personality, Jurinis?")

Because the personality still is near, I suggest that I give you that information in your next session. The emotional contact with Ruburt has not yet been completely severed; and you have that fact to thank for my presence.

("Just how do you mean that?")

I have come through to help Ruburt sever the emotional contact, and at Ruburt's request. Overall I am pleased. This was an experiment, and worked very well. I thought Ruburt might like to get some information directly from someone who had a greater interest in such matters than I, and I paged our good friend.

Now I will end the session, even though I did not begin it.

My heartiest regards to you. *(Smile.*

("Good night, Seth."

(10:45, Jane left trance quickly, in comparison to last break. She said she felt good that she had heard from Seth.

(A curiosity: Carl Watkins said he felt there was a definite mass change in Jane when she was speaking as Seth. When she rocked back and forth as Seth, Carl said, the floor beneath the rocker creaked. But the floor did not creak when Jane rocked as herself after 10:45 PM. Carl said he carefully watched to make

sure the chair had not been moved. Jane weighs 105. Carl weighs 188. He sat in the chair now, without shifting its position; when he rocked back and forth the floor creaked.

(I had heard the creaking of the floor while writing, but hadn't noticed when it took place and when it did not.

(We thought the session was now over but this was not the case. As the three of us discussed it Jane began to get more impressions on her own again. At 11:05 she began to speak in the same quiet and controlled trance manner she had used at the start of the session.)

...An encyclopedia of mathematical knowledge... Edinburgh... would have this guy's name in it. It would seem to be in Latin. This theorem came up again in 1831. The particular volume or edition of the encyclopedia came out in the fall, and at the time this guy was working there was some kind of mathematical dispute going on, and a schedule set for some kind of conference to be held at the university for mathematicians from all around. The dispute had mathematical and philosophical connotations, because the ideas were wrapped up with science somehow.

The name Sturgeon connected also with it, and Litargeous, this is as close as I can come with the name. It was popularly called "The conspiracy of numbers" under the auspices of the primature. *("I'm not positive of the name." I thought Jane might be trying to get at imprimatur, meaning sanction or approval.)*

Pius, doesn't sound right to me, 8, 1... I'm getting... I guess it's Pius the 6th. But it doesn't sound right but seems to be what I'm getting.

(A check of the dictionary shows there have been 12 Popes, but our source does not list most by date. Pius the VII was Pope from 1800-23, Pius the IX was Pope from 1846-78, etc. We have no dates for Pius VI and VIII.

(At the end of the session Jane said she was getting Roman numerals here; then she had the impression that what she wanted was "2 digits this side of 8, which would make it Pius VI."

(The data appears to be distorted, or Jane's interpretation of it. Jane thought that if she followed through as she began with the Pius data she would have said Pius IX, but she didn't do so.)

...Somehow this whole controversy almost seems to have been thought of in the nature of a conspiracy, that would overthrow, I suppose, current ideas at the time. M I N N I U S *(spelled)*, did I give the name?

Eight men sat in judgment on this guy I was talking for earlier, and he got kicked out. There was a Thaddeus involved, and the nature or characteristics of the zero in problems in infinity.

According to this guy, this bunch overrode, through their ignorance and stupidity, the true nature of the constants involved. This guy's name was removed from the following two editions of the encyclopedia as a result... Oh, we're going to break it right now.

(End at approximately 11:30. Jane said she quickly ended the flow of data because as she spoke she could feel the guy getting furious all over again at the mention of the encyclopedia; this following a growing anger fueled by the previous data. There was a strong emotional reaction growing, so Jane ended it.

(None of us have any information pertaining in any way to this data.)

NOTES BY JANE BUTTS ABOUT SESSIONS 449 AND 450

(Intrigued by giving such different and difficult material, Jane checked a few reference books before Pat Norelli's Thanksgiving visit from Boston. Pat did take copies of the two sessions back to Roger Sullivan who sent us his opinions of them in later December. But first, here are the copies of Jane's notes.)

Websters Dictionary

Democritus - 4633 (Dictionary 1020)
460 BC - Greek philosopher

Fermat - de Pierre 1601-1665
Fr. Math.
pg 4633 script. person says the man mentioned earlier, found 'my' theories.

Spurgeon? (Sturgeon) - 1834-92
Eng baptist preacher (4635)

Crotoniatae - gr/latin name.

Democritus - 123 Infinity 116 -
formulated atom theory -
(book: in passage devoted to matter & its properties and magnification, he said all atoms alike. (& molecules).

inner structure of matter
& connection with alchemy.
title chpt MICROCOSMOS

166 - somethn. about cohesion of
molecules

151 - spks of annihilation of ?
35 - NON-EUCLIDIAN geom -
most "PURE" - & INCAPABLE
of application

35 - one large system of math -
called 'crown of purity" -
called "theory of numbers'
meaning INTEGER Numbers -
oldest & most intricate
product of pure math thought.
I CANT GET REST.

FERMAT pg 37 41 (CANT UNDER).
40 - the GREAT theorum of FERMAT
the roots of this problem go
back to Egypt - (all about
INTEGERS. More about 7 1621
about the formula we were
given. He wrote a note in
A BOOK - a MATH BK

Giving hint. Died: new Branch
Math Result called theory
Of Ideals—
I never read this part
goes into negative numbers

151– pair formation of (positives & neg.)
152. electron pairs
INVERTED scheme?

149– Indefinite ... movement
sphere — ?

Quadrants?

The Universe
Asimov –
pg. 246-7. Bruno Rossi Italian
1905 –
By 1935 – pg 246 – Neg. charged
particles.

251 – Ital Amer Enrico Fermi
1901-54

255 – Color Bands – yellow 2.0 ev
(whatever that means!)
291 – Geoffrey B. Burbridge · Amer Astron–

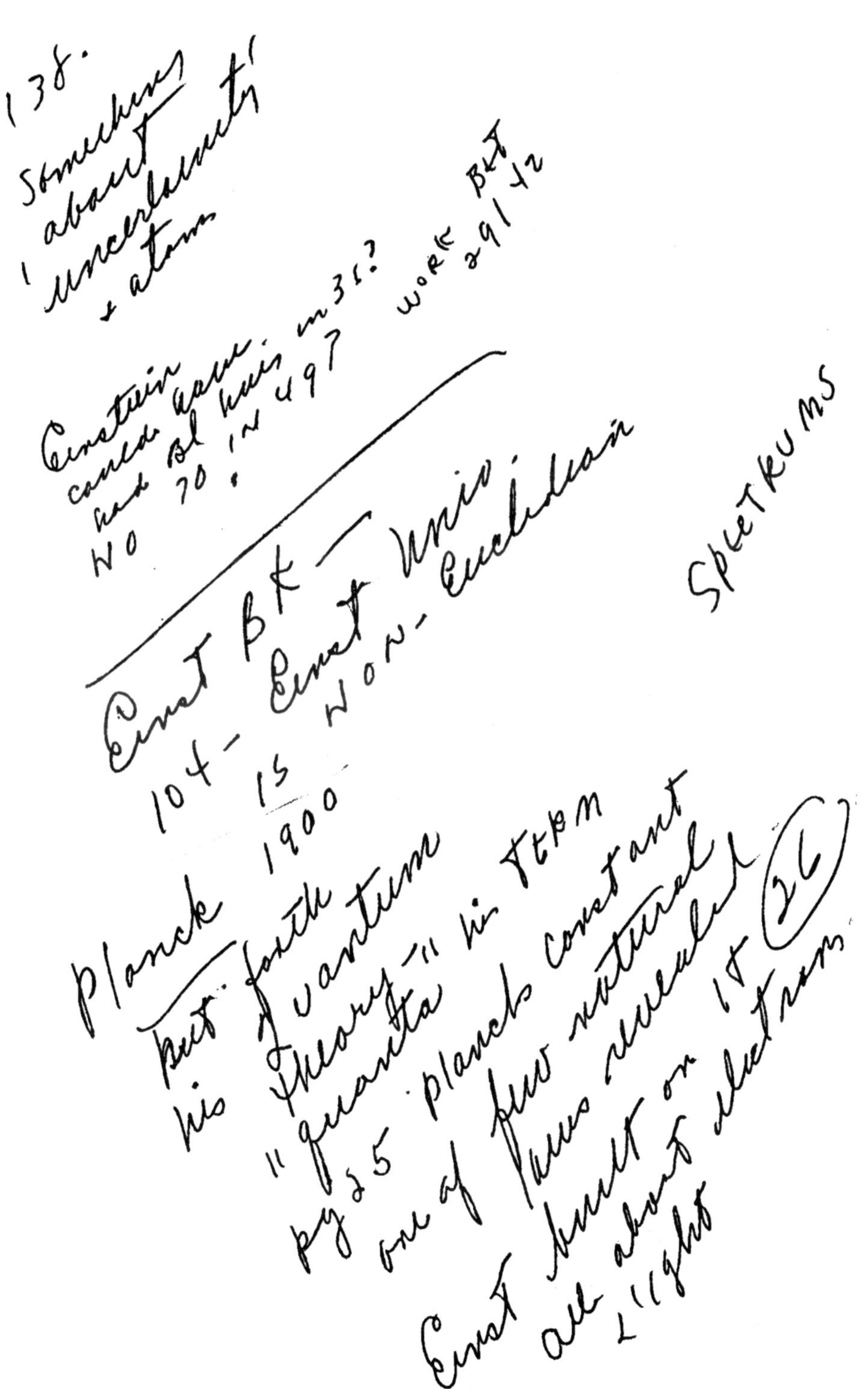

(Now here is the reply Roger wrote to Jane on December 21, 1968, after he'd studied sessions 449 and 450. We hadn't sent him copies of Jane's own notes.)

P.S. (1-12-69) I still haven't had a chance to do library research, so I think I'd better send this as is. I shall write again if I find anything more.
Sincerely, Roger

A. M. C. HUT SYSTEM

ELEVATIONS	
MIZPAH	3,800'
MADISON	4,825'
CARTER NOTCH	3,450'
LAKES OF THE CLOUDS	5,000'
LONESOME LAKE	2,743'
GREENLEAF	4,200'
GALEHEAD	3,800'
ZEALAND FALLS	2,700'

DIRECT ALL CORRESPONDENCE TO:
HUT SYSTEM HEADQUARTERS
PINKHAM NOTCH CAMP
GORHAM, N. H. 03581
OPEN YEAR ROUND

TELEPHONE
GORHAM, N. H. 466-3994
AREA CODE 603

32 Emerson Gardens
Lexington, Mass. 02173
December 21, 1968

Dear Jane and Robbie,

Thank you very much for considering my questions. I turned in my thesis on Dec. 12 and am now skiing in the White Mountains. I hope that you don't mind my writing in longhand from Pinkham Notch!

I am not able to provide a "paragraph-by paragraph" analysis, since most paragraphs were unintelligible to me. Rather, let me make some comments relating to the two sessions as a whole; I hope that this will be of help to you.

I'm afraid that nothing in this testimony "rings a bell" with me. I am reasonably sure that it is all gibberish. It reminds me of the sort of talk I often hear in my dreams: while I'm dreaming, it all seems terribly sensible and important, but when I wake up, I see that it is gibberish. More significantly, I see nothing here that suggests any mathematical

A. M. C. HUT SYSTEM

ELEVATIONS

MIZPAH — —	3,800'
MADISON — —	4,825'
CARTER NOTCH —	3,450'
LAKES OF THE CLOUDS	5,000'
LONESOME LAKE —	2,743'
GREENLEAF — —	4,200'
GALEHEAD — —	3,800'
ZEALAND FALLS —	2,700'

DIRECT ALL CORRESPONDENCE TO:
HUT SYSTEM HEADQUARTERS
PINKHAM NOTCH CAMP
GORHAM, N. H. 03581
OPEN YEAR ROUND

TELEPHONE
GORHAM, N. H. 466-3994
AREA CODE 603

— 2 —

expertise beyond that of a typical layman. Although I retain the *hope* that evidence of a world beyond our senses will someday manifest itself, I am not yet convinced that it ever *has* done so. In particular, I'm afraid that this material seems indistinguishable from what might result from a "dream" that a person had while conscious (a trance?). Jane may have remembered certain key words from my questions, and these, along with other sub-conscious memories, ran through her mind in a "stream-of-consciousness" which seemed somehow to make sense. No other intelligence need have been involved. Another reason I suspect this "stream-of-consciousness" theory is that, often in the material, the speaker confuses questions (1) and (2). (2) deals with pure mathematical logic, which should certainly be independent of physical quantities such

A. M. C. HUT SYSTEM

ELEVATIONS	
MIZPAH	3,800'
MADISON	4,825'
CARTER NOTCH	3,450'
LAKES OF THE CLOUDS	5,000'
LONESOME LAKE	2,743'
GREENLEAF	4,200'
GALEHEAD	3,800'
ZEALAND FALLS	2,700'

DIRECT ALL CORRESPONDENCE TO:
HUT SYSTEM HEADQUARTERS
PINKHAM NOTCH CAMP
GORHAM, N. H. 03581
OPEN YEAR ROUND

TELEPHONE
GORHAM, N. H. 466-3994
AREA CODE 603

-3-

as the speed of light or Planck's constant; yet somehow these latter appear in answers (apparently) to (2) [20, 28].* I suspect (don't you??) that this would not have happened if (1) had not been asked at the same time.

Now let me comment on some specifics.

(1.) Names: Various names and words are mentioned: Bainbridge [19,20], Minopelis [24], Rufunt [34], Sturgeon [35], Litangeous [35], Thaddeus [36], Crontonomous [32], Juris [32], Tominaria [33], Minnius [36]. All are meaningless to me. Of course I have heard of Euclid [30], Democritus [33], the Popes Pius [36], and Edinburgh, Scotland [32,33] but I don't see their relevance. However, I shall check the MIT library after New Year's to see if I can find anything of interest.

(2.) History: The speakers refer to the years 1831 [32,35], 1872 [32], 1936 [23], also to "a little man with dark hair [23,31], also to someone who apparently

* I shall refer to page numbers this way; i.e. this means pp. 4620, 4628.

A. M. C. HUT SYSTEM

ELEVATIONS	
MIZPAH — —	3,800'
MADISON — —	4,825'
CARTER NOTCH —	3,450'
LAKES OF THE CLOUDS	5,000'
LONESOME LAKE —	2,743'
GREENLEAF — —	4,200'
GALEHEAD — —	3,800'
ZEALAND FALLS —	2,700'

DIRECT ALL CORRESPONDENCE TO:
HUT SYSTEM HEADQUARTERS
PINKHAM NOTCH CAMP
GORHAM, N. H. 03581
OPEN YEAR ROUND

TELEPHONE
GORHAM, N. H. 466-3994
AREA CODE 603

-4-

got in trouble with the authorities because of his mathematical beliefs [35,36], also that "Michigan was the place of birth" [28]. Again, none of this rings a bell.

(3.) Science: References are made to quadrants [22,25, 28,31] and the psi factor [25,26,28,31]; again, familiar, but with no apparent relevance. I also infer some mathematical relations:

$$\frac{x^9 y}{\pi} = \frac{c\hbar}{4} \quad [22]$$

$$\frac{137}{4^9} \quad [31] \quad ;$$

and a great significance to the 9th power [19,20,21,24,26, 27,28,29,30,32]; but again, no bells.

(4.) The symbol on p.4634 represents the looking glass of Venus, hence is used to symbolize Venus (goddess or planet), or the female sex generally. Again, no bells.

(A note: as of now my original single and/or double spaced typewritten record of the Seth material is 4,636 pages long. Sessions 449 and 450 take up the last 18 pages— hence Roger's references to numbers in the 4,000 category.)

A. M. C. HUT SYSTEM

ELEVATIONS	
MIZPAH	3,800'
MADISON	4,825'
CARTER NOTCH	3,450'
LAKES OF THE CLOUDS	5,000'
LONESOME LAKE	2,743'
GREENLEAF	4,200'
GALEHEAD	3,800'
ZEALAND FALLS	2,700'

DIRECT ALL CORRESPONDENCE TO:
HUT SYSTEM HEADQUARTERS
PINKHAM NOTCH CAMP
GORHAM, N. H. 03581
OPEN YEAR ROUND

TELEPHONE
GORHAM, N. H. 466-3994
AREA CODE 603

-5-

(5.)* There is one concrete item. If Jane's weight actually changed [35] it should be measurable. Could she possibly stand on a scale, or place her chair on a scale, so that this interesting effect could be confirmed quantitatively?

If question (1) or (2) were to be answered in a form understandable to human scientists, it would have to be a page full of equations, starting with what we know and ending with a derivation of the equations in my questions. Is it possible for Jane to receive such material through "automatic writing", rather than verbally?

I have enjoyed very much reading the material and writing this critique, which I certainly hope has been of help to you. If you wish, someday I should be happy to call on you personally; perhaps, together, we might shed more light on this fascinating field!

Sincerely,
Roger
(Roger J. Sullivan)

* Sorry, they don't have any ink here!

LETTER TO ROGER J. SULLIVAN FROM ROB AND JANE BUTTS FEBRUARY 3, 1969

Dear Roger:

Thanks very much for your letter of December 21. Please pardon our delay in answering it. Jane has been snowed under with work, correspondence, classes, etc., so I have taken it upon myself to help her out re letters. When I get a free minute I answer the next one on the list.

In view of what you say about the material we sent you, we see why a paragraph-by-paragraph rundown isn't necessary; this is perfectly all right, and we thank you for your effort in going over the material, and the time you spent answering. We have studied your reply to some extent—not as much as we would like—and intend to do more with it. Jane's experience in receiving the type of material we sent you is quite limited, and we have many questions.

One episode like the sessions we sent you, held after those, turned out quite well; another, involving California, didn't, as far as we know. It is difficult to check out sometimes. If we ever meet we could ask you a lot of questions, but we have learned it's tough to do much of a job by letter, so we'll content ourselves with what's been said above.

However, if you and your wife ever get to Elmira, you know of course that you are welcome any time. Don't wait for an invitation. Pat, for instance, knows she can stop in any time. By the way, we have been so busy we haven't written to her, either, lately—and we sincerely hope that she is doing well.

We don't know how things work re turning in a thesis, etc., as you mention in your letter, but you have our best wishes. We assume it means you have done all your work and are now just waiting for formalities, etc., re that great day! If you find a minute, please keep us informed.

Thanks again,
Rob & Jane Butts
458 W. Water St
Elmira, NY 14905

SESSION 451 NOVEMBER 25, 1968 9:05 PM MONDAY

Good evening.

("Good evening, Seth.")

Now. A few more remarks concerning the center of the self, before I continue with a longer discussion.

You will find evidence of the center of your self in your paintings, of course. There is a continuity that follows through all existences, and shows itself in the endeavors and creations of the individuals involved.

There will be a core within your own paintings, from which the whole composition springs, and it is here that you can find rapport with the center of your self. The center contains condensed knowledge, not only of seemingly past lives, but also of the future. Of this, in your work, you create a new dimension.

That center is like a road that you can follow inward. Remembered faces of those you have known, and remembered scenes from other existences, form the nucleus of your experience; the forms that you bring, seemingly out of nothing, into actuality. Although you are not consciously aware of the past familiarity, nevertheless you use the knowledge to your conscious advantage.

In one way you are the steps leading up to yourself, or the spirals leading in to yourself. The painting spirals outward from your inner reality, and it brings forth energy and previous connections and interpretations. You form these anew, however, adding to them the knowledge and vitality of your present self.

It is somewhat easier for the artist or poet to find this center of the self. The intuitive symbols can be better recognized. Now you can grab a hold of the original inspiration for a painting, and ride it outward, or you can look at your own completed painting and ride it inward to its source. Do you follow me?

("Yes.")

In either case when conditions are right, you should feel a sense of recognition, a sense of grasping a portion of the center of your own reality. This is not a nebulous experience, but vivid, powerful, and direct. You will know it at once.

When you have achieved this oneness with your own center, then you automatically free additional energy and vitality into your life.

Your painting itself will seem to expand, for the channels will be opened. The symbols that you work with will grow in depth and validity, for they will be symbols that will be recalled to some degree by all men. There may be a definite memory recall, a few curious moments when time dissolves, when even beneath a portrait you have painted you will see another face.

Now when you, with your love of images, look at a face, relax for a moment. Slightly let yourself fall out of focus, look away, and then back to the face of the subject. Tell yourself that you will see the features and the structures shift. You will see the face behind that face, the image of the person as it was in a past life.

(Smile.) You need not paint one neck with ten heads, but the one portrait

can be made to suggest previous structures and characteristics that have merged to produce the present head. You can look through the face therefore, as an archaeologist would look through rock. Such a portrait will immediately be fascinating, particularly of course to the subject, who will intuitively and unconsciously recognize its components.

Are your fingers tired?

("No.")

A too-rigid rendition can frighten the subject by imprisoning him within the moment, from which it seems he cannot escape. Obviously the technique can be as realistic as you like, however. It is that the lines, seeming so realistic, also symbolically suggest what the viewer himself cannot see in his own face, but knows is there. And so the landscape, not one but many landscapes in one, for while it is unique in a given moment, still it is a composite in your terms of the pasts that have formed it, and the futures that act upon it even now.

In that respect the landscape has its center. Your own thoughts are like the outward spokes of a wheel. They are not at the center of yourself, but have traveled a long way from the center of yourself. You may therefore follow them backward. We have been dealing so with the diversity of the self that I want to assure you that within all this diversity the center can be found and recognized.

It is after all the you from which you spring, and the impetus within the present self. You may take your break and we shall continue.

(4:35. Jane came out of trance quickly. I was yawning, and Seth came through briefly and humorously:)

I hope it is not the company.

("No."

(Resume at 9:47.)

The mathematical material was in the nature of an experiment, and to this extent was a demonstration.

(See the last two sessions.) There are various ways in which Ruburt's abilities can be used, and various purposes they can serve, according to circumstances and conditions. As I told you, I was present, though in the background; Ruburt's tutor—and it was I—who showed him how to return when he felt it desirable. *(Very humorously, eyes open:)* He needs a guide. Often when he supposes he is out by himself, or working alone, I am there to keep an eye on him.

He is learning to use his abilities now in various ways,, though you have only begun to learn what they are. Ruburt is just beginning to learn how to handle different conditions. Experience is the one teacher. And I am the next. *(Smiling, but serious.)*

Now, I will give you additional data as to the source of the material. *(Seth promised to do this last session.)* I prefer we wait a short time, since our friend is only too willing to return and speak his own piece, and Ruburt has had sufficient experience for a fortnight.

(Here Seth refers to the source, as yet unidentified, of the mathematical data—not to Jane, Ruburt or himself.)

I am showing him *(Ruburt)* how to open and close doors, how to answer knocks without letting the whole world in. *(Pause.)* I am letting him do a good bit of his own work, however, rather than doing this for him. The ability is his, and it is he who will use it. I will always help him in such endeavors.

Though he does not understand what he does, he is learning control at other layers of consciousness, and he will be able to utilize his abilities far better in our sessions and in other experiments. In other words, various types of such experiences, within reason, are highly beneficial, for he learns from them.

They are also in the nature of little tests on my part, for I can tell by his performance where his strong and weak points lie, and in what direction he needs my support.

In the episode with the Craigs, *(see the 447th session)* he was freely roaming the fields of their experience, and did quite well. I commend him. Such episodes add to his confidence, and give him an inner subjective touch. Later this will grow so that he will be able to tell when he is hot or cold.

These abilities have their counterparts to some extent in any creative endeavor. You know when you are on to a painting. Ruburt knows when he is on to a poem. The same psychic directional sense can be perfected, so that as he roams over fields of experience Ruburt will know when he is on to the proper signals.

The saying, on the beam, applies. *(Smile.)* Sometimes I give him a nudge in the proper direction, when he thinks he is on his own. Then I let him alone, and see if he can tell by himself when he makes an error, for it is this inner manipulation that we are interested in perfecting. It is somewhat like teaching a child to walk, except in this case *(smile)* you cannot see the surface.

Now this will not be a lengthy session. I will not forget to give you the necessary information on the mathematician. *(Pause.)* I found the affair amusing.

("How come?")

I was following Ruburt's performance, knowing full well that the person who gave the information would not be willing to stay in the background. I wondered how well my student would follow my direction, and he did well.

In the past, you see, it would have been highly improbable that Ruburt could have received that kind of information. He would not have allowed himself the highly focused sort of trance necessary, for rather specialized data. Now, some of it may not make sense to mathematicians as yet in any case, but portions will.

(I began a question: "Well, you were still present, even with this highly focused trance—" when Seth motioned for me to wait.)

We were not concerned merely with simple formulas, but with certain issues that lay behind them. *(Pause.)* Implied questions were also asked hidden within the formulas. These we attempted to answer. Now your question?

("I just wanted to comment that this highly focused trance of Ruburt's wasn't so specialized that you were shut out. It wasn't that extreme.")

I was here to help Ruburt handle the mechanics of the affair, and to see how well he could do with such a highly focused trance. It can be used for many purposes, and was as I told you a demonstration on several layers.

As he almost discovered, such a trance is highly effective for projections. There is a more intense focus of concentration, high use of energy, a merging of capabilities, intent, direction, directly from the center of the self, that can be compared, properly used, to a laser.

It can also be used in healing, when it is developed. Without realizing it Ruburt has had several other very brief experiences with this kind of trance in the past. In those instances a necessary familiarity was achieved, though the results in terms of information were negligible.

There is a subjective feel to such a state that he is beginning to recognize. It is like a strong beam, and he must learn how to use it, and how to change its direction. In this case he must learn to be in command of it. It is like a tool of perception. It turns on brightly and intensely, and has a boring quality. In many ways it is an aggressive tool that the consciousness uses to pierce through time and space as you know it.

It is more aggressive than receptive, in contrast to some other trance states that are used to receive, rather than go out after, information. *(Long pause.)* It pierces, opening up dimensions through which the consciousness can then perceive events or on occasion travel through the dimension to experience the events more directly.

In the case of projection, this trance forms a safe channel through which the consciousness may travel and return. It is associated with the pyramid effect, usually going outward from the center of consciousness.

I did not intend this session to be lengthy, and therefore if you have no questions we will bring it to an end.

("Okay.")

My heartiest regards.

("The same to you.")

You have been doing some traveling in your dreams. Let yourself remember.

("I've been having trouble, all right.")

I took you on a good trip two nights ago.

("Where to?")

To meet some of your previous acquaintances.

("I don't remember it.")

If you meet your father in your dreams, he will be quite transformed from the person that you know, so you need not fear remembering your dreams on that account.

(Pause. Then: "Good night, Seth."

(10:26. Jane left trance easily. As Seth left, Jane said, she got from him that the particular trance he was discussing tonight could, or would, be used in sessions; it would let Seth come through "stronger," though Jane then questioned the use of this word, and said "immediate" might be a better one.

(At various times in the past I have heard Jane mention this same sort of intense focus in trance, but not to this extent previously.

(Seth could have gone on for hours, Jane said. When I asked her why the session ended if both seemed able to continue, Jane paused, then said: "I know why we ended it." She continued, that it was because the same intense focus was partially used in the session tonight as in the last two sessions; Seth didn't want her to overdo it, just to get used to it. Jane didn't hear Seth tell her this within; she merely "got" the information.

(Jane said now that there was a "tremendous amount of energy" available, but that it was being withdrawn slowly so that she wouldn't feel any letdown.)

SESSION 452
DECEMBER 2, 1968 9:17 PM MONDAY

Good evening.

("Good evening, Seth.")

Now. Children build houses of cards and knock them down. You do not worry about the child's development, for you realize that he will learn better.

You may even smile at the child's utter sense of desolation until he finally connects the motion of his own hand with the destruction of the paper, cardboard house that is now gone, and in his eyes gone beyond repair.

Now, mankind builds civilizations. He has gone beyond the child's game.

The toys are real, and yet basically the analogy holds. I am not condoning those violences that occur. The fact is that they can never be condoned, and yet they must be understood for what they are: man learning through his own errors. He also learns by his successes, and there are times when he holds his hand, moments of deliberation, periods of creativity. *(Pause.)* Identities take many roles in many lives.

There are periods, cycles if you prefer, through which such identities live and learn within your system. To some extent they are taught by others, practice teachers if you prefer. *(Amused.*

(Today the newspaper carried the story of the violence attending the Democratic presidential convention in Chicago in August, 1968, telling of the many clashes between police and various groups of demonstrators; and a guilty verdict re police behavior was rendered by an investigative commission. Jane and I had discussed the report at the supper table.)

The race of man is far more than the physical race however. You see him in but one stage of development. When an individual leaves your system it is for other systems. He has learned his A B C's, but that is all. There are some exceptions—identities that choose, then, to return and teach. They are not in the same league, so to speak, as those whose reincarnational cycles are not complete.

They may return, even enduring violence, as a man might set up a school amid a jungle of savages. And yet even with this there are advances made within the system itself. A nuclear weapon in the hands of the inhabitants of middle-age Europe would have been used almost immediately, and with nary a qualm, to wipe out all but Christendom.

Christendom may well have perished along with the rest of the world, but this possibility would not have been considered, so narrow and evilly self-righteous were the governing powers at the time.

In those days neither did a sane, righteous man give thought to sharing his wealth, or even consider the plight of the poorer classes. Not only was charity not given, its practical nature was not considered. The archaic concept of God nicely covered such matters.

The poor were obviously sinful. Poverty was their penance, and it was considered a sacrilege to try to help those whom God had so cursed. Animals were tortured in sport. Compassion for living things in males was regarded as a weakness to be plucked out, to a degree that you can barely realize now.

Women were scarcely thought of as human creatures, but in very select circles. The progression through the centuries would be far more noticeable if you knew all the facts. There is one aspect here that I have not previously mentioned. Man was not allowed to play with the more dangerous toys until certain evidence was given that he had gained some control.

This does not mean that he could not destroy the world that he knew. It simply meant that such destruction was not inevitable. You do not give a child a loaded gun if you are certain he is going to shoot himself or his neighbor.

Now the weapons and the destruction are the obvious things that you see. The counterparts are not so evident, and yet it is the counterparts that are important. The self-discipline learned, the control, the compassion that finally  is aroused, and the final and last lesson learned, the positive desire for creativity and love over destruction and hatred. When this is learned the reincarnational cycle is finished.

Now there is a reason why these lessons must be learned in just this way.  Elementally there is only creativity. Destruction is merely the changing of form. A cloudburst or a tornado knows nothing of destruction. This same energy encased within a human form is something else. There are different kinds of creativity, then, to learn, and a specialization in energy is focus and feelings that emerge; elemental energy becoming conscious of itself, and aware of issues that did not exist for it earlier; millions of molecules momentarily united with the living consciousness *(pause)*, filled with primal energy, now learning love, and forming highly sensitive psychic patterns, electrical charges that now form emotions instead of clouds; the innocent chaos of undifferentiated personality that exists behind the highly specified and truly sophisticated mechanism of one thought. And all of this before an individual is born within your system. In terms of time this is behind us all.

Little wonder that psychic battles wage, and yet beyond your system there are refinements impossible to describe, and further developments more miraculous than those that have gone before. And through all of this, the entity formed from that massive chaos retains its identity and the knowledge of its pasts, and continues to grow in creativity.

This is some of the most important material that I have given you, for you have wondered about the purpose, and have been able often to see but one small speck of time and space.

The violence that you were both speaking of this evening opened up a chasm within each participator's soul, through which he glimpsed the dizzying origins that were behind his identity. There was the fear, then, and afterward, of falling back into that mindless chasm.

Now a storm at times will fascinate many, and so will such a violence, but a highly destructive storm will find few going abroad in it. Each participator sensed the chaos to which he had direct access *(emphatic)*. He feared it then and afterward, even in his fascination, because he was bound to recognize that it would sweep he and his enemy into insanity or death. *(...him and..?)*

Many of the participators have never known that they had access to such energy, therefore the notion that such energy could be used creatively never entered their heads. Many of them felt tiny, alone and powerless. Now the energy alone was exhilarating. For the first time many of the participators realized intuitively that such energy was also the source of creativity.

Many will try various methods of re-experiencing the energy, in order to release creative feelings they did not know they possessed. Their energy of course was neutral. It was their use of it at the time that caused the destructive elements.

The energy that was liberated has already changed your national scene, and will continue to do so. Such massive liberations of energy will be used, but not in your lifetime, to begin to unify the whole planet, in peace. This will not happen before disasters also occur, but when it does happen it will represent the first such time within the planet's history where there was peace with equality for all.

There have been various periods that were peaceful, but there was no equality. There have been countless other civilizations that have destroyed themselves in the planet's past, and before this when another planet was approximately in earth's position. There were however civilizations that endured, that outlasted their planet, and went elsewhere.

You may take your break and we shall continue.

(10:09. Jane paused for a few moments, then resumed, after I had thought she was out of trance, and had called her name.)

There were 9 planets once, grouped like jewels around the sun. They were evenly spaced one from the other, and they were evenly distributed outward from the sun. And this was the first system that knew the race of man. These were in your corner of the universe, but in your terms they would have seemed to have drifted off so far that none of your instruments could ever find them.

They exploded, and were recreated many times, disappeared and returned. They would seem to pulsate. To you they would seem to disappear for eons. To them their existence was continuous. As atoms and molecules give your chairs a reality within your system even though the atoms and molecules come and go, so this planetary system still retains its reality. *(Pause.)*

Your astronomers may receive a ghost image of it at the edges of your universe, but only a reflection from a reality that you cannot perceive. Now take your break.

(10:19. Jane left trance easily, eyes opening after a bit. She said she had been far-out though, and had had a vision of the planets and sun.

(I made a quick mental count of the planets we now know to be in our solar system: Mercury, Venus, Mars [not counting the asteroid belt], Saturn, Jupiter, Uranus, Neptune and Pluto, for a total of 9; the same total mentioned above by Seth. Naturally Seth's data gave rise to many questions, but tonight wouldn't see them answered.

(Just before break ended Jane said: "I just got a whole chunk of thought from Seth." Resume at 10:31.)

Now. Existence uses form. When a planetary system is disrupted, in some cases entities who are attracted to it or consider it their home, simply change their form, regroup their forces, and if they consider it worthwhile, put the house back in order.

They enter then such forms as are available, or make such forms as could survive. This has been done within your own system on several occasions. It is not done often in such a way, since with the materials at hand often a complicated-enough structure cannot be formed in which consciousness can fully-enough express itself.

There can be in your terms some loss of memory, complications that confuse the knowledge of origin. When the situation does occur, there is always a division of forces, some entities returning to form, and others not entering the process. These watch, keeping their memories and knowledge intact, and acting as directors, against whose memories the new models are formed.

Again, this happened within your own system. Many entities have no need for form, in your terms, at all, but we will not be concerned with them this evening. *(Pause.)* This original system of which I have spoken will at least be theorized shortly, but the idea will not be taken seriously enough to cause any deep controversy.

The energy of this system was enormous, far greater than any you know, and the debris thrown off constantly from its pulsations gave birth to other systems. *(Long pause.)*

We are struggling with Ruburt's vocabulary. *(Pause.)* The speed of its motion was also far greater than any you know, though it speeded up and slowed down in a cyclic manner.

(Jane paused again. Her pace was slow in here, and she used many gestures, drawing pictures in the air, frowning at times.)

It possessed creatures of consciousness, but not as you know creatures. *(Pause.)* Energy, entities... *(long pause)*, continually transforming massive roytans...

(Or perhaps roetans; my phonetic interpretation. I was not sure of the word Jane or Seth used and didn't press the point beyond one question, which wasn't

answered.)

...We are working with Ruburt's vocabulary...

("Do you mean roentgens?" I meant here the international unit of X-rays.)

They originated from themselves, massive units of energy, that reacted automatically, and in an explosive manner upon the form of the system. Their energy caused the behavior of the system.

There was a direct and instantaneous reaction between consciousness and matter. *(Pause.)* An outburst of electromagnetic power, strong enough to seed a universe. Your universe is but one of many, and you perceive but a small portion of the universe in which you do exist, for there are dimensions within it that you do not perceive. *(Long pause.)*

Now. I will end the session unless you have questions.

("I guess not.")

The evening's material has come to a natural breaking-off point, but we have also reached some subjects that we have not discussed in sessions earlier, and this can serve as a preparation. My heartiest good wishes to you both, and a fond good evening.

("Good night, Seth."

(10:52. Jane left trance quickly, though it had been deep. She felt a strong energy flow at the session's end, she said. In fact, she added that she had also been aware of this flow during the day while writing, etc.)

SESSION 453
DECEMBER 4, 1968 9:06 PM WEDNESDAY

(Sue Mullin was a witness.)

Good evening.

("Good evening, Seth.")

Thank you for inviting me to your party.

("Okay.")

Now. The planetary system of which we spoke in our last session was the first one within your universe, when you are speaking in terms of time.

It is very difficult to explain to you that the universes that you see, the stars and planets that you view, are one-dimensional, comparatively speaking. You only perceive the portions of them that are apparent within your own system of reality.

You are seeing shadows upon a blank and a black screen. The three-dimensional system is like a shadow of realities that you do not perceive. Now.

(Pause.) The heavy hydrogen molecules had a large part to play in the birth of that system. Consciousness had first to create the void, or the dimension in which the system could exist, and also to endow that void with all the probabilities for development that have come about in your time, and are to come about.

The void, in other terms, can therefore be compared to a mind, and who can predict what images or thoughts will be given birth there? There are as I have told you, many, indeed countless such systems, and yet within them all there is identity, and there is direction.

This vast void, this infinite mind, came out of another that was greater than itself. *(Pause, smile.)* The possibilities that have come to reality within this universal system have each given birth to other systems and other realities, as one tree bears a thousand seeds. *(Pause.)* You yourselves through your own mental actions create realities of which you yourselves are unaware, and you give birth to more than physical children.

You do not understand the dimensions into which your thoughts drop, for they continue their own existence, and others look up to them and view them like stars. Now I am telling you that your own dreams and thoughts and mental actions appear to the inhabitants of other systems like the stars and planets within your own; and those inhabitants do not perceive what lies within and behind the stars in their own heavens.

Though they probe their own universe, they will not wander into your reality. They will only perceive the shape and form that your own mental acts, thoughts and dreams take within their own system.

This is some material that we have not given you, lest the implications lead you to thoughts of insignificance. But you are not simply receivers, you are also givers. As your own universe was formed by entities that you do not presently understand, so the discards of your own consciousness form realities for entities that are scarcely aware of your existence.

In this abundance nothing is meaningless nor wasted. There is interrelationship, intertwining realities, and connections that cannot be denied. I told you that dream reality consisted of more than you knew, and that the dream universe continued whether or not you perceived it. Within that context those inhabitants dream in turn their own dreams and form electromagnetic realities. You are not at the top nor at the bottom of the heap of consciousness, so to speak. You are not at the center. You are not at the rim.

The inner self is intimately connected with each reality, though you are not aware of it, and the inner self can trace its own connections through the network of any existence, and still keep its identity. When we speak then of the beginnings of your system, we speak only in consideration of your own ideas of time.

All obviously then exists at once. To your way of thinking some lives are lived in a twinkling, and others last for centuries, as some huge trees. The perception of consciousness is not limited however. I have told you for example that trees have their own consciousness. The consciousness of the tree is not as specifically focused however as your own. To all intents and purposes the tree is conscious of 50 years before and 50 years hence.

Its sense of identity spontaneously goes beyond the change of its own form. It has no ego to cut the I identification short. Creatures without the compartment of the ego can easily follow their own identity beyond any change of form. The inner self is aware of this integrity of identity, but the ego focused so securely in physical reality cannot afford this luxury.

Any consciousness is therefore innately aware of its basic identity. The inner self knows what is behind the stars and planets that the eyes views, but the ego would be swept aside in panic. This system spoken of earlier, the sun and original 9 planets, in your terms, have long ago passed into and formed other universal systems. The whole cosmic structure however was the materialization of one original thought, for the thought, the real reality, must always exist before the representation of it.

There was intelligence therefore within that first system, for without the intelligence there would have been no system. Now you may take a break and we shall continue—and *(to Sue:)* my heartiest wishes to our friend.

(9:36. Jane came out of trance quickly, but said the trance had been a good one. Seth came through rather stronger than usual, and somewhat rapidly in a louder voice. Resume in the same manner at 9:44.)

Now. Each thought forms its own electromagnetic reality, and is composed of energy which can never be dissipated, but only transformed.

The subjective reality of one man, left alone in the universe, would emit enough energy to seed another. That sentence is not distorted.

The energy that is within you is inconceivable to you.

Now you are going to have some extra sessions this weekend. I do not want to overdo Ruburt's resources. Nor do I want to keep you strapped to the typewriter for three weeks. Therefore this will be a very brief session, to supplement the material in our last session.

(Humorously:) I will still get the better of the bargain.

My heartiest good wishes to you all then. I will remain awhile to enjoy your conversation. *(Smile, eyes closed.*

("Good night, Seth."

(9:48. It took Jane a while to come out of trance this time. Her eyes finally began to open, after much urging on my part. "I may be done," she said, "but I'm not back. I hate it when I'm half in and half out . It's like I'm in a cone—I can hear what's going on out there, and I have to get out."

(By 9:55 we thought she was out of it but this proved to be an overestimation. Seth, or the trance state, lingered for some time. Jane showed definite tendencies to go back into trance, notably a rolling up of the eyes, and I continually talked her out of it, made her tea, etc.

(One circumstance that kept her in this state came to my attention when Jane casually mentioned, as she sat in her rocker: "Seth's still here—he's over to my right now," and she reached out to her side with her arm. When I asked about this phenomenon she said she'd never thought to tell me about it before.

(Seth, it seemed, occupied a space about five feet high—a "blob" of space into which I could step, just at the limit of Jane's reach, without disturbing him or without Jane sensing me as a separate entity within Seth's province. Seth's presence lingered into the evening as the three of us talked.

(Jane said she never sensed him above her—that would lead to the pyramid effect, she said. Either side seemed to be the rule, not front or back either. He's either in me or to the side," she said, "and boy he's having a ball tonight!")

SESSION 454
DECEMBER 7, 1968 APPROXIMATELY 1:15 PM SATURDAY

(This a long session, given for Tam Mossman and Eve Naudain, of Prentice-Hall and New York City. It began at approximately the time noted above, and continued through most of the afternoon.

(Some of the material obtained is verbatim, some is not because of Seth's rapid delivery. I made no attempts, seriously, to slow him down. The very beginning of the session is not recorded because I was working in the studio in the back of the apartment when Seth came through as Jane, Eve and Tam sat in the living room.

(The stage had been well-set for the afternoon session, however. Tam and Eve had arrived in Elmira the day before, and much of the ensuing conversation had been about matters psychic. Tam had witnessed a session before—the 434th on September 6, 1968—but Eve had not; she was a little nervous before the session began, and like many others was surprised by the session's actual beginning and its manner of presentation.)

(One section of the session was missed by me entirely, since I had left the house thinking the session over. This will be noted. When she spoke for Seth, Jane's pace was

somewhat faster than usual; eyes open often and quite dark, voice about average. There were no strong voice effects. I indicate breaks in my notes by the usual symbol: ...)

... I have been looking out for you. Not 24 hours a day, but I have peeked in on you now and then.

My friend here, Ruburt, is my mouth, and speaks for me. You may at some time be in communication with others. I will never speak through anyone other than Ruburt, simply because there must never be any doubt of the origin of the Seth material.

(The above data refers to some questions Tam had asked Jane earlier.)

Now, in your dreams you have made certain contacts that you do not recall ... when you are ready you will remember... and that you have known them.

I was here last evening. *(Humorously:)* Far be it from me to frighten a young girl *(to Eve)*, although the girl is not so young and the girl has not always been a girl.

... Ruburt has spoken to me: I am aware of social environments.

(To Tam:) Your inner attitude could slow you down. There must be an inner security, a quiet ... No agitation. Allow the door to open, do not kick it. You will be given a full reincarnational reading, whether now or later. It will be yours to follow.

I cannot promise you that you have been a king, or that you will be one *(humorously)*, nor a story reading in which you are a hero... but a reading in which you can learn from past errors. It will also make clear the relationship between you both. I have been amused, last evening and this morning... like a stranger at the window; first open and then closed.

(Here Seth refers to various moments during the visit of Tam and Eve, when he was ready to come through, but for various reasons did not do so.)

Give me a moment here. *(Pause.)*

Your enthusiasm is excellent. However, your enthusiasm can cause waves that can go up and down. You want a quiet surface. It would help you if before bed you imagine your mind like an ocean upon which you could walk. All feelings are on the waters, you are above. Then imagine yourself walking on the water, listening with your inner ear and using inner eyes. You should hear voices and see a figure on the horizon... let the figure come closer... Do not run. Relax and let the figure come to you.

When the figure comes closer let him speak first. You are then using your own enthusiasm and are in control of it. If you develop properly you will understand when the figure speaks. The figure is a person you have known who will help you in your own endeavors... It will not appear until you are ready... Your own abilities must be developed enough so that the meeting takes place.

When this meeting takes place you will know how to proceed, and the figure will indeed be three-dimensional in this mind image of which I am speaking. Now this person is an old friend—and I mean <u>old</u>—of mine... He will help you.

Follow the exercise... each night. It need not be lengthy... just before sleep. Do not strain if for a while you see a dark figure and the horizon... This is a symbolic exercise... but there is truth in the symbolism.

Some of this concerns data I gave you in the last session you witnessed... It will give you confidence and control. Take careful note of sights and sounds.

I am not pleased with Ruburt's hairdo.

(Seth's remark stemmed from the fact that Jane's hair was continually falling over her forehead and eyes; she had taken to brushing it back often; usually her glasses would keep the hair out of her eyes, but as a rule she doesn't wear glasses in trance.)

...Exercises in recent sessions are good if not overdone. *(A reference to projections.)* You shouldn't do these however until you have tried the water exercise at least 30 or 35 times.

(Seth has never suggested this water exercise to anyone else.)

I do not suggest now that you work with tables alone. In your enthusiasm you send out messages to all kinds of guests ...but you should be selective, and be careful of the company you keep.

The exercise of the self above the waters will put you in control enough so you don't have to worry.

Now, you may take a break, eat lunch, listen to records, walk upon waters...

("We'll just take a break, Seth."

(1:34-1:45.)

Now. I would simply visit with you now ... for friendly purposes ... I am a teacher and I have this work. It must come only from one source.

That has been done before. All of this has been done before. Through many ages, in one way or another, I have spoken. *(Humorously:)* I never shut up. And others have spoken ... And there is always the difficulty in maintaining the integrity of the material and keeping it free of distortion... I have worked very hard to help Ruburt condition himself to provide for the material's integrity and cut down on distortions *(Smile:)* I would be appalled at going through <u>that</u> all over again.

Now. Give me a moment. Joseph—

(Here Seth asked me to get "whatever it is one uses" to keep the hair out of Jane's

eyes, meaning her barrette. Jane was still in trance when I handed it to her, and she thrust it into her hair above her right forehead in what was not the neatest way, but it did the job.)

A moment. *(Pause. Then to Eve:)* This will have to be filled in later. Ireland—you were an Irish lass, and a minstrel. Now I do not know offhand when St. Patrick was roaming—at a time however before Christianity was introduced—you lived in the country now called Ireland... before the Christian Era...as a man given much to wandering and without a permanent abode.

A very good sense of rhythm *(pause)*, but a great difficulty in communicating with words, a verbal incapacity. You could compensate for this however strongly enough *(pause)*, in your occupation, in that when words were mixed with music you followed the rhythm and could speak clearly and well.

In conversation you stumbled and gave the impression of being stupid. Nor could you communicate with the townspeople. The verbal facility came easily in song, and so you wandered, singing, from town to town, using for your songs the news that was happening . Stories of events, a musical newscaster.

To some extent you even gave commercials, for wherever you went you spoke of the superior powers of a people to the north. *(Pause.)* You came before an invasion. You also had some clairvoyant abilities and used them to spice up the day-to-day news.

In relationships with other people you did very poorly however because of the lack of verbal communication. You did very well in a group with music, but not individually.

We cannot give you all this in one afternoon, for I wander like a minstrel through your own past. In a life just previous to that one however, you were a woman with a bitter tongue, who spoke too often and too harshly, and so you set yourself among other things the task, in the Irish life, of speaking only to music. This is highly simplified of course, there were other reasons, but in singing you were not harsh, and in singing you communicated in a way that you could not in the earlier life, and in the singing also you gave of yourself in a way you did not earlier.

You were also highly involved with what was going on in the country at the time, where in the life immediately previous you cared little for any but your immediate family, and rarely moved beyond your house. In the Irish life therefore you chose to roam freely and to inform others as to the happenings of the time.

You had no children in this Irish existence. You often perceived clairvoyant information without knowing it, giving the news ahead of time, and then being surprised yourself when the events did indeed come to pass.

(Jane now held up her right hand and indicated the first two fingers on it.)

You lost this finger and this finger in a brawl, cut by a knife. The brawl being over a woman. *(Pause.)* Now you played an instrument in which these fingers were valuable, and you were no longer able to play the instrument after the accident. Therefore you took on a helper, who played for you while you sang.

This helper is known to you in this present existence, but is not our friend here. *(A smiling gesture to Tam.)* It would make a lovely story. Give me a moment. *(Pause.)*

The helper now is a woman. This is not clear, we will see what we can do, and if we do not get it clearly we shall at a later time. The woman's name now has a strong R sound. Such as is the word star... R...

There may now be a blood relationship, though it is distant rather than immediate. At that time this woman was also a male, and also known to you in the lifetime immediately previous, and as a man.

Now here you became involved in teamwork, learning how to work cooperatively, closely, with another individual. In the immediately previous life you see you were quite different, and thought only of yourself. The two of you then worked together.

Now there were invading forces from the north and you moved ahead of them, warning the people; and sometimes because of your clairvoyant abilities you could tell just where the invading forces would be in a particular area. And so finally you warned the people, and so the people moved ahead of the forces.

Now there were ruins there of a previous civilization, and you hid in these ruins, in some viaducts that were beneath the earth. Now you may take a break and we shall continue.

(2:09. The break was a long one. We didn't know whether the session was actually over or not. Once again I happened to be in the studio when Seth came through again, at 3:55.)

...Do not be overanxious to develop your abilities ... *(To Tam:)* You must be in control... This is extremely important. When you work with tables, work with those who are experienced in such things...

Meditation is good for you, and my exercises ... At no time do you want your abilities to work full blast without control... Difficulties arise because the individual is not in control... You do not want to drive your car at 90 mph without brakes, for example ...

(Here, speaking rapidly, Seth went to some pains to emphasize to Tam the importance of the individual being in full control of his abilities, letting them develop slowly and naturally at all times so that the individual would feel at ease with them. He used the speeding-car analogy to hammer home the point.)

The telepathic abilities are good for you. Also the meditation... You have healing abilities and should use them... You are strongly gifted... Otherwise, you wouldn't have to be so careful. This data is more important to you now than reincarnational material.

Give us a moment. *(Pause.)*

(To Tam:) Personally, your healing abilities are stronger in early evening, as opposed to the rest of the day. You should practice using them daily... even when passing someone on the street. This opens new channels... helps you learn to handle them...

Do not concentrate on symptoms, but on feelings of health... Do not get caught up in sympathy... abilities won't be as effective. Before sleep direct your thoughts to those who need help... The healing abilities will automatically teach control in other areas... To help others also helps maintain your own control, and will inspire others...

You can automatically choose good friends through the use of your abilities... Don't bother now with thoughts of the origins of your abilities... Avoid cultism. Also don't let your imagination follow along the lines of possession... Fear of this creates a state in which a <u>semblance</u> of that can be caused. Most cases of possession are not caused by spirits... although it does exist in those terms... usually caused by those who request it or are too lazy to live their own lives within ... Such people then issue a blank invite to control the body they no longer wish to control.

If you are in control you need have no fears of possession. *(Humorously:)* I do not want you falling off any psychic ledges.

([Tam:] "Thank you, Seth. Thanks again ...")

(4:05. We now thought this might be the end of the session. Jane's trance had been good. Tam told us that he now does try direct healing on persons he passes on the street—one of the points mentioned by Seth. Tam hadn't mentioned this to Jane before. Tam said a lot of what Seth commented on concerned ideas he, Tam, had been speculating on to himself.

(I ran an errand to the store not long after this. When I returned Jane and Tam informed me that Seth had come through again. This time the material concerned, among other things, plants and thoughts; Tam being very interested in plants and related subjects. Since we have no notes on this material, Tam said he would send us a brief resume of this last delivery, to include with these notes.

(On this visit also Tam read the 418th session, of June 24, 1968. In this session were perhaps a page and a half of Seth's clairvoyant data re Tam and Miss Carr. This was given before any of us had met, and when any kind of communication between Jane and Tam was just beginning. Tam was able to verify quite a lot of the

data; some of it referring to Miss Carr was good. The last name of Cecile Grossman, an editor at Prentice-Hall, was mentioned by Seth, for instance. Tam noted the correct data in the 418th session, so this material has now been checked at least once.

(The delivery by Seth concerning plants did mark the end of the afternoon's session.

(After session Eve verified her stated love of music & rhythm by Seth, etc.

(Tam & Jane experimented also, feeling heat from hands without touching.)

POSTSCRIPT TO SESSION 454
DECEMBER 7, 1968

(Tam Mossman and Eve Naudain, witnesses.

([Tam's Notes:] The following represents a spontaneous session that occurred after Seth had been kind enough to come through three times for Eve and myself. Robert Butts had gone out for a while, and Jane, Eve, and I were chatting. I could feel Seth's vague presence in the room, which Eve apparently didn't. Jane went into the kitchen to see about the chicken she was cooking and — as she later told us— felt Seth coming through and hurried to get back to her chair.

(This session was unusual; even though I have only seen Seth on a few occasions, I noticed that Jane kept her eyes open much more than usual. Seth's voice was precise, but quick and conversational; also, we had the opportunity to exclaim in a brief conversation, which I of course found most gratifying.

(We can't remember everything, but I'll try to give a precis of what he said, based on what we both remember. Actual dialogue, where included, is not precisely accurate, since we have tried to fill in words that were not clear in our memory.)

(Seth had some trouble putting down Jane's glasses. He finally set then down aside an incense burner and sat back.)

Now...you need not take notes...

([Tam:] "I'm afraid we can't.")

But I wanted to clarify some points... *(Previously, Eve had wondered how Seth felt about her, so Seth turned to her.)* You are a delightful young lady... *(He advised her to assert herself more, to be less cautious in going after goals. He said she should use her "abilities"—though he was not specific.)* And you will. You will.

(Seth reiterated what he had said before about my healing powers.) When you pass people in the street, go to work immediately. *(He went on to say that the same power could be applied to plants as well, and that I had apparently used same in my previous existence as a gardening monk.)* A plant cannot fight back, *(and it would be good to practice on something whose subconscious could not give me trouble. It*

would be "interesting" to make experiments, using this power, that could be recorded.)

We will be treating this same topic in our own sessions...imagine the ill plant as being able to use sunlight more effectively during the day and continuing to make use at night of that energy which has been absorbed. *(Picturing the image of a healthy plant is)* something that the plant will be able to use in its own fashion ... The plant will give you a kind of "thank you" in the form of energy... You ought to try to work with plants also in the early hours of the evening.

(He then paused and went on to other topics at random:

(As I have said before, Seth has a way of answering questions that come up in conversation or even confirming or clarifying thoughts I have worked out for myself, without mention to anyone. A few of his following remarks apparently represent such "answers".)

Healing powers and the exercises I mentioned earlier direct your energies outward, where you have more control...

You have nothing to worry about in terms of possession. *(He then implied that spirits that had left the earth were seldom responsible in the first place.)* Worry itself will, however, induce *(he may have said "duplicate")* a state similar to the preliminary stages of possession. *(A person)* never becomes possessed unless he has requested it, *(when he is not interested in, or afraid of life, and would like another to take over the job.) (Eve recalls that at this point, he added:)*

In your enthusiasm *(meaning table-play)* you issue a blanket invitation to all.

(Humorously:) But you should issue only se-lec-tive invitations, and be careful of the company you keep.

I should emphasize that it would be better for you not to play with tables at all, except here or in the company of others who are already familiar with such work.

([Tam:] "Don't worry, I'll stick to bonsai!"

(Seth smiled, closed his eyes, and opened them, leaning forward intently.) You wear a cloak *(gesturing)* to protect yourself while flying in the cold night air.

([Tam:] "Do you mean the cape I had on in my dream?"

(Note: earlier that week, I had a dream in which I had crawled through the air, wearing a light, felt-like beige cloth over my shoulders. I had ascribed it to projection.)

Precisely. In the future, you will probably imagine it as a magic carpet.

([Tam:] "Like the ocean image spread out underneath me?")

Yes.

(Note: Later that week, I had a similar dream, but the cloth was folded under-

neath my thighs, bearing me along in a sitting position about six feet above the ground.

(We can't remember anything else, but the session was short—only five to six minutes—and probably little if anything was added. Seth withdrew rather abruptly, and noticing the change in Jane, I added, "I'll help Ruburt get back if there's any need." Jane didn't, fortunately, and woke up with no trouble and a pleasant smile.)

SESSION 455
JANUARY 6, 1969 9:20 PM MONDAY

(The session was witnessed by John Bradley and Bill and Peggy Gallagher.

(As predicted by Seth in the 420th session for July 1, 1968, Prentice-Hall is to publish the first book on the Seth material. Jane was notified of this over the Xmas holidays, and signed a contract earlier this month. See Volume 8 of this series.

(Seth spoke briefly and spontaneously once during the holiday break, with Sue Mullin and Carl Watkins as witnesses. He spoke to Carl about a game involving mathematics and drama that would make millions for Carl, should he succeed in working it out. Some clues were given.

(Seth also said that Jane and I would die within a short time of each other, when our earthly work was finished. No date or sequence was given. Seth said that Jane would publish 5 books on the Seth Material; 3 novels; 3 books of poetry; plus 2 books to be dictated by Seth himself. I do not recall if the dream book, now at Ace, was mentioned; or if others were.[Jane died in 1984. I'm publishing Volume 9 in 2002.]

(Seth was in a particularly good mood this evening, after the long holiday break, and because of the presence of witnesses. Jane entered trance easily and spoke vigorously, rapidly and with much humor. Her eyes opened often. The pace proved to be so fast in the beginning that I soon gave up trying to keep abreast. I also discovered, to my surprise, that I was somewhat rusty at taking notes.

(I settled for sentences recording the gist of the session, then, and will add notes where necessary. Peggy also took notes.)

Good evening.

("Good evening, Seth.")

I am idle and curious... My best wishes to all of my friends. My best wishes also, Joseph, to Ruburt. I am still not pleased with the hair arrangement; it does not suit me.

(A reference to Jane's hair falling over her right eye. She had to keep brushing it back as she spoke.)

Ruburt was correct. He received a message from me this afternoon. There will be another development, and a good one for him.

(Earlier today Jane had said she thought this development referred to the dream book, now at Ace Publications, and that a sale was quite possible.

(Humorously:) I have not been on vacation. Very shortly now in our own sessions I will begin writing my own book, and it will be as mentioned earlier.

(See the 418th session for June 24, 1968. There was an interruption now as the paperboy called, while making his rounds collecting.)

Now. When we are finished publishing Ruburt's books and my books, we will have some library.

(To Bill G:) I was here the other evening *(1/3/69)*...looking over your shoulder... The Jesuits do not miss anything, you see... They are always given to specific answers... We are oftentimes amused, but always delighted.

(I missed material in here to some large degree.)

Now, I have the framework for my own book in my mind clear enough... I even have the chapter presentations; and if I mention my friends you may or may not recognize yourselves, for I shall present you through my own eyes and not through Ruburt's.

The format of the book shall be simple, and it shall be a supplementary to the Seth material itself, for it shall be my own... subjective interpretation. For if Ruburt finds it mystifying to speak for me, so do I find it mystifying to speak... through him... It is some experience, indeed, for me...

(Much humor here, and again I missed material.)

The book will yield a tremendous amount of psychological knowledge, for little if at all has been done to explain the subjective personality ...

(There was more here, and it led into an exchange of jokes between Seth and Bill G.)

Now, Ruburt has largely dispensed with the negative state of mind that has so long plagued him... He is no longer blocking his own opportunities, so the further development for which I have spoken will shortly come about.

(To John:) There is also a development to come about here ...

I am in fine company. I am honored... *(to Bill:)* you run away. Jesuits are not that bad... We could get rid of all of your symptoms, but... to please you I will make a bargain with you: I will not mention your problem if you do not want me to—*(There followed another humorous exchange between Seth and Bill.)* Some Jesuits are sorrowful jokers, and laugh while the tears roll down their cheeks. That is all right... They will learn...

([Bill:] "I don't know Seth... I'm 43 now... worried about learning; etc.")

You do not remember what I have told you.

([Bill:] "I remember clearly.")

Then you would understand more about your present inner attitudes ... And when I stand at your right shoulder you would hear what I whisper in your ear ...

(There was more here that I missed. Then Seth spoke to John:) I warned you. You could have avoided the condition, you see... *(Gout.) (It came about)* through your mental attitude... It was not fated... but a matter of probabilities...

(9:30. Jane now took a break, I wished for full notes because of the humor flying about, but had fallen way behind. Seth then returned briefly when John, during break, asked Jane a question related to the causes of gout.)

... There is always in such a condition the struggle between the desire to move quickly, and the fear of movement. In such cases the desire to move is paramount ... The...

(Jane's trance was a good one, she said. Her pace here was quite fast. After a break she resumed as Seth at 9:45.

(To John and Bill:) Now. This applies to anyone, so if I look at you consider yourself the symbol of everyman. And this applies also to you. *(To Bill:)* You have very simply two alternatives. You either take the time and the effort to look into yourself or you do not. If you take the time and the effort, then I tell you, Jesuit, you will have no terrors of the flesh. While you do not take the time you must put up with it, and depend on your doctors...

This is not only personal. It is a law. Because I am your friend, I can help you... That you do not take the time and the effort is the reason why you still have the symptoms. *(Ulcers.)* ... There is no other way. When you are ready to look inward you will rid yourself of the symptoms. This applies to every man.

(To John:) The pills that you dispense... These to some extent mechanically and chemically bring about changes that can be brought about mentally.

([John:] "I can't argue that point." John sells for a drug company.)

You must be in a good mood this evening. *(Humorously.)* ...You had some questions...

([John:] "Not specifically. [Pause.] I can't formulate a question right now. You go ahead. I'll ask you later.")

Now, I am pleased that you have kept copies of the material so carefully. And when we are done ... Then you will see that we have done very well indeed.

(Here Seth refers to the copies of sessions concerning John and his company, Searle, that John has carefully kept. John is also to make a tape for us, correlating all the data, predictions, etc., that Seth has given him to date.

([John:] "You say a development will occur shortly."

(This refers to events within Searle.) I did indeed. Give us a moment.

(Pause.) There seems to be a man this time with very dark hair. It may be tinted hair, for he is older than the hair would suggest. He is not directly connected with those in your immediate area.

He seems to be either a relative or a very close associate to one near the very top of your firm. You might say like a brother to him. He has been dissatisfied of late, and there will be suggestions made concerning a change in organizational structure in one particular area, and this will affect you indirectly but definitely.

There is a June date here insofar as your knowledge of the development is concerned, and there are two partners, or two allied men within your firm who will break apart.

My symbolic impression is of twins. But they will break up, pull apart, and exert separate pressures. They will disagree on matters of policy. Now the date of June 18 comes to mind, and it seems to be connected with an anniversary or get-together of some sort. The chips will be down, but another man will pick them up; that is, these two men will drop the chips and another man will pick them up. *(Humorously:)* Empire makers are always looking for a toehold... and this will give you one... You can use some of your tricky footwork... *(More here that I missed.)*

There is something else here, completely divorced. A female relative I believe, perhaps an aunt of yours or of your wife's. A name perhaps like Evelyn, in connection with a trip, and a rather unfortunate circumstance.

(To Bill:) I will try to give you some practical suggestions. Take your break... I dare you, Jesuit, to look into yourself. I have never led you wrong, and I tell you, you can be a healthy man.

(10:00. Jane's trance had again been good, her pace a bit slower but still usually faster than I am used to as far as note-taking goes.

(John Bradley said much of the data was good, and he will cover it in detail in his projected tape. There are two regional managers in the Searle organization who are brothers-in-law. One of these, Steve Chase of Los Angeles, has black-tinted hair. The other, George Striker, is in Skokie, Illinois. John thinks Chase is the more progressive of the two, and is of the opinion that in any clash between these two men a southern regional manager, Don Robinson, would be in a position to pick up pieces. John told us more that is not covered in these notes.

(John's wife's sister is named Evelyn, and so would be the aunt of John's children. This family has been involved with travel, and at the moment lives west of us, in Ohio. John said there is a tie-in here with some earlier material given by Seth concerning family travel and Hawaii. This data will also be covered via tape.

(Resume at 10:10)

Now. My friend Ruburt always knows what he is doing. *(Humor.)* Do not fall for that line... Give us a moment. *(Pause.)*

Now, I like you *(to Bill)*, but I do not intrude when I am not invited, and as a rule I do not offer advice when I am not asked...

([Bill:] "Seth, you have an open invitation from me, anytime...")

But you are not ready... demands effort... The results would be spectacular in your case. Your life and destiny is in your own hands... Wouldn't feel the need to punish yourself ... I am ready to give you help—

([Bill:] "I need it all.")

Then you shall get it, and if you do not follow it that is up to you. But I will give it to you. *(Amused:)* For one thing you deserve it, and I like to see you work... and there is a peaceful man within you. You have only to find him... and you can do it. I can help you find him.

He is not driven, but he knows his abilities and how to use them, and he knows how to retain his integrity in society... Not to fear selling his soul to the devil. Then I will definitely give you information that you can use.

Whenever you come to a session I will begin a reading for you that you can follow. I throw our Jesuit a challenge: I dare him to be a peaceful man.

([Bill:] "I wouldn't know how to begin, Seth.")

Inside yourself you know.

Now give us a moment. *(To John:)* I am not sure here, so I will go slowly...

There seems to be a drug you are taking into your own system that is going against your system. An occasional thing I believe—having to do with a retention of fluid. Ruburt has no medical vocabulary. Let us see now; you should take those fruits that are strong in vitamin C, but are not acid. You should avoid acid fruits taken in one meal with milk. You should avoid all chocolate in any form. Now this is not forever, merely until the condition vanishes. You should not eat grapefruit now under any circumstances. Cranberry juice however is beneficial. You should avoid aspirin.

You should avoid natural butter, and much malt. You should not, for example, indulge in beer, breads or cereals over much... need not cut bread from diet... Rice is good, fish is good.

Pork is disaster.

([John:] "This is true.")

Fatty foods should be avoided. You should eat almonds. And watch your intake of sugars. Honey will not bother you. Give me a moment. Now. Symbolically in your case, and opposed to our Jesuit's case, the retention of fluids has to do with the fear for your position, of refusal to give up, or the fear of giving up, prerogatives. *(Pause.)*

...Obviously an inability to relax, because you feel by relaxing you let down your hold... You should imagine in your spare moments, even driving, that poisonous fluids are disappearing from your system and leaving it free. The fluids represent bitterness that you will not let go of, and so you must tell yourself that your inner self possesses the answers—as it does—that it will guide you... You can therefore afford to let the bitterness go, for the bitterness is your enemy... The fluids are not in themselves poisonous, only their retention that makes them act upon your system.

(To Peg:) Ahead of time, I thank you for our interview... and I should be perfectly willing to hold an interview with you myself...

([Peg:] "That's not a bad idea...")

(Peg is planning an interview with Jane for the Elmira Star-Gazette *concerning the publication of Jane's book on the Seth material.)*

—and any time you want to try your tricky camera... We will see what we can do—

([Peg:] "I'll do that.")

(There was more to this humorous exchange that I did not get down.

(Jane took a break at 10:28. Her trance had been good. John Bradley said at first that he knew of nothing he is taking into his system that would encourage fluid retention. He said he very occasionally takes Metamucil, which is inert.

(Seth was hovering about as John talked. John then said the Metamucil contained dextrose, a sugar, which could lead to fluid retention.

("I beg your pardon," John said, "the Metamucil would then—")

The inert substance is not inert. Within your system you activate certain elements... The stress reaction changes the substance... so that it is no longer inert.

There is an interaction with salt and sugar—an activating principle... and an extra charge of electricity, noticeable perhaps when you are combing your hair...

(There was more here I did not get down. My notes do not indicate what, if anything, John said about the possible electrical effects. A long break now ensued.

(Jane, during break, began to get impressions from/for Bill Gallagher, and Bill signaled me to take them down. There follows an accurate account of what Jane said, not quite verbatim however.

("Tom C., he's got hair like spikes on his forehead...Tom Crompton. He's 36. Connection with a grocery store ... produce of some kind. There's a woman connected with him, a sister, who helps him somehow. There's a Detroit connection. Spikes. A group of 4 people; he and a woman are one... Bill's one; a female relative the other

one."

("There's a connection with a lawsuit, or trouble along those lines. A guy who's a jokester. Two little kids. September, 1943. Then the present..."

("I don't know why I get this..." [In answer to Bill's question.] "A close relative. I don't know... I leaped to the death of a father. A connection between this guy's father and yours [to Bill]—because I know your father's dead. Either that, or there's a real connection between this guy and his father."

("The words, don't do it—you'll screw your ass." [Laugh.]

("A family interaction with this Tom and perhaps your father. Not a pleasant one ... the family situation."

(Bill Gallagher told us he knew a Tom Crawford in college; Bill and Peg verified, or made connections with, much of this data. Lengthy explanations were required and I did not record them; the Gallaghers said they would write out the data for us upon receipt of a copy of the impressions, so the material can be included with this record.

(A few impressions that were particularly apt were September 1943, the Detroit connection, the spikes-for-hair, the lawsuit type of trouble, the family situation similarity, and the profanity. Tom C. was a prolific profanity man, according to Bill.

(Resume at 11:02.)

Now. We have been coaching Ruburt in the use of his abilities. We do not want him to feel inferior, and the information is basically legitimate. *(Pause.)*

There is some information in our sessions having to do with Prentice-Hall, long before the sale, that you should reread, for there will be a long relationship involved; and there is some considerable significance to your relationship to your friend Aerofranz. *(Meaning Tam Mossman, editor at P-H.)*

They will also publish my book, though by then there will be some changes in the company, and eventually our friend Aerofranz will change his allegiance to another company.

(To Peg: An exchange here followed which was too quick for me to get down, so it is here summarized. After joking with Peggy about interviews, cameras, etc., Seth said in time that he would interview Peg, who by then would be "notorious," or better known. I don't believe he said just how this would come about. Seth also told Peg there was some data she would need, that she would request it herself, about the crisis in her own life approximately 6 years from now.

(Seth said his use of the word crisis didn't necessarily mean that there would be disastrous circumstances, but again he didn't elaborate. To Peg again:)

Now. I hope you will use the material that I gave to Ruburt's class, for it contains within it the heart of my message.

(To John:) No specific questions...?

([John:] "Does anything depend on what goes on at the meeting next week? Is anything going to happen?")

No. Nothing that will be of true or lasting import to you, next week. Remember the whole sentence.

Now I come from a long way to speak. You do not have to come a like distance to listen. When through Ruburt's open eyes I observe you, I observe more than the person that you realize that you are, for it is difficult for me to pinpoint you in your time. In your terms therefore, I see both your present and future selves, though probabilities operate.

(To Bill:) It is the probabilities that worry you, though certainly you can put up with them... *(After a humorous exchange:)* You play hopscotch beautifully...

Do any of you have questions? I will answer them to the best of my ability.

(When no one spoke up:) Give me a moment. *(To Bill:)* Now. An appointment... Do not say yes. Forget the unprincipled... You have more to offer than that. Three men seem to be involved, and one you cannot trust. Forget the arrangement. It is a bed of nails. You can seem to be accommodating while holding your own on the one main issue... And do not back down on that one issue. To back down would... be weakness.

Unfortunate implications... seem to be accommodating, but stall... within 2 or 3 days I believe, the circumstances will have changed.

Now you may not be certain of my existence, but be certain of my knowledge. *(Humorously.*

([Bill:] "I've never doubted either. It's the context...")

You may take a break... *(To Bill:)*

Forget the referendum, and look in the back of your desk drawer for a bit of information you have forgotten. Your initial analysis was correct.

(To John:) Your Stan now has four counts against him, and he has lost his fifth. *(There was more here.*

(11:16. In contrast to earlier breaks, Jane now came out of trance rather quickly. Bill and Peg didn't particularly want to talk about the data given above, but said it had a direct bearing; something, we were told, about a meeting tomorrow...

(Bill showed Jane a page of pencil drawings he had doodled while Seth spoke. They were heads, in various stylistic poses, small in scale. He told Jane they were not cheerful. After a short discussion Seth returned.)

You are getting rid of morbid aspects of your nature... *(More here.)* The lower right drawer, of your desk... to the very back...it contains some information that will be helpful... A card with a name and address...

([Bill:] "Do you know what the name and address are?")

A connection with Cincinnati, and an account and a withdrawal, and a circular ...

([Bill:] "Do you mean a circular in the graphic sense, or in the Sears or Montgomery Ward sense?")

Something that is circulated ...

(This after quite an exchange between Bill, Peg and Seth, as an attempt was made to lucidly describe the item in question. The discussion proceeded rapidly and I missed most of it. At the moment Bill could say nothing about Cincinnati, etc.

(Very shortly after this exchange the session ended. 11:25.)

SESSION 456
JANUARY 8, 1969 9:12 PM WEDNESDAY

Good evening.

("Good evening, Seth.")

Now. We are back on our schedule.

You will find that a creative, placid and yet fulfilling time is beginning, when you will both begin to do some of your best work. Certain elements are leaving your lives now, and with the signing of the contract Ruburt feels socially, economically and creatively justified, and accepted.

The resulting inner freedom will also free his own creative energies, and his career will continue to expand. It will no longer be as restrictive. He will find himself writing in other areas as well. His release will also have its effect upon your own subjective life.

He has passed over the hump of early adulthood, that you passed through some time before, and you are both ready to give yourselves to your work. There will be an added placidity, as well as spontaneity. We will return to our material. Much work that we have done however in terms of the Philip *(John Bradley's entity area is Philip)* readings, will be of great value, and serve to add to the authenticity, in other people's eyes, of your adventure.

I do intend to begin my own book now, very shortly, for this will give a new organization to the material, and direct the flow of information. There has been a very marked improvement in Ruburt's condition. There will shortly be another equally remarkable improvement—another stage, in other words, and this one will be followed in a matter of two months or so by complete recovery —that is, two months after the next improvement.

You should recall that I told you that this one would occur.

("Yes." See the 442nd session, page 107. October 14,1968.)

I will then give Ruburt some suggestions as to normal living habits that if followed will enable him to stay in good health. One of these will be a mental exercise, taking no more than ten minutes, and if done properly, only three times a week, will be of great benefit in keeping joints and muscles loose and free. *(Pause.)* I should perhaps give you that exercise now.

When resting, and in a tranquil state of mind, he should simply imagine the limbs slowly stretching out, becoming somewhat longer, and then slowly returning to their original length. He should then imagine the neck revolving easily and normally three times in each direction; mentally here doing the yoga neck exercise that he recalls.

The lengthening exercise to be emphasized with the arms particularly. The toes and fingers should be visualized as lengthening also, easily and slowly, and then returning to normal position. The joints should be imagined as moving easily. At the same time, he should dwell on the idea of flexibility and freedom, mental, spiritual, psychic and physical flexibility. That is the end of the exercise.

It will do good also if during the day occasionally he imagines the exercise as he goes about his chores, but he should not do this willfully, with an intent to command physical performance. The whole thing should be done with a mental lightness, more as if it were a children's game, and he must remember this for it is the whole point of the procedure.

The potato is effective, and highly. The symbolism in holding the potato, you see, is that tensions and poisons pass from the fingers into the potato, which is a root vegetable. It is symbolism, but highly effective for that reason, and for that reason it does indeed draw out tensions and poisons.

I am giving you this information because it is useful. I do not intend to keep you long this evening however, being content with the resumption of our schedule. Ruburt's decision in regard to his classes is a good one. There will be no difficulty in holding students, or in keeping the same income, with only one class.

At one time two classes met certain needs. He needed that extra, outside contact as others came here. Now he does not.

You may take your break and I shall continue. One remark, however. Once we begin my book, there will still be some interruptions for the other personality may sometimes also speak. There are other experiments with concepts with which you will be involved.

I also suggest that when we are holding regular sessions, then for one session a month we deal with a session for someone like your Pitre, Norelli, or whoever needs such a session at any time. This need not be a rule.

There are some remarks about healing, both for you and for our Aerofranz *(Tam Mossman)* for example. Such sessions will serve us all well, and one out of eight sessions would hardly be too much. In helping others you help yourselves.

(9:38. Jane left trance quickly. Her pace had been good, eyes open often. She said she could see how to do the exercises while Seth was describing them.

(A subject came up at break that hadn't been anticipated; I explained to Jane some of the troubles I had had lately re my oil portraits. I thought the remarks would bring forth some response from Seth, but since a shorter session had been announced I didn't think such a lengthy response would materialize.

(Jane resumed at 9:58 at a slower pace.)

Now. Give us a moment, dear friend. *(Pause.)*

You are working with portraits, and portraits are of people. Here is where some of your difficulty lies. *(Pause.)* You should try to probe the mystery of individuality with love. You are overimmersed, presently, in the technique and the painting.

A portrait must contain a searching and a deep statement of the human condition, a reaching out toward the mystery that is another person, whether the person exists in your mind, or physical reality, or both. A portrait must contain a journey into personality, and the technique and the form will then follow naturally and spontaneously.

(This is very good philosophy, and I have been aware of it.)

As you know you are apt sometimes to use a problem with technique as a substitute problem, as a way therefore of escaping from, rather than facing, certain issues concerning the nature of emotion. *(Pause.*

(*This I have been suspecting recently, but hadn't said anything about it to Jane.)*

Now laughing loud and heartily, or crying deeply—either would serve you well, help release inner feelings and help clear the inner channels. You are trying too hard, as you know. Being an artist is a natural way of life with you. Paintings can and should emerge from you easily.

You do not need to justify your existence by painting. It is impossible to do so. *(Pause.)* There are two approaches, either of which would be highly beneficial. The first is to paint a portrait of a person whom you know, trying to portray the essence of that person, their deepest agonies and highest joys, their highest capabilities and fears of failure. *(Pause.)* This would induce on your part an honest effort to face the raw emotion of another personality, and portray it.

The emphasis would not <u>necessarily</u> (underlined) be upon technique nor detail, though it <u>could</u> be, but upon portraying in one portrait, if you will forgive the phrase, the agony and the ecstasy of individual existence. This is what you often avoid facing.

Now. The other approach in many ways is completely opposed to the first one. Indeed it may not seem like an approach at all to you. Using this approach however, for ten days minimum, you drop the work you are doing. You drop the idea of work as work during your usual work hours. You capture as much as possible and in whatever way you choose, a careless, childlike, playing attitude.

Look at the scenes outside your window in this light. Think of your painting as a spontaneous play of the godlike self, who paints or plays for the pure joy of doing so, without effort, without questions, and without plans. Sketch whatever comes into your head. Do not limit yourself in any way whatsoever in terms of intent as far as subject matter, medium, technique. Indulge in a spontaneous childlike game. When you feel like sketching or painting, when an idea springs into your head, try it immediately. When it does not, when an idea does not come, then walk, play with your cat, do anything you want to do.

(I don't believe there has been a time when I didn't have plenty of ideas. This has never been a problem with me personally, but I didn't interrupt to make a point of this. I thought the data excellent.)

Give me a moment. *(Pause.)*

The idea, again, art as a spontaneous play of the godlike self. Do not dictate to it. It knows more than you about the game. Now either of these techniques will serve you very well and refresh your creative energies. They are equally valid, and equally geared though in different ways, to your peculiar dilemma. Do not mix the approaches however. Plunge into one or the other wholeheartedly, and underline wholeheartedly fifty times.

If you choose the first approach, then you must plunge wholeheartedly into the person you are using as model, and immerse yourself in his reality, and from this let the painting flow.

Now you may take a break, and we shall continue. *(Pause at 10:20.)* In the first approach you become completely immersed in the subject. In the second approach you become completely immersed in the idea of spontaneous play, which is true blessedness and creativity and there is no focus upon subject. Do you see the value and similarity of the approaches?

("Yes.")

Either will be some experience for you, I can promise you. *(Humorously and emphatic.)* Both demand a concentration and focus into the basic reality from which painting comes, rather than upon the painting itself. They will acquaint you with their source.

(10:22. Jane had been in a good trance, and was bleary when she came out of

it. She said that whenever I ask questions about painting she "really goes out." Jane said that at some time when Seth explained the two approaches she strongly felt what he meant.

(A note. It is January 12th as this is typed. I have already begun the second approach, as might be expected. I can say that it is working well. This session was held on January 8, 1969.

(Jane's pace was back up to its faster rate, and remained so when she resumed at 10:26 as we discussed the material.)

Now. Something else here: you are overly concerned with the physical idea of time, and focusing wrongly, and this is affecting your work.

You feel rushed by the years. You regret past time, and that your abilities, you feel, have not come to fruition. This serves to tighten you up and overwhelm you with a sense of desperation at times, and is highly restricted.

This restriction will show in all areas of your work if you do not break it, and you can do so. Its effects literally color all of your painting activities, and serve to reinforce the restrictions of an emotional nature. So solving one issue helps both.

Give me a moment here. *(Pause.)*

You must realize, and tell yourself, that creativity is timeless in a basic manner. You must completely cease inner speculations and regrets and questions as to why your abilities have not come to fruition. This must positively be done. The negative suggestion works constantly against you. When such thoughts come to mind, instead tell yourself that that trend of thought will not help your painting, but hinder it, and that it is constricting. Then immediately imagine a time when you painted very well and spontaneously, and tell yourself that you are now free to use and develop these abilities. *(Pause.)*

You need not hammer this. The feeling is what is important. Think of yourself as being flexible creatively. Psychological time, if you contemplate it, will set you free, so that you feel value fulfillment and durability within the time that you know. Do not think in terms regretfully that you have only afternoons in which to work. This restricts you in two main ways.

One, you are limiting the time in which you can be creative or get ideas. You are saying, effectively: I can only get my creative ideas in the afternoon. Instead tell yourself that creative ideas for your paintings can come to you at any hour of the night or day, and that creativity knows no time barrier.

In this way creative ideas can even come to you at your job, or on other occasions, and be used at a more convenient time. The negative thought that you have only afternoons (underline only), also tends to limit the value of the time that you do have, and restrict it.

Your attitude should be, I have the whole afternoon to myself in which to paint, and all the rest of the time I have for creative abilities to bring me inspiration and ideas.

Now this information, properly used, plus your use of one of the two approaches given earlier, will be of great benefit. Not only now but for the rest of your life. Do you have any questions?

("Not particularly until I can study this material. At break though I was telling Jane that yesterday I had an intuitive flash similar to the second approach you described. Happened while I was taking a nap.")

My approach is freer than what you had thought of, and more effective for that reason.

("Yes, I can see the difference.")

If you have no more questions I will end the session... If you have questions ask me at our next session. You realize that you can call upon me in between regular sessions, or instead of a regular session when you feel the need.

("Yes.")

You may then end the session or take a break as you prefer.

("We'll end it then.")

My heartiest wishes to you both. You have been given advice geared to you and to your needs. If you follow it you will be amazed at the difference in your attitude and in your work. It must not be a willy-nilly trial, a one-or-two day affair, but a wholehearted plunge into whatever approach you choose, and you should also follow the suggestions given later concerning time and your attitude. This is your artistic prescription, and half doses will not do a full job.

("Okay. Good night, Seth, and thank you."

(10:48. Jane's trance was deep, but she left it quickly. She remembered little of what she said.)

SESSION 457
JANUARY 13, 1969 9:06 PM MONDAY

Good evening.

("Good evening, Seth.")

A few notes. *(Pause.)* Our friend Ruburt must be entirely committed *(pause),* in order to succeed, but once committed his success is assured.

He is now committed. His diverse abilities had to be gathered together and focused. The deepest needs and desires of the personality had to be aroused and deeply involved in an endeavor that would allow the personality to use its full strength in a focused and emotionally intense manner.

The process could or could not have developed, according to the probabilities and the circumstances. Even the early environment, so abhorred by the ego, were chosen in order to deepen the desire for truth and to force the personality to face the issues of life and death, evil and goodness, full face. Ruburt's ego would have avoided the questions and taken the easy road, and this easy road would not have developed the full potentials that were necessary if the personality were to use its creative and intuitional abilities in any important manner.

Only now does Ruburt see the consistency and how the path as he knew it brought forth the impetus that is now his present. I told him sessions ago that the poetic and psychic portions of his personality were deeply united, and now looking over his old records he knows that I was correct.

The ego would have chosen an easier road, through fiction. *(Pause.)* Through easy success, through in fact a far more shallow route, but the intuitive self would have suffered drastically in your future, and there would have been severe difficulties.

Instead Ruburt is involved in our endeavor, and his daily life entwined in the search that fiction cannot approach. This endeavor, involving you both so deeply, all also lead you toward the full development of your own abilities. Both of you must be fully committed, for your personalities have been formed in that direction.

(Loud music was blaring up now from the apartment below us.)

The commitment also unites the two of you in a passionate philosophical concern. All probabilities now point toward success for you both; but remember, as you know, I do not mean a sudden showering. When I speak of success I mean that now you will be able to use your abilities to their fullest. That is success.

You will to some extent change the thought of your error, and in so doing of future errors, in your terms. You will put rungs down for others to follow. If you wonder, you will be financially comfortable, but the energy now being gathered together, and focused will be felt in all your endeavors. It is more powerful than you realize, and it will bring great changes in your lives.

The changes will bring responsibility and stress, and great potentiality. The challenges will further allow you to use your abilities, and you will gain strength from them. Your work as an artist will be well-known. This will not happen overnight. It will become well-known first because of our sessions. It will then quickly be recognized on its own merit.

Your own early environment should also be considered for what it was, a challenge set by you to bring out your full potential, through making you face problems from which you would have only too readily isolated yourself. In a recent session I outlined the books that Ruburt will write. He will be free, you see, to work in fiction, and will do so in the future, because fiction will be something different than it was.

(See the notes on page 194, preceding the 455th session for January 6, 1969, re the books Jane will write. These notes contain a brief summary of an unscheduled session held over the Xmas holidays, with Sue Mullin and Carl Watkins as witnesses. I would now like to add to those notes.

(I neglected to add that after this unscheduled session, which was held at night, Jane also spoke as Ruburt. This was the first time I had seen this take place, although it has happened a few times before, usually in ESP class. See the notes on page 122, 444th session for October 30, 1968. On the occasion I witnessed, I do not recall what Jane said as Ruburt.

(In the 444th session also, Seth deals with Jane-Ruburt at length.)

I am of course aware of your Christ's head. You would not have felt free enough to do it in the past, for you did not realize what it represented, or rather, you did not see the implications.

(Here Seth refers to a painting I began yesterday, in line with approach two of the suggestions he gave me in the last, 456th session, I am following his suggestions and they are working well.)

There is something I will tell you someday about your art.

("Oh?")

I do not want to make any suggestions now, for what I am thinking of will come from you.

("From me or from Joseph? Not that I object, either way."

(Amused:) If you want to be that picayune, it will come through Joseph, but since you are Joseph you should hardly quibble. Like Ruburt, only more so, you have avoided religious symbolism, strictly avoided it, and for many years you did not see beneath the obvious hypocrisy and distortions inherent in religious organizations. The hypocrisy of the organizations blinded you to the inner truth of the symbols.

The symbols have great meaning to the inner self. They also serve as intuitional springboards, opening up channels through which insights can flow. They can also serve as vehicles for energy.

You may take your break.

(9:35. Jane came out of trance rather quickly; her eyes remained dark, her manner subdued, and she said: "Yeah, I'm pretty Seth yet, but I'm also conscious of that music." The music was still noisy from below us.

(While moving about in the kitchen during break Jane got this within: "Ruburt is only now beginning to start upon his life's work." Sitting down a bit later she said: "I'm trying to get back in," meaning trance, "but that music downstairs bothers me." Resume finally at 9:48.)

Now. The search for answers, and this passionate yearning toward truth, has driven Ruburt's personality, and he became ill only when he was afraid to continue the search, because it led him into byways that he had not planned upon; or rather, upon which the ego had not planned.

Until then the ego and the intuitive self had not come into conflict, as far as basic philosophy was concerned. The intuitive self presented the ego however with a new line of development that it was not prepared to follow.

The ego did not see the consistency. It did not see that then previous questions that it had set, that it had asked, led inevitably to intuitive answers and to psychic experience, and for some time it refused to see this, in quotes "quite logical" consistency. For the psychic development made logical sense as well.

You suggested that Ruburt put his records in one place for quite sound intuitive reasons. He could have read his old poetry over 50 times in the past two years, without realizing what he has finally realized now.

(Recently we have been moving all of Jane's old poetry, novel, short-story, psychic, and other manuscripts and notes, dating back to her grade-school work, out of the upstairs storeroom into our roomy front-room closet. In the process she has come to read over a lot of her earlier work, with eye-opening insights, etc.)

One of the reasons that the intellect refused to see, that its own search was bound to end up in this fashion, was Ruburt's inability to see beyond organized religion's hypocrisy. This was mentioned earlier in tonight's session in regard to you.

He spoke honestly when he said that he considered it intellectual suicide to accept even the possibility of personal survival of death. The conflict brought him to a point where he simply could go no further intellectually, for the intellect would not follow where the intuitions led. This caused him to think of our sessions in stereotyped ways, putting an either-or aspect to our relationship, and closing his mind to my own explanation of my existence.

He is quite free to question the basis of the sessions, and to question my own source. *(Pause.)* But he did not even do this with any true (underlined) logic, while he distrusted himself, or distrusted the intuitive and revelationary (underlined) aspect of the material. Now his intellect is accepting the revelationary aspect of the material, and the word appeared in his own writings about it for the first time. *(Recently.)* It is a highly evocative word to him, and even his intellect has always trusted revelationary knowledge as long as it was given to him through channels that were egotistically accepted. *(Emphatic delivery.)*

As he himself suspected, there has been a personality reorganization on Jane's part, and for the abilities to be used fully, such reorganization was necessary. A reorganization would have occurred in any case, only it could have resulted in diminution of effective ability, instead of a magnification. He recognized this, feeling that while he highly enjoyed science fiction it was a dead end, for the answers he sought could not be worked out even through philosophical fiction.

Poetry came the closest, and yet the form of that art still could not carry the full weight of the knowledge he knew was available. The high points, yes. *(Pause.)* Poetry could not however express in a consistent way those intricate patterns so that they could be clearly understood.

In our sessions I use, with Ruburt's permission, his intellectual abilities also *(pause),* in an organized fashion. Poetry was far less *(humorously)* dependable. Now. Many of these reasons are the personality's own reasons for *(louder, abruptly)* opening up the revelationary channels, and they would be legitimate regardless of the nature of my existence.

Were I only his personality's method of gaining revelationary knowledge *(pause)*, then he should be content with that, recognizing his need of me in that endeavor. I am however far more. Now there is a need on my part also. Any personality has a psychological makeup, whether or not they are equipped with physical form, and I am a teacher.

In time Ruburt will recognize fully my independent nature, but he did not completely (underlined) even admit the revelationary source of the material until quite lately. He knew it, but the ego did not admit it. Now the intellect is free from the only tie-up it would encounter, for again, it has always accepted the legitimacy of revelationary data.

In other words, your friend's ego has declared me legitimate now. On the other hand, I have always counted upon Ruburt's ego as an ally in this fashion. It kept Ruburt in strong protection under its wing, and if it was overly stubborn, it was so because it always recognized Ruburt's intuitive abilities, and the full strength of Ruburt's sense of commitment, once given.

Now it adds its strength. I made no attempts to browbeat it, recognizing its purposes. Ruburt chose a strong ego as a necessary guardian in adolescence, and as a balance to the strong spontaneous self, until a mission made itself known, and the correct mission. It simply did not recognize the mission for some time.

Neither of you realize the strength of the abilities as yet, and the need for forging a strong personality who could learn to handle them wisely, and hold its own while using them. The ego feared that the abilities could sweep Ruburt away in the past even before our sessions, sensing the great but as yet unfocused energy. When it was assured that this was the mission for which the personality had waited, and only when it was positive, did it free its protective hold and give its blessings.

It is still protective, but now it realizes that it has nothing to fear.

You may take your break.

(10:23. Jane just about had time to leave trance, say to me, "The session isn't quite over yet," sip some wine and offer a few ideas, when she resumed at 10:29.)

The ego now, once again, sees the whole personality's search as its own, and will wholeheartedly take part.

It understands quite well that I am more than a subconscious extension of the personality. I would not be satisfied, either, with a highly simplified version of my existence, accepting me as a long-gowned spirit in those terms known to it, and knows that I am far more than that, that the truth is deeper, and it will work with the intuitive self to search for answers. *(A bit jumbled, Seth!)*

It recognizes the answers given in the sessions as legitimate, and also that these answers involve intellectual as well as intuitional effort. The ego is pleased, for it now finds itself at the helm of a much stronger personality, and with more challenges, free to use its abilities, to question and wonder at will now that it accepts the basis of the sessions.

It is far more permissive, while still retaining its dominance in those areas that are its natural ground. It also realizes the experiences open to it that would otherwise be unavailable, and it can now itself grow in understanding and development, and as a willing and able protector, but not a jealous one.

Now I will let you end the session, but this is information that is highly valuable. The spontaneous self is also highly relieved that it is on good terms again with the ego, and that the personality is establishing itself and the main work is beginning.

For you and Ruburt both are now beginning your work. Ruburt's physical symptoms will entirely vanish, and within now a relatively short period of time, as given in a recent session. My heartiest regards to you both from your legitimate Seth.

("All right.")

One small note. I believe there will be extra freedom in out-of-body experiences for Ruburt. Tell him not to be frightened at any new developments in that area. I will be there whether he knows it or not. No, there are not any phantoms out there, Ruburt. It will simply be a new environment. You will return safely. A friend wants to meet you. My friend. A long trip in a brief time. You

Communication from Seth—

will be protected all the way. I would hold your hand, but that would probably frighten you more than anything else. Be assured, it will be a safe trip.

You will be given information and you will remember it. And again, I will be your guide.

("Good night, Seth. Thank you.")

(10:43. Jane snapped right out of trance, quite alert; she remembered the last part of the data and said she "got scared" while giving it, re astral travel. Yet after supper tonight she said she wished Seth would help her out while projecting.

(This session was held on Monday, January 13. It is Friday, January 17. To date Jane has had no such unusual projecting experience as outlined above by Seth.)

SESSION 458
JANUARY 20, 1969 9PM MONDAY

(Sue Mullin was a witness to the session.

(For a while now Jane and I have been considering the question, aloud, of Seth's availability to us whenever we choose to hold a session. This would take into account our physical time system, etc. We thought the question would have many ramifications. Note that I didn't specifically ask that the question be discussed this evening.

(As is often the case Jane had no idea of what material would be dealt with this evening. Sue told us she had no specific questions. Jane began speaking in trance at quite a fast pace, eyes open often, etc.)

Good evening.

("Good evening, Seth.")

Now. As to my availability at your sessions.

You know the nature of personality now to some degree, and I am always to some degree present at your sessions. *(Smile.)* Now give us a moment.

You are able, within the conditions that we have set, and with my assistance, to call upon those elements in my personality with which you are acquainted. Sort of a vitalized 4th-dimensional letter or communication, in which, if you will forgive the term, the medium is the message. *(Humorously.)*

In some ways then Ruburt is turned into a vitalized telegram. My regard for you, and the material, are always interbound with my own identity, however. When you send a communication or a telegram, you send merely words, in your terms. I send portions of myself.

My entire essence however need not always be involved. *(Pause.)* I need not be entirely focused within your dimension in other words, but I am focused sufficiently to meet our appointments.

The psychological bridgework of which I have spoken serves us well, however, and this exists on Ruburt's part as well as my own.

(Much of the data on psychological bridgeworks was given at least a couple of years ago.)

A certain portion of my reality is therefore available to you during our appointed times, and the bridgework of which we have spoken is always available; and using it Ruburt can call upon me on other occasions.

Using it, I may call upon you on other occasions. This does not necessarily mean, on either of our parts, that such a call will always be met by an affirmative answer, or that contact will be made.

(Jane now began to gesture with her hands and arms.) It is as if there were two portions of a bridge, like a toll bridge or a drawbridge, and these two portions you see must meet. When you wish to contact me at other than appointed times, I may or may not be easily (underlined) available. Your own emotional need and impetus will however be made known to me. Therefore if that need is strong I would of course be here, even as you would not disregard the need of a friend. I am not automatically available however any more than you are.

(This is a refinement of the question, and a good one. When Jane and I wonder about Seth's seeming availability, we mean the scheduled Monday and Wednesday evening sessions, an occasional appearance at one of Jane's ESP classes, and an occasional dropping in at an unscheduled session, perhaps on a weekend, etc.

(This is a different thing than Seth being available say at 8 AM, or noon, or other capricious hours we may choose. We have not conducted any tests to see if this is possible. We do know however that Seth would be available at any time under emotional stress, if we asked.)

I am however, again, automatically a part of the message that I bring to you. At times, for various reasons, I am here more completely than in other sessions. These reasons however have to do with circumstances that are usually beyond "normal" control: electromagnetic conditions, psychological circumstances—the psychological climate for example. All of these could be considered as atmospheric conditions through which I must enter.

As I have told you, to some extent then projection is involved, both on my part and on Ruburt's. The question, am I always available to you when you want me, is based upon the old limited concept of personality *(pointing to Sue, humorously)*, for even our friend here can be in two places at the same time—and I have had more training.

(This is a reference to Sue's projection experiences.)

When it seems to you that there is a difference between the focus in sessions, then it is simply that the reception conditions are poor. There is also a complicated psychological, very delicate manipulation that must occur. Sometimes there are small errors, so that the reception does not come as clearly.

(To me:) I have told you that your own presence is also involved here to some extent, and whether or not you are present at any given session.

Give us a moment. *(Pause.)* Now when you watch, say, educational TV, you see the teacher, and he speaks. He may or may not actually be speaking at that time, for you may be watching a film. But the teacher exists whether or not he is speaking at that time, in your terms, and his message is as legitimate. So now see Ruburt as my TV screen. I must come through much more clearly, and you have here the essence of the teacher.

The teacher transforms the TV screen until the TV screen becomes momentarily the teacher. Now it makes little difference, you see, when the transformation is worked, in your terms, or what dials are turned, or whether or not I as myself am at this moment within Ruburt speaking in your terms, or whether I did this *(meaning this session, being delivered by Jane now)* last evening in your terms, and tonight is a film or playback.

For again, the medium is the message in the spacious present, and whenever the time for the program arrives I am here in your present, regardless of where I am in what you would term my present.

For in my present in your terms, I am also the personality who is not speaking this evening, the Seth who does not have those characteristics with which you are so familiar. It is unfortunate that I must use terms of time to explain this to you, but as I told you many sessions ago, my time is not your time. *(Humorously.)*

You may take a break and we shall continue. *(To Sue:)* I give you my welcome.

(9:26. Jane left trance easily. Resume at the same rather fast, and active, pace at 9:32.)

Now. I may prepare my film in advance, in your terms, when consciously Ruburt is not aware of it, and when no impression is made upon his conscious mind.

Again, this does not imply that such a session is less legitimate than others. It simply means that I use what you would call time in a different way than you.

Now, some part of Ruburt is of course aware, for I would not intrude, and he has long since given his permission for such an arrangement. Nor, because you ask specific questions at a specific session, and I answer them, does it necessarily mean that the program has not been prepared, in your terms, earlier; for on many occasions I will see the questions within your mind, or the minds of your witnesses, and will therefore answer them, in your terms ahead of time.

(There must be much more data available re the above paragraph. This is a reminder for future questions.)

Even on such occasions however I look in closely on the classroom to see how my pupils are behaving, and whether or not my message is coming across clearly; and I also learn. *(Pause.)* If you study this material closely, you will see that I have answered your question more clearly than you realize, and indeed in the only way that would make any sense at all.

Give us a moment. *(Pause.)* This does not mean however that I use Ruburt as a puppet, and stuff his mouth with tapes as a recorder, and that you are always listening to replays, or that emotionally I am not here during such sessions. It means that in such multidimensional communications I can be here emotionally. I can be here in your terms at appointed times, for the medium is also more than the message.

The teacher is within the tape. The personality is condensed. Your question stems however from the idea that if I am here I cannot be somewhere else at the same time, or that all of my energies must be focused here at the session. There are aspects of my identity with which you are not acquainted, though you may be at some later date in your terms. *(Smile.*

("I see.")

This should not make you feel cheated. All the channels are not yet working on this set yet, you see.

("Yes.")

I use certain facets of my personality, for they are helpful as a teacher. You know all of me that you are able to know, at any given time in your terms. *(Pause.)* It would be <u>relatively</u> (underlined)but certainly practically impossible, for me to make my full reality clear to you, now, in our sessions, for your understanding would not contain it.

Now you may take your break. We would not want to blow a tube.

(9:47. Seth ended on a humorous note, and Jane was out of trance quickly. This proved to be the end of the session.

(Continuation of Session 458, January 20, 1969, after break at 9:47. This material is not included in the records.

(Resume at 10:01 PM. Point at Sue Mullin.)

Now, give us a moment. Some information for you...

Your child, in a past life, this child was an uncle, and in an accident you killed him. You were in a carriage, driving it. He went to adjust a bridle.

England, 1451. Give us a moment.

James. He was James Talbert. You were his niece. Matilda Montage. You were from a side of the family with French connections, and at that time flighty, easily upset, with some ability as a musician in piano, but without the discipline or drive to use the ability.

He was taking you to a concert. I do not know now, or see now, what initiated your reaction, but something happened that frightened you. You yelled at the horses and screamed. Your uncle fell. The horses panicked, and *[he]* fell beneath a hoof. You never forgave yourself, and now in your first reincarnation as a woman since that time, you decided to be the vehicle through which he could enter physical reality again, and so became his mother in physical terms.

This was the extent of what you felt to be your responsibility.

You had not been a mother of a male before.

Now. While the inner self is aware of this connection, the present self has been fooling itself to some degree, for it did not accept the intuitional knowledge. Regardless of what you thought consciously therefore, you still inwardly blamed yourself for letting the child go, and therefore the difficulty with the womanly organs.

You blamed yourself for financial reasons, though consciously this would be the last thing to come to your mind. You think of yourself quite free of financial conditions, and as an adult now in independent terms set yourself free of your parents. But subconsciously you wondered what social environment your child would really (underlined) encounter, and whether or not you deprived him of the social and economic benefits that you have convinced yourself, consciously, you do not need.

You also wondered about depriving your mother of a grandchild now, for though you tell yourself she would not understand, still you wonder if interest in the child would not give her additional impetus and interest.

Now these are things, some of the things, that you do not want to face consciously. Your uncle did not blame you for the accident at the time. While there was a past family connection, you were not the closest of friends, and there was no need or desire on either of your parts for a family connection of any duration in this life.

At one time you and the child were also brothers. He was impatient with you at times, for he remembered you as a companion in male pursuits, and bitterly resented your femininity.

For various reasons, and because you did not understand, you held it against yourself that once you accidentally killed him, and then when he was a child you gave him away. You gave birth to him however when you did not have to, in order to give him this reentry. There were other entries available, but he understood your purposes, and accepted you as a mother to show you that he held no grudges. *(Humorously:)* There were two accidents, then.

Even the first had its psychological implications, for the uncle at that time was dissatisfied with existence, and with his accomplishments, and the carelessness that helped result in his accident was also partially his own. But the fact that the conception was accidental, and the death was accidental, has its own intuitive logic.

There is in other words no need for you to punish the organs of your body that were involved in that birth.

You may take a break.

(10:24. Jane was out of trance easily. She said she could see horses' hoofs and cobblestones beneath them as she talked. And possibly stone-type houses, close together, on each side of a street, crowded houses. This was not a country setting.

(As Seth talked the witness felt a series of intuitive jolts that led her to believe the information was good. She likes horses this life. Jane resumed at 10:37.)

Now. I cannot give you your entire reincarnational history in an evening.

The father of the child however was a sister of yours in that life. Give us a moment. *(Pause.)* Your mother died when you were very young. The sister was older than yourself, and you felt, favored over you by your father.

You were also fascinated by her clothes in particular. You felt that she had taken your mother's place in the affections of your father, and she lorded her position over you. She was not that much older than you, you felt, to be put in charge of you, since there was only a five-year difference.

You used to wonder what there was about her that so captivated your father, since he had an obvious preference for her, and you would watch her secretly, trying to find the answer. You disliked her heartily but the fascination kept at you, so that you studied her mannerisms, and even at times tried to copy them.

You used to stand in a mirror and copy her expressions. *(Pause.)* She married a man whom you also have known in this existence. Your father simply preferred her because she did remind him of his wife. In a past life you had no use for women, and therefore chose an existence in which you were feminine; not only feminine but endowed with those qualities that you had particularly disliked; because you feared those qualities you therefore lived with them and to some extent learned to understand them, though you are still left with some impatience when you see them in others.

Your sister was also fond of the uncle, and therefore was instrumental in this life in allowing him new entry; but you joined for that purpose only. The fascination was an expression of a past fascination of a different kind, though you were pleased that this time you were older.

Both of you realize this intuitively. *(Long pause.)* As personalities however you have worked out your relationship. When you come together, one or the other insists upon domination. You have decided not to work out any further relationships together. Often problems with one personality are worked out by relationships with another, different personality.

You felt that you wanted to give a life for the one you accidentally destroyed, but it need not have been the life of the same personality, had you chosen otherwise. You also still remember that the father of your child was a woman, and your sister, and so in this life you have found the relationship ambiguous.

Now you may end the session or take a break as you prefer.

("We'll end it then.")

(Pause.) If you take this information to heart, you should then intuitively realize that by giving birth to the child *(pause)* you performed a kindly gesture, and opened a door. The system should then realize that there is no need for the symptoms, and release you from them.

("Good night, Seth.")

(10:58. Jane left trance easily. The witness said the data contained many intuitive insights, etc., citing especially the material re ambiguous relationships, etc.)

SESSION 459
JANUARY 22, 1969 9:50 PM WEDNESDAY

(At 9 PM tonight Jane said she felt a "massive presence" behind her chair. Not that she thought Seth was there to be seen, but she did sense something out of the ordinary. She knew the session was about to begin, and we hoped to learn something about this presence. The effort was cut short however by the arrival of company.

(The effect did not return after company left. Jane held the session in the usual manner.

Good evening.

("Good evening, Seth.")

Now. We will have a brief session.

A short note to Ruburt first however. There was no suggestion meant that he had made any decision to give up the poetry. It will always be one of his main creative endeavors. There will be further developments in his use of poetic form.

Now. As you have a tendency to think that earth is the center of the universe, although you know this is not true, so you have a tendency to think that the ego is the center of the personality, and that other aspects of the personality exist for the use of the ego, that all else revolves about the ego. This is not true.

In my own book I will describe the makeup of personality from another viewpoint indeed. You take it for granted that each individual has but one ego, and therefore perhaps understandably you ascribe to it more importance than it possesses.

I have told you that through many existences you don egos for the purposes set by the inner self. It is necessary of course that you believe in your role. The difficulty is that you must believe in your role, and yet also realize that it is a role that you, the inner self, have chosen. Otherwise your connections with the inner self are nearly forgotten. The ego forgets that it is only a part of a much more complete personality structure, and therefore cuts itself off from abilities and insights that are necessary, even for its own comfort and stability.

In my book therefore I will show the personality from the inside out, so to speak. I am simply waiting while Ruburt gets himself settled in the book he is beginning. Within at the latest a few weeks I will have my own book begun.

To some extent it will also relate my own experiences, but in a larger sense I hope that it will be able to give a picture of the nature of reality as seen by someone who is not imprisoned within the three-dimensional structure.

The book will not require any additional work on Ruburt's part, taken from his own, except for the final putting together, which will be simply a matter, I suppose, of typing. Give us a moment. *(Long pause.)* This book however, written by me, will therefore be entirely Seth material. Ruburt may make minor corrections if he feels them necessary, but the I in the book will be my own so interpretation will not be needed.

The book will begin when I first tried to contact you, although, there will be back flashes into my own previous experience in your time. It will also include in the opening chapter several occasions when I tried to reach Ruburt in the dream state, and the ways in which I was able to insert several ideas into his dreaming consciousness, and the ways in which the conscious mind utilized and distorted the information.

(End at 10:09.)

SESSION 460
JANUARY 27, 1969 9:10 PM MONDAY

(Jane had a strong experience this morning; when I came home at noon she

was still going through phases of it. She has full notes on it, so it will be briefly summarized here.

(She said it began when she tried psy-time this morning a short while after 9 AM. It culminated in a massive feeling of smiling relaxation, she said, combined with a strong experience of relief. It was as though she had passed through some great experience in triumph, she said, and would not be called upon to repeat it—all the travail, etc., involved.

(The dream book, which is now at Ace for consideration, was involved. Jane wrote during the morning several pages of notes, ideas and impressions. The gist of these seemed to be that the dream book, its struggles in creation, etc., was involved, and that it was to be accepted, finally, by Ace. This would be a triumph. More than this seemed to be involved however—there were feelings of health improvement tied in also.

(A nap after lunch seemed to restore Jane to a "workable state," as she put it. Naturally we wondered what, if anything, Seth might say about the experience. I also read to Jane just before the session two questions I had written out recently for Seth's consideration.)

Good evening.

("Good evening, Seth.")

Now. There is some instability of elements this evening, having to do with a natural, overall change taking place in Ruburt—a beneficial one, I add hastily *(humorously)*; but his system is in a state of change.

He is not entirely aware of this as yet, for remember when physical improvements show themselves the inner, causal, change has already occurred.

Now. *(Pause.)* I will continue with this in a moment.

First of all, briefly, an answer to your second question.

(There follows the question as I had written it earlier:

("Why is it that in cases of specific information, such as names, dates, places, etc., you [or Jane or Ruburt] will often delay giving the answer. That is, the answer will be put off until the next session. I have often noticed in such cases that if I don't insist in the following sessions, the subject in question will not be voluntarily referred to again by you [or Jane or Ruburt.]"

("Many instances could be thought of—re Van Elver; the mathematician in Edinburgh; re my telepathic experience in Wyoming last year; the auto accident data involving Bill Macdonnel in California, etc. The question is not intended as criticism, but merely to get information that can be developed more fully later.")

When impressions are given, the emotional impetus behind them is particularly strong. We are tuned in, so to speak. It is sometimes difficult, later, to retune as precisely. If the material is important enough to you, then the emotional impetus behind it is communicated to me, and I attempt to get you your information.

If the impetus on your parts is not that strong, or if fear operates, if Ruburt is afraid for example, of being put to a "test", in quotes, then of course the proper stimulus is not present. The best time to get information is when it is mentioned initially. This does not mean that further information cannot be given. It is simply not as easy to obtain. Ruburt's own change of attitude will be of great benefit to us from here on however, and such incidents will diminish.

(This gave rise to another question, which I did not ask but will note here: Seth has said on occasion that Jane was too close, too emotionally involved with data to answer clearly, and that it is then best to wait. This would leave only the recourse of going back to the data later, if we want more information, when it is "cold.")

Now. Ruburt is always under my protection in his out-of-body experiments. There is nothing to prevent his seeing me on such occasions but his own attitude, as I have said before. He progresses at a natural rate however, at his own rate. He will not overdo, for in this his ego is an aid and it will see to it that overexertion does not occur. When experiments fail this is usually the reason, and also the reason for the rhythmic effect.

Your other question, to me, is a curious one.

(I had asked: "Please redefine the ego, briefly, as a part of consciousness in our terms."

Your ego, in common ordinary terms, has changed as a result of our sessions, in that it is now concerned with other realities also. In common sense terms, the ego handles manipulations within physical reality, and focuses brilliantly within a rather narrow range.

I used the term *(ego)* often myself for your convenience, and I use it now for the same reason. I believe that I will tell you this for your definition: the ego is the portion of identity that is presently focused within an apparent now—that is, it is primarily designed as a mental tool, focusing within time as it is known and experienced by physical creatures.

Divisions between portions of the self are primarily arbitrary however. They do not exist. It is only to speak of them to make meanings clear that we use such divisions.

Obviously then ego is a part of identity, rather than the other way around, and it is only a part of consciousness. It is when ego attempts to confuse itself with identity that difficulties begin.

(Pause.) Give me a moment.

(Pause at 9:30. Seth now spoke about some remarks I had made earlier today, concerning my poor success in remembering my dreams and projections over a peri-

od of months now.)

At times you become jealous of your energies. You fear that direct psychic experience in terms of projections could rob you of the energy you should put into your painting and quite unconsciously, though not entirely, when you are focusing upon your painting strongly with particular inner vigor, then you close the door to personal psychic adventures out of a misplaced jealousy for your art.

You feel that all of your energy must go into the painting at hand. In this way you also close the door unknowingly to additional energy and refreshment *(pause)*, to some extent (underlined). You cannot close one creative door without closing all of them to some degree. I qualified this statement twice on purpose, for naturally your main focus is to be your painting.

However, dedicated psychic exploration of such a nature always brings with it increased intuitional powers, and new energy and a spiritual understanding that can be used then in any creative endeavor. The two go well hand in hand. Understanding these reasons should help you therefore.

You *(smile)* with your peculiar interests, can (underline) roam quite freely, art galleries and museums, in either the past, present and future, in those terms, and a sufficient impetus will help you do so. In other words, if you tie your psychic endeavors with your love of art there will be no difficulties. Simply the knowledge that the psychic endeavors will help your creativity should be a sufficient impetus.

Now you project in your sleep whether or not you know it. But this feeling of jealousy prevents you from using consciously what you have gained. Unconsciously of course the experience does sift through, and like any other experience you use it in your work. But you could use more.

Do you have any questions pertaining directly now to what I have been telling you?

("No, not at this time. I think it's very good.")

You may take your break. You must not consider psychic endeavor as a rival to your art, but instead as an aid, with which the best of artists have always been blessed. *(Emphatic, leaning forward.*

(9:42. Jane was easily out of trance. Once, she said, she felt that she was growing "smaller" as she sat in her rocker while Seth spoke. She felt that she was an old man, little, tiny... at the same time as Jane she knew she wasn't shrinking but that it was a subjective experience. Seth kept on talking, and the feeling passed.

(Sometimes when I make notes I don't have enough time to consider the material being received. Now is a case in point. I somewhat misinterpreted what Seth had said concerning projections. I commented aloud to Jane about how I thought that I had *been using my psychic abilities in my paintings, quite consciously and deliber-*

ately as a most welcome aid.

(Seth was still around during break. As I spoke, Jane said later, she could feel him responding to my conversation. Jane, who was in the kitchen, hurried back to her chair just as Seth resumed at 9:44.)

I was speaking of psychic endeavors involving projection. Endeavors which you felt involved a greater production or use, rather, of energy. You have been much freer in opening of channels, and passively receiving and becoming receptive to inner information and experience.

You felt that actively going out however, in terms of a projection involved a greater effort and energy, and this particular aspect you had not tied into your art. You may continue with your break.

("All right. Thank you, that's much clearer."

(Humorously.) My telepathic abilities must not be operating well this evening, for I took it for granted that this is what you meant by your question; knowing what I did of your use of the psychic knowledge in your present works.

("You're right. It is just that I didn't fully understand while I wrote."

(9:50-10:01.)

Now. Give us a moment. *(Pause.)*

Ruburt is working out toward a complete symbolic understanding in a poem he began yesterday, and he will know the one to which I am referring.

For some time he has identified himself with the dream book, and projected his own problems upon it so that it bore the brunt, so to speak; and if it was a failure, then he was a failure and in very definite terms.

The identification no longer exists, and he realized today that his success is not dependent (underlined) upon the dream book for once and all, you see. He is no longer vulnerable in that manner. It was like his albatross around his neck, and it is no longer so.

For that matter the book has changed you see from what it was, as he has changed from what he was. He also knows that the book will be published, and this inner information has been given to him in one way or another time and time again.

(Jane has a long list of dreams, psy-time experiences, messages from Seth and herself, to the effect that the dream book will be published.)

It is an example of the way in which his abilities came to his aid, giving him inner assurances when they were most needed. He realizes that he is a creator of the book, not its prisoner, and he once thought that he was. He has stepped clear of it *(pause),* its fate no longer seen as his fate, regardless of what happens to the book.

Now he is so concerned however that I tell you whether or not Ace will take the book, it is difficult for me to speak clearly on the issue. *(Pause.)* Give me a moment. *(Pause.)*

He has freed the book also from the negative ideas that he had earlier projected upon it, ideas which were picked up by those who read it. *(Pause.)* We will see if we can get around him. Now. *(Pause.)*

He will hear of its publication soon. That is, within a short time he will know physically that it will be published. *(Pause; smile.)*He will be working on it through some stages of the Seth material, also. *(Pause.)* Wollheim will be involved in it. With it. It will be an <u>ace</u> of a book. *(Smile, eyes closed.*

("Yes.")

He has made a sale and now goodnight.

("Good night Seth, and thank you."

(10:15. Jane popped right out of trance. It was a funny situation. She knew what she had said about the book, under consideration at Ace Books, where Don Wollheim is editor-in-chief, and was at once concerned about distorting material, etc. "I wish I hadn't said it," she commented wryly, after I remarked that we hadn't pushed for any answers from Seth; or even asked any questions about the dream book specifically, before the session.

(The next day, January 28, after some debate, Jane called Ace in an effort to learn the status of the dream book. Don Wollheim hadn't seen it yet. The editor in charge of psychic books was not available; her assistant told Jane a report on the book hadn't been delivered yet. If Jane's experience this morning does include the sale of the dream book, the event can be called precognitive to some degree.

(Don was delighted to learn about the sale of the Seth material to Prentice-Hall, and urged Jane to stress this sale to the dream book editor, Evelyn Grippo, in the letter he suggested Jane write.

(Speculation: Did Jane's phone call today tinker with the experience yesterday? Did the experience lead to the phone call, and will informing Ace of the sale of the Seth material result in the sale of the dream book? On the other hand, can the sale to P-H have an adverse effect upon the hoped-for sale of the dream book to Ace?)

SESSION 461
JANUARY 29, 1969 9:15 PM WEDNESDAY

(Before the session tonight Jane and I discussed the excellent manner in which Seth was able to relate to the various people who have witnessed sessions. This ability escaped us for some time, until we finally realized the various approaches used by Seth to make the material given meaningful to the very different personalities

involved.)

Good evening.

("Good evening, Seth.")

Now. As to your remarks of a few moments past: I always knew what I was up to in class.

I told you that if this material and information was ultimately to mean anything in your terms, then it must be related to people. I will see that it relates to many kinds of people. It will be given in many ways. There is no reason why the less intellectual should not have access to it, or that it should discriminate against them for their lack of gray matter. *(Humorously.)*

The material is quite legitimate, regardless of the ways in which I may choose to present it at various times. The basic principles of it will rest in our own sessions where those who are curious enough and gifted enough intellectually may find the arguments and reasons upon which it is built.

There will be those who cannot understand. For them the material will not be watered down, and has not been. But it will be given in simpler terms. You need not worry about a Seth Reader. There will be one, and I will write it.

(Before the session I told Jane, half jokingly, that she should publish a Seth Reader, said volume to contain Seth material on many subjects, presented in a rather more simplified way.)

It will be written to the intuitions and the emotions, and so it will be done somewhat differently. Intuitive truths, as Ruburt should know, can also be revealed in other than highly intellectual ways. Some will intuitively understand the material far better than others who may grasp it intellectually but without emotional comprehension.

The whole body of the material, by the time that we are done, will speak in various ways to various types of individuals who may not be able to speak to each other. Ruburt becomes intellectually scandalized when I speak simply. I have no need to worry about my intellectual superiority. I am perfectly free to communicate what should be communicated. He is however still at the stage where he takes pleasure in intellectual superiority, and somewhat looks down upon those who are not so intellectually gifted. *(Amused.)* A common-enough failing.

The attitude however could automatically make the material unavailable to many who need it, can understand it intuitively, and will use it well. There will be others, like Ruburt himself and like yourself, Joseph, who will be intrigued by those fuller developments and arguments given in the basic material. And upon these, again, the logical framework of the work will rest.

In the past because of Ruburt's own difficulties, I merely hinted at future developments. I will tell you now however that within our own framework of sessions, and with what I call contact sessions with others, other books will materialize. There will be several in which the basic principles will be given simply, directly, with many examples to the ordinary man and woman.

They will be given with great emotional rapport, and I hope of my own depth of compassion and understanding for the human condition. Some will appear simply as Ruburt collects class sessions or witnessed sessions together. One at least will be specifically written by me for that purpose.

(A couple of days ago we began to collect the sessions given by Seth in Jane's ESP class in a separate category. This work, just beginning, gave rise to the idea for a Seth Reader, etc.)

One book will deal primarily with metaphysical realities, and will be designed for those more intellectually gifted. The audience for that particular book may be somewhat more limited, but it will be a fascinating endeavor; and in it I will hope to present a multidimensional theory of morality for those too sophisticated to accept any longer outdated concepts concerning the God concept.

This book however will also point out the truths that do exist within the tattered garments of organized established religions; rip apart the crumbling fabric of dogma to the body of revelationary knowledge that was always there.

(The phone rang at 9:35 and interrupted Seth's delivery. Jane herself answered the call before I could do so. The call nicely pointed up the material for the session given above, re making it known to others, etc; the call was from a prospective ESP class member.

(Jane resumed in the same fast, active, eyes-open manner, with a good amount of emphasis, at 9:53.)

Now. Individuals within your system have difficulty relating to those with whom they do not have some fairly strong bond, either of common experience, general beliefs, cultural similarities—the list is endless.

In this respect you and Ruburt fall generally into that category. You like those whom you understand. In my position however there are many aspects of my overall personality structure and experience upon which I can draw, and therefore relate.

It is from the bank of knowledge then that I can relate to others, and they realize intuitively that on such occasions I am not speaking down to them. Impediments do not get in my way, for I do not throw up impediments of that kind. I do not throw up distortions of my own making, and therefore misinterpret the reactions of others. When I speak to them I am thinking of them, and to some extent I can indeed enter into their psychological reality. Therefore I can phrase what I want to say in a way that is highly meaningful to them.

As a painter you use many mediums. You may portray a basic idea in various ways, and produce many excellent paintings in doing so. And using the English language I can still speak in many tongues, and present the material.

There will be several books that simply result from our sessions, beside those that will be specifically dictated. There will be books of Ruburt's own as his personality grows and evolves and correlates what it has learned and will learn. There will be developments in your own painting that will follow naturally, and sometimes directly (underlined) from our sessions.

(Long pause.) Now, our friend Aerofranz *(Tam Mossman, of Prentice-Hall)* is indeed progressing. *(Small smile.)* The extent and potential of his healing abilities are considerable. It is therefore all the more important that he always try *(pause),* to use discipline and caution, that he think in terms of helping other individuals, and that he not glorify his own position egotistically, thinking, "Since I can heal you, I am therefore superior to you," even though the idea is partially hidden from his own consciousness, and even though he feels kindly—put in here that I smiled—while feeling so superior.

His abilities are considerable in the healing line, and again for this reason it is extremely important that he is understanding of himself as well as others. His ego is (underlined) a kind one, but the structure of any ego is such that it considers, or can consider easily, psychic ability as a sign of its own power; or feel possessive of the ability, and overly proud of it, even when it knows it originates in other layers of the self. We want our friend to have a strong and healthy overall personality balance, for this will allow him to use his abilities well, and then the abilities themselves will further add to his own development.

He has—are your fingers tired?

("A little bit.")

You may take your break.

(10:10-10:25.)

Now. Our friend *(Tam)* is in contact with another layer of his personality, and as I told him over the infernal machine *(a humorous reference to the telephone)*, a dependable layer. This is an advancement.

I would like him to keep Ruburt informed. I do not suggest that he do such writing *(automatic writing)* more than twice a week for now at the most, however. Ability always demands responsibility. I know that he knows this, and I do indeed commend him. I do not want his abilities to run away with him however.

I do not mean to speak as if there were any great danger involved. It is only that I want him to progress at a steady rate, with the overall personality in good balance all the while. The personality must learn to understand and use the abilities.

Now I give our friend my most fond wishes, and I enjoyed, in quotes, our "mechanical" communication. He must also make sure of the integrity of his motives, and learn to recognize his own motives. This is not to imply that he does <u>not</u>, but it is a necessity for any personality who is working with psychic activity of this kind.

(Yesterday, Tuesday, Seth spoke over the telephone for the first time. The occasion took place during a call from Tam, in New York City, to Jane in Elmira, at about 9:30 PM, and lasted at the most perhaps five minutes.

(Tam has written Jane a letter covering the above episode; the letter will go into our files, etc.)

Now give me a moment. *(Pause.)*

We will close the session. Ruburt is doing well with the book. I did communicate with him last evening, though he did not remember.

(Jane had requested that Seth communicate with her during a dream, and that she remember the dream. Next morning however she could only recall that such a dream had taken place; no details appeared.)

I will do so again this evening, at his request.

You are doing well. I see paintings that you will produce. *(Smile, eyes closed.)* What I have told you this evening should also help you understand the use that emotion can have in your work, and its value. And when you are finished with the large painting, I will tell you something about it that you may perhaps realize subconsciously. *(Smile.)* And I should say no more.

(Here Seth refers to preparations I am making to paint a larger, 3/4-length portrait. Jane has seen a pen and ink drawing I did recently, which is the basis for the painting.

("Why not?")

Because if I tell you now the spontaneity could be interrupted. As it is you have no real conscious conception in any meaningful way of what I will tell you; and yet you are using intuitional <u>and</u> emotional depths that you have not allowed yourself to use before, and I will tell you, when you are finished, the reasons.

You may ask me directly, if you wish—

("I will." Meaning that as soon as I finished the painting I would be after Seth for the information. I felt that by insisting I could get the data now, but decided to wait.

(A note: After the session Jane told me that she knew what Seth was going to tell me when I had finished the painting under discussion. I asked Jane just how she

knew this; was Seth telling me one thing, and Jane another; did Jane divine the information from Seth as he spoke through her, or what? We can learn more about this later; this is the first time we have been aware of information being given and received in just this manner, though it may have happened before. But as Seth told me about the painting Jane knew what he was to tell me.)

Now, I will be glad to set up for you a definite program, geared to you specifically, toward the release and use of your psychic abilities whenever you are ready to take some session time to do so.

("Session time?")

I will give it to you in session, or at any time you request. It will be relatively easy for me to help you in out-of-body experiences, incidentally, when you are ready.

("How about tonight?")

Then we have an appointment, at three in the morning. Give yourself the suggestion before you sleep that you will remember what happens, and that even while sleeping you will be alert to my presence, and ready to follow my directions. Also, tell yourself that you will be enriched immensely by a memory of the encounter and the journey, and use those words.

("Okay.")

One note before I close. The Saturday-night excursions, regardless of your activities, are necessary and beneficial. Sundays, if you do not go to your mother's, then the two of you should at least for an hour or so also leave the apartment, if only for a walk or ride. *(My mother lives. Jane's has died.)*

Another brief note, perhaps mystifying to you: the mistletoe *(pointing)* over the door is also beneficial.

(We left the spray of mistletoe in place over our hall door lintel after we took down the rest of our Christmas decorations.)

I know you are tired, and so I bid you a fond good evening. The fortunate financial changes will continue, because of the change of inner attitude on Ruburt's part, and the reorganization of personality structure.

("Good. Good night, Seth, and thank you.")

(Leaning forward, eyes wide, humorously:) This was not a replay.

("Very good." See the 458th session, when Seth dealt with his availability to us during sessions, etc.

(10:44. Jane left trance quickly. She said Seth could have continued for an hour, etc., in his excellent mood. His presence had been immediate this evening.

(As instructed, I gave myself suggestions for dream-projection recall, though I was tired. In the morning I was vexed to realize I had a memory of an experience involving Seth, but it was such that I couldn't recall enough consciously to make notes.)

SESSION 462
FEBRUARY 3, 1969 9:17 PM MONDAY

(Sunday, February 2, 1969, a group of articles and photos, totaling a full page and a half, was printed in the Elmira Star-Gazette. The stories by Peg Gallagher dealt with the origin of the Seth material, Seth himself, and quotes from various sessions as well as the way the material is gathered, etc. The photos were of Jane and of the painting I did, in oil, of Seth.

(Much work went into this presentation, and a response has been materializing through phone calls, personal visits, and the mail. The series was built around the acceptance of the first book of the Seth material by Prentice-Hall.

(Before the session Jane and I discussed the reaction of Roger Sullivan, of Lexington, Massachusetts, to the two sessions dealing with his mathematical questions. See sessions 449 & 450, and the attached correspondence, etc. We also talked about the California session involving Bill Macdonnel, auto accidents, etc., and other material—see the 435th session.

(Strictly speaking, these episodes could be called seances, since they were given by Jane herself rather than Seth. The math material meant little to Roger, and we have no way, as yet, of checking out the California data. I wondered why the method used was chosen by Jane, and what was involved emotionally and intellectually. We didn't think subconscious fabrication was the answer, or that a total lack of control on Jane's part was involved. These would be extremes. We didn't insist that Seth discuss this material this evening, instead merely saying we had much to learn here.

(Jane began speaking as Seth in an active manner, often humorously, with emphasis and gestures, eyes open, voice good, pace faster than usual, etc.)

Good evening.

("Good evening, Seth.")

Now. My thanks to your cat lover. *(Peggy G.)* Our friend Ruburt learned something from that article, in that a simple presentation works very well.

The excerpts that were chosen were divided almost evenly: some appealing to the intellect, some to the intuitions, although to some extent of course each excerpt appealed to both. That is what we want. *(Emphasis.)*

The sense of work, dedication and commitment has finally been given on Ruburt's part, and the energy and vitality that has always been available to him can now be practically used to both of your advantages.

I will thank our friend personally for the work that went into the article.

There was something rather important that I could not and would not force, and I have mentioned this before. There were several in quote "keys" that could unlock, direct and focus the full abilities in Ruburt's personality. Our sessions were one of these keys.

He had to use the key himself. Symbolically you have both solved many problems in the past few years. You particularly *(to me)* had intuitional releases, rather delicate ones, that are in the process of taking place—that is, the process is still being completed. In such a way will your own full abilities be released and focused, this being largely accomplished through your work, and the benefits being reflected there.

Now give me a moment. *(Pause at 9:26.)*

As I told you *(humorous)* the medium is the message, and more than the message in many ways, and therefore for best results the medium should not be too hot or too cold. Information can rarely flow like crystal-clear water, with the medium a faucet, to be turned off and on at will.

Information quite literally must be sifted through the layers of the medium's personality. *(Pause.)* The nervous system reacts to the information even as it translates it. Nothing is neutral. Nothing can be neutral in those terms. The information is received and translated, as it must be, into mechanisms which the nervous system can handle and interpret and translate in physical terms. The information then, like any perception, becomes a part of the nervous system's structure. It cannot be otherwise.

Any perception of any kind instantly alters the electromagnetic and neurological systems of the perceiver. In your terms, physically, that is what perception is—an alteration of neurological structure. The perceiving mechanisms themselves change and are changed by that which they perceive, and I am speaking now of your physical system, and the physical nature of any perception.

It is literally impossible for you, and it is a logistic contradiction to imagine, with your physical structures, that any perception can be received unless the perceiver's own inner situation is altered. I am trying to make it as clear as possible that information automatically blends with, is intermingled with, and enmeshed with, the entire *(pause)*, physically-valid (hyphen) structure of the personality.

Now. I am on my way to answering one of your questions—

("There's no hurry.")

—and you have every good reason to want your answers.

Now. *(Pause.)* Any perception immediately blends, then, with the entire system of the individual. Any perception is action, and it changes that upon which it acts, and in so doing it is itself changed (underlined.) This applies to any perception.

The slightest perception to some extent alters every atom within your physical structure, and this in turn sends out its ripples, so that as you know the most minute action is felt everywhere.

Now with this background, give me a moment. *(Pause.)* I simply want you to see where we start from.

("Yes."

(Pause.) Some individuals always see the worst side of things, and interpret any given perception in the most pessimistic light. In a low mood any individual is much more likely to react to pessimistic suggestions, and to interpret data in the same manner. Now this applies to any data, whether it be physical in the usual sense of the word, telepathic, clairvoyant or otherwise.

Fear will often sensitize individuals however, so that fear for a loved one will bring about clairvoyant knowledge of a disaster. They are not concerned over joyful events, you see, and do not therefore as easily perceive these clairvoyantly.

Now in any ordinary clairvoyant event, in a low mood, Ruburt or any individual may, according to time and circumstance, overemphasize or misinterpret information, overstating say, pessimistic elements. *(Pause.)* Personalities strongly (underlined) given to the need for self-punishment will consistently misinterpret such information, or any information.

Now all of this is not meant to apply to specific incidents mentioned by you earlier, but only to clear several matters that we have not discussed thoroughly enough, involving the normal psychological aspects involved in clairvoyant information. Most of the remarks I will make can be applied to any perception, however.

To a large extent you are what you perceive, and not symbolically. I forgot your fingers—

("They're okay.")

Now. *(Pause.)* Information does not exist as I have told you independently of consciousness. There is not therefore any particular event, say an automobile accident, that exists independently of the consciousnesses of those involved in it, for a given perceiver to perceive.

It is more than a simple matter. It is more a simple matter of having a clear channel through which neutral information can flow. Now you will I am sure have further questions concerning that last remark—

("Yes.")

—for it has all kinds of implications that we cannot cover in an evening, but it will be more than worthwhile for us to pursue them. Now whether or not a medium is in a trance that is as deep as the Atlantic Ocean, the medium will not be a pure channel. The ego will simply be bypassed, but the other layers of the self, the neurological structures particularly, will continue to operate as always. They will be altered by the perceptions that flow through them.

You may take your break and we will continue.

(9:55. Seth/Jane leaned forward, smiling and emphatic.) And I will sit more formally for my portrait some day.

("Good."

(9:56. Jane was quickly out of trance, but it had been a good one, fast and active and emphatic and humorous. I said I thought it was a contact session, as Seth calls them, meaning that he was present with us at this time, rather than having given Jane the material earlier. See the 461st session.

(During break we discussed some of the aspects of precognition and telepathy, clairvoyance, etc., that would be called upon in cases where witnesses attended sessions, but the material for the session had been given to Jane by Seth in advance, in our terms.

(Resume at 10:05 in the same manner.)

Now. It is true that much of our work is done outside of session time. Session time often represents the end result of our work. In projections other portions of Ruburt's personality leave your system. They are not portions needed for physical manipulation. The ego is not even aware of them. There is nothing particularly unusual in this. The unusual aspect, comparatively speaking, is that the information gained can be translated and used within your system.

There are simple stories that can be told, symbolically true enough, but they do not begin to explain the reality, and so I do not use them. The question of my availability, again, is a pertinent one only when you think of personality in terms of one individual, who cannot be in two places at once in your time.

In your terms therefore I can be in many places at once, and conscious of so being. It does not mean that I am less in one place than another. *(Pause.)* Now in some way that you are not ready, or should I say able, to understand as yet, I help Ruburt to perceive clairvoyant information more clearly, in that I help to direct the kinds of alterations that occur within his neurological structure.

I do this for him in many instances. *(Pause.)* What I perceive *(smile)* is still dependent upon my own identity. It cannot be otherwise for any consciousness. In your terms I help keep to a minimum distortions which might otherwise occur as Ruburt's own mood or circumstances might otherwise misinterpret.

My own identity, in simple terms, has fewer hang-ups than the personality that is operating in physical terms. My range of perception is far greater, as is my range of activity and the kinds of energy I am able at times to direct. Even the quality of that action is of a different nature.

Now the California data was fairly correct, and in one session I gave you a possible description of what it represented. *(Pause. See the 435th and 436th ses-*

sions.)

The mathematical data I have also somewhat explained. This is more difficult because of Ruburt's lack of mathematical vocabulary, and the fact that conceptual patterns were given in intuitive mathematical language—not in a precise narrow range at all, and answering deeper questions than those asked. Nevertheless the answers to the particular questions are inherent within the material given, I believe, and become obvious by reference.

(See the 449th and 450th sessions.)

In other words, larger mathematically intuitive, pure-theory ideas were presented as well as circumstances would permit. *(Pause.)* Theories and ideas are far more important than details, for the detail comes from the theory and not the other way around.

Ruburt worked rather hard, and did learn to achieve a more intense focus. *(Long pause.)* I fail to see, however, that the most precise mathematical data will enhance the spiritual, psychic, creative condition of mankind *(smile)*, unless it deals with issues that throw light upon the nature of existence, in basic terms.

Ruburt could not have cared less, and tried simply as a favor. A strong emotional basis did not exist therefore, and under the circumstances the results were surprisingly good, and they will make sense, if not now then later.

We will have more to say concerning the nature of perception, and the ways in which such information is perceived and used.

Now I tell you that while the perceiver is changed by what he perceives, he also changes that which is perceived. Perceiver and perception, in a basic manner, are one and the same. Here we come close to the meaning of value fulfillment and moment points.

You may take your break.

(10:31-10:38.)

Now I will not keep you much longer.

We should go deeply however into the nature of perception before we leave it, or you will have that left hanging. An amazing amount of energy was released in the article, that will affect others, and Ruburt is only slightly beginning to realize the force behind it and within it.

(See the notes re the article, on page 231.) It insures its own success, and contains its own vitality. Now, I have endowed it with this. *(Pause.)* The other books you see already exist, and wait only to be given physical form. *(Pause.)* Your own masterpieces exist, and only wait for you to find them and give them physical form.

Painting is as natural to you (underlined) as breath. You breathe with a beautiful technique, and yet effortlessly. *(A smile, leaning forward, for emphasis, etc.)* Paint with the same confidence and belief with which you breathe.

Now, if you have no further questions—

("I guess not.")

—then I will end the session. And unless you have further questions we will resume on perception, on Wednesday.

("Will you help me project tonight?")

Will you remember if I do?

("I'll try." See page 230, containing an account of my failure to remember projecting the last time Seth offered to help me.)

Then I will help you. Do you recall the suggestions I gave you?

(I nodded.) Use those, and keep them foremost in your mind as you fall to sleep. Even more, inspire your enthusiasm for projecting, for desire is extremely important. Imagine yourself doing so. You may find it of benefit also to imagine a flying dream, or form a dream consciously in which you feel me waiting for you to let go the cares of the day, and ready to help you leave your body.

("The last time, in the morning I felt I could almost remember projecting, with your help.")

I helped you, and you projected. Tell yourself that you want to remember as much as you want to project. Even imagine the rising sensations as I help you out. This as you fall to sleep. Other suggestions: tell yourself that a portion of you will remain alert while your body sleeps.

This <u>will</u> (underlined) enable you *(to have)* greater freedom. Ruburt's own old suggestion—be critical in your dreams of your dreams. When you know you are dreaming you can indeed project. But I will help you this evening. *(Leaning forward, humorously:)* Am I that hard to remember?

("I don't really think so."

(However, my efforts to project, or rather the remembrance of projecting, were again dismal failures. I remembered nothing in the morning.)

My fondest wishes to you both. *(Amused.)* And this is not a recording.

("Good. Good night Seth, and thank you."

(10:55. Jane was out of trance quickly. She was smiling, and explained that near the end of the session she'd had an amusing image. The painting I've done of Seth hangs on an inside wall of our living room. Jane saw Seth's painting move, intact, to and then through our large center window in the living room.

(The gesturing hand in the painting beckoned to me in three-dimensional form, Jane said, as the painting moved through the window—this was a clear invitation to me to project, accompanied and guided by Seth. But as stated, to no avail this evening.)

SESSION 463
FEBRUARY 5, 1969 9:10 PM WEDNESDAY

(Before tonight's session I read to Jane this question: "In the 462nd Session, page 232, you say [meaning Seth] that any perception, however slight, alters every atom within our physical structure. Not to be nitpicking, but others as well as ourselves are sure to want to know just what you mean by this alteration."

("Do you mean changes in the atom such as the number of electrons and/or other particles, literally; or are you referring to the nonphysical content of energy within, or carried by, each atom? Or is this a concept difficult to put into words? Jane doesn't have much of a scientific vocabulary."

(Jane began speaking for Seth in a fast and active manner, voice good, eyes open often, etc.)

Good evening.

("Good evening, Seth.")

Now. A few remarks. The material need not be presented in one way only, as I have told you in the past.

Do not attempt to force it to follow preconceived patterns, or insist that it be presented in any given manner. To do so is to lessen possibilities, and to limit the good that can come from it, and the number of people that it can reach.

It carries within it certain propelling forces, possibilities of development, and possibilities of presentation.

Do not insist that it be published in chronological order, in other words. Now, large portions of it will be published in chronological order, but not if you insist upon this now. *(Pause.)* It is in one way the natural order of the material, but also your own development was my beginning point. Though you were not acquainted specifically with such phenomena, you were good readers, and my presentation was, if I may say so myself, shrewdly and cleverly geared *(leaning forward intently)* to your own individual possibilities.

The material is wide-ranging enough so that it can be used in many ways, and this is my idea. I have told you this before in my analogy of the stream and the streambed.

Now Ruburt's ego, so hard to win over, is now up in arms because it regards me as its exclusive property. *(Smile; pause.)* It need not worry. It took me long enough in your terms to set up our communications, and our relationships in the past helped in this behalf. *(Reincarnational relationships.)* It is quite natural that others in your acquaintanceship who are experimenting should go through a stage in which it seems to them they are receiving information from me.

Suggestion operates, and any trance deeper than ordinary for them can be interpreted in these terms. He should understand this, and explain it simply to his students.

(Pause.) Now. The material is like a touchstone from which other creations may flow. Working with it Ruburt can use his own creative abilities as he attempts to make a work of art from any given book. Psychologically his interpretations and comments add another dimension that he scarcely realizes at present.

Creatively and intuitively, he relates much better to others than he realizes, and this will also add to the manuscript on which he is working. Addressing himself as a writer to ordinary people will enlarge his own creative abilities. Many of his short stories, so addressed, are products quite as good as the poetry.

His idea of intellectual merit sometimes presupposes a lack of emotionalism. Speaking to the reader releases his intuitive and emotional and creative abilities.

Now give us a moment. *(Pause.)* Returning to the material on perception, there are changes in the positive and negative atomic charges, alterations of movement inside the atoms in the smaller particles *(long pause)*, a change in pulsation rate. *(Long pause; eyes closed; smile.)* The activity of molecules actually is caused by perceptive qualities. To begin with, atoms do not just move within themselves because they move because they are atoms.

The constant motion within them is caused by the constant perceptive nature of any consciousness, however minute in your terms. Does that answer your question?

("Yes. I could ask more questions, but at the moment that's quite good."

(Pause.) Each of the molecules or particles within the atom are perceptively aware of all the other particles within the given atom. They move in response to stimuli received from each other, and to stimuli that come from other atoms.

(Seth slipped up in the first sentence of this paragraph; being busy writing, I did not catch it at the time. Molecules are not within atoms; it is the other way around, molecules being composed of groups of atoms.)

Each molecule within a cell, for example, is aware of the activity of each of the other molecules, and to some extent of the stimuli that comes to the cell itself from outside it.

(Long pause, hand to closed eyes.) Perceptions in general physical terms usually seem to involve information picked up from an arbitrarily designated structure, of an event seemingly occurring in another structure outside of itself. In

the entire act of perception, however, there is a oneness and a unity between the seemingly objectively perceived event and the perceiver.

The entire act has its own electromagnetic reality, and the event is actually electromagnetic motion. The movement within the atoms mentioned earlier therefore is a part, basically, of the entire perceived event. Does this make the issue plainer for you?

("Yes.")

Egotistically you make arbitrary designations of necessity, perceiving only portions of any given action; again, the ego attempting to separate itself from overall action, and to see itself as an entirely independent structure.

You may take your break.

(9:41-9:55.)

Now: Perception is constant. There is no place where one perception begins and another ends.

Remember that you are a part of what you perceive. Now in many instances of so-called paranormal perception there is what would seem to you a reversal of focus. It seems to you that the burden of perception in on your part as perceiver.

Your in quotes "unity" with the event that seems to exist outside of you is not understood. In paranormal instances you change your focus largely, throwing it into the seemingly independent event. Do you follow me here?

("Yes.")

There are constant interchanges on all levels. I will try to explain this to you more clearly. Remember also in your terms that the seemingly independent perceived event and its nature is changed and altered by your own perception of it.

Any physical perception is actually an action response at a psychic level to thoughts and emotions, and these exist independently of their physical counterparts. The thoughts and emotions however also have their own electromagnetic reality. *(Pause.)*

Physically then you perceive an approximation of an inner event. The inner event basically is not physical. *(Pause.)* Now, as simply as I can put this, thoughts and emotions form, of their own electromagnetic reality, vitalized physical products called atoms and molecules. This is basically what I told you in our early analogy with the mazes and the wires.

(This would be in early 1964.

(Long pause.) Any questions that you have from this material, ask at our next session and I will answer them.

("Yes. I want to read this over first.")

From your viewpoint, you only see the physical product.

Now. To some very valid extent in our sessions, changes occur then within Ruburt's physical organism *(pause)*, for in responding to my communications, electromagnetic alterations are therefore in inevitable. You have however more of a merging. I do not for example completely take over. There is a complementary merging with my patterns however predominating mentally and psychically, and to a large extent emotionally.

On occasion the change can be noticeable enough however so that the physical resemblance *(pause),* changes, Ruburt looking far less like Ruburt, comparatively speaking.

(Yes, I have seen some striking demonstrations of this; so have other witnesses. See the 68th session, for example, in Volume 2.)

On the one hand his own personality is enlarged in that the self structure includes far more perceptions than ordinarily. Further actions are recognized and interpreted. The speaking systems however and mental faculties have to be trained to handle the additional data; this of course causing some distortions along the way.

They are unavoidable. The emotional system of the medium must also learn to handle further stimuli, and then also learn to do so in such a way that balance is maintained.

Another dimension in your terms is simply added, a more extensive one, and when this training is done properly, as I have tried to do, then the medium's personality is not only strengthened but its abilities used far above the usual normal. The process however is highly involved with perception, and is largely a

matter in learning to handle, recognize and use constructively perceptions that other personalities are not equipped to handle.

Now you may take your break. *(Pause; smile.)* Ruburt knows of my fond regard for him.

(10:22. Jane was out of trance quickly. She remembered the last sentence Seth spoke. This was a reference to the fact that Jane got "mad" at Seth—one of the few times this has occurred—at an ESP-class session last night, for some remarks Seth made concerning Jane's tendency to intellectually categorize people. See the 461st session in this respect. I had found the situation rather humorous.

(10:32.)

Now, when you see what Ruburt can do occasionally, and the troubles I can have with distortion, then you can be sure that I would not double or triple the chances for distortion by attempting to speak through anyone else. He need not worry. Beside, I like him too well.

There is also something else that he seems to have forgotten—that your own relationships, yours and Ruburt's and the relationships between us in the past, do much to make our communication possible. You transmit also, or rather you act as a transmitter whether you are at a session or not. So unless there is another identical (underlined) Ruburt and Joseph combination, I am stuck with you. *(Smile.)*

Now in the past, in your distant past, when I spoke through others, or portions of my entity did so, then such personal connections also existed with those through whom we communicated. Do you follow me here?

("Yes.")

Now I bid you good evening, and my fond wishes—

("The same to you.")

—and I thank Ruburt for the class sessions. *(Elaborate, courteous amusement.)* He learns as much from them as the students, but of a different nature; and he also knows that if he did not give his permission, such sessions would not be held. A hearty good evening.

("Good evening, Seth, and thank you."

(10:40.)

SESSION 464
FEBRUARY 10, 1969 9:19 PM MONDAY

(Jane did not feel much like having a session; she finally decided to hold one at 9 PM, and of course I left the decision up to her. She said she decided to have a session because sometimes when she didn't feel well a great session resulted.

(A very interesting session developed tonight, also. Thinking Seth would speak as usual, I read to Jane another question that had come to mind as I typed up last session. The question wasn't answered however so it will not be quoted here. Nor did Seth speak. His entity held the session instead.

(The last time Seth's entity spoke was in the 446th session for November 6, 1968. We had wondered at times why the entity hadn't spoken more often; Seth has said little about his entity, and we did not ask that this personality speak tonight.

(At 9:16 Jane said she was waiting to see what developed, that she was getting a hint of the pyramid feeling; which usually means that Seth's entity will speak in place of Seth. See the 406th to 412th sessions for detailed material on the circumstances involving the personality we call Seth's entity.

(Jane didn't get the pyramid feeling in any strong way this evening, she said later. She sat upright in her rocker, hands clasped, head back somewhat, eyes usually closed; her lips began to form words silently, as is usual in these instances. When she began speaking the voice was high and distant, with little inflection, and as usual

ended on a peculiar upbeat so that at times it was hard to detect the ending of a sentence, etc, Jane moved very little as she spoke; her glasses remained on. There was no greeting.)

Looking into your system, into your physical system, to us is like looking through one *(pause),* of innumerable windows.

(Eyes open briefly, slitted.) These windows are always available to us, as the windows in your room are available to you. In your terms some of the windows would contain probable realities within your physical system. To us one is as real as the other.

We have to select your proper window. You could not understand us if we did not speak through one of your kind. We try to give you information for your benefit and that of your world. It is necessary that we rely upon the mental equipment of the person through whom we speak, and at times we are able to activate the intellectual capacities many times above normal, in order that certain concepts be given.

But we must still rely upon the mental structure of the person through whom we speak. This has disadvantages but without the method such communications would not be possible.

While the speaker, or speaker-system, necessarily loses many meanings, the very distortions that do occur make the messages decipherable. We have no language in your terms.

(A hint of a smile. The pace was good, pauses brief. I thought the above paragraph very well expressed.)

Seth, as you know him, is a medium through whom we speak, as Ruburt is a medium through whom Seth as you know him speaks. This is simplified, but basically an adequate explanation. *(Pause. Jane's upright, almost prim posture was unchanged.)*

Seth's intellect and abilities are far beyond Ruburt's, and with Seth as you think of him, I can to some degree directly communicate. *(Long pause.)* We dwell in dimensions that are far beyond your comprehension, and in many instances what we say is squeezed, as if through a tube, so that the knowledge may enter the relatively smaller dimensions of your present existence.

It is not that your being exists in a lesser reality. It is that *(eyes open occasionally, slitted again)* you have not learned to recognize the extent of the reality in which you do exist. So our information must somehow appear within the small scope of what you recognize as reality, or you will not perceive it.

(9:35. No break was called for. Instead after a long pause Jane coughed; she then began to come out of trance rather quickly. After she had blinked her way clear, she began to remember things to tell me.

(After the session began, she said, laughing, that she had the image of "a bunch of spooky-looking guys, looking through windows and windows and windows." More seriously, Jane said she had the feeling during the delivery that Seth was helping the other personality to reach us—that the entity's messages were like "handkerchiefs or clips of paper, that they had to be thrown out right in front of us or we wouldn't see them."

(Jane now recalled that just before she began speaking, she received the gently chiding thought—addressed to her from she knew not what source—that since "we" were going to so much trouble to get this material through to "you" [meaning Jane], that she shouldn't be concerned about explaining it to others. That is, Jane shouldn't worry about this. There was no disembodied internal voice speaking to Jane here; but a distinct thought, not angry or impatient, addressed to her in terms of "we" and "you."

(Resume in the same high, formal voice, at a slower pace, at 9:47.)

The speaker at your end must necessarily do the translating, and the purity of the translation, relatively speaking, is determined by the speaker's own development.

Such sessions as yours aid in such development, and automatically begin to alter certain electromagnetic patterns inherent in the personality: so that in your terminology the circuits can receive greater charge quite safely.

More energy is therefore available for the communications, and additional energy is always at your own disposal. Certain portions of the personality in your terms are able to climb up further, as on *(the)* steps of a ladder. Inner attunements are refined, and to some small degree you can look out through the small end of your own window, and glimpse the light at the other end.

There are such lights throughout the entire universe, but this one is at your own apex point, to which your consciousnesses are attuned. You can see but dimly but some vision is better than no vision at all. When you are no longer blind, all possibilities that belong to the sighted *(pause)*, come at least within your grasp. You are learning inner sight.

(A note: at times Jane's head would shift or vibrate slightly from side to side. moving rather rapidly perhaps only half an inch. After a few repetitions the head would then be still again. This has been noted a few times before when Seth's entity speaks. I neglected to ask Jane if she was aware of this movement, but do not believe she is because she hasn't mentioned it.)

This knowledge is being given to you in terms that you can understand, and it must be given to others in terms that they can understand. In your terms you are one in many in an unbroken chain, and what is given to you, you pass on.

(Long pause at 9:59; head lowered briefly, then upright again.)

A light bulb in your terms cannot hold the light within itself, but when it receives the current then it must share its light with others. *(Pause.)* And it shines indiscriminately, and does not turn itself off for those who cannot read. It shines even upon the wood which has no eyes.

(10:00 PM. Jane's head tilted; she stopped speaking, then nodded that she was coming out of trance, if slowly, when I finally spoke to her. Her eyes opened slowly.

(Jane thought this was another break, but it proved to be the end of the session. She said she feels "distant" when she comes out of trance when the entity speaks; she seems to have to travel back to her physical body, to warm it up. She goes someplace, and we wondered about some kind of projection being involved. With Seth, Jane said, it's the opposite; Seth "comes in," and there's no doubt about it.

(With the entity, contrasted to Seth's immediacy, Jane feels she travels but doesn't know where she goes. She feels distant from the voice, "like signals are far away from my mouth that does the talking."

(At no time during the session was there much of a pyramid effect. Jane said that as she left trance last time she got the feeling that "this personality felt that he was able to use some of my processes, that we were clicking together better, to get his ideas across."

(Jane now felt somewhat better than she had before the session.

(I wondered aloud about a couple of points: What decides when Seth's entity is going to speak? And whether the entity could help out in things like health. Jane then received: "Health is overall efficiency," without knowing where this came from.

(At 10:20 Jane said she got a few bits and pieces of things, then said she thought the session was over—she "slid down." She could say but little about what she had picked up: Since consciousness creates reality, reality is not independent of consciousness; but there was more here.

(Jane said she got up into the pyramid to some degree, but not high enough to make contact. Seth wasn't involved in this, she said; she'd "know him in a minute."

("...something to the idea that knowledge was meaningless if it wasn't applied to consciousness..." This was the last bit Jane could recall.)

SESSION 465
FEBRUARY 17, 1969 9:12 PM MONDAY

(Jane didn't feel particularly like having a session, but decided to anyway. I asked no questions before the session, nor did Jane, but we were still surprised at the subject matter.)

Good evening.

("Good evening, Seth.")

Now. To you ... *(Long pause, eyes closed.)* Your paintings are your own, and I am no artist. If I read your inner intent correctly however, your prophet will dominate the background, and seem almost to come out of it. At the same time the background itself will be alive, so it is difficult to tell whether the living background propels him outward, or whether he himself, from his own power, seems to rise out apart from the background. Or whether he has been thrust outward from the background of which he is part, a living focus rising out of the background, a part of consciousness rising out of a larger, undifferentiated consciousness implied in the background.

And with implied words, for the words that are sensed but not spoken, will rush out with color rather than with sound, and behind the implied words those emotions upon which the painting must be based. *(Pause.*

(Seth here refers to a large painting I have planned and made a pen-and-ink drawing for in small scale. Tonight I explained to Jane the problem involved in determining the correct relationship between background area, and the prophet, who is in a standing position. In this particular painting the background will play an important role, since it is designed to indicate a play of light and shadow. The prophet looks upward to the left, lips parted in speech.)

Do you know what he is saying?

("No.")

Is he saying: "Let there be light," or "My God, my God, why hast thou forsaken me?"

("I don't know."

(The idea had come to me intuitively while I was at work at Artistic. I made the pen-and-ink drawing then. I hadn't tried to consciously decide what the prophet might be saying as he looked upward. The only conscious decision I had made was that I would let such designs remain in the subconscious if they did not spontaneously present themselves.)

The particular words are not important, but the emotion behind them is important, for they will—the words and the emotions—be reflected in every muscle of the face, as well as in the thrust of the head and the hands.

The face, in <u>intense</u> (underlined) joy and in intense terror, may often be much the same, but the <u>emotion</u> still will speak within it, and you will know clearly despite the similarity of some muscular effects, which emotion is being expressed.

Between those extremes of terror and intense joy however, where the intensity itself can almost form the same sort of grimace, there are infinite varieties of emotions, these being reflected in every minute shadow and gesture.

Sorrow or fear obviously show different faces—not only *(long pause),* the anatomy and the structure [*that*] forms the living face, but the emotions within that give the muscles and the structures meaning, and that play upon them. You want the force that feels the form and so the figure must indeed dominate the painting, as the force within must fill and move within the figure itself.

(Just before the session I had said that I feared I would have to revise my preliminary planning, and allow more background area in the painting than at first planned.)

The power must fill the image, and the image then fill the painting so that the very force of the figure seems hardly contained within it. It is the emotions beneath *(smile)* that give meaning to the image, and yet these emotions are held and contained and given direction and force by and through the image. *(Leaning forward, emphatic delivery, eyes open.)*

Now as men wonder about what was Mona Lisa thinking, so let them be so intrigued and so involved that they want to hear your prophet's unspoken words. Put yourself in his place, and with all of his capacities, and with his wisdom, and what would you be saying, and what emotion would move the muscles of your face?

(At this moment I then consciously knew what my prophet was saying in the painting; the words came clearly to mind: "My God, my God, what am *I?" I was tempted to speak them aloud next chance I had, but did not. I hadn't tried to conjure up these words; the emotional climate set up in the session by Seth had made their release from the subconscious effortless.*

(An interesting example of knowing something you did not know you knew.)

The emotion always provides the movement.

Now there are several ways of taking care of such matters. You can build form or a structure with lines, or a face, and leave it and wait for the emotion to fill it up, and then quickly with a touch here and there bring out that which has appeared, the movement that was within the form, that you barely sensed. Or you can perceive the movement, the emotion and the power first, and then paint the form that grows about it to form it.

The painting itself, and any painting, rises out of the empty board through the force of your own emotions, and the board becomes the focal point that collects, draws together and directs the energy from your inner self, into form.

Your prophet's lips move. To whom is his implied speech spoken—to a god he understands, to a god he does not understand, to the elements or to a part of himself that he knows exists and cannot reach. *(Smile.)* You should sense or know the answers, now, or as the painting progresses.

By the time the painting is done you should almost be able to hear his words, even though they are in a language you do not know. But what power moves him, and is it the same power that moves you, and that moves those who will look at the painting? *(Smile.)* For unity's sake it should be. Is he only aware of those who will later look at the painting? Is he only aware of the unseen power or person his lips address? Is he speaking words not only for himself but for every other individual?

You may take your break.

(9:45. Jane was rather slow coming out of trance. She said "Seth really put me out. Like a thunderbolt. He always does put me out strong when I talk about anything to do with you and paintings."

(Jane had no visions while speaking, but sensed some things. She felt the background in the projected painting as being alive, she said, with the figure being the important thing and materializing out of the background, while yet a part of it .

(She was on the whole quieter than usual at break, as though not quite all the way out of trance. Resume at 10:02.)

Now. Become your prophet as you paint him.

Look out through his eyes, and cry out through his lips. I had my reasons *(smile)* for introducing these questions pertaining to the painting this evening—to make available to you certain information that you had, the kinds of questions to ask yourself in other paintings in the future.

(The technique certainly worked well—see my notes on page 246.)

And perhaps in painting your picture the answer to the question asked by your prophet will also come to both of you. Does the question provide its own answer, or is there another who will provide the answer, or does the prophet question in vain? Does anyone hear his question but himself?

(At break of course I had told Jane about the answer I had received concerning what the prophet was saying. See page 246.)

Do his words go back into the background from which he himself emerged, and does the answer emerge also? Or is there any clear answer to his question? *(Smile; pause, eyes closed.)* Or is the question itself the important thing, whether or not there is any answer to it in the terms in which it is asked? All of these issues are a part of your painting, implied in every line of its conception, but I want you to see consciously the implications of the figure, and the overall implications of the figure in context with the background.

For now the figure rises from the background and dominates it, is thrust forward and you catch it; but may it not also once more return to that background in the instant that you turn away, and emerge anew. The question itself is significant, and indeed universal. *(Smile.)* And look even further: what is the nature of one who can ask such a question?

This is somewhat different from the original question. Do you see?

("I guess you'd better elaborate a little bit." This is one of those instances where Seth was speaking rather rapidly; I was so busy writing that I had no real time to think about the content of the material. Later upon reading it over it became clear.)

You will understand when you read it through.

"What am I?" is one question. Then comes the wonder—"What am I that I can even ask such a question?" And the answer to the second question answers the first.

("Yes.")

"What am I," question three, "who can conceive of a painting in which the first question is asked?" The three questions automatically show the added dimensions of the questioner, and the various stages through which the original question can develop. *(Long pause.)*

You ask yourself the same questions as you paint the painting, and the directed unity and focus will provide exhilaration and strength to it. And the need, so strongly implied, will <u>also</u> provide the answer and the means.

You identify with the prophet, not only as yourself but as the representative of your kind. Therefore the question is yours with all the intense yearning to know within it. But it is also every man's question, and herein lies its strength.

Let the prophet therefore be yourself, and yet let him also stand for every other man. In speaking honestly for yourself, you therefore speak also for others, and intuitively they know this.

If you speak for yourself only, or for mankind only, there is a short circuit. Yourself <u>as</u> mankind—this is the answer *(pointing to me)*—not to the original question but to the identification in art.

Now you may take your break.

(10:25. Jane was out of trance more easily, but it had still been a deep one—she remembered nothing of the material just spoken. Resume at 10:30.)

Now. I would not want to keep my sleepy babies awake—and so I will close the session.

("It's been very good.")

The main points I wanted to make I have made, and I hope they have been of help.

("Very interesting.")

I do not know art, but I understand the nature of perception within your system, and I understand what you are trying to do and such hints as I can give you can also be applied to other areas.

("Yes.")

And your interest in art has aroused my own curiosity—

("How come?")

—and so I set myself to learn what I can about its nature, in order to help you.

("I can think of a lot of questions about that statement.")

I will answer them.

("Well, I'll get them all together..." I didn't ask any questions here because I knew Jane was tired. "Have you been in touch with Van Elver lately?" See the 414th session.)

I have not of late. But do remember now that you are interested in him.

("Yes.")

We have plenty of time. I will try to get him here some evening here for you.

("That would be good." And this too brought many questions to mind. After the session Jane and I speculated about just how this might be done. It would be a new situation, as far as we knew. Would Seth relay my questions to Van Elver, then deliver the answers, or what? There were lots of possibilities.)

I wish you then a hearty good evening, and my best wishes to you both.

("Good night, Seth, and thank you."

(10:34. Jane was soon out of trance, but again it had been deep. Her manner had been strong, active and emphatic. She said that before the session she didn't "have the slightest idea of what I was going to talk about tonight."

(Jane said she was "little and tiny inside the voice," which always means that Seth's presence is strong and immediate. To Jane while in trance, the voice seemed "to be booming all around, with me inside.")

SESSION 466
MARCH 10, 1969 9:05 PM MONDAY

(The session was witnessed by Virginia and Tom Milligan, both of whom are members of Jane's ESP class. They had no questions for Seth prior to the session; Tom said he had been giving Seth questions mentally earlier today, and also earlier in the week. The Milligans have known for some days now that they would witness the session tonight.

(Note that this is the first regular session since February 17, although Seth has given material in ESP class since then. Jane had felt the need for a rest.

(This session was recorded.)

Now, good evening—

("Good evening, Seth."

([Tom and Virginia:] "Good evening, Seth.")

Good evening to my friends. *(To me, humorously:)* And welcome back to the sessions.

There are several issues that have been left hanging in our own sessions, and material that we shall get to. This evening there are several remarks I want to address to our friends here, and some material that they should find helpful.

Give me a moment.

(To Tom:) Now you must stretch your intellect as well as your intuitions. Your intellectual abilities are higher than you believe them to be. They have grown with the impetus of intuitional development. You can use your intellect now in ways that you could not earlier.

You will find it easier to understand concepts, and to apply them. You must not let this go to your head, but use your head. You should find also that rereading your own earlier material you will find it easier now to pinpoint distortions and subconscious data.

There is still considerable coloration, but this is to be expected, and you will work through it. Much of the reincarnational material that you have is symbolically valid. The psychological insights are valid in that material although you do not always understand their true validity. The reincarnational material in one way is still codified, and you have not yet the key, but you will find it.

There is no need to keep questioning the names and dates. In any case they are not important for an understanding of yourself. Later you will be able to receive such information more clearly. This applying to specific names and dates.

The psychological understanding of yourself is hidden within the reincarnational data that you have. You must still however learn to interpret that material, and look behind for its implications. Now much of the stability in your endeavor is also being provided by our other friend here *(Virginia)*, for without the bedrock you would not find it as easy to lift one spiritual toe from the barren ground. You did not trust the ground, seeing that it was not always so fruitful, but at last you felt you could trust it.

You know that our other friend is here when you return. There is also available from her a strong creative energy that she willingly shares with you, and you use in these endeavors. As such she is therefore a definite part of such activities. This is not to negate your own quite personal involvement, but only to show that other strong issues also help make that involvement possible.

The interrelationships of your personalities in past lives is quite legitimate.

You will learn to apply your own material more effectively in community relationships. You are still quite timid in that you do not allow yourself to fully comprehend the changes in your behavior within the community that should result. To some extent your own quite natural hesitations and fears and conscious ideas still limit the full and comprehensive nature of the material that you could be receiving.

When you are working alone in psychological time experiments, you do not so fear emergence of the subconscious, and you trust your material more. You feel that the experiences are at least your own, with no Bega who must speak through you as in your writings.

Your feelings here largely result from a lack of understanding as to the nature of the subconscious. As I have told Ruburt often you cannot be a pure channel, through which information miraculously flows. You are a personality, and you must interpret the information that you receive.

You can indeed misinterpret it at times, but you cannot divest yourself entirely of personality any more than you can entirely drain a room of air.

Now you may all take your break, and we shall continue.

(9:21. Jane left trance rather easily. Her pace had been a bit faster than usual, eyes open often, gestures active, etc. At times because of the faster pace during this session, I may have missed a word here and there, but only to a slight degree; this can always be checked against the tape the Milligans made.

(A wide-ranging discussion followed at break. Jane resumed as Seth in the same manner at 9:33.)

Now. *(To Tom:)* You have a tendency at times to water down certain ideas because they would suggest alterations in your attitude that you are not as yet willing to accept. And when you are willing to accept them, then you will allow your material more freedom.

There is no need to be so uneasy on that point however. They will come with time, as your ideas on religion have changed...

There was no inference made or given, and certainly not intended, that you forsake your Bega sessions. *(A point discussed at break. I missed a few words before the last statement.)*

I simply meant that at times you still worried as to whether or not he was a subconscious fiction in the writing sessions; but you did not feel this as strongly in your psychological-time experiments, because of the mental activity of your own that they provided.

Now our friend here *(Virginia)* is telepathically aware of most of your inner activities, and it is in a large part through her also that there is an expansion of psychic activity from the two of you outward. This is not immediately obvious. She does not have her guard up as high. Also however she is not as adventurous, for it is after all your endeavor: you carry the main issues and personal involvement. The symbols will give way to other symbols. There are roads within the roads, and rooms within the rooms, and wholes within the wholes. But we do not want you to get lost within the mazes, and so we are giving you maps, and when you get where you are going you no longer need the maps.

Now give us a moment. *(Pause at 9:40. A slower pace now.*

(To Virginia:) There seems to be on your part a relationship with another woman, either an older woman or a woman you feel to be older. A relationship that can stand some clarification, and further application on your part. I would say an aunt, but I am not certain here, and that does not seem to be correct. Yet a relationship that has a family connotation certainly; an overexertion on your part that can lead to tensions. *(Pause.)*

An issue here, it seems can arise within a 6-month period, that you should face with tact. *(Pause. Seth now looked at Tom.)* And his initial reaction, his initial ideas to this issue, will give way to a more reasoning attitude. His initial idea therefore will not be the best one.

Give us a moment. *(Pause.)* There seems to be another younger woman connected with the older woman and in the background. Perhaps, though I am not sure, a daughter or sister. Rather thin.

The letter G—we will try to pick this up later.

(Pause. Then to Tom, who laughed:) Now. Another point. Do not expect windfalls. The point is, the information in your own material is meant as constructive suggestion, to get you in the habit of thinking in terms of abundance, and such attitudes can indeed be highly successful. Within your own material you will find reasons if you look hard enough for them, intuitive reasons for <u>some</u> (underlined) information that would seem highly distorted or influenced by the subconscious. A particular fact may be entirely wrong or distorted for example, but there may be also highly valid reasons for the distortion, and truths within it that are more valid than physical fact.

When distortions occur therefore and you recognize them finally as such, look for the reason for the particular distortion, and you will find the truth. Examine your material for what it says and for what it does not say.

Now you may take your break and we shall continue.

(9:52. Jane was again out of trance easily, but said it had been a good one.

(Virginia and Tom verified Seth's data concerning the family relationship, tensions, two women, etc. In fact, with the exception of the 6-month prediction, they tied all of the data together quite easily around one family situation; they explained the situation to Jane and me, but it will be but briefly summarized here. Any clari-

fication or reference to this material will be furnished by the Milligans because of their intimate acquaintance with it.

(The older woman referred to by Seth is Virginia's aunt, the younger is the aunt's daughter-in-law. The older woman is Virginia's mother's only sister. The data refers to a long-standing family relationship involving older relatives, a farm, furniture, a sale of land, etc. The farm, the house now owned by Virginia's brother, seems like home to her. The G, the Milligan's said, refers to Geneva, where both the aunt and the daughter-in-law live. The daughter-in-law, Virginia said, is "rather thin," as stated by Seth.

(The tensions, Virginia said, are really below the surface, but are there. These are usually passed over by Tom and Virginia. I read a summary of these notes to the Milligans at break, and they agreed to their content. This typed version can also be checked by them and any necessary changes made.

(Resume at the slower pace at 10:05.)

Now. *(To Tom:)* If you have any specific questions you may ask them.

([Tom:] "I'm wondering what G A R or D A R may mean."

You have more important questions than that.

([Tom:] "Yes."

That is not important.

([Tom:] "Other questions might take the format of what opportunities might arise in business; the Bega development; etc..."

(There was more to the above question that I missed, but the Milligans have it recorded.)

The guidelines will have to be your own, as you know. Give me a moment however. *(Pause.)*

There seem to be three main branches here, or possibilities. There could also be a merging of three into one.

(Tom interspersed a comment here.)

Now. The three-into-one has one inherent weakness, and strong organization would be needed or the venture could be severely weakened. The weakening element would be largely concentrated in the choice of one individual within the organization as a focal point.

Give us some time here. *(Pause.)*

That person's ability to handle public relations would be highly important. Either there is an individual already in mind for that position, or the individual that would be chosen for it would not have the capabilities that it seems he would have. An overestimation of abilities, therefore. You seem to be the third man in this particular setup that I am now trying to describe.

Give us some time here.

However there could be a complete turnabout, I believe in procedure; and if so oddly enough in the light of present circumstances, you would be the man to whom they would turn. There is something it seems that you should follow up. A conference with three men, perhaps in April, is involved.

You can be too conservative, not following up sufficiently your intuitive understanding of the business. There is one man important in the three-in-one merger, and the best man has not yet been found.

A small committee is too turned-in upon itself, and you are at least partially involved here. A gray-haired man with glasses has other ideas. You have freedom within the framework that you have if you use it creatively. There seems to be a large loan, out already overlong, due, that is somehow involved here also.

An S. A foreclosure that is an issue. *(Long pause.)* There is the opportunity to change your own position, and you can and should do so, but there is another opening that you have not seen.

(Break at 10:21. Seth didn't call a break, but merely took it. Jane was far- out, she said.

(Tom said that on the whole the data meant quite a bit to him; he could interpret it, and did so at break. It concerned his job in banking, about which Jane and I knew very little. Tom did very well in making connections; the material was quite specific, and the longer Tom and Virginia discussed it with us, the more connections they made. "Except for the last two bits of data," Tom said, meaning the opportunity to change his own position, and another, unseen opening.

(Some of Seth's data was symbolic, Tom said, and explained just how he felt this was so. Again, Tom and Virginia stand ready to interpret the data in detail should the need arise. During break also, Tom expressed concern for his son in Vietnam. Resume at 10:39.)

Now. Give us a moment. *(Smile; long pause.)*

The boy will return, as probabilities now stand.

We will return briefly, ourselves now, to the business world. And to our lady *(Virginia)*, who prefers to stay in one place. There is creative opportunity for you here, within the framework in which you are now involved, within the general framework.

(To Tom:) Neither Ruburt nor I are bankers, so you must let us sort out this material. I would make a fine bank president, if I do say so myself, even if I do not know banking. *(Humorously.)* These jovial remarks are simply to take up some time while we look into these matters.

Two mergers would seem to represent your best opportunity, two rather than three, and you could maintain excellent control here. One element therefore would be dropped, and it would prove in the overall not as effective as it would seem—one could be a liability, and might need to be discarded even if at first included. Two mergers would be much more effective.

(The above paragraph is abridged somewhat because of Seth's rapid pace. Later Tom agreed quite definitely with this material.)

You could also serve more brilliantly *(humorously)* in that capacity. The third aspect could end up draining your energies. This second possibility therefore is a good one and would work highly to your advantage. The third is a one-man show. A department initiated by you, and a relatively new service in this area—I believe it has been adopted and sometimes discarded in other areas—but it is not an ordinary issue, and it is something that you have considered yourself in the past, though not seriously.

It is a new service, and would take place generally speaking within the same framework within which you now operate. In one way it could be called an offshoot from another department, but it is too novel to be so described. It would set you up, and would be not so much a merger as a completely new development of your own initiation.

(Again, Tom agreed with this data.)

It seems you have either read of, or met, or heard of, someone else who tried this, with mixed reaction. There is a public-service issue involved in here, and a way of squaring away old debts. It involves the creative use of money through diversification, and diversity is the key word here.

You focus accounts from diverse sources. *(Long pause.)*

This does not make sense and yet somehow the impression is legitimate: that interest rate *(pause)*, is tripled somehow.

(Later Tom agreed the intent of the above statement was correct. Interest rates for such monies as discussed above were not, or would not, be tripled, Tom said, but such money was expensive, and instead of the usual six percent would cost eight or nine percent.

(It might be added here, or at the end of the session, that Jane has no knowledge of banking, nor had she discussed any of this material with Tom before the session, or at any other time. In fact, as Tom remarked, "She doesn't even know what my job is, except that I work for a bank."

(As Seth, Jane now pointed to Virginia, and dealt with a problem mentioned at last break.)

Psychologically, when you are filled up, you have physical difficulty, and it is a psychological reaction that activates the physical structure. When you need release you find it then in that physical means.

In trying to play down issues, and to avoid dissatisfactions, you have a tendency to store up bitter feelings that are unexpressed. They turn to bile and gas, and you are relieved of them in that fashion. While you hold them you are also uncomfortably aware of their reality. Honestly admitting your own feelings to yourself will help give you release from the symptoms. Do not brood upon the feelings but admit them as your own, and then simply let them go. It's holding them too long that causes the pressure.

Now we cannot cover too many issues in one evening.

([Tom:] "I've got to do some thinking for myself.")

You are doing very well, and you know that I commend you for it.

([Tom:] "I've got a week to go on community chest."

(If I recorded the above correctly.)

Bega is also doing very well.

You may take a break. If you have other questions you may then ask me. *(To Virginia:)* There are other issues involved here that we will try to give you, now or later. I will enjoy listening to your social chatter, and will in any case have a few remarks before I leave you for the evening.

(11:00. Again Jane emerged easily from a deep trance. Virginia agreed with Seth's interpretations concerning her. Tom said Seth gave "some terrific material" regarding banking; he then proceeded to explain some of the details to us. They are not listed here, being rather complicated, but Tom has stated his willingness to explain them. Some of the material reaches back for years, Tom said, and involves his ideas re a "finance clinic," etc.

(The merger material also applied, and Tom explained how he had been thinking of the second possibility suggested by Seth, the merging of two rather than three. Elmira and Syracuse banking facilities would be merged, with the Utica branch left out; according to Tom this would be a better arrangement, etc.

(The pace was again faster after break, and I missed data here and there, though not extensively by any means. Resume at 11:10.)

Now. The word clinic was a good one, and an intuitive, one, and it is a key for you.

As a man brings a body to a doctor, then let the businessman bring his business to you for a checkup—find out how healthy it is, and how you can further its productivity.

Such a service could be born within your framework, and become an important part of other banks. You would have your finger on the economic pulse-beat of the area, and you could diagnose business ills <u>before</u> they occurred —banking preventative medicine, you see, and you could have the preventive medicine at your fingertips and be ready to apply it.

Not only would you be helping individual businessmen but you would also be protecting the economic health of the area. You were quite correct in thinking of small business and the informal atmosphere. A thorough knowledge of the tax structures would be invaluable.

Often such men do not know how to invest the earnings that they have. You could also focus such investments so that they could help the community at large.

Now I am almost giving you the advertising that would be effective, for the imagery is important. And as a doctor guides the growth of a child, so you could begin at scratch to guide the growth of new companies, and even you see to consult with them before. You could also consult there and aid those who intend to go into business, have capital, and do not know precisely how to proceed. This would automatically bring new funds and fresh blood into the economic structure, and into your particular bank.

Now give, me a moment. *(Pause.)*

We will have a session some evening for our friend here. *(Virginia.)* There is no particular benefit to your moving at this time, and the venture of which I have spoken would do best if begun here; and if it is begun here it would spread, but this would be its focal point and the point of overall management. It would need you see an informal hand, and every effort should be made not to intimidate the small businessmen who would be coming for help and service.

([Tom, humorously:] "Everybody in our bank likes the prestige of a million-dollar loan.")

The overall commitment would be high indeed, and the general structure would be diversified and secure. The security itself, because of the diversity.

Now give me a moment. Probabilities always operate, and free will. I am merely pointing out the probabilities.

The inner possibilities are far more important however, and your inner development more important than any decisions having to do with your occupation. For your inner thoughts are the only realities, and from these you form your physical circumstances, including those in the occupational area.

Again, you are doing very well. Bega is learning my material in our own classes, but he must also interpret this, and as I said earlier he tailors it for you, knowing you so well. Now, I adopt the personality that you know, and it is quite legitimate, but it is only one of my personalities. Know then that other personalities are also here, and in ways that you do not understand, and that is the end of the sentence. *(To me, humorously.)* The familiar human component is necessary, and it is by my characteristics that you know me, but the entity is an ancient one, and we are far more concerned with other things than your position at your bank.

([Tom:] "I thank you for letting me get it out of my system, though.")

I wish you a fond good evening. *(To Virginia:)* We will have a session for you, and I will tell you when.

Good evening, Joseph, and tell Ruburt it is good to have him here again.

("All right. Good night, Seth.")

([Tom and Virginia:] "Good night, Seth.")

(End at 11:28.)

SESSION 467
MARCH 12, 1969 9:08 PM WEDNESDAY

Now, good evening.

("Good evening, Seth.")

The regularity of our sessions is important. Some freedom and spontaneity is also important.

If Ruburt misses sessions and then feels guilty about doing so, little is gained and the regularity is also lost. I suggest therefore that you hold six weeks of sessions as always at your regular time, then feel free to miss a week with my blessing and your own, and then begin another six-week schedule.

This will allow for regularity, and also provide for some release from regularity. This does not mean that a session may not be missed now and then. It does mean that variety would be allowed for within our framework.

If there is a class session, a long one, and if Ruburt feels tired, then the following session of my own may be a briefer one. But all in all the regularity should be maintained, and the suggestion I have given will allow both schedule and freedom from schedule.

There is a difference in the various work done in different kinds of sessions, and subjectively Ruburt may be aware of this. The class sessions have their place, and they are meant to serve as illustration. While they each are legitimate within themselves they are each meant to show how the material can be applied. The source however is always in your private sessions.

We were discussing the nature of perception some while back, and its relation to clairvoyant activities. We were discussing the fact that no knowledge exists apart from consciousness. I told you that any perception alters the perceiver. Not only mentally and emotionally but also alters the electromagnetic reality of the internal physical structure.

In a very literal manner then you are the knowledge that you have. The interchange is constant. Now. Initially and basically perception is not dependent upon your senses. Any perception is first of all a psychic one that is then translated in ways meaningful to the physical organism. To other organisms in different realities perception would therefore be translated in an entirely different manner.

Relying upon such external perceptions therefore, communication between members of various systems would be relatively impossible. You might not perceive each other to begin with, or realize that there is anything to be perceived. Such contact therefore would always take place beneath so-called normal perception, and even then you would have to translate this inner perception, as you do any into terms you could understand as physical creatures.

That translation would be bound to be distortive, and yet it would be the only kind of perception or understanding that would be possible under the circumstances.

Now to some (underlined) degree, this also applies to the information that I give you in our sessions. It must come through the available channels of the physical human mechanism in order that it be at all meaningful. As I mentioned some sessions ago, on the one hand you can say that the method involves distortion, but without the distortions there would be no meaningful knowledge for you to understand.

Verbalization is not a basic method of communication for in quotes "higher" forms of consciousness, nor is it for lower forms of consciousness. It is only at your particular intermediate state that verbalization as such is so important. It is a main basis for your species. Because of its importance at your particular stage it is an excellent method for our purposes. In many other systems of reality it is never adopted, for it is in many ways restrictive.

In some systems colors are used as a prime method of communication. They are sent out telepathically, each gradation of such variety that you cannot now imagine it. These intricate color communications follow the almost endless emotional shadings possible. It is difficult you see to verbalize this concept. They have to begin with more spectrums than those with which you are familiar. They live in an entirely different sense universe.

As you for example attempt to blend colors to give an effect, they telepathically send out a continual stream of ever-changing colors. Such a concept as a sentence would be meaningless to them, and yet pattern is involved in the colors so that the shape and form of a color also has meaning.

The analogy may be a poor one in that it says so little, and yet it will be helpful in giving you the idea. Instead of nouns for example you would have the shape of the ever-moving pattern, instead of a verb the pulsation of the color, or rather of its transmission. Instead of a time sequence of tenses, which they would not need, you have the intensities and depths of color.

These are not to be thought of as colored pictures however, for neither do they use that kind of imagery, and yet a high degree of preciseness is communicated. In your terms there would be, in quotes, "words" for all kinds of subtle emotional states for which you have no words.

Now were I to communicate with someone in that system, I would have to affect their sense mechanisms, and therefore the material would be delivered in a way, again, that would seem to distort it, and yet without the method it could not be given.

(Pause.) You may take your break and we shall continue. I should mention first however that the inner self is always free of whatever camouflage structure it may presently inhabit.

(9:39. Jane left trance easily. She remembered parts of the material. Seth was pushing data at her, she said. She had no idea before the session as to what Seth would discuss; nor had she been reading about any such ideas as those presented tonight before the session.

(Resume at 9:52.)

Now. Any conceivable method of perceptions is possible to the inner self, latent within it. It can adopt any method of perception it chooses, according to the environment in which it finds itself.

In psychological time therefore it is at least possible that you can have some experience with other methods when you close off habitual methods of perception. The ego is firmly attached to the use of the physical senses, however. In the dream state there can also be other methods at least slightly experienced.

In deeper dreams and fairly unusual projections, you can and do leave your own system entirely. Even though you are out of your physical body however, you will attempt to translate experience with its learned patterns rather than switching into the inner senses. This is why many such experiences, even if recalled, seem chaotic and without meaning.

Now. There are indeed a body of symbols that are more or less basic within all kinds of perception—bridgeworks from one form of perception to another, since beneath all perceiving systems there is consciousness. Certain symbols therefore will have meaning. I do not see any particular purpose in giving these to you now, but at some time I will do so. *(Long pause.)*

They are the root assumptions from which all communications spring. *(Long pause.)* The trouble is, again, that in trying to give them to you certain alterations are necessary. Knowing them at this point will not help your development. I wanted to mention them in our record however for later reference.

Some systems use methods of perception that cannot be explained, since they contain nothing that is familiar to you. Within most systems death as you know it, with the meaning you attach to it, has no importance. The advanced consciousness can focus within one in quotes "life" while already sending portions of itself into the next quote "life," as for example you might in school take advanced calculus while still remaining in an elementary philosophy class. Do you understand?

("Yes.")

The whole psychological structure is therefore entirely different. It is also more demanding. The emotions and intuitions are the basis of experience, and the means of getting knowledge in most other systems. They have their own in quotes "reasoning processes" of which you are little aware, since at your point of development you use the intellect as a rule in its place, and make a clear distinction between the two areas.

The intellect forces you to interpret data in a highly specialized way for the use of the physical organism; and while adopted particularly because of the time structure, your kind of intellect only has value within your particular kind of time structure, and its type of logical thought is much slower and limiting. It moves at a snail's pace along the line of consecutive time.

Emotional reasoning however rises far above this. The inner highly precise nature of the in quotes "emotional intellect" is hidden from you, for the physical intellect cannot follow it. The emotional intellect therefore would seem chaotic. Most of its richness and depth would not be perceived by the physically oriented brain.

The emotional intellect for example is not time-oriented, and this alone makes no sense to the physical brain. It finds it highly difficult to assimilate any information not time-oriented, therefore it labels it as meaningless. Now this information is helpful to your development, and we shall continue to discuss it, for you can to some degree, with my aid, understand how this emotional intellect works if you try to understand the material intuitively, use your imagination with it, and try to feel it out.

Now you may take your break and we shall continue. *(To me:)* You particularly however, because of your own background, have felt the emotions to be reasonless, and so you have to some extent feared them. When you discover that their "logic" in quotes is far more effective and meaningful, and purposeful, your attitude will change.

One note for Ruburt, who has been waiting for it: he is not pregnant. *(Humorously.*

(10:17. Jane's trance was a good one and she couldn't recall the material. Resume at 10:38.)

Now. Emotion, a particular emotion as you know it, is the result of information and deductions already made of which you are aware. Because all of this information is not available to the brain, it sees the emotion as a sudden thing, appearing within the brainscape's reach, often unexplainable and therefore to some extent threatening.

Emotions, to the brain, are also somewhat frightening, because of their vividness, which seems out of order to the brain. To the brain something in the past seems dim, yet an emotional feeling that occurred in the past may suddenly appear again within the brainscape's awareness, as vividly as its first occurrence, and the brain feels disoriented.

The brain however often does not see the inner logic of the emotion's reoccurrence, or the inner connections that make it again pertinent. Any given  emotion itself contains within it multitudinous perceptions that the brain has not perceived, and as a result indeed of in quotes "calculations" the brain could not follow.

Any current emotion contains within itself memory patterns, interconnections and interpretations, that are far more dazzling in their meaning and content than any, for example, highly precise mathematical data. Particularly are memories enclosed within, gathered together from in quotes "previous" experience, all cunningly collected with utmost attention and high selectivity.

I will give you examples of this, for the general statement tells you little, and we will continue with this material unless you interrupt it with other questions, for some sessions.

I want you to understand the complexity that lies within emotional feeling, for you can then use it to better advantage, and it will add dimension to your own present experience.

I will close our session now however unless you have questions.

("I guess not.")

At the end of our next session *(smile)* after I have delivered the evening's material, I will devote some time to explaining Ruburt's figure of lights. Now my best wishes to you both. Remember my suggestion given earlier, and positively enjoy a week's vacation after six weeks of session.

("Good night, Seth."

(10:40. The "figure of lights" describes an apparition Jane recently experienced, at night, and we are interested in getting Seth's explanation of it.)

SESSION 468
MARCH 17, 1969 9:45 PM MONDAY

(Notes: Last night, Sunday, March 16, a rather long session was held for Dr. Subadh Roy, who is a professor of philosophy and comparative religion at Mansfield State Teacher's College [PA]. Dr. Roy, who is blind, was driven to Elmira by his friend and student, Mike. Dr. Roy is from India but has been teaching in the United States for some years.

(I made some notes during the session but they are incomplete because of Seth's fast pace, the exchange of questions and data, etc. If a transcript is needed I will make one and insert it prior to this session. The session ended at midnight.

(Tonight's session was late because of the discussion Jane and I had beforehand.)

Good evening.

("Good evening, Seth.")

Now I will not keep you for a long while.

You paint because you want to paint, and you set aside certain hours for your painting to insure that you will have sufficient time to do what you want to do; and this should be the reason for the regularity of our sessions.

Ruburt's attitude is his own. I have not imposed it upon him. He reacted last month when he had an experience of release and joy.

(See the 460th session for January 27, 1969.)

He was still afraid to accept it. He did not know whether he dared yet trust his spontaneity, and imposed upon himself symptoms as limitations.

These remained until another intuitive realization *(tonight)* would free him. Our sessions have also had their basis in spontaneity and creative energy, and the spontaneous nature always shows itself. You merely set the form through which the spontaneity flows.

There is no time when the sessions should be held merely from a sense of responsibility, and the sessions could not be held merely for that reason.

(Pause. Humorously, because of my comments re the fast pace last night:)

Am I speaking slowly enough for you?

("Yes.")

Now my humor and my sense of joy are obvious. I would hardly then impose responsibility as opposed to joy upon Ruburt. It took him some time to accept the fact of the sessions, and when he did so nothing would do but that he <u>overdo</u>, and accept them as a task rather than a joyful creative endeavor.

This resulted in uneven attitudes. I know him, and hence I have suggested the periods mentioned in our last session, with weeks set aside for sessions, and time off from them. He knew he was free to take time off at any time, but he was afraid that if he did so he might be deprived of the sessions entirely, and such is not the case.

You have both greatly changed as a result of the sessions. Intuitively and creatively new avenues will be opened to you. There is no either/or situation however. Ruburt need not think in terms of grim responsibility. *(Pause.)* And now he will not. This evening for several reasons his thoughts became clear on these subjects. And the point, buried somewhat in the past, came to light of consciousness, for within intuitively the necessary connections had already been made.

Our material will flow clearly now along those lines that are most important. To me this means that I am able to deliver to you information concerning the nature of reality which you can then pass on, and apply.

Do you have any comments or questions?

("No, except that I'd like to know what we're going to do now in the sessions.")

We will continue for now with the nature of perception.

Now under this heading I include other types of perception beyond those which you are acquainted with. The organization of such a topic therefore is mine. It may seem to you that the subject should be limited to physical perception, or so-called paranormal perception. With my wider viewpoint however I include perception in other realities. Often there is organization where you do not see it in our sessions. Nor have I forgotten the book of which I have spoken. Are your fingers tired?

("No.")

We will begin then when the intuitive time is right.

Subjective freedoms may seem slow to appear on Ruburt's part. There is however an inner rhythm that is not apparent. In his last trial he faced and is conquering many important issues, and it was better in the long run that they be fought and won during one period rather than stretched out. It has been a compressed period of high activity, with the inner attitudes <u>clearly</u> (underlined), concisely and quickly made visible in the physical form. The learning process was far more effective in this manner—the symptoms serving as immediate checkpoints. He has learned therefore to look within for the reasons as soon as symptoms appeared or reappeared.

The answers are not all at once apparent, but they become apparent.

Out of due regard for your fingers, take a break. Or you may end the session if you prefer.

("No.")

You see, I am making an effort to speak more slowly...

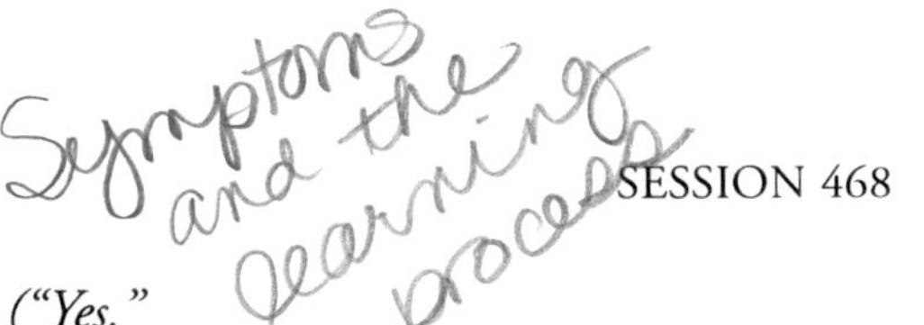

("Yes."

(10:13. Jane's pace had indeed been slower than recently. Tonight in addition, Seth's voice was very quiet. Resume at 10:21.)

Now. I told you that I would not keep you this evening.

Tell our friend however that when he is light-hearted he is light-limbed and moves lightly. Responsibility, in a certain sense, always got his back up.

He has been able to see for himself how inner heaviness of spirit is instantly reflected in his physical condition. He knows this. He is now free enough so that the spontaneous method of working on our book came to him, and he began working upon it in that manner today.

It is no coincidence that he also began working upon a novel idea, and no coincidence that further insights appeared to him this evening, and that the physical organism was almost immediately relieved. The changing of the room is also symbolic, and beneficially so.

He is not so frightened of others now that he must shield himself from them the moment he opens the door. On the other hand the moving of the bookcase to divide the work area showed even before his novel idea that his spontaneity was emerging fully within his work again, and that the work area was therefore to be separated from social activities.

At the same time in his mind, the work area was enlarged, since before he considered it to be composed psychically of his table area alone. It has been extended therefore, you see.

("Yes."

(Jane was gesturing to indicate how much larger an area was now set aside, beyond the new location of the bookcase, for her workroom.)

Now, inner realizations have been made, and I have tried to make them clear to you.

One point: your friend the Jesuit *(Bill Gallagher)*—his symptom is hidden within his tissue, and not physically observable. Its buried nature, the ulcer being hidden, is an added indication that he does not want to face his problem. Ruburt chose more observable symptoms. He was more determined to discover the reasons for his problems, and the learning process is much faster. The kind of symptom and its observability is often a clue as to the problem and to the individual's attitude toward it.

We will end the session. I wanted to make clear the fact that illness can be a method of learning *(long pause),* and to tell you that Ruburt's subjective feelings this evening were legitimate. New freedoms will follow. Intuitively you also provided clues that he needed this evening, but he was also ready to put them together.

Now my hearty good wishes, and a fond good evening.

("Do you want to say something about that apparition Jane saw recently?")

Now. Give us a moment. *(Pause.)*

The sense of fun and joy and spontaneity—all of these things are as important in the dreaming as in the waking state. He felt a responsibility, in his terms, to be psychic. Therefore he carried this attitude into the dream state, and rebelled against the idea of working while he slept. *(Pause.)* It is no more his duty to be psychic than it is his duty to be human, or creative. It is simply his nature. For some time therefore he curtailed his own dream activities, projections and other such adventures. He could hardly negate them entirely however.

On that particular evening I was in the room. He and I had been discussing his development. He was in a dream state, and in the dream I appeared to him in the form of a pyramid of lights. We were communicating telepathically.

The form was generally a figure. The pyramid for example could have been a robe, though no robe was present. The lights were my thoughts *(pause)*, in their electromagnetic form. Yet the form of the pyramid represented in other areas the three of us. The form had its own meaning therefore. The form did not disappear when he awakened. He simply switched to physical sight mechanisms that did not perceive it. The freedom of his dream activity will now return. *(Long pause.)*

I often appear in his dreams as a form or symbol, for he accepts me more readily. I often appear in such a manner in your own dreams, but as various people. Do you have further questions?

("No, I guess not." We were both tired.)

Then we will end the session. *(Smile.)* Look at your own dream notes more carefully, and perhaps you will find who I have been in them.

("Good night, Seth."

(10:50. Seth, above, seems to say that the pyramid of lights Jane saw was a dream image, that she did not see when she awoke. Yet Jane woke me at the time and told me she had just seen an apparition, while awake. I did not catch this, above, when Seth spoke, or I would have asked about the discrepancy. Next session.)

SESSION 469
MARCH 19, 1969 9:11 PM WEDNESDAY

Good evening.

("Good evening, Seth.")

Now. The inner self has a much richer and deeper heritage than the intellect or ego. Its perceptions are of a different nature, varying particularly in scope and depth. *(Long pause.)*

One note: Ruburt was correct in the interpretation he just gave you. He could use his inner senses fairly frequently in his waking state, as he did momentarily during that incident.

(See page 266 of the last session, concerning Jane seeing Seth's apparition. I had interpreted Seth's material as indicating that Jane saw the apparition only while dreaming, and not in the waking state, as she has maintained all along.

(Tonight Jane said she interpreted the data to mean that she momentarily saw Seth's apparition after waking up, before she switched to usual use of the outer senses. Note that Seth agrees with this.)

There are things he does not remember from his childhood, when he was warned against telling lies—apparitions that he spoke of. He was punished. This has something to do with an intellectual reluctance to admit truths delivered to him psychically and intuitively.

Strong abilities show themselves, and Ruburt's inner life is a full and rich one, his inner perceptions well-developed. The intellect it seems is continually being scandalized.

Give us a moment.

(Pause.) True and basic perception is a highly complicated phenomena, in which the line between perceiver and perceived vanishes. There is a strong correlation in what happens when the medium feels that a surviving personality has taken over the personality itself.

The medium perceives so clearly the reality of the surviving personality that the medium to some extent directly perceives that reality. You see the correlation here with what I told you in the past about experiencing concepts. That is one thing. To experience the reality of another does not necessarily mean that the medium negates her own personality—only that momentarily she allows it to perceive as directly as possible the experience of what it is to be the other. This involves a high degree of cooperation from the other person who does not exist in your physical terms, an opening of his reality to the medium rather than an invasion of the medium.

Now this is pertinent since the medium-communicator language can be legitimate in many other areas beside the one in which it is involved. In the simplest perception in those terms you are involved in the same way that a medium is. You are receiving data that is not basically physical, and translating it into terms meaningful to your own physical organism.

Regardless of the field of reality from which the data is received, to a large extent the mechanisms are the same. It is only because so-called mediumship is more unusual than simple perception that it appears so striking. Ruburt, reading from a book, would still have to receive and translate that information without knowing the endless manipulations necessary. The same sort of inner calculations would have been involved by the author of the book.

The information contained therein in such bulky printed form, is not physical. It is a matter of knowledge, electromagnetically coded, psychically valid, but you cannot hold knowledge in your hand and perceive it directly. You take its usual transmission in daily life for granted, overlooking the fact that all the physical aspects of its transmission and appearance serve to hide its basic non-materiality, and that words and printed data and moving pictures, all visual or physical symbols, are not the knowledge itself. These only serve as physical carriers. *(Long pause.)*

You are used to acting on knowledge only when it is so physically passed on, and the more numerous the forms in which it physically appears the greater your trust of it. Mental images, though they may occur within the physical skull, are not in themselves physical. The images, again, are only the symbols, the physical symbols, of inner knowledge. They are not the knowledge but the symbols of them.

Therefore you accept them for they make sense to the physical mechanism. The inner self has the knowledge behind these physical perceptions. The brain is responsible for these physical symbols. The mind has no need of them, but passes the information to the brain, who then interprets it.

The words that I speak to you transmit information, but the words themselves are not the information but verbal carriers. Now you may take your break.

(9:42-9:56.)

Now. Ruburt has always perceived with the inner senses.

He was considered an overimaginative child, and turned much of the inner information into poetic form as he grew from childhood. He felt free using this information in writing.

If it were not creatively transformed into writing however he felt, as a child, threatened, for he would be accused of telling lies.

Now. In your system of reality you are learning what mental energy is, and how to use it. You do this by constantly transforming your thoughts and emotions into physical form. You are supposed to get a clear picture of your inner development by perceiving the exterior environment. What seems to be a perception, an objective concrete event, independent and apart from you the perceiver, is instead the physical materialization of the perceiver's own inner emotions, energy and mental environment.

As long as scientists insist upon considering the perceiver and the perceived event as entirely separate, then the true nature of perception will not be understood.

Physically speaking now, there are mechanisms that interpret physical events. The scientist's field of inquiry involves these. The methods by which emotions, concepts, and energy are projected out from the individual to form the physical environment and events, mainly occur in nonphysical terms, but there are nervous system connections that aid in this projection.

These connections are not even suspected, simply because your scientists do not seriously consider that physical reality is the result of any such interrelation. The fact is however that the full function of the nervous system is not known, for the proper questions have not been asked.

Basically then there is little difference as to the manner in which normal perceptions or extrasensory perceptions are received. Now the sources of the data may be different, but in both cases they are basically nonphysical.

Give us a moment. *(Pause.)* The brain is capable (underlined)of interpreting and transmitting far more inner information than it does. It is the ego's idea of what is possible, the ego's concept of reality, that determines in a large manner whether or not the brain will interpret any particular data.

Now some inner data cannot be perceived or translated by the brain, practically speaking, but as minds develop so the physical brain will develop, and in some individuals to a large extent this has occurred.

Changes in the physical structure of the species will always follow inner need, and the inner need is anticipated from the beginning of the seed. Therefore large portions of the brain, now unused, lie latent for these developments. So-called psychics put some of these portions to work. Otherwise information such as ours would not be received clearly enough to be understood.

To a large extent you create what you see or perceive. This does not mean you are the creator in that respect. There are many realities of whose existence you are ignorant, but they nevertheless exist. Now you may end the session or take a break as you prefer.

("We'll take a break.")

I saw your yawn.

("I thought so."

(10:17-10:29.)

Now. You attempt to translate all information in physical terms within your system.

Your inner environment is the total of your inner (underlined) perceptions of inner reality. This is what you have to work with, and the raw material practically available. You then project this into physical events which you then physically perceive.

When you perceive more and more with your inner senses, you have more extensive raw material, better supplies, more available data. This should automatically bring about refinements within the physical structure to carry the additional data, and provide new outlets for materialization. The physical structure then to some extent is altered.

Latent potentialities, always present within the system, are activated as they are needed. The physical self can, it is true, become somewhat bewildered, but the ego also learns and expands so that it is able to accept and use the new information, and benefit from it. It quickly learns methods for example to utilize such activities for the purposes of the psychological structures that it recognizes and feels responsible for.

In Ruburt's case it has been some overprotective. Also since earlier conditions taught it that such knowledge could bring punishment. The ego of course also has more data to handle and works quickly to assimilate such data within the reality structure it recognizes.

Inner perceptions enlarge the ego's idea of reality however so adjustments are made. It is the ego that insists upon separating itself from events, preferring to imagine itself a spectator above events, rather than a participator in events.

You remember this from our material on action and the personality. The ego therefore is pleased when information is proven correct. *(Long pause.)* If the nature of perception were clearly understood then the nature of reality as you know it would also be understood much more clearly. Only half the process of perception, so-called, is even considered, however. Only half of the circle is known. The entire circle consists of those projections outward that form events, as well as the mechanisms by which the events are then physically perceived.

It goes without saying that telepathy is one method by which events are formed as well as perceived, but telepathy hides so far beneath physical perception that it is hardly detected.

Unless you have questions I will end the session.

("I guess not.")

Resuming on the nature of perception on Monday.

My heartiest regards to you both and a fond good evening.

("Good evening, Seth. It's been very interesting.")

(10:45.)

SESSION 470
MARCH 26, 1969 9:45 PM WEDNESDAY

Good evening.

("Good evening, Seth.")

Now. There is, then, a constant interaction between the perceiver and the perceived event.

I use the word event here to include either object or happening. There is a field that combines both perceiver and perceived event, a communication and a system of similarities set up between them. Obviously this holds true in each case of perception. It is for this reason that the perceptor and the event change each other. The field reaches out from you, say, as a self, to all the things that you perceive —and physical time does not enter in.

You are only aware of any such changes when your present conscious attention is directed at any object or event. Objects or events known to you in your past still exert their pressures upon you even as your own effect still changes them. The same holds true for what you would term future objects or events.

Your intense specialized focus within a highly limited present shields these other activities from you. You are bound by an entire spectrum of events, some that have already grown dim in your memory, and others that have not yet occurred in your time. You also affect these same events, shaping and altering them, and then reacting.

This highly intricate web or field obviously reaches out from you as a self to all the persons you perceive, and you also participate in the same sort of web, projecting outward from the other individuals. These webs have an electromagnetic structure as well as a chemical basis. They act like infinite pathways, and have a definite construction, though you do not perceive this.

Nerve impulses travel outward from the body, invisibly along these pathways in much the same manner as they travel within the body. The pathways are carriers of telepathic thoughts, impulses and desires that travel outward from any given self, altering and changing the seemingly objective events.

In a very real manner events or objects are actually focal points where highly charged psychic impulses are transformed into something that can be physically perceived, a breakthrough into matter. When such highly charged impulses intersect or coincide matter is formed. The reality behind such an explosion into matter is not dependent upon the matter. An identical or seemingly identical pattern may reemerge in quotes "at any time," again and again, if the proper coordinates exist for activation.

There are all kinds of events traveling along the same pathways, equally used, that do not appear physically. Physically then you do not perceive them. They may be transformed and emerge as realities or events within entirely different systems, in which they are then accepted by the inhabitants as vivid events.

Whether or not such an activation into physical actualization occurs or not, nonphysical portions of the self will to some extent react. There are certain similarities here both to the behavior of electricity as you understand it, and the behavior of the nervous system as you understand it, and I have tried to hint at this through the vocabulary that is available to me through Ruburt.

Now you may take your break and we shall continue.

(10:11. Jane's trance was a good one although she came out of it quickly at break. "I sort of had images while that was going on," she said, "but I couldn't tell you what they were." Resume at 10:22.)

Now. Give us a moment.

(Very long pause.)

Tell Ruburt to do relaxation exercises again for a while each day, and also to allow himself to act in a more impulsive manner, in strong bursts of activity, and particularly to imagine himself moving swiftly and lightly.

He is receiving larger doses of energy due to the season, and his own natural reactions to it, but he is not acting or reacting with the spontaneity that is natural to him in early springtime. Therefore the additional energy is blocked up and not released.

He is doing as well as he did a month or so ago in his reactions, but now that is not good enough. There is additional energy to be used. Do you understand what I am saying here?

("Yes.")

Quick physical action, such as that he involves himself in, even in housecleaning, is beneficial. An idea he had earlier this week along those lines was intuitional, but he did not put it into practice.

The condition now is due to this need for readjustment due to the season: bursts of impulsive and yet directed behavior followed by relaxation.

Now I am not going to keep you this evening, but the information on perception and its relation to physical events and objects will continue for some time. You do not understand as yet the prime part played by the nervous system in the transformation of psychic material into physical matter.

Ruburt's condition is temporary. The hints I have given him should clear him up within a matter of several days. Now do you have any questions?

("No.")

We will then close the session. My heartiest wishes to you both and a fond good evening.

("Good evening, Seth."

(10:35.)

SESSION 471
MARCH 31, 1969 9:05 PM MONDAY

(Jane wanted information from Seth about her struggle last night with what she believed to be a thought form she had created while sleeping. The experience had been somewhat frightening, and she was quite certain it was not a nightmare.

(Instead however Seth began to talk about Jane's evident conflict with an editor at Ace Books. Last Thursday, March 20, Jane had written Ace demanding the return of her dream book manuscript because of the delay in hearing from Ace—but once—since last December.)

Now. Good evening.

("Good evening, Seth.")

We are going to hedge about for a moment, until Ruburt's state is such that he is completely unconcerned.

In the meantime I will tell you about your Miss Grippo *(the editor in question at Ace)*, and the name is an apt one. She did enjoy Ruburt's first book, but is very angry that Fell held out financially, thinking then: "Who does Fell think Jane Roberts is? Why does he think we would pay so much when the name is unknown? He," meaning Fell, "is out to bleed us."

She projected this feeling to Ruburt also, particularly because Ruburt knew Don Wollheim. Fell was asking an exorbitant rate, she thought, for the first book; and Ruburt, she reasoned, would expect special privileges because of her contact with Wollheim, and so she got her back up and made sure no special privileges were given. In fact she bent over backward in the other direction.

There was something else. She resented the authoritative tone of the dream book as she first saw it, thinking again: "Now my God, this Jane Roberts imagines herself an authority." Wollheim did not overstate what she told him. She never thought that Ruburt would revise the book. *(Pause.)*

Beside this, as you felt, there was a fear of Ruburt's abilities. She is overly sensitive, feeling that psychics know more about her than she would wish, and this applies generally speaking, but particularly to women. This added to the other resentments. She does not like to speak to Ruburt on the phone, fearing the direct contact.

There does seem to be some involvement with Ruburt and that house however, in the future. Wollheim is rather afraid of Grippo.

(In the 460th session of January 27, 1969, Seth predicted the sale of the dream book to Ace, considering present—at that time—probabilities. It follows of course that drastic action such as Jane took last week could radically alter the probabilities.)

Now give us a moment. *(Two-minute pause.)*

Ruburt may study astrology, but he will not feel easy with it. He does not need it. As a matter of interest it is perfectly all right, but because of his particular nature he will have a tendency to let the charts impede rather than help his clairvoyant information.

It is too closed a system. Now astrology has its merits, and many good ones. An excellent astrologist can help people to better understand themselves. Understand that individuals themselves between lives choose the time of their own birth, adopting ahead of time those characteristics that they feel will best aid their development, and challenge their abilities.

Ruburt could involve himself however needlessly. His abilities will follow a different line entirely, though there is no harm in his study. The difficulty would lie in the drain upon his time, for people would want readings: and again, look for miracles rather than self-understanding and self-development.

Now I suggest that you take a brief break and I will continue with some other matters.

(9:25. Jane seemed to leave trance quickly, yet as it developed she did not really do so. She was quite sleepy at break, and said Seth was "putting her under" in order to talk about the thought-form and projection experience of last night with the least amount of distortion. Jane of course has a full account of the experience written down in her own records.

(Resume at 9:34.)

Now. Give us a moment.

Our friend attempted to choose a different battleground last evening. He decided to think of his symptoms as an enemy, and to give them form in another plane of reality where he could do battle with them. Now this was not an astral plane, but a lower one.

I am referring of course to his "black thing" in quotes, and the struggle. The energy behind the thing was the energy of hidden fears, but such a thing could be formed by anyone, for there are fears in every man. Ruburt tried to isolate them, give them form, and fight them all at once.

The thing was actually then a rather clumsy lower-dimensional animal, a provoked dumb dog of other dimensions who then attacked him symbolically enough, by biting. Any "thing" in quotes so created entirely of fears, would be frightened, and particularly angry at its creator, and it could do nothing else but attack; in one way to protect what reality it had, for it knew Ruburt created it only to slay it if possible.

It did have a reality therefore. Ruburt leapt back to his body to safety and normal consciousness. The thing therefore dissipated, for when Ruburt ran home he automatically withdrew his energy from it. Give us a moment. *(Pause.)*

He attempted to separate from himself all those elements he considers negative, and fight them at once, almost as if in doing so he removed or could remove evil from the universe. This was the result of his tendency to regard reality in terms of absolute (underlined) values.

He attempted to destroy the animal of evil, and it bit him back. Now evil does not exist in those terms, and even illness or fear is not necessarily an enemy, as much as an aid to understanding and the means to a greater end.

Even his desolations, of which I know, lead him to continue a search for understanding, and serve as an impetus to further development. You should try to help him understand them in that light.

Those who seek answers desperately want to find them, both for their own sakes and for the sakes of others. They care deeply and emotionally, and it is because they find little sense in the world as they understand it that they are driven to look elsewhere for answers.

Now the evil which Ruburt imagined he was projecting outward does not exist, but because he believed it did, he formed his materialization from his fears. It was the shape of the desolation he had felt last weekend. Now in larger terms, and in the deepest sense, there is no evil, only your lack of perception, but I know this is difficult for you to accept. But this fact is Ruburt's safeguard in his astral travels—as long as he remembers it.

The words: "May peace be with you," will get him through any difficulty in other layers of reality, for as he formed that image others also form images, and he could encounter them on occasion. To wish them peace will be to give them some comfort, for they do have a kind of reality. To fear them is to put yourself into their realm of reality, and then you are forced to fight on those terms, and there is no need for this.

Now Ruburt was attempting a legitimate projection, and the Grant book, in the overall, was good for him; but he got the idea for such a materialization by playing around unconsciously with an idea in the book. He thought of turning his symptoms, or the fears behind them, into a demon which he could then slay and conquer for good. *(An autobiography by Joan Grant is referred to here.)*

The suggestions he gave himself as to healing, you see, were connected here. He formed a poor creature with the purpose of destroying it. The symptoms were worse following the episode because of the impact with which the creature's energies were withdrawn and then reabsorbed. They had been already isolated from other aspects of Ruburt's personality, so the fears flew back in with an explosive impact.

Now in the first place the symptoms are not evil nor his enemies, but methods of instruction that he has himself chosen; and if ever he imagines them isolated in such a fashion, they should be imagined instead as being projected out from him into the whole of the universe where they are absorbed harmlessly, and their energy used to the greater good.

The earlier episode involving the man *(the same evening)*, is something different. The man was dying. Ruburt entered him briefly. He was going to comfort him and help him readjust. Instead the man's fears reminded Ruburt of his own, and he became sidetracked into the production of the other.

Now give us a moment.

(Pause.) The man had a connection with Poughkeepsie *(NY)*. I am not certain here. It was a man Ruburt knew in the past, and considered evil. This had something to do with his reaction, therefore. Do you follow me?

("Yes.")

The man may have been Ruburt's Father Doren. If not there is quite a psychological connection between the man who died and this Father Doren in Ruburt's mind.

Now, if he is worried about a recurrence *(pause)*, I suggest that he say quite simply: "God's peace be with me," before he sleeps, without worrying or arguing with the meaning of the term God.

This will always protect him in any out of body endeavors, or any other unearthly realities. He was actually getting rather tricky, and the accomplishment, while misguided, shows the growth of his abilities. Now had he been in severe difficulties someone would, have helped him. He has many friends, but it was best that he followed through on his own for his own confidence.

You may take a break, ask questions, or end the session as you prefer.

("We'll take the break."

(10:10. It was hard for Jane to open her eyes. As before, she did not leave the trance state completely; she was very sleepy and quiet, but when the session resumed her manner was once again quite active and energetic, eyes open often, voice good, pace rather fast, etc. Resume at 10:15.)

Now. Do you have questions?

("Why don't you just continue?")

Give me a moment. *(Pause.)* Now it will help if you take it for granted that under some circumstances—and underline some—dealing with Ruburt's idea of authority, he has difficulty expressing dissatisfaction, or expressing any normal impatience.

I know you realize this. It would help however if you simply remind him of this when such occasions arise, for your reminder, given without rancor, would be enough now to let him make a suitable adjustment at any given occasion. You need not force an issue, but remind him of the fact. You fear overinfluencing him, but since your influence is considerable in any case, this is a good time to use it.

His intellect will then begin to take over. When you say nothing he uses this as an excuse, thinking: "Rob has said nothing, therefore he must agree with what I am doing."

I have mentioned before that the two of you have been highly involved in the past, and that your combined efforts aid in the sessions. You do not have to feel that you have forced Ruburt where he does not want to go, even inadvertently. He does need and thrive upon your support. Without it he would have chosen other pathways perhaps, but they would not have been as beneficial nor as helpful to both of your developments.

He feels a new freedom, realizing, because he can be such a knucklehead, though a beloved one, now that he has freedom to do as he desires, to hold sessions or not to hold them. Because he does at times use you as an authority figure, he did have a tendency to think that he must have sessions because you wanted them.

The rigidity was in his mind however and not in yours, and he knows this now. Give us a moment. *(Pause.)* You are to him in this existence a figure for lover, father and child, but he is also a figure to you of mother, mistress and child. And all of this energy in both of your cases unconsciously understood, is then at its best, joyfully bound together and projected into your works.

You are handling much more than most people however. Do you have questions on this?

("No, I'd like to read this over first.")

The very impetus and charge of the energy propels you both in to new byways in your arts and in our work. Were the energy and emotional impetus materialized instead for example in parent-child relationships, with you as parents, in your particular cases it would be lessened in your work.

You have chosen to divert and use tremendous charges of energy in your final reincarnations, and your own art will make its way for this reason. *(To me.)* What seems to you as inner difficulties or problems, or lack of success, like

Ruburt's desolations, serve as the very impetus to development.

God himself did not create reality easily. We will get into that matter at another time *(humorously emphatic)*, though in the past we have given you considerable information on it.

Now if you have no questions I will end the session, but I will be glad to answer any that you have.

("I guess not, Seth.")

As far as the information concerning Ruburt's symptoms, I have this to say. *(See page 272 of the 470th session, March 26, 1969.)* He must be open about them, and they will vanish. I do not mean *(be)* pessimistic about them. When he attempts to hide them from you he builds up the mood that they so dismay you. He takes an aspirin behind your back as if he were a secret alcoholic because he fears that you would be annoyed. Then this builds up within him the feeling that he is alone, and the mood builds up to which you then react.

If he is open with you then he feels that you are with him, and this alone does much to dissipate the difficulties.

Now do you have questions?

("You seem to be answering them as you go along."

(For the last couple of pages it had been quite noticeable to me that Seth was anticipating my questions and then answering them. This can't be demonstrated of course, but my feeling was apparent subjectively.)

It took me some time to get our friend in the proper condition.

("I'm satisfied for the moment.")

We will then close the session. My heartiest regards to you both. Have Ruburt read this session several times.

("Yes.")

You know, I know, that your compliments quite go to his head, when they are real ones, and this also sends his symptoms running. Now I will leave you. A fond good evening. Were it not for time involved in your typing of my immortal words, I would stay with you longer. Now, I wish you well.

("Thank you.")

Talking is good for him, with you.

("Good night, Seth, and thank you."

(10:42. Jane came out rather quickly, but was still very sleepy and relaxed. "He's being real affectionate and sweet... and I don't know if I'll ever make it to the bedroom," she said. "He could have gone on and on.")

SESSION 472
APRIL 2, 1969 9:10 PM WEDNESDAY

Good evening.

("Good evening, Seth.")

Now. You condition your body to behave in general overall patterns. You condition it to react in certain ways. It mimics perfectly your psychic and mental reactions.

Concentration in any given area predisposes certain elements within the nervous system toward that particular kind of focus or concentration, as many footfalls hollow out a pathway. Now this is somewhat understood in your scientific circles.

What is not understood is that the same sort of conditioning also operates, not only in the reaction to events but in the formation of events. You predispose yourselves toward the construction of events of a particular nature, to which of course you then react.

You also help maintain and form constructions or events of others that fit in with your own particular varieties of interests. Now again I am not speaking symbolically. Very definite portions of the nervous system that you do not understand are the receptors of impulses that go outward from you to form events.

There are of course mass constructions, psychic pools whose energy is derived from many individuals, all predisposed because of their own inclinations toward specific areas of activity. Various groups of individuals therefore, massed together, help form and maintain particular areas of your reality.

This sort of behavior continues of course whether you are waking or sleeping, and is highly involved in the construction of dream images and constructions. There are areas of activity to which you do not react simply because you have not activated sympathetic pathways within yourself. These require much more effort on your part, but even the physical brain has latent within it the possibilities for many kinds of activities that still remain generally unknown.

The inner self therefore uses the physical system to express its own inclinations and ideas of reality. It is the inner self that unfolds those patterns of behavior spoken about in the article you read on infant growth. *(In a recent issue of* Time *magazine.)* Such unfoldings always occur from within, responding to signals not from the exterior but from the interior environment.

The interior self causes the physical challenges that then seem to spurt further bodily activity. The impetus for any developing and latent action is incipient in the unborn infant. The child's first steps are latent within the first flickering of the infant's eyes, for the events follow as naturally as the opening of the petals of a flower.

These are unfoldings, as the inner self materializes what is already latent into physical actuality. Now there may be areas in which the inner self is simply not interested. There may be areas in which it is simply less proficient. The inner self is a developing entity, not a finished product. The whole idea of physical reality, individually speaking, is the emergence of experience within your particular system.

The inner self is acquainting itself with reality as it exists there. In many cases it is emerging into a new world. Since the learning process is involved, there are errors. Any faulty constructions however are used by the inner self in a feedback system and as a part of the learning process. Your system is not the most elementary, but it is one of the most elementary, and it is a way that the inner self acquaints itself with certain basic facts.

It therefore provides itself with a large variety of environments in various reincarnations, with problems of various natures, and with diverse circumstances. It does not try to form life conditions that offer no challenges, quite the reverse in fact. It is getting used to its own abilities and learning how to use them. What happens in the case of willfully used destructive energies? It finds out by using them.

It knows full well its own indestructibility, and that of its fellows. What happens in the case of constructive psychic energy when it is purposely denied aggressive outlets? It finds out. What does it feel like to be the brunt of aggression? It forms another life situation and discovers the answer. How strong and potent is the energy that is at its command? How can it best be used? It is quite necessary that all of these questions be answered, for the inner self is composed of energy, and in other fields of activity thoughts and emotions are instantaneously translated, their results instantly seen. There is no saving time lag, as within your own system, and there is no physical body such as you know it.

There is form. The very mechanism of the body however is so constructed that it can bear the brunt of many errors, and free itself from them, though this may not seem to be the case at times. Nevertheless yours is a slow-motion world in many ways as far as your perceptions are concerned, while you are within it. Your body is much like a sculptor or a sculpt, never really completed, the inner self trying out various techniques of creativity on its first test piece. The results are not always of the best, but the sculptor is independent of his product and knows there will others.

Now you may take your break and we will continue. Ruburt for example has found out what certain mental patterns will do to his image, and he is now attempting to undo the damage that became apparent. Without the damage he would not have accepted the obvious truths. Now the sculptor does at times identify with his sculpt, but never entirely, and it will help him if he remembers that he did the damage, and therefore can undo it.

Not only that, but the lesson will prevent him from doing more serious damage. Tell him that he has, or he is, learning a lesson in perspective, whether he knows it or not.

(9:47. Jane quickly left trance although it had been a good one. She remembered only the last sentence. Resume at 10:01.)

The inner self then has an entirely different perspective upon your reality than you do, and it sees purposes which are not apparent to you.

Do not forget however that you are a portion of the inner self. It is not using you. You are the portion of it that experiences physical reality. Now physical illnesses that are not critical but observable, that do not involve the loss of say of a limb or of an organ, generally (underlined) represent problems that are in the process of being solved, problems that are in quotes "out in the open."

Now these particular kinds of illnesses are the end product of a process of discovery. Inner problems are literally brought out into the open when they can be faced, recognized, dealt with and conquered, using the symptoms as measuring points of progress. A trial-and-error system is (underlined) involved; but inner processes are reflected rather quickly in these cases upon the physical condition.

Now ideally the means have been given, with the problem out in the open, for correct solution. A healing process is definitely involved, even with the initial emergence of the symptoms, for the psychological system finally forces the problem out into the open. I am speaking now of the kind of illnesses I have described.

In other cases where the symptom is interior itself, as in ulcers, this is a sign that the inner self has not yet come to such a point. The personality is not yet willing to face the problems even to that extent and the symptom itself is shielded from physical sight, quite rightly symbolically speaking. The relative observability of a symptom is a clue therefore as to the personality's attitude toward its problem.

Your friend the Jesuit you see does not want his problem out in the open so he can deal with it, for he is not ready as yet to face it.

Now this material has important psychological implications that I will follow up, and it is also connected with our material on perception. Ruburt physically perceives as well as feels the symptoms. Our Jesuit will not see the problem, even to that extent, and so it is buried even physically within him.

Now there are other layers. Many problems are never materialized as physical symptoms. They remain as blank spots, uncultivated and unproductive areas within the psyche—areas in which there are no problems because there is no experience permitted. Curiously vacant areas in which very little perception is allowed. A lack of development, lacking any challenge or possibility for fulfillment.

There is then a mental, psychic, or emotional lack of sight. An idiocy of a kind, and a complete blockage, a denial of experience along certain lines that is far more detrimental than a specific problem, for there is an inability of the personality to express itself to any effective degree in that area.

Give us a moment here. There are also problems within the psyche and in the emotional context that are not understood by the individual, or that he is frightened of or that he will not face. Now any of these distort his ability to perceive and to create. They limit his effective area of psychic and creative activity.

Now this was Ruburt's state before the emergence of the symptoms. The explosive first emergence represented the first forceful emergence of the problem into physical terms, but as such was actually productive and of a healing nature—much more beneficial, say, than if such emergence had not occurred.

Old negative patterns of thought, always present beneath an exterior optimism, had gone unrecognized by him, and were like a thorn in his side. Until these emerged physically he was not aware of them sufficiently enough to handle them effectively. They distorted his reality and his perceptions without his being aware of them.

I am going into this rather deeply because while we are dealing with perceptions we will also be discussing distortions, because the information will help Ruburt, and because personal examples serve well for your understanding.

When he is finished you see he will understand something extremely important for him, and experience a corresponding relief. For seeing that he creates his own reality now, he will understand that he also helped form the environment in which he grew, and that his mother was not entirely responsible.

The despondencies that he encounters also should show him that these feelings emerge into his conscious awareness now, to be dealt with, where in the past they festered beneath consciousness, and he would not admit them as a problem for he was not that aware of their existence.

They are negative feelings, deliberately exaggerated so that he can understand their nature and handle them as such. Your therapy was highly successful. I refer to your shopping endeavor *(on Saturday March, 29)* and the therapy of delight in small things, and laughter.

Now you may take a break, though I hope your fingers are not broken.

("No.")

(10:27. The trance had been good, the delivery fast, etc. Resume at 10:40.)

Now. The information I am giving you this evening will be far more helpful to many individuals than any information I could give you this evening concerning your student or his family; for the boy at this point would not put my advice into practice. He is not ready to understand it, and the father has still to realize that no one can bail him out except himself. I will not give him ready answers, and I have told him this.

Ready answers for he or his son would only betray them. They would use them as excuses. Now give me, a moment ... I will tell him that many of his worries concerning the boy are projections of his own fears, and will not materialize. The boy is reacting telepathically for one thing to the father's worries. The best thing the father can do for now is to be simply kind to the boy, but relieve the child of his heavy-handed thoughts mentally. Leave the boy alone. He is picking up the father's negative attitudes telepathically.

(Long pause; one of several, etc.) He is at this point a repository for them. Another positive suggestion is for the father to involve himself in creative endeavors with his painting. He will feel he is doing something productive, and this will help break his feelings of guilt and frustration, and therefore help the boy.

Now the information given earlier this evening, along with other material, will someday provide an effective measuring stick by which individuals can understand the nature of their difficulties, and is therefore quite important.

In many situations one individual within a family will serve as the family symptom. Do you see?

("Yes.")

In such a case the difficulties are not being faced by others, but only projected by them upon another. In many cases the other is a younger individual who is more resilient, has more energy, a more instinctive use of the life force, who is better able to bear the problems for the whole unit, and who will actually escape from them. Sometimes he can solve the problem. Often when he leaves the problem simply falls back where it belonged originally—upon the shoulders of the parents. It is for this reason often that parents have difficulties when the children leave. Now unless you have questions...

("I guess not.")

We will end the session. My most fond wishes to you both, and an affectionate good evening.

("Good night Seth, and thank you.")

One note. Ruburt need not bear the weight of the world upon his shoulders *(humorously throughout)*, nor take the responsibility of the universe. This is high egotism. God can handle his own problems and take care of his universe. Ruburt need not judge him, for he does not know all the facts, and it is sheer nonsense for him to suppose that he does.

(10:53.)

ESP CLASS
MAY 6, 1969

(Notes by Jane from Murphy's Power of the Subconscious Mind: *"The power of your subconscious is enormous. It inspires you, reveals to you names and facts and scenes from the storehouse of memory. It started your heartbeat, controls circulation of your blood, regulates digestion, assimilation, and elimination. When you eat a piece of bread, your subconscious transmutes it into tissue, muscle, bone, and blood. Your subconscious controls all the vital processes and functions of your body. It never sleeps or rests. You can discover the miracle-working power of the subconscious by plainly stating to your subconscious mind, prior to sleep, that you wish a certain specific thing accomplished. Here then is a source of power and wisdom that places you in touch with omnipotence, or the power that moves the world, guides the planets in their course, and causes the sun to shine. Your subconscious mind is the source of your ideals, aspirations, and altruistic urges."*

("Whatever thoughts, beliefs, opinions, theories, or dogmas you write, engrave, or impress on your subconscious mind... you will experience them as the objective manifestation of circumstances, conditions, and events; what you write on the inside, you experience on the outside."

("It is a universal truth that whatever you impress on your subconscious mind is expressed on the screen of space as condition, experience, and event. Thought is incipient action. The reaction is a response from your subconscious mind which corresponds with the nature of your thought. Your subconscious mind can be likened to the soil which can grow all kinds of seeds, good or bad. Every thought is a cause and every condition an effect."

("As you sow in your subconscious mind, so shall you reap in your body and environment. Whatever your conscious mind assumes and believes to be true, your subconscious mind will accept and bring to pass. Whatever you habitually think sinks into the subconscious. The subconscious is the seat of the emotions and is a creative mind. Once the subconscious accepts an idea, it begins to execute it. Whatever you feel is true, your subconscious will accept and bring forth into experience.")

(Seth:) When he *(TM)* gets the gold tassel, I will pin it on him.

My friend Ruburt has been correct however, and we must have a tighter ship! And I will see to it that we have one. I do not see your party faces—you had them on earlier. You may sing "happy birthday" to me—I will give you a list of my birthdays and you can have a party at every class.

Now I am only speaking because many of you have known that I was here. And it ill behooves me not to bid you welcome when you felt my presence. But in many of your discussions, there has only been surface thought and surface feelings... and we do not walk on the surface in this class. I would push your heads collectively and individually underneath... for you still do not understand that you create your physical reality! You form your blocks and shove them up upon the surface of the earth. You cannot solve the problems of your world on a surface level. If you could, you would have done it centuries ago. You must step out of your present perspective in order to see your world clearly. Here you are not to hide within the closet of 3 dimensionality and cry, "It is dark and I cannot see!" And refuse to use the inner light that can alone aid your vision.

SESSION 481
MAY 12, 1969 9:10 PM MONDAY

(Below, Seth discusses a projection experience of Jane's on Friday, May 9, that involved her perception of my astral presence in the apartment although I was at work at Artistic Card Company that day.)

Good evening.

("Good evening, Seth.")

Now. Ruburt's experience involving you was quite legitimate, although you were not consciously aware of your activities.

(Jane has her own full set of notes re the experience.)

You were nevertheless largely responsible for the encounter as it took place. You were thinking both consciously and below consciousness about Ruburt's appointment at the dentist. You wanted to give him confidence and to reassure him. This acted as an emotional impetus.

Ruburt was working and without realizing it telepathically was aware of your emotional presence. It was this that gave him the idea of a projection experiment that morning. He wanted to see if he could become aware of your form.

You did not want to project, per se. You wanted to be here to offer reassurance. The desire got you here. Your conscious mind was taken up fully with your activities, giving the inner self full rein. In the same way do you travel in other realities without being aware of your journeys. You were not frightened, either of you, because of the familiar surroundings, and you were unusually free to express your feelings for each other, released from restraints of time.

You perceived in a normal fashion, which should tell you that perception is not dependent upon the physical image. You were well-aware of your relationship. You have both traveled together in such a fashion often from the dream state, without your knowledge. There is no reason why you cannot try such experiments by trying to project at the same time.

If you try to do this from a dream state then you must set aside two and one-half hours, for the first portion will be used as preliminaries. You can also give yourselves such suggestions before you sleep. You might begin by making an appointment to meet each other, say at three in the morning in the living room.

You would feel more comfortable if your initial journeys were within the apartment. You sleep more deeply as a rule than Ruburt, hence you must be sure to give yourself the suggestion to awaken and remember. It might also help you to place an object to which you are strongly attached in the living room. Impress yourself with the thought that you want to get up and retrieve it.

For your own purposes an unfinished painting on your easel would help you project to your studio, for you would psychically wish to return to study it. You have in fact often done this, though you do not remember. It would be to your advantage to try some experiments together however. Besides this the two of you travelling together could help each other retain proper consciousness and purpose during projection. If Ruburt knows he is projecting he should try to remember you, and to rouse you astrally.

He can be of great help to you here when he learns to remember. You can also suggest dreams in which you are flying in an airplane, and tell yourself you will awaken to project. You will know the plane is a dream image but be able to retain it for your convenience, so that you do not fear falling.

Give us a moment. *(Pause.)* In such instances you are withdrawing your perceptive abilities from the physical body. They will seem to operate as usual, but they are more vivid and far-reaching. Your thoughts instantly attain a form that you can then perceive. If you think of a dog for example, quite unconsciously you form the image of a dog, which you do then perceive.

It is because of this instantaneous creation and projection of inner reality into form that you experience time within the physical system—to train you literally, to give you time to learn to handle your own creations. Projection experiments should only be adopted therefore when you are in a peaceful state of mind, as Ruburt should know after his creature experience.

Now there are, in quotes, "objective" realities that exist, within astral reality itself.

There are more than your thought forms in other words. Your thought forms however can be used as definite aids when you are in the proper mental condition, and they can impede your progress if you are not. In physical reality a man in a desperate frame of mind is more apt to emphasize horrible aspects in the news, for example, and to see desperation rather than joy in the faces of those he meets. He will ignore the contented playful child on one side of the street, and notice instead a dirty ragged boy even though he be further away. So your frame of mind when projecting will largely determine the sort of experiences you have, and the environments you visit.

You may take your break.

(9:45-10:00.)

Now. The original intensity behind the construction determines the length of its existence, in your terms, rather than the duration. Do you follow me?

("Yes." During break I had wondered, for instance, how long it would take to supplant a negative habit that had existed for say ten years, with a positive one.)

Left alone, any such construction will eventually vanish. It will however leave a trace. This does not necessarily mean it will leave a trace in your consciousness. A trace in electromagnetic reality, where it can then be activated by anyone when certain conditions are met, or are favorable.

Denying energy to such a construction can be like pricking a balloon. It can instantly disintegrate, be deflated. The prick however is comparable to a conscious and subconscious denial of the construction's validity. Then all attention must be taken from it, for it thrives on attention.

To replace it with a new construction, it is a good idea to suggest that the old construction has indeed vanished, and in its place a new more acceptable one is being built. Now symbolism may be used here. The following mental exercise is most effective. It may be varied according to your interest.

In your mind's eye however imagine a run-down, shabby, deteriorating shamble of a house with rotting floorboards and sagging porches. Then imagine that it is burned to the ground and the remaining rubble carted away and burned. Imagine the land now free beneath it, open to the blessing of wind, rain and sun. Then imagine a new house being built there, of your preferred choice, with all new materials, of splendid design, and see this always in your mind where before you saw the previous image.

Imagine the summer winds that blow over the land that now fills the interior of the house with scented air. Let the first house represent all negative ideas or constructions, and the new house represent the desired ideas or constructions. Have it firmly in your mind however as to what ideas these refer, specifically.

The first object must be seen as completely destroyed, and the area cleared before the new object is imagined in its place. The first object should be deliberately destroyed. What relief to see it vanish. The symbolism will help activate those forces that are necessary in any replacement of ideas. Any object you see can be used in place of the house. Do you follow me?

("Yes.")

If the exercise is done correctly it is literally impossible for the old idea to obtain any energy for its continuance and your attention is directed to the desired end. The object should be something you can visualize easily however. If you have difficulty imagining the deliberate destruction of the negative object, this is merely a sign of its hold. You may then instead imagine its destruction by an act of nature. The house being struck by lightning for example. If this is the case then the exercise should be continued until you imagine you yourself deciding upon and bringing about the destruction and replacement. If you are not ready to burn down the structure itself, imaginatively, then you are not prepared to rid yourself of the negative behavior, you see. The symbolic destruction is the real destruction. The symbolic creation is the real creation. Such exercises will cut down the physical time involved however.

Now there is no doubt that you cause your dream environment as you cause your physical environment. As I have told you negative patterns of thought are reflected in both states. Proper suggestion before sleep can doubly work to your advantage then, for you are holding your ground in two worlds at once.

The same exercise can be done while dreaming, you see.

This is entirely different from Ruburt's attempt with his creature, for he was trying to form an evil creature, in those terms, to slay—a thing conscious of its own evil in those terms, and that is always dangerous. Do you see the difference?

("Yes.")

Now you may take your break. Or if you have a question ask me.

("We'll take the break."

(10:25-10:37.)

In a very real manner, all conditions exist in your mind.

The amount of conscious thought given to any construction obviously reinforces it. Ruburt became a writer because he thought of being a writer constantly. He became ill, generally speaking, for the same reason.

If a desire for health leads to an emphasis upon symptoms to be overcome,

you would be better off to avoid all thoughts of health or illness, and concentrate in another direction such as work. This follows regardless of the desired end, be it wealth, fame, or so forth. Such an emphasis can lead to a focus upon the obstacles that stand in the way. This reinforces the negative condition.

Confidence is extremely important. It will lead to more confidence, and of itself wipes out the fear that causes most negative conditions. In the exercise you see the house can simply represent fear, for a basic therapeutic method, and the new house confidence.

While Ruburt tells himself he is weak or sick, he causes the organism to behave in that manner. Dreams of health are of great benefit. He can tell himself that his dream self becomes his physical image. He knows his dream self is real. *(Long pause.)*

The energy from any construction can be weakened if it is countered by another strong energy force. The desire to work well, enthusiastically and emotionally held, can offset bad health for example. You do not need the direct opposite. Do you follow me?

("Yes.")

—but something of equal or stronger intensity. Womanly pride in Ruburt's case is a help for example. *(Long pause.)* Other elements also come into play. As your inner environment changes you also begin to attract others. You will begin to attract people who want to buy paintings for example. There is a snowballing effect—an acceleration, that is quite evident as soon as the first groundwork has been laid.

First you are clearing up negative debris, you see, and reversing a trend. When the results show they appear magical.

Now I will end our session unless you have questions.

("I guess not." Pause. I asked humorously, after waiting to see if Jane was coming out of trance: "Did you hear what I said earlier this evening, about growing new teeth?")

If you want new teeth that badly, you can grow them. If I were you, I would concentrate upon the easy use of my abilities rather than my bite.

A fond good evening to you both.

("Good night, Seth."

(10:55.)

(The following private sessions have been deleted from this Book 9, the last one in this series of The Early Sessions. *Except for Session 494, however, those sessions will be presented in* The Personal Sessions *series that New Awareness*

Network will soon begin publishing. See my note about The Personal Sessions *in the front matter of this book:)*

473 - April 7, 1969
474 - April 9, 1969
475 - April 14, 1969
476 - April 16, 1969
477 - April 21, 1969
478 - April 28, 1969
479 - April 30, 1969
480 - May 7, 1969
490 - June 25, 1969
494 - No copy available

SESSION 482
MAY 19, 1969 9 PM MONDAY

(No session was held on Wednesday, May 14. John Bradley was a visitor.

(On Sunday, May 18, John Pitre called Jane from Franklin, Louisiana and asked that Seth hold a session for his wife Peg; she is in the hospital, in poor condition, with muscular dystrophy. John told Jane it "might be a matter of hours" etc., and wondered whether Seth could give some data on Peg's psychic activities at the moment, whether she would be helped after physical demise, etc.

(Last night Jane had trouble sleeping. She was out-of- body often, she said, and on at least one occasion was aware of my own astral presence with her. Jane recalled at least three episodes of astral travel. She had experiences involving caskets, death, etc...but said these episodes were separated in time, at least one of the times being quite long ago. Jane said she was aware of wanting to contact John's wife Peg during these travels, without the experience being "unpleasant" for either of them...

(Re John and Peg, see sessions 394, 416, 441, etc.)

Good evening.

("Good evening, Seth.")

Now. A few comments only regarding Ruburt. Overall he did well on Friday.

(When Jane spent the day with my mother in Sayre, PA on May 16.)

A few days earlier, knowing he had progressed, he ceased doing the psycho-cybernetics exercises however, and these are an excellent and enjoyable way of focusing conscious energy in constructive directions. This is active prayer, with him, and a definite training device. Since little time is involved, twenty minutes, this should be continued.

There would have been all kinds of complications as a result of the Friday episode had it not been for your combined prayer activities and new understanding. He made some errors. These were so small in proportion to his success that he should forget them. And he did very well, tell him, in his encounter with Mr. Fisher, and with your mother's friends in the hospital room.

He should remember to recognize resentment when he feels it, and then to realize that the resentment can be dismissed, can fall away from him. The initial recognition must be made, however. Then have him imagine plucking out the resentment by the roots and replacing it with a positive feeling. But he must imagine the plucking-out process.

(I slipped up concerning the Friday episode, not realizing it could have psychic consequences for Jane. She herself suggested the idea, that I take her to Sayre for the day so she could go to the hospital with my mother, while I returned to work at Artistic Card Company in Elmira. I returned to Sayre at supper time. We ate there with my mother and then I brought Jane back home. Other arrangements could have been made to get my mother to the hospital, and in the future will be done so.)

Now this is the difference between repression and positive action. In repression the resentment is shoved beneath and ignored. With our method it is recognized, imaginatively plucked out as being undesirable, and replaced by the thought of peace and constructive energy.

Work on the book will now proceed. Last week's poetry served to refresh his creative energies, and in commitment to the book and to our work, and with your prayer activities. You will indeed find success in the health endeavors. Energy given in commitment will rob the symptoms. There' will be no room for them.

For your own edification: I hope you have seen the increasing improvement since the prayer activities began.

("Well, he's cut them down to four days a week.")

(Pause.) I did not hear you.

(I repeated my comment. I had in mind that we now held no prayer sessions on Fridays, Saturdays or Sundays.)

There was a reason, of which he may or may not be consciously aware. When he began to cut them down it was because of mistakes he had made: an overemphasis, a concern, so that he was watching himself too closely.

He had a tendency by the end of the week, during prayer period, to become overanxious looking for signs, and found himself concentrating upon the symptoms that still remained. He has conquered this however, and also varied his prayer technique to advantage.

The periods can now be continued, as you planned. Have you noticed the improvement since you began your prayer period?

("Yes.")

I have told you some of them. You should not need me to tell you. Now, give us a moment. *(Pause.)* Do you have questions on our present discussion?

("No.")

The following is for our friend.

His wife has already established contacts in another reality. Some of these include friends and relations from other lives. A few are persons with whom she seemed to be superficially connected in this life, but the encounters provided deep emotional support that was not obvious.

There is a Sonja connected here in this regard, only a girl that she knew in eight or ninth grade, briefly. The last name began with an M, and was something like Monshard. *(My phonetic interpretation.)*

Trouble at the base of the neck.

An Aunt Nellie. Now this Aunt Nellie may have died in 1936, but the date in any case is closely connected with her.

These are simply odd bits of information that have sifted through Peggy's mind as she reviews memories... Something about being outstanding in a speech class, or in a play, in grade school. About sixth grade. Something that pleased her very much—her performance—it may only have been a time when she recited well, but she smiles about it.

(Jane now gestured to her throat and collar.) A connection with an iron, and the collars of her dresses being ironed. It is a small white collar. Something about "John, forget the misery," and, it seems, the word peppy.

("How do you spell it?")

I do not know if this refers to a name, or if it was a way she had of pronouncing the word peppy, as full of pep.

Now these are disjointed images from her mind. A recital. Now, N O R... Something about a ring on her finger, or on John's finger, and the initial A, I believe, connected with the ring.

"It has all been worth it." *(Pause.)* Victoria, the place. "When we danced one night I had a headache—do you remember?

"On a Christmas morning you pricked my neck with a pin, trying to fix my dress."

Now, an Anna is waiting for her, and a Steve K.

("The letter K?")

Yes. *(Pause.)*

She is already running about where she is now, and laughing, but she does not want him to be sorrowful. She is collecting her memories, and putting them in order. She laughs and says: "It is like juggling letters in the alphabet, and trying to hold them in an open kerchief." She has them all. She is trying to make them neat, so it is difficult to tell him things clearly, now, but she is not worried.

There seems to be something about a doctor. I cannot get it clearly from her. The name seems to be something like Mesh, or the beginning of the name. Something about his eyes, either that she wants John to notice or that she has noticed. Does one eye look off in another direction?

She says: "He says he will keep an eye on me," and laughs. She jokes, and says she does not want another eye on her.

Give us a moment. My attention seems drawn to a bottom dresser drawer, of dark wood rather than light. It seems to have clothes but with a portion of the bottom of the drawer showing between, and somewhere in there a small notebook of some kind, or photographs that mean much to her.

I get a large letter P here that I do not understand. The dresser seems to be taller rather than short. Perhaps with divided drawers at the top. Something about a small calendar. It may stand on the top of the dresser. I am not sure.

Something about a party. She says: "You really took me for a ride." The letter A here. The party at a girl's house. The A may be for Anita. She says: "How nicely you tie bows in my hair." *(Long pause.)*

I think she uses the term: "Little Jesus knows we have done our best.

"There was a fountain with an apple on it—do you remember?" *(Long pause.)* Something about a missal or prayer book, with dates, black, and a connection with a grandfather.

You had better take you break.

(9:50. The session had begun at 9 PM. Jane's eyes were heavy as she came out of trance. She told me she "could sort of see" a bureau drawer while Seth was giving the related data. She now added that although Seth hadn't said so, the dresser was against the south wall of their place, "like the south wall of our apartment here, to my left," Jane said.

(Resume at 10:00.)

Now. The information I have given you I derived from a certain portion of the girl's consciousness. Disjointed memories, thoughts and ideas.

Her whole reality is far greater, and she is endeavoring to put these memories in place, in perspective, as you would put furniture into a new house. Time as you think of it has little meaning for her. You could compare the different time concepts in this way:

In your dimension it is as if events, remembered events, were like pieces of furniture, all arranged in one room, in a given order. Living in the room, you can find your way between the pieces of furniture easily.

Then you move out into a much larger and different kind of room, and here the furniture may be arranged in any fashion—arranged and rearranged to your heart's content, and you may form different combinations from it and use it for different purposes. So Peg is rearranging the furniture of her mind; and as you might visit a new residence and move some of your belongings into it before you have officially made it your own, so she has for some time been examining her new environment, and been in tie process of transferring her self to the new location.

There have been guides to help her. She will hardly notice that she has entirely moved in, for she will feel so at home. In her case, she has been forming memory pictures of her childhood, and entering into them, and of days before the physical illness, and she has had help in these endeavors. She is learning that events that seem to be in the past can be recreated. She does not *imagine* that she is a child. She is enjoying the freedom of revisiting and re-experiencing certain events. This is also a sort of spiritual therapy in her case, so that she loses the identification with illness, and does not carry it with her.

I mentioned that she was solving many problems in this, the last reincarnation within your system, and shortly training periods will begin. It will be her turn now to help others and be their source of strength. She has already begun a new life therefore, though presently her experience is being monitored to some degree by guides.

She sees herself supported in a religious sense by conventional figures from the Bible. These personalities will explain the nature of reality to her in vocabulary that will make sense to her. She has solved the problems that she set, and brought forth in her husband compassion and understanding—qualities that greatly help in his own development. *(Pause.)*

I have appeared to her as a very gentle John of the Disciples, and spoken with her. This is not trickery, but a method of helping that she can accept. It is not unusual for those trying to help, to assume such comforting forms and images. This is a period of new learning for her.

You already have a way prepared for you. You have already made your inroads long before the time of physical death. Only the ego is usually unaware of these activities. John has himself been with her in his sleep state, and does not remember.

She is used to movement now, and in the past. Returning to the body she would become confused with the body's behavior. Give us a moment. When the transition is complete for her, and she is fully organized, she will be able to visit John, but she will also be involved in rather intensive training periods of her own, and will be more alive than ever.

She says: "It will be fun to learn again."

Now you may take a break or end the session as you prefer.

("We'll take the break.")

(10:30. Jane's trance had been a deep one. When she was out of it I mentioned several questions that occurred to me during last delivery, and that I thought John might like to have answered were he present. Seth proceeded to answer the questions after break ended at 10:43.)

Now. The new body is of course not a new body at all, but simply a body not physical in your terms, one that you use in astral projections, one that gives the vitality and strength to the physical body that you know.

Your flesh is embedded in it. When you leave the physical body, the other body is quite as real to you, and seems as physical, although it has many more freedoms. You can do things with it that you cannot do with the physical body, for example.

Peg is delighted with this body, particularly in comparing it with the physical one. She is trying to cut off any identification with the physical body, whether it be alive or dead in your terms.

John must tell her that she is free to leave, and that he joyfully gives her her freedom, so that even after death she does not feel that she must stay close to him. She knows now for certain that they will be reunited, but she knows that he cannot be as aware of this as she is. She is also aware of their previous relationships now however, though all of this information is not yet clear to her. So she sees him as the self that he knows, and also as the people he has been, and already looks upon him with new eyes.

Unless you have questions I will end the session.

("I guess not then." Jane was getting tired.)

My heartiest wishes to you both. A fond good evening. And Ruburt has been helping you project.

("Yes. Good night, Seth, and thank you.")

(10:55. Jane had been "far-out" this time; it took her awhile to come fully out of trance, etc. We'll be sending a copy of the session to John Pitre.)

SESSION 483
MAY 21, 1969 9:10 PM WEDNESDAY

(Yesterday afternoon and evening, May 20, we had as guests Reverend James Crosson and his wife; they visited us at the end of a lecture tour that had taken them

from their new home in Florida to their summer camp in the Berkshires. Reverend Crosson has read Jane's ESP book, helping her publicize it in various ways, contact editors, etc., and we were pleased to meet.

(Yesterday was ESP class night, so the Reverend attended class; a session was held during class, which was recorded; when received a copy will be added to these records. Part of it was addressed to the Reverend and his wife, and was quite successful. Jane also gave impressions on her own for the Crossons, and again these were also successful. The Crossons stayed until about 1:30 AM.

(Reverend Crosson has met many of the leading figures in parapsychology, including Eileen Garrett, Arthur Ford, Martin Ebon, etc. He had many questions for Seth, which that gentleman answered with his usual aplomb.)

Good evening.

("Good evening, Seth."

Now. Yesterday's meeting will have some beneficial results.

Your good reverend was far more impressed after his visit, and he will speak about our work to many others.

(Reverend Crosson took some copies of sessions with him. He also asked Jane to speak to a series of meetings in the Berkshires [in MA] toward the end of June.)

The idea of which you were speaking earlier this evening is a good one, and shows already that you have begun to change habits of thought. Such a venture would also help Ruburt feel that he was holding his own financially in the universe. This would be good for his confidence as well as for the bank account.

(Jane brought up the idea at the supper table: Having the sessions printed up for distribution as a course which could be subscribed to. Advertising, printing, editing, etc., would be involved.)

Now certain changes have occurred within him. If he now uses psycho-cybernetics as applied to his work and to the *(Seth)* book, and makes a definite effort with those methods to focus all of his energy into the book, the symptoms will simply fall away, and quickly. They will dry up. Somewhat earlier his energies were so depleted that it would have been more difficult for him to do this in a rather sweeping manner, and this is what I suggest.

This incidentally is the same as effective prayer. To do all the things that he should do, to put in the writing hours that he should, inspired writing hours, then he must automatically be in good health, you see. By seeing himself doing this and by imagining it vividly, he is taking good health for granted, and this of course is what he must do.

The venture that you spoke of earlier can begin in your minds now. It can be an exciting venture, when this book is finished, and now mental preparations can begin for it. It will be good for Ruburt to throw himself into this. I cannot stress the importance of the suggestions I am giving this evening. He is quite capable now of throwing himself wholeheartedly, with his full passion, into the book, and doing so will automatically release him from the remaining symptoms.

It is fortunate that his most creative periods come in late spring and through into autumn. Have him read this and tell him I said to put it in practice. Your present life is like a book that you are writing. You write it. Your ideas are the words and the chapters. Intelligent use of the imagination, focused use as suggested in psycho-cybernetics and other such methods, provide excellent training. They straighten out the first draft *(humorously)* so that you do not have to do so many revisions.

Now for many reasons your success, both yours and Ruburt's, will come later in your lives than those who achieve it in their young adult years. In other words it is ahead of you. It will be solid however. The nature of your particular achievements has something to do with the period in your life in which they are accomplished.

Creative understanding is necessary. The quality of your achievement demands unusual understanding. Despite the errors that have been made, you did set about to gain the necessary knowledge, and all the episodes in your life have been used in this behalf. Your creative abilities, coming into full flower, will maintain you mightily however until the end of your lives, and serve as the same kind of impetus that usually spurs the very young onward.

The main problems will not be there, unsolved, to rear their heads. Do you understand?

("Yes.")

The ramifications of our work will be far greater than either of you usually imagine. It is only natural that the work which will bring so much to others will also serve you abundantly. Otherwise it would be impossible for you to give it as much time as will later be required.

The work itself will also sustain you both in other ways. When Ruburt's symptoms are a thing of the past you will see how insignificant they were in the overall scheme of your lives. You are far luckier than most. Ruburt has been given abilities. You have been given abilities, both in creative fields.

Our work has given you additional purpose in life. Our work should also show you how to enjoy your life. You have been given the means. You are literally on the threshold. The suggestions I gave to Ruburt this evening are most important. This session is not to be filed and forgotten.

Let him remember that when he is entirely engrossed in discussing our work or explaining it, he hardly knows he has any symptoms at all—this even when his attitudes may not be of the best at any given time.

Few are offered the opportunity to use abilities with which they have been honored, the opportunity to help others, and provided with a purpose in life in one full sweep. This applies to you both.

You may take your break.

(9:40. Jane's trance was deep. She said, "He's here real strong tonight. I can tell, I feel light... I also got the feeling that somebody's been laying down the law..."

(9:48.)

Now. Do not be misled by the simplicity of the suggestions I have given.

They will have powerful effects if followed. They are useless if they are not followed. Ruburt has said this to his students often. Let me remind him to give himself the same advice. *(Long pause.)*

There is no reason now why your main problems should not dissipate. You know what to do and how to do it. *(Long pause.)*

Continue your combined prayer periods. During the time have Ruburt concentrate upon all those other functions of body, organ and mind, that are in excellent condition, quite obviously filled with vitality. This automatically concentrates his attention upon health, which is what you want.

He can think along these lines for example: "Of course I am healthy. I have excellent digestion, a strong heart. I can feel the vitality of the universe as I breathe in and out. How beautifully my body operates, and I do not even have to think of it."

This insures that he does not inadvertently concentrate upon symptoms.

Now this will be a short session unless you have questions, but it will be a very important session if it is not simply filed and forgotten, but followed. I wanted this to be separate, so that it can be read in that manner. You should frame it and put it on the wall.

("Okay." Actually, I made an extra copy of this session so that Jane could pin it up on her bookcase beside her work table, for easy reference.)

Do you have questions?

("No, we'll leave this session just as it is, then.")

We have done well this week. Ruburt's various self-images have just about merged into one good one, and I want him to see this as effective. I have already given him some mental images that will help him, and you gave him some in an earlier discussion this evening.

I bid you then a fond good evening, and I hope you will reap from this session all those benefits that it can bring.

("All right, Seth. Thank you and good night."

(10:00. Attached is a transcript of the ESP class session held last evening, May

20, 1969, for Reverend Crosson and wife. Session typed by student WL.)

ESP CLASS NOTES
MAY 20, 1969

(Reverend James Crosson and wife Muriel, guests.

(Jane introduced Jim as a "rock drummer." His presence was advanced as a possible reason for the quietness of the class.

(Seth:) —and I thought you were on your good behavior because I was here. I will have to learn to be a Reverend Rock Drummer—and, I will keep the beat with you.

Now, I bid you welcome. They are not at their best this evening for you are a minister and they are frightened.

He seems like a very nice gentleman to me. You do not have to be so intimidated

Our Lady from Venice over here is filled with questions that she would ask you. The questions tumble from her mind indeed like heavy blocks. And yet, you have not asked them. He is a good one to answer them for you. And he has answers for them.

Now, we have been sliding along again. Our Lady from Venice has made some progress, for since I spoke to you last, you finally took me to heart. I hoped for <u>more</u> from you. . . and you will surprise yourself. I am speaking to our young merchant from Venice over here.

Our other friend is playing with his crutches...tossing them in the air a bit...practicing a two-step without them. But we need more than that. You have book one of the material. I tell you that that information is practical information. You can put it to use. I am flattered that you pick it up and look at it now and then. You may have it bound in gold or leather and keep it as a keepsake. But it will do you little good unless you use it. You must become more aware of your inner selves.... They are not all <u>that</u> horrible. You still fear, as our Lady of Venice, that there is a cellar door... a cellar door to your mind—to your inner self. And, if you open it, all sorts of demons will emerge. And if there are any angels, the demons will gobble them up before you get to see them. Instead, I tell you, as I have told you before, you are more than you know. And it is up to <u>you</u> to find your own reality. <u>I</u> cannot give it to you. I can point you in the <u>direction</u>... but the <u>experience</u> is personal and the experience is subjective and the journey is one that you must make and that you must make alone. I cannot make it for you. I have my own journeys to make... and detours here. And any problems that you have I have had them... so look at me and know how indestructible you are!

I tell you now—and for the sake of our guests—that death is not sober and it is not death. You simply take a giant step forward. And as my friends know that I will, I will tell you that all vitality rings... and it rings through this frame and it rings through your own frame... and it is lighthearted... and it is joyful... and it knows not sobriety... As you know, it is a lighthearted thing.

Consciousness left to itself is like April left to itself. It is you who project disasters into the month of April... whenever disasters occur. And it is you who project disasters into consciousness when those disasters occur.

I use Ruburt's body with his permission because he is a friend of mine. You use your own bodies... they are the vehicles that you wear. As Ruburt would say, they're the space garments you don in order to dwell upon your earth. They are not you... you use them... use them joyfully and gladly and well but do not identify with them for they are not you. I have used and discarded more bodies than I would desire to count. And had I really died with even one of those bodies, I would not be speaking to you now... and you would not be sitting beside me. For you have also spoken with many tongues. But again, coming here once a week may help you find yourself... it may point you in the right direction... but you will only find yourself when you journey inward. And by journeying inward I do not mean a quick and hasty and apologetic trip to your child memories. I do not mean an attempt to find out why you are frightened of spiders or have boils on your arm. I am speaking of a more extensive journey. And all of you know to what I am referring.  Open up the gates of your consciousness while you sleep! You know you are more than what you refer to as your conscious I. But you should know it through experience! Open up the barriers in your daily lives... step outside of the self that you know—and you will solve your difficulties! You will solve them and you will know that you have done so. You will know that the ability is within yourself and you have used it—then you may hit me over the head with your crutches and I will laugh!

I will let you return to your social discourse.

You may ask me any questions that you like. I do not guarantee that I will answer them all. But I will answer some of them.

([Jim Crosson:] "When we leave the physical body where do we go?")

You go where you want to go. Now. When your ordinary, conscious, waking mind is lulled in like your sleep state, you travel in other dimensions. You are already having experience within those other dimensions. You are preparing your own way. When you die, you go into those ways which you have prepared. There are various periods of training that vary according to the individual.

You must understand the nature of reality before you manipulate within it intelligently and well. In this environment and in physical reality, you are learning...you are supposed to be learning...that your thoughts have reality and that you create the reality that you know. When you leave this dimension, then you concentrate upon the knowledge that you have gained. If you still do not realize that you create the reality that you know, then you return and again you learn to manipulate and again and again you see the results of your own inner reality as you meet it objectified. You teach yourself the lesson until you have learned it. And when you have learned it, then you have begun to learn how to handle the consciousness that is yours intelligently and well. And then you can form images for the benefit of others, and lead them and guide them. And then you can continue, you can continue to enlarge the scope of your understanding and consciousness...and as you do this, you take on a more conscious awareness of your responsibility. And your responsibility is not difficult to understand.

([Jim Crosson:] "What determines the time between reincarnations?")

You. If you are very tired, then you rest. If you are wise, you take time to digest your knowledge and to plan your next life even, you see, as a writer plans his next book. If you have too many ties with this reality and if you are too impatient, and if you have not learned sufficiently, then you may return too quickly.

It is always up to the individual. There is no predestination. And there is no one who tells you what you must do. The answers are within yourself then as the answers are within yourself now.

([Jim Crosson:] "How do you discover those answers for yourself?"

Now, there are many ways ... but only one real way. And the way is to begin the journey, as Ruburt told you, into the nature of your own consciousness for the answers are within you and not out from you... and no one can tell you the answers. Now in one way, each individual will find his own answer... and yet all answers, in another way, are one.

You must try to forget for a period of time each day the self that you think of as yourself ... the adult pretensions, the adult bignesses. You must remember the childhood spontaneity. You must think of the freedom that is within a flower. Now it seems to you that a flower cannot move, and therefore has no freedom. And yet I tell you, you must think about the freedom of a flower.

You must dissociate yourself from the person that you know. Close your eyes. Imagine anything that you like that is pleasant to you. It makes no difference what it is. Then imagine yourself stepping apart from yourself in whatever way you choose. And then imagine that all about you there is another dimension and you need only take one step at a time ... and you will find your answers.

You have only to begin. There is an adventure and it is within you. And there are answers, and they are within you... and you can find them. Now. You have more questions?

([Jim Crosson:] "How do you develop the power of spiritual healing?

You already have the power of spiritual healing. You want to know how to use it. Now you use it whether or not you know that you do. When you think thoughts of peace and vitality, and when you wish a man well, then you help heal him.

Now in order to direct this power consciously, you must again get used to the feeling of your own subjective experience....so that you can tell subjectively when this energy is pouring through you and outward. You can use your imagination and imagine perhaps that you hold an arrow and want to direct it to a proper location. But with practice, there is a subjective knowing that you will recognize and understand. But you use the ability whether you realize you use it or not. You are a healer, whether you realize this or not.

Now. I have some questions. It is more difficult for me to form questions than for me to answer them. My question is this... and you do not need to answer it now. You do not need to answer it at any time, to me.... It is a question for yourself:

Would you not be freer to pursue your work out of the framework with which you are now involved?

([Jim Crosson:] "You mean the church?")

I do indeed. Not the church... but any church. Do not your ideas already leap over the fences and the fields? And do you not already feel hampered within the environment in which you have spent so much time? And are you not only now and even reluctantly .... taking small steps where you would take giant steps? You do not need to answer.

([Jim Crosson:] "Yes, I will answer that. Yes, it is true.")

Your answers to the questions that you gave me will come from within. They will come in an easier fashion if you can free yourself. For you have formed barriers without knowing it... where barriers do not exist.

Now. I will let you return to what I hope is pleasant social discourse.

([Jim Crosson:] "It has been very pleasant.")

I have enjoyed it.

([Jim Crosson:] "So have we. Thank you.

Now, dear friends, you all dwell in the same unlimited dimension....you simply have not opened your eyes to see it. You think that you are blind and so you do not see. The universe in which I dwell is the universe in which all of you dwell. Some of you have better eyesight than others and the vision is not physical. Now. You have done well with theories *(addressing Reverend Crosson)*; Now, I tell you forget them. Forget the self that has the theories...and begin to experience. To do this, follow the directions that I have given, but also get in the habit of looking about you morning, noon and night ... and realizing that there is more within every environment than each small room that you see.

Realize that there are personalities that you cannot see physically, yet they are there. And look positively for them. Realize that there are voices you cannot hear with your physical ears, and listen for them inwardly.

Now. I have been in my many pasts an intellectual gentleman and a frivolous female. And yet I will tell you, that as a frivolous female who loved to play with a ball in the bright afternoon and had no chores to perform, seemingly an idle life and seemingly a quite useless personality .... I was not burdened with intellect... and yet in that one particular life I learned more about the nature of spontaneity and joy than in many of my ponderous intellectual existences.

The trick is not to try too hard, to realize that the answers are available, that they are there, that you can find them. All that is necessary is given to the flower. And all that you want will be given to you, but you must want what you want desperately enough, wholeheartedly enough. An intellectual curiosity will give you some answers but it will not give you the deepest answers.

You must be willing, quite willing; not only willing but anxious to travel in dimensions that you are not acquainted with on an egotistical basis.

And into this reality, you do not go as a grown man with preconceived ideas. You go as a wonderer without preconceptions. And you become acquiescent and the answers are given to you... and to you.... and to you. *[By WL.]*

JANE'S IMPRESSIONS FOR THE CROSSONS
MAY 20, 1969

(Fourteenth-century France ... Riding academy... Saw riding accident by an academy when you were about 14...You were held up, crippled in some way, for a couple of years... You had a brother and the brother was with you at the time of the accident.

(I saw a brick structure... don't know whether or not it was a riding academy... had a very wide entrance... related to the accident mentioned before.

(You had a brief life as twins... Some definite clear-cut divisions within yourself have to do with this life when you were one of two... one going one way, and one the other... One twin had a strong leaning toward military things... a soldier... The organization of the church now serves the same purpose I believe.... security within

the organization... The twin who was in the military found his sense of identity as a soldier within the system, but he had great faith in the system... in what he was doing... The other twin was more given to a statesmanlike sort of thing... and was in fact an orator although he had another profession...It included oration to people... The two of you had a very strong telepathic relationship... and this time the church has provided the same kind of organization... You sort of resented the fact that this twin brother of yours had this organization in which he found support and in which he felt so a part because he was absolutely certain of the aims and goals of the organization and he was a good soldier within it... and at that time you envied him that security and that sense of identity within the system in which he believed. This time the orator part of you is still strong in that you want to teach and like to talk and to discuss issues... but also at the same time you wanted the sense of security that you felt the other brother had... Also you picked up his desire to go to battle for, only in this case you are using battle for ideas that you are struggling for. The other brother was battling for what the organization wanted, and served the organization well... You are now battling the things the organization wants and you feel the division... This division is bringing up memories subconsciously, in this past life where there was this division between you and your brother.

(Greek name... Ostinatious... I am getting also 12 B.C.... This would be his name, not the other twin; that is because he had this telepathic communication with his twin, he has this sense of wanting unity within himself very strongly, at the same time a sense of being divided. A strong inclination to go ahead independently with his ideas, balanced by the desire to find security within the system, and the fear to leave it. His intellectual freedom, he feels, exists only so long as it is cushioned by the feeling of security of the organization... and if he cut loose he would be too panic-stricken to be an independent thinker leading to a dilemma...which you reached just after 30 in this life.... You, Muriel, were the twin brother.) [Typed by WL.]

SESSION 484
MAY 26, 1969 9:10 PM MONDAY

(John Bradley was a witness to the session, and part of the material deals with John's relationship with his employer, Searle. The first part of the session however takes off on various matters Jane, John and I were discussing before session time, and so is unplanned. Remember that Seth's entity name for John is Philip.)

Now, good evening.

([John and I:] "Good evening, Seth.")

And good evening to our friend, our empire builder.

Now when you think of problems such as you have been discussing here this evening, concentrate, Joseph, upon probable solutions, and imagine the solutions that can be worked out. Do not project the problem as it exists, accelerated by future negative developments, for you only add to the difficulties.

Give me a moment. *(Pause.)*

Concerning the overpopulation problem, remember that more than physical mechanisms are involved. The problem will be solved by mankind indeed; but mankind is composed of reincarnational entities. It is quite within the probabilities that the statistics will reverse themselves and that for no reason that scientists can discover, children are born stillborn, as in a mass epidemic, and that entities simply refuse to inhabit the bodies made for them. The bodies then remaining empty to decay unused. *(What a grim situation, I thought.)*

When you think in terms of mankind solving its own problems, remember that reincarnation is involved, and not a group of persons in existence for only a particular time. When the personality is thoroughly ready to leave the body, nothing, including transplants, will keep it within the body. And if personalities refuse to inhabit a new body, then no science will be able to give life to the newly formed but uninhabited body.

Now this is simply a possibility that you have overlooked.

As a matter of fact there has been such a population problem in the past, in your terms, on several occasions and involving your planet. An earthwide epidemic took place on one occasion. On another occasion the number of conceptions was drastically reduced. The women's fear of bearing children alone made them barren when starvation loomed. The third time artificial means were utilized to prevent birth.

("Can you tell us when this was?")

The third time involved Atlantis. The first time I mentioned with the epidemiclike disaster, was 14 centuries after Atlantis. Give us a moment. *(Pause.)* A pre-Inca type civilization.

For many reasons at various periods in your time there has been particular work to be done requiring numbers, a broad stratum, a physical pool, that would serve as a basis for future generations. In many such instances there is a ferment of activity, a birth of new ideas, and an unstructured psychic activity, that is freewheeling and explosive.

It is a period of great activity, telepathic communication, an overcrowding physically, but forces great new developments and a new synthesis, and this is your present situation. *(Humorously:)* It is not difficult for neighbors to understand each other when they live 50 miles apart. When you become overcrowded in severe circumstances, you must learn to understand your neighbor or lose your mind. You are forced to relate.

And so in the present circumstance the overcrowded conditions will still be further accelerated, until a new synthesis is formed—and it will be. The psychic activity engendered will finally form the basis for a greater understanding. It will be quite obvious that telepathic thoughts travel quicker than good news or faster than a pestilence. Man will be so shoved together that the impact will literally explode into a new level of consciousness, a new development in those terms.

Our friend here *(John)* spoke of communications, and their effect upon you. Here you will find an almost instantaneous system of communications. The individual will find himself surrounded by more stimuli than he knows what to do with—but using this as impetus he will learn to handle it, using portions of the brain that now lie latent.

The change will amount to a new kind of consciousness, certainly in quality.

Now you may take your break and we shall continue.

(9:45-10:03.)

Now. If you will forgive me, I will for a moment continue our discussion, or if you prefer monologue.

There have been changes through your ages that have given birth to enlarged or expanded consciousness. The oversaturation of your atmosphere that will be brought about as a result of overpopulation, the increased psychic activity, the greater communications, will have the result further of pressing inward upon the individual until he is forced to find a new way to handle stimuli, and to respond to events.

A concentration will occur. When atoms and molecules are heated certain changes happen. When they are artificially crowded certain changes happen. When they are frozen certain changes happen, and when the psychic atmosphere is saturated there will be a metamorphosis of a kind and a release of abilities that have been latent.

Because of some of mankind's curious characteristics, often it does not change unless his life depends upon it, unless survival is threatened. He will be forced to recognize, use and develop his paranormal abilities simply to survive, and in so doing will release them finally for his own benefit and the benefit of his fellows.

Initially fear will be the impetus. He will want to know what is going on in his neighbor's head so badly that he will realize he already knows. When the transformation is completed mankind will be operating at an entirely different level than you now know.

Now give us a moment, for overpopulated Chicago.

(The following material concerns questions John asked at last break.)

Three men, three we have mentioned in the past. Another man is now ready to move into the third man's place, and there seems to be something somewhat surprising in this movement.

Take this down, and I will try to clear it: S C A R. An initial development, greatly lauded and spoken of, either will not happen or will turn out badly. This may involve policy that seems to be already settled.

A man with glasses and a scar, or a scar connected with the name, is retreating. Either he is getting weaker in position, is stepping out, or is dying. In any case he will be replaced by a man with white or whitish blonde hair—light hair, initially from the Midwest, and he may have an accent. He has heard of John, our Philip here, and met him at a meeting or conference, perhaps in 1964.

Give us a moment. *(Pause.)* Now either there is a woman, or a man with a name like a woman, who will shortly step up and come to Philip's notice, either generally in the same sort of position as Philip, or slightly above.

This person will move quickly upward however, taking Philip's ideas along. Philip has either been offered another job in the immediate past or will be in the very immediate future. The initial M—I am uncertain here. The name Midol *(my phonetic interpretation)* and a connection with an unscrupulous kind of lawyer or associate. In any case definitely the feeling of a treachery involved, not on Philip's part but using Philip.

This is on the sideline: the approach has been made or will be made on a Tuesday. If it has not happened in May then around the fifth of July perhaps.

([John:] "Is this the lawyer you're speaking of?")

There is something about a product that is overestimated, and legal difficulties that will be taken against the company, for which you have been asked or will be asked, to work.

([John:] "Another company I will work for?")

If you have not been asked in the very immediate past, in this month, then you will be asked in the month of June.

([John:] "For a separate company?")

Yes.

([John:] "Would they ask me or would I be expected to approach them?")

Give us a moment. It seems to be something not completely surprising. Either you thought of this or they have thought of you, and some communications, though of an informal nature, may have happened in the past. Read what I have said more clearly, for there is an immediate issue involved.

(After the session John told us that he has informally been approached to work for a rival drug concern—Abbott, recently.)

Now give us a moment. I will shortly give you your break. The name Alice, this is something definite now, 1943, perhaps a classmate. Some items here will come to your attention. You may take your break and we will continue.

(10:25. This proved to be the end of the session. A lengthy discussion ensued, during which John said that a number of items given by Seth seemed to fit in, stating with the three-men data, the Midwest, etc. John said a number of possibilities are applicable here, and that we will have to wait to see how some items work out.

(After the session Jane found herself giving some impressions on her own, again involving John and his company and related personnel. Some of the data was very clear, she said, but she spoke so rapidly I did not take notes. Most of it was precognitive, involving Detroit to some extent and a group of men there; although the data was quite clear to Jane, John could offer little help re interpretation.)

SESSION 485
JUNE 2, 1969 9:18 PM MONDAY

Now, good evening—

("Good evening, Seth.")

—and give us a moment here. *(Long pause.)*

Your friend Leonard's return has changed the environment to some degree. It was his belief, quite simply, that brought about the mowing of the lawn. He is sending constructive telepathic suggestions to the landlady, and they are being received. She is highly suggestible.

(Long pause, one of many, etc.) Some of your own attitudes still escape you. You do not recognize them as negative because they are so familiar that you glide over them. Some of these operated in your reactions over the raising of the rent.

You must remember, once more, that expectations are the blocks with which you build your reality. There are no exceptions to this rule. I merely wanted to point out these matters this evening.

Now. Take any single event or perception. I want you to see what forms an environment. We will take the simple example of the high grass. Most of the people in your house took it for granted that your landlady would not take care of the place. She is highly suggestible. She is also insecure and very on guard against threats of any kind. Her houses represent security to her.

She has accepted the advice of two men in whom she puts great trust. At the same time she is afraid that in several instances their advice has been poor. She dislikes change, and is afraid of it, and does not trust her own judgement. She is upset when she distrusts the judgment of those in whom she has put her trust.

The resentment felt by the tenants was picked up by her, and felt as a threat. If everyone moved out she would have to force the issue with her advisers. Her advisers have told her to raise rents, since they handle her estate and money. She means well enough but in her insecurity she believes them when they tell her that she would be a fool for not raising rents. Money does mean security to her. She has no other and this does play into their hands.

She was very sensitive therefore to telepathic suggestions sent her way by tenants, and felt that they did not like her, highly resented her as the new landlord. When Leonard returned, all unknowingly he sent out constructive thoughts to which she also reacted; but he loved his lawn and his yard, and in his mind's eye he saw it the way he wanted it, clearly, and it did become an event.

The event itself was an interaction of thoughts and emotions and images, a group of communications in which actually many people were involved. She is not a puppet, simply carrying out the telepathic wishes of others. She also has a love of yards and gardens, and a love of beauty, so that Leonard's wish met with fertile ground. *(Humorously.)*

There are points of correspondence you see between people that can be used to set up constructive communications and bring about constructive events. Leonard's planting of the flowers has more than symbolic significance. Now give us a moment.

He ignored what seemed to be a fact of reality, built his own constructive expectations, and made them the reality. He expects good things, and receives them. Now he also gives. At his own level he gives in his relationship with his students, and primarily his turn toward counseling is directed by a desire to help others. There is no one to whom he wishes ill.

Now in his own mind Ruburt has been highly critical of that neighbor, and so have you at times. There is one area you see where he *(Leonard)* is thus far entirely blocked, for he cannot love another person wholeheartedly, nor imagine himself in that position. This lack is always with him, and it is caused by a particular shallow area in his personality that is not developed.

("Who are you talking about here?")

I am speaking now of Leonard. Now your landlady is in somewhat the same position, and it is for this reason also that a corresponding sympathy is set up between them. I am trying to give you some insight into how a seemingly trivial event takes place, how telepathy and expectation enter in. These intertwinings take place all the time, beneath notice. Any physical event is the result of them.

You may take your break.

(9:48. During break Jane and I entered into a discussion that was vehement at times, covering various people, subjects, etc. Jane's trance had been good. Seth finally interrupted us at 10:00.)

Now—if you are ready for me—

("I suppose.")

—I will tell you. First of all there is no need feeling resentful. You knew the rent was going to be raised, and you wanted it raised. You wanted it raised because you were ready to change your environment, but not ready enough to move on your own, without the additional impetus.

You said often enough to yourself: "I'd move if the rent were raised." That is one point. The raise was meant to be used as an aid. Now this does not mean that your landlady knew this, but in a way she did, for all of your intentions were subconsciously taken into consideration when such a decision was made.

Now give us a moment.

Leonard will want to buy a house. When he finds he can afford the rent easily, he will realize he can afford a house easily. Your lawyer wanted to get out of a bad situation in the front apartment, and the increased rent serves his purpose. The woman in the back over the garage, the whole family, is also involved. One daughter is paying the rent. Other members of the family live there some of the time. She wants a smaller place so the family cannot visit overnight. This will give her an excuse shortly to move.

(Note: This session was held on June 2. On June 5 we heard that Leonard was going to contact a real estate agent about buying a house.

(The lawyer's apartment downstairs front presents another problem. According to the above his rent was raised. Today Jane learned that his rent has not been raised, peculiarly enough, as of today, June 5. The lawyer never lived in the apartment, for whatever reasons of his own. Now however he has allowed a friend of ours to move in for the summer. Perhaps time will tell how much rent she ultimately must pay ...)

The two unmarried people on this floor are also involved. Dick wants the young lady to marry him. The high cost of keeping the two apartments will be used by both of them as an issue and excuse. The man on the top floor always feels persecuted: for his own reason she seeks out situations where his feeling is justified.

Now I am giving you an apartment-by-apartment version simply to make my point. The elderly widow fears living alone now, and hopes her children will take her in. She hopes the additional rent will help convince them.

The only person who was more or less entirely neutral in the whole affair was the woman above, who had little to do with any decision. Now this does cover only one issue that you mentioned. Give us a moment.

The landlady chose, unconsciously, houses in which the deeper needs of her tenants would in one way or another correspond with her own. This does not exonerate injustices. Nevertheless the lacks that exist, for example in your landlady, will bring about further lacks, and resentment on your part only hurts you. Does this answer a few of your questions?

("Yes.")

Now I can go into each issue that you mentioned in detail—

("No, that's not necessary.")

—but each event is formed by those involved in it, for their own reasons, and it is foolish to feel resentful because also the situation serves ends of your own that you may not consciously recognize. If you can take this for granted then you will be much more at peace; and beside that you will most likely be much more correct in your overall assessment.

There were also reasons why the same thing happened in the medical line, with the offices. Many of the men involved were imagining how happy they would be in a medical building, and subconsciously hoping for an excuse to move into one. The people drew the landlord then as much as she drew the houses. There is always a give and take. She will discover that without inner security money is no security, and she will discover this without your resentment to help her.

You will say later: "If the rent hadn't been raised we might have been in that place the rest of our days—who knows?" and laugh, but at times you still feared that that might indeed be the case.

Now you may take your break and we will continue.

This material, while it is personal, should give you an excellent example of how ordinary events occur.

(10:18. Jane's trance was, she said, very good. She had been "far-out" again, with little or no memory of what was said. We intended this to be but a break, but once again our own discussions ran so late that this proved to be the end of the session.)

ESP CLASS
JUNE 3, 1969

(Note: The first few words were not recorded. Transcript by WL.)

... to solve your problems and triumph over your challenges.... and the impetus is this: you must not journey into inner reality until you feel secure in physical reality.... for you cannot live in two worlds at once unless you are secure in one. You need a firm groundwork... a groundwork that you can trust. And then you can travel through these other doors, but you must be able to stand on your two feet in this universe.... And then you will go consciously where your body cannot follow... and you will find your answers. But you must have something secure to hang onto. Now there is no better reason to solve your problems.

When you are certain that you feel at least reasonably secure, where you are, then we shall take you to where you are not and you will find yourself. You are already there, but in order to go there, you must start from somewhere. You must start with, you see, a balance and a degree of security.... You must start with confidence. And if you travel too quickly and too far, you will not have confidence, for in the back of your mind you will think: if I do not feel secure in physical reality, then why should I feel secure here... and you will not have the daring that is necessary, nor will you have the peace of mind... and the peace of mind is the key to the door.

So when you are on the way to solving your situation here, I will give you some new ones to solve... and I will give you a push along the way, and you can count on it... and you can count on it when you tell me that you are making true progress here. Then I will give you a gigantic push.

(The above was addressed to WL. WL's recorder failed to record a part of the above, and in ascertaining what portion was missed, a short burst of singing emanated from the recorder's previously used tape. Seth reappeared and said the following:

If I could sing that beautifully, I would sing for you through our classes. Now I wish you *(DM)* a bon voyage. And I did not mean to hurt your *(class)* feelings; far be it from me to hurt your feelings when you hurt your own so well you do not need help from me. I will have a message for you *(VMcC)* through our friend Ruburt shortly in any case. I simply wanted you to know that I was here and I did have a specific message that I wanted to deliver to our friend *(WL)* on this side. And if you do not have the words recorded, they are recorded there *(pointing to WL's head)* and you will not forget them. And when I make promises I make promises and I keep them. And when I say I will give a "push" at a certain time, I will give a fine push... though then you may not need it. I've come through this evening in any case simply as a friend. I wish you all well. I am not going to keep you until two o'clock in your morning. Some evening I will keep you until two o'clock in the morning just so you can say that I have done it. But you would not bless me the following morning... of that I am sure.

(At this point, Tom said, " I am in good shape tonight, Seth, I'm ready.")

Now, indeed you are. And... as a piece or chunk of physical matter... you are indeed immediate and here. You do not understand the ways in which you project the physical matter of yourself into this room, however. When you understand that completely and fully, you will no longer be within physical reality. But that is of little notice. You will never notice the difference. In any reality, you create the image that you see. And the reality that follows this one will seem as physical to you as this... and as real. But you will have freedoms within it that you do not have now.... Not unless at 8 o'clock in the morning you leap from the rooftops and fly through the windows to your death.

You can do things with the inner image that you cannot do with the physical image. But while you are doing them, they appear physical. Do you follow me?

Now. In this existence, when you see a picture in your mind, and when there is strong emotion and vivid desire behind it, it will be constructed. There will be a time lapse within this system, but in other systems there may be no time lapse... and your thought may be instantly transposed into reality. Therefore, now you must learn the nature of your thoughts and how to handle energy.

([Tom:] "Because now we have time to do it.")

Indeed.

([Tom:] "But between the time of thinking about it now and the time it becomes a reality, other thoughts can come to bear on that idea and change it before it becomes a reality. Is that so?")

Then the ideas merge.

([Tom:] "I see, and form a compromise... composite.")

Now as a compromise, but not as a composite. I will leave you, but I will give you more information on that topic the next time we meet. And I will keep my eye on you *(DMC)*, but I will not bear tales.

(Summary for Jane:

([Tom:] "He talked some more about physical matter... an elaboration on the things we've talked about during the evening. The reality on another plane or in another dimension is just as physical as what we experience as physical here... just as real, seems physical to them. But the freedoms are greater, so that when we think of something on another plane, it happens instantaneously. Whereas here, there is a time lag between the time we think of something and it results in a created action or object. In the time lag on this plane, there are other thoughts, projections on the same idea or object; Seth declined to go into their effects on the final idea or object until a later time.

("By our projecting our thoughts to this finished product, we can influence our

health, our future, our position, etc. We should picture ourselves as being in a state of good health. Now I would assume that this same thing applies to a station or vocation...")

But never as a finished product. For a state of health is not an end product.... or an unchanging station in those terms. It is the ability to effectively handle energy in a constructive way for your own benefit and the benefit of others. The state of health is a poor term. You should indeed imagine yourself, therefore, able to handle your energy effectively for your own good and the good of others; to imagine yourself as a channel through which the creativity of the universe can express itself. For when you harbor negative ideas and resentments, then indeed you set up a block and the block causes distortions. Now you call them illnesses in many instances. They are distortions. The energy is being distorted and misused and misshapen.

([Tom:] "But to want good health or position just for the sake of that is not the end of the line. That, you are saying, is just the beginning of...")

It is a beginning, and health is not a static state in any case...

([Tom:] "We should desire good health because it makes it possible for us to do something else... to serve or perform some other role...

You should desire good health because it is a natural state of your being. You should trust in the innate intelligence of your own being... which produces good health. Health is a natural state of your being. Through your physical image the energy of the universe expresses itself. You as an individualized consciousness are a part of this, and you cannot express yourself fully nor fulfill your purpose as an identity, as an individual, if you are not in good health... for the effects of the body are felt in the mind... and the effects of the mind are felt in the body. You distort the picture. Now I did not intend a question and answer service this evening, but I seem to be involved in one. And some evening I will turn the tables. And when I ask you questions, I will expect some answers. And they will not be easy questions... and they will not be general questions. And I will make you search for the answers... and the answers will form steps upon which you can walk and will serve as foundations within which you can travel within yourselves. But they will be your answers and not my answers.

([Tom:] "Now it has been suggested that the next time I go to New York I might see a man...")

It is indeed possible!

([Tom:] "But the point is... I guess the question I'm asking is: am I really more interested in the certain possibilities of status, and that would not be the positive way of looking at things... or should I be seeing that man within a framework of, just as we were talking about health as just being a stepping stone, should I be seeing this

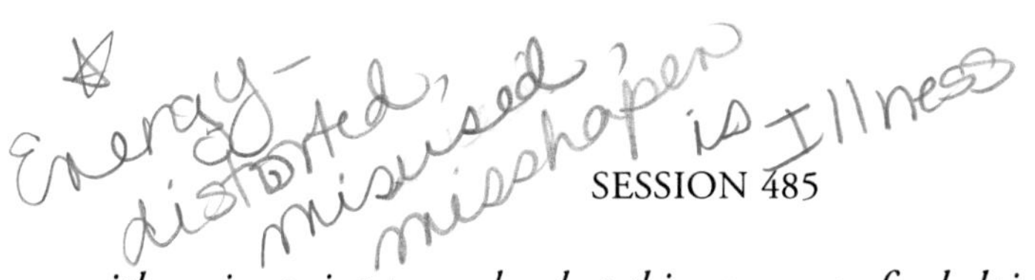

man with a viewpoint towards what this can mean for helping other people be part of a constructive arrangement?")

You have answered your own question. Your latter statement applies.

Now I will bid you a fond good evening... particularly to our merchant from Venice who is going to travel afar.

There are other ways to travel, and we will see that you learn of them. There are other fascinations and foreign countries upon your planet, but it is good that you learn of those also. We will get you used to the idea of foreign lands and then we will teach you to travel into lands that are really foreign.... And we will give you an idea of the vocabulary used... and it will not be as simple as "Good Morning" and "Good Evening" or "Where can I find a can of beans?"

(Pause. [Tom:] "My interpretation of what he said is that (1) good health is a natural part of ourselves, and so we should naturally desire it, and (2) good health in itself is not the objective at all. It is what you can do when you are in a state of good health. We carried it into another dimension besides health... vocational aspects. We project ourselves ahead mentally to vocational status we are interested in, and by doing that, accomplish it. It is not the status itself that is the end. It is what we are able to do through it, that we should really be aiming at.

([Dave:] "Tom made the analogy of health vs. occupation. His implication was that the product of good health was the ability to do good more efficiently. Taking it over into occupations, then, I don't know how it would be ... advances an occupation, I guess is the closest.

([Tom:] "...Choice or advancement ... and advancement maybe.

Now I am going to leave you. However, I want to clear up an issue. If you are in poor health, this does not mean that you are an evil person. It means that you have a block in that particular area... in which you are unable to utilize energy constructively. And if you are not at the top of your profession, the same thing applies. It does not follow that those in excellent health are more blessed than others. It does mean that in that particular area they are able to utilize energy more effectively.

And theoretically, theoretically, if you are using energy the way you should, you would indeed be at the top of your profession and in excellent health and filled with abundance. Now various kinds of lacks can show up in many ways... in mental deficiencies... A man or a woman who has strong and definite mental deficiencies... who has strong negative habits... such a person has blocks in those areas. You may not attain perfection... I have not attained it. But it is the ideal toward which we work.

I do not want you to have the attitude, however, or make the implication, that your health or status in any way automatically, and alone, is an indication of your spiritual wealth... or lack of it.

Some of you for example, do well in certain areas and are blocked in others. We want to get rid of the blocks. You are working toward this ideal, and the ideal is—and you will achieve it—to use all your abilities, all of your capabilities... and in doing this, you will help others automatically. And you will help the race of which you are a part. And you will add to the creativity of All That Is ... and I said that you would add to it. This is for you, for the anticipated argument that you will think of. *(To VMcC.)*

And now I do wish you a fond good evening. And store up your questions... and store up your answers... for I will grade you!

You have been involved in this examination for many years!

SESSION 486
JUNE 9, 1969 9:26 PM MONDAY

Good evening.

("Good evening, Seth.")

Now. Before I launch into a discussion on another matter, let me remind you that you can also make the error of concentrating upon Ruburt's symptoms, and ignoring improvements, and this does not help him.

Make sure that you do not project any negative attitudes toward other issues into the situation. You can see when Ruburt does this, so do not do it yourself. And your prayer sessions have helped you, as I have told you.

Warm encouragement are the key words. Now give us a moment.

I have told you that portions of your personality exist in other realities. Other portions of the self are focused within different dimensions than you own. If you can, imagine a huge building with many rooms, each room entirely different from the other. The environment, the methods of perception, the reality system within each room is unique.

The building shares some common passageways, however, as well as a common cellar and attic... There are devices within each room that enable a dweller in one room to communicate with those in other rooms. But the guests are so engrossed by the wonders of their own quarters within this strange hotel that many of them do little investigating.

Sometimes in their sleep they sleepwalk and come upon the passageways, and meet, but in the morning they do not remember. Now their maintenance is provided for. The hotel is beautifully equipped, and all pains are taken to insure their comfort and survival. Each guest has a peculiar and unique uniform, suitable for his own room environment, and no other. And every care is taken that it is kept in good repair.

Each room of course is so arranged that it has within it the illusion of many rooms. He is given tasks and each room, again, has been planned so that within it all methods of learning are available that the guest will need to perform his task. On our rather bulky analogy the guests are all portions of the inner self, who is the unseen attendant who maintains the building.

Now it is often difficult to see yourself clearly, and your situation, because you seem so close to it. It is quite possible however when you know how to use one of these passageways and look at yourself and your situation from a different viewpoint, to see it in greater perspective and from outside your particular room—to see it perhaps more clearly in its entirety.

You can do this quite alone. It is easier however if you have the help of one of the guests in another room who is more used to the passageways, someone who has been investigating a while longer.

Following our analogy, you will be his guest and from his rooms look down into your own with some greater objectivity. This is possible, feasible, since you are all portions, in our analogy, of this same inner self who maintains all of the rooms. While each of you are egotistically focused within your own reality, the deeper layers of the self are aware of the quote "family" relationship. Now give me a moment. *(Pause.)*

There is another portion of your whole inner self, another more advanced. I mentioned earlier that in one probability system you were a doctor who painted as a hobby. His name is P I E T R A. *(Spelled out.)* In psychological time or simply when you are still, close your eyes and imagine your physical universe as one room in our analogy, and his as another with a passageway between. Tell yourself that you would like to travel through that passageway, and that he will be there to help you do so.

You may be interested in hearing some information about him, for he is working with art, painting, in terms of therapy. He is not only working with patients and using art as a therapy for them, not only having them paint as therapy, you see, but he is also working on the idea that some paintings in themselves have a healing effect.

All of his interest in painting is used as a supplement to his interest in medicine. Certain paintings can capture the psychic energy of others, and certain paintings can release the psychic abilities and healing abilities of the viewer. The painter's intent is embedded in his medium and in his painting.

Not only this however, but certain colors as you know have their own soothing or inflaming qualities. Now. I have told you something about this other portion of yourself so that you will be able to relate to him and see how your interests merge. Think of him when you are thinking of the room and the passageway and ask that you meet him there.

He is a man of some psychological insights also, and he is like you enough so that he can understand many of your attitudes easily, and unlike you enough so that he can see you much more clearly. You should be able to go with him, and from his vantage point observe your own reality and situation, to see you and Ruburt and your lives for yourself from this different vantage point. You should find it exciting and most instructive.

Are your fingers tired?

("No.")

You may take a break if you prefer.

This other portion of yourself will also view his reality from your vantage point, and your ideas will stimulate his own, and both of you will gain from the encounter.

Now there is no reason why this cannot be conscious on your part, although portions may take place in the dream state. He will also be able to help you in the use of healing energy. Some few encounters may occur in which he shows you the various ways that paintings can also be used as healing agents.

I repeat: some of this can be conscious, if you use a psychological-time framework. You should be able to see him rather clearly. In his reality he is embarking upon a series of experiments that will lead him to you, if he proceeds properly.

Now you may take your break and we shall continue.

(10:01. Jane was out of trance quickly. Yet she said the trance had been quite deep, and also—unusually—she could remember what she had said. She'd had an image of a "huge building with many rooms."

(My father had a brother, Ernest, who died a bachelor in Florida quite a few years ago . At break now Jane told me she had a "flash" that my "Uncle Ernie was, or would have been, the son that Dr. Pietra would have in this reality."

(Jane said she had an image, an amusing but quite clear one, of a large arrow arching south over the continent toward Florida, so as to emphasize that location in relation to Uncle Ernie.

(I told Jane that I had been tempted to ask Seth if I had ever painted a picture of Dr. Pietra. Resume at 10:13.)

Now. You will model for each other, and as you see him in your studio, so he will see you in his.

His experiments involve drugs of much greater precision and stability than any that are known in your environment. The drugs enable him to isolate certain portions of himself, of his psyche, and to send the isolated portions on journeys of investigation.

The drugs not only help him but they also have the effect of emphasizing his presence on his journeys, of concentrating his essence, isolating and focusing those portions of his psyche. Therefore they will help make him more observable in sense terms to you.

You must be looking for him however. He knows of your hypothetical existence. He believes he has such a probable self, and is endeavoring to visit this probable universe. He has no idea however that you might be told of his visits, or that you might be planning to meet him. He has been working on the drug himself along with two others.

He will be perfectly able to manipulate in his own system while he is gone. Your state of mind and the receptivity will be communicated to him and serve as a beckoning area that he will recognize. The sympathetic, and to some degree similar, aspects of your personalities serve to open up clear channels between you. The passageway you see is of course not physical, and yet molecular structure is to some extent involved.

Now Ruburt was correct in the impression he gave during your break, and this other portion of your personality also has a sister. Give us a moment.

You should see him visually either entirely objectified, or in an unusually vivid inner image. But more than this there should be an inner word communication between you that will actually be of telepathic origin. He is also visually oriented you understand.

He may be able to show you images from his own reality. He should be able to take you there in a projection, and from that point you should be able to look down into your own system, and in a series of flashes to see your life and Ruburt's with greater clarity.

I gave you this information this evening because he is experimenting now. I believe that within seven hours he will be within your environment, whether or not you perceive him.

The drug may have the effect of coloring his image, so do not be surprised at such an occurrence—a yellow or purplish tinge. For various reasons we will not discuss this evening the experiments being conducted now over a period of some weeks, and they will not be tried again until your autumn. This has to do however with the conductivity of cell structures and your particular atmosphere during these periods.

Now you may end the session or take a break as you prefer.

("We'll take a break."

(10:31. Again Jane's trance was deep; this time she was really out, she said, and remembered nothing until tile last line of the data.

(This session was held on Monday, June 9, 1969. It is now Friday, June 13 as I finish typing up this session. So far neither Jane nor I have in any way perceived Dr. Pietra, or had any kind of experience that we would connect with him or this data. This includes our use of suggestion and psy-time each day since Monday. The initial 7-hour period mentioned by Seth would have placed Dr. Pietra within our environment early on the morning of June 10, perhaps an hour before our usual rising time. Jane and I gave ourselves suggestions that we would perceive Dr. P at that time, but nothing developed.

(10:40.)

Now. There is as I mentioned some natural sympathy between you.

There, is also a loose correspondence in the ways (underlined) that you use your cellular structure and utilize energy. He is working from the medical principles you see. This is a very loose analogy, but he is hoping to shoot himself toward you like an arrow, hoping that those correspondences that he suspects will help draw him to you. He has made some errors, and your receptive state of mind will give him more leeway.

The receptivity is of a creative nature, you understand as if you were clearing land so that a primitive airplane could land, or setting a beacon in a window. In other words your state of mind can help guide him to you, much to his surprise and delight and gratitude, for he did not count on that boost.

Your own abilities are quite adequate, with his knowledge, to enable you to project to his reality with his help. He has no idea that such a thing can be done without the use of drugs.

Now Ruburt may be able to see him.

Unless you have questions we shall end the session. But read my suggestions over well, so that you are prepared.

("Yes.")

The class tomorrow night might be of benefit because of the focusing of energy, although it is possible that you will encounter him earlier. Do you have questions?

("No, they can wait." Actually I had many.)

I give you then my heartiest good wishes and a fond good evening—and take heed of the very early suggestions given at the very beginning of the session.

("Okay.")

He may have a friend with him.

("Good night, Seth."

(10:52. Jane outlined the content of this session to her ESP class on Tuesday

evening, June 10, and a focusing of energy was tried re Dr Pietra, without result as far as we know.)

SESSION 487
JUNE 16, 1969 9:09 PM MONDAY

Good evening.

("Good evening, Seth.")

Now. On two occasions since our last session *(June 9)*, near contact was made. *(With my probable self and Dr. Pietra in another more advanced reality.)* What happened was a very momentary merging on deeper-than-conscious levels.

Neither of you knew how to handle it. You were afraid of blurring your own identities, and were rather frightened by some of the similarities within them. It was the similarities however that made even that contact possible. Give me a moment here.

(Pause.) It was a time when your inner thoughts veered off at a tangent from their familiar ways. I believe you had an image of the inside portion of a human body, or a thought having to do with inner organs. This happened as you picked up on a deep level the presence of your probable self.

(This is possible. As an artist painting human figures, I am often concerned with anatomy, though usually of the head and features. I don't recall any strong inner image of the interior of a body, but at the same time I know I have thought of this recently.)

Fuller contact is still possible. Even during the experiment he is not here for example all of the time. His focus is not certain, and the intensity of his presence varies. You could sit quietly. Automatic sketching might facilitate contact.

His controls are not good. He is actually between various probable systems, in which however each of you have an interest. It is as if you were, say, distant cousins. Oddly enough your neighborhood, with a rather high saturation of doctors, is a help here. Perhaps I should mention that in your terms (underlined) he is an older man.

He has more time for such experiments now than he did when he was younger. This particular probable system, generally speaking, exists within the same space framework as your own. Now you know of positive and negative matter. There are also other kinds of matter forming other systems of reality, invisible to your eyes, as is negative matter.

There are in fact infinite varieties of matter, existing in what you would call (underlined) one space framework. Using the physical senses, you can of course never perceive the existence of these other systems. Advanced training with the inner senses can lead to such explorations however. Your friend is more advanced—his system is more advanced than yours in this respect.

Give us a moment. In the same way that thoughts can be sent through space, so individual consciousness can be sent through systems, using various methods. As a seed can fly through the air enclosed in a sheath, you see, so can individual consciousness travel through systems. But it must be protected. Certain drugs can protect it.

Now they are like time capsules, cutting down stimuli for certain intervals, and then injecting stimulants as destination points are reached. The process is highly involved. The injections are made into the physical being, affecting therefore the physical brain. Consciousness projects in an out of body experience. The physical brain is cushioned against shock because in this case consciousness travels at such a fast pace that ordinarily contact between it and the body would be severed.

Certain injections, given to the brain, actually help consciousness outside of the brain, and act as nourishment. This is simply one way that is being used however. You may take your break and we shall continue.

(9:38. During break I told Jane I had a couple of questions for Seth, but would wait to ask them until he said all right. Resume at 9:43.)

Now. The drug allows for regulated periods of highly intensified consciousness, operating at peak levels, with all of the mental faculties accelerated. Between these periods however there are periods of unconsciousness. These are of a protective nature. During the periods of unconsciousness the drugs injected into the brain give increased nourishment to those areas of the physical brain that are involved in such ejections of consciousness. Therefore even though your probable self is within reaching distance, so to speak, he is sometimes involved in such blackout-nourishment periods.

In your time the periods of high conscious activity would run approximately for three days, followed by a day and a half to four days of inactivity, according to the circumstances. This involves a transfer of conscious energy from a home system to an alien one, and certain more or less automatic changes must be made from system to system, involving the use of brain waves; certain patterns being normal in different systems. There are other brain patterns for example than those discovered by your scientists. The brain patterns simply reflect the kind of mental or psychic activity, and other kinds of activity will give you different patterns.

The drugs also help in changing the patterns when it is necessary. If the brain patterns were not changed on entering and leaving a system, then theoretically at least the consciousness could become trapped within any given system. Acceleration or de-acceleration, you see, but mentally. *(Decelaration.)*

The drugs also insure that consciousness will not come back to the physical brain too quickly, to shock the system. There are methods by which the relative behavior and condition of the travelling consciousness is monitored at the other end. In case of any severe dangers the consciousness will be pulled back, but this is highly dangerous.

In this case the sleep-nourishment period is activated as a cushion. There have been no such difficulties however in the case of your probable self. Now, you may try to range about, as you have before sleep. Thinking of medical drawings you have done may be of benefit.

Now, what are your questions?

("I'd like to know what's been going on with Jane and her teeth.")

Give us a moment. *(Pause.)* Nothing new. Originally he set a rather massive assault upon his physical system, that did involve among other things, infection. Literally he was infected by negative ideas. As he rids himself of these he rids himself of infections. The words used make little difference.

("This is what the dentist noticed?")

Had the man seen Ruburt's mouth two years ago he would have been outraged, and told Ruburt he would not have a tooth left in his head by now. And Ruburt most likely would have reacted to the suggestion.

("Should Jane go back to the dentist?")

It makes no difference whether or not he does. Give us a moment. *(Long pause.)* I do not suggest that he has any work done at this time. If he wants to learn the nature of his X-rays he can call. Have him remember to relax the jaw.

Negative thoughts running rampant do cause infections. Negative suggestions however can also keep them going. I suggest that Ruburt concentrate as much as possible on his work, even in his psycho-cybernetics exercises.

Did you have other questions?

(I hesitated. "Well, I don't want to use negative suggestion, or ask this the wrong way; but I was wondering what Jane's symptoms would be called medically.")

I would prefer not to answer that the way you have asked it.

("What happened in Sayre yesterday?")

Ruburt has a good idea of that from his work with the pendulum.

("Okay." Sayre, PA is my home town, 15 miles from Elmira, NY.)

We will give you more on some of these issues at another time.

("All right."

(10:08. Jane's trance was good, but she was aware of the questions I asked. I

hadn't told her beforehand I planned to ask them. I explained that I thought the information could be helpful in answering questions other people come up with occasionally; giving Jane something to use as a guide, etc.

(Resume at 10:15.)

Now. There are groups of symptoms which are given names. The names help physicians to categorize and treat, but the names are also dangerous when they are used as labels.

The body is always in a state of changing. By labeling a group of symptoms you add to their idea of permanence, and give a name to certain aspects of bodily activity, distinguishing them from other activities and therefore giving them rather dangerous focus. They are seen as apart from other bodily activities and gain prominence.

If a doctor tells you you have a particular disease and names it, then tells you he has something to cure it, your belief may cure it. Do you follow me?

("Yes.")

If however his treatment involves drugs, these may further upset the inner processes, causing further imbalances. These imbalances may be labeled with a name also. Ruburt's symptoms would therefore be called arthritic, since they fit into that category, so named. To concentrate upon the term however is dangerous, for it gives a specific identity or implies a state of permanence to a group of varying and impermanent symptoms.

States of mind are not permanent. Their reflections upon the system are not permanent, generally speaking, though they can be cumulative. It is much easier to pass through such periods if names are not given to symptoms, and many people pass through many so-called diseases without ever being aware of it.

The label often helps the individual adopt the position or role of a "sick person", in quotes, rather than of a well person momentarily indisposed. This should answer more deeply the questions that you asked me.

("Yes. How's John Pitre's wife?")

There has been a momentary brightening that will I am afraid be followed by darkness. I believe a period of six months is involved here.

("Is Dr. Pietra active at the moment?")

He is.

("I'm still trying to contact him consciously. Do you think he'll be around tonight?")

Give us a moment, please. Now there is an exaggerated fear on Ruburt's part of the word arthritic, for in his mind it is connected with his mother's chronic state. He should understand it does not have this meaning to other people necessarily. He feels threatened by the term. *(Long pause.)* It's being used in the context it was, in your parent's home and under those circumstances, was unfortunate.

On the other hand he did take steps to free himself. The other negative suggestions involving health, given during the entire afternoon and evening, contributed. The effects however were highly reduced from what they would have been in the past.

Now you may take a break, ask questions or end the session as you prefer.

("I guess we'll end it then.")

I give you my fondest good wishes, and a hearty good evening.

("Good night Seth and thank you.")

You might try right after noon tomorrow for contact also.

One further note. Your apartment hunting had a favorable effect, simply because of the complete change of focus and the swinging of energies into a different area.

Any new venture of course or interest serves the same purpose, as will your vacation or any endeavor or pursuit that captures Ruburt's attention. Energy is automatically drawn away from negative areas and from the symptoms.

(End at 10:39. Jane was far out, she said.

(I had no luck in trying to contact Dr. Pietra the next day, etc.)

SESSION 488
JUNE 18, 1969 9:35 PM WEDNESDAY

Good evening.

("Good evening, Seth.")

Now. Give us a moment.

Ruburt is attempting to rid himself of poor habits of years' duration. He is progressing. Certain incidents, trivial in themselves, will at times carry a tremendous charge, not necessarily because he is repressing thoughts about the particular incident, but because the incident recalls unresolved past issues that he has psychically associated with it.

He pulls out part of the thorn but not all of it, working with the pendulum, in some cases. When the symptom hangs on this is usually the case. The general overall condition of his body represents his general state of inner health. Specific complaints represent usually local reactions brought about by a current problem or current incident.

If the local symptom does not disappear or subside within a day, then there are hidden or repressed elements connected with it, to which he is still reacting. Give us a moment.

I mentioned earlier that strong focus of activity in other areas is of benefit. Your apartment hunting, because of its novelty, and his interest in decoration and arrangement, stirred his imagination in new way so took energy away from symptoms. He imaginatively arranged you and your household in each new apartment he saw. This added to his inner sense of mobility.

Such activities, and you can think of others—I am simply using this as an example—are therapeutic, even though it may seem that they are beside the issue. They automatically sweep his consciousness into other areas of activity, away from issues to which he may have been sensitized in the past, and serve to give him a breathing spell and refreshment.

You saw for example the therapeutic effect of your brief shopping trip to the mall, and the overwhelming effect of a simple emotion like laughter and different surroundings, to break up a difficult depression. Your vacation plans can serve in the same manner. Different environments simply give consciousness some new material to nibble on.

This allows the inner self to work much more quickly and effectively. You can trick normal consciousness quite easily with baubles, take its attention into other areas so that the inner self is left alone to do its work. Now give us a moment.

It may seem that response to a particular episode is out of all proportion in intensity, but attached to it may be past material which does carry a heavy charge. Now Ruburt can learn to use his subjective feeling also as an aid in this manner. He should not identify with it to begin with. It would help him if he could imagine it as having a shape or form, or a weight.

He is in possession of it. He has this mood. Say it is a mood of defeat. He should realize that he is not defeated but that he has a mood of defeat. See it as a form, then as you work with the pendulum close the eyes and see whether the form or the shape is disappearing. The image idea here will be an added reinforcement and help.

When this is working well the emotion will diminish as the image fades; an episode such as this latest one should be considered as a local condition, and not exaggerated. He has had an intensified condition in the knee, and it should be considered in this light, using the methods given.

The jump from a local condition to a statement like "I am a mess," should be avoided. An inclination to project a local symptom on the body in general—do you follow me?—is very poor, and takes focus away from very definite advances which go unnoticed.

When the knee is bad, today for example, the tendency is to focus upon it, and the difficulties involved, and to ignore entirely the other portions of the body which are not affected. Then in the overall he sees himself in his terms generally as a mess. The attitude should be: "This area is affected, why? We can find out."

The points of sensitivity are diminishing. This he often forgets. Now you may take a break and we will continue.

(10:00-10:10.)

Now. I have another suggestion.

When Ruburt is in good spirits and physical condition, at the end of the day let him note down, briefly, what he has been doing and thinking about. Let him use those days as models, the focus of attention being upon them rather than upon the poor days. The idea being to reproduce those daily activities and thoughts that naturally reinforce his strengths. He should not overanalyze, but generally speaking keep such days in mind as models to follow.

The twenty minutes of psycho-cybernetics should be particularly maintained when he is not feeling well, for in themselves they help him change his mood and give a breathing spell. Often on the days when he needs this exercise most he dispenses with it. As a part of his routine it is an excellent automatic way of mental reconditioning. Now do you have questions?

("No, I guess not. I'll wait.")

Give us a moment. There are three days left during which communication is most likely between you and your probable self. He is aware now of your existence, rather than only your probable existence.

(As of June 24, 1969, I have had no success communicating with Dr. Pietra on a conscious basis. This session was held on June 18.)

He is himself trying to make contact after finally discovering where you were. There are some problems here we have not discussed that are rather involved in having to do with time relationships. He may make contact with you in his now during this visit, but this may not be known by you or experienced by you until some time in your future.

He is aware of this, but you are real to him in all of your Robert Butts time periods. From his vantage point it is a matter of when contact can best be made. He does not realize you do not perceive yourself as one in these separate time intervals. He realizes this about himself but he has not taken it into consideration in his calculations.

I will let you know very shortly what is happening if <u>you</u> are not aware yourself of contact. Conceivably he could make contact with you in the past, and you would have forgotten, but this is not the case. Although both of your realities are physical ones, the environments are entirely different. The forms you make out of matter are only generally similar. His consciousness has been perceiving this sort of unfamiliar environment with some awe. *(Meaning our own.)*

The medicinal possibilities take up his interest. He intends to communicate with you again, and I would say that in your time this would occur at approximately three o'clock tomorrow morning.

("Will I know it?")

We hope that you will. *(I didn't.)* I suggest that you give instructions to the effect that a portion of you will remain alert in sleep to such an encounter. Give us a moment. There may be a change of air pressure in the room that could alert you. Most probably it would be a telepathic communication, but he may touch you, to see if you feel physical to him. He will only appear in apparition form. The true stuff or material of his body of course will not be here, since its kind of matter cannot exist within your own, that is within your own system.

It is quite possible for you to see his apparitional form.

(I have been trying without success, daily.

("Is he humanoid in our terms?")

The answer would be yes. There is a difference in your terms of skin color, his being of a purplelike cast. As they age in their system incidentally the skin turns grayish. I do not know precisely how to explain this: the atoms of their matter weigh more than yours do.

You may take a break, ask questions, or end the session as you prefer.

("We'll take the break."

(10:24-10:45.)

Now. We will shortly close our session. A few added remarks however.

If a specific local symptom arises, it will help if Ruburt says to himself: "Of course I know the reason for this; it will come to me as I go about my work." Simply that attitude would bring about an improvement. His attitude is often: "Now what in God's name caused this?"

He overestimates the difficulty of finding the causes, and this prolongs the process. He should not overwork with the pendulum. In one day, often, he stirs up many issues without getting to the bottom of any given one. It is highly important that both of you remember the gains. He is working well now, and this was at one time a major issue.

His spontaneity is being released in his writing. The deep depressions have largely vanished. Only echoes remain. The hands have regained some considerable strength. The feet are greatly improved. Other symptoms have entirely disappeared, so that he has almost forgotten them. Now he must remind himself, and so should you, of the progress made, particularly on poor days.

He should also imagine the future when present symptoms have vanished like the others. Anything but projecting them into the future. You can help him by reminding him of improvements and saying something like: "You used to worry just as much about your—say—feet, and they are fine now." But remind him of gains. At least keep the gains in your own mind. It may be better not to mention specific past symptoms, while still dwelling on the improved condition. Do you follow me?

("Yes." This is the method I try to use.)

Now do you have questions?

("No.")

We will then end the session. My heartiest wishes to you both. The idea behind the psycho-cybernetics exercises is that in the future such thinking will become automatic.

He has automatically changed many areas of thought over the past year. These are changed for good. And a fond good evening.

("Good night, Seth."

(11:00.)

SESSION 489
JUNE 23, 1969 9:10 PM MONDAY

(Seth's entity, who is nameless in our terms, spoke this evening, rather than Seth. See the 464th session for February 10, 1969; this is the last time this entity spoke to us. Seth's entity hasn't spoken many times; the 464th session and earlier ones contain detailed notes as to the manner of speaking used by the entity, etc.

(At 9:09 Jane told me that for the first time in a long time she felt like "the other personality," meaning Seth's entity. She looked up, then said she felt the subjective pyramid above her head. Waiting, she began to move her lips silently, as though forming words. Her eyes closed and remained so until break. She sat upright in the rocker with her hands clasped in her lap.

(Her pace was good. The session began with no greeting, as usual. The voice was very high, thin, formal, quite distant, and quite faint when contrasted against Seth's delivery. The windows were open to the sound of traffic close by; this made hearing this faint voice difficult at times.)

You do not understand the diversity of life-forms within your own reality. Their scope escapes you. You perceive them stuck like living specimens on the glass of present time, with no comprehension of their multitudinous expression elsewhere.

Even physically you have not categorized all of the life-forms, and there are many co-inhabiting your system that you will never physically perceive. You do not understand the multiple reality of your own thoughts or thought forms, and you are not able to follow them out of your own mental home.

The multiplicitude of your own system is but one small example of the infinite realities that exist outside it. The gradations in physical matter forms alone escape your scientists. That matter exists in other forms is scarcely understood. There are gradations in matter as there are gradations in your color, realities that blend one into the other, and probable systems in which various representations, reflections, shadows and echoes, all probable creations of any given self, mature.

They are all interwoven and yet separate, and if you look closely at your own physical universe you will see that here also matter is interbound with matter. You see but one form of matter. There are diversities within each system as there are diversities within your own, that are chemical universes where thoughts are patterned in ways that would be incomprehensible to you.

There are frameworks so tenuous and so divorced from your concept of reality you would ignore them, and yet they are richer and more varied than your own. If these universes were not interwoven then we would have no communication, but each has a mirror in each, and one reaches out to all the others, and I speak a million words to you for each one you hear.

You are a part of other systems that you do not know, and dreaming portions of your processes exist as thoroughly in other systems as your physical body dwells in this one.

You could not consciously handle these existences with one mind, as you think of mind, segmented. Your self exists in various compartments, and while all are one, you could not now bear an opening of the doors between.

Ours is the voice that whispers through the corridors. The very matter of your physical brain has its greater reality in the mind, and behind that mind is another mind, and behind that another, and yet all of this is your mind. The mind of the larger self you do not know.

There are no presents or pasts to these minds, only simultaneous experience, and a creativity that constantly of itself and its existence creates more. Consciousness of itself forms all of these realities and systems. It does not forget as you forget, that you form all the dimensions within your own system.

You forget what you know. Larger mind does not.

Translated for you, the eye *(spelled)* is the symbol for this greater mind, for it sees through all systems, and looking outward sees infinities of itself dancing into its own eyes: the glances themselves vital creations and dimensions of consciousness.

(A few words missed here because of rapid delivery. Then:)

... Creations are formed within your closed eye, in the dreaming wisdom, and thrust into actuality as the eye opens. This symbol explains the workings of the probable system, all possible variations being formed, and each creatively bringing forth another.

(9:35. There was no announcement of a break by the entity. Jane merely stopped speaking. Her eyes were a long time opening. Jane said she had the usual pyramid feeling, described in detail in earlier sessions, and that as usual when break came she felt herself coming down through it.

(At 9:50 Jane said she was "just beginning to feel him again," though as far as we know sexual definition of the entity is meaningless in its terms. As before now Jane began to sit quietly, hands again folded in her lap; her mouth and lips began to work again, and finally the high thin voice emerged once more. 9:56.)

And when you sleep you are in accelerated periods of creativity and concentration, making with thoughts and images the world you know, forming from inner experience the physical story that will unfold, the events that you will encounter physically.

You are also receiving information from other probable selves. You are planning earthly reincarnations. You are making contacts that will be used in other realms. When your eyes close therefore, you bring realities to earth, and when your eyes open you also thrust them out into actuality.

You visit with travelers from other systems. You plant thought forms in other systems, and you tend them. You hold congregation with the many segments of your own reality. Your world is like a thought form in my experience. Your physical system exists in many intensities, and can be perceived. Probable selves can be viewed by myself and others like me, for we see your reality in all of its dimensions, and you view it from the small present forms that you know. *(Pause.)*

In all of this there is purpose. You are being watched by others. This evening's session is a brief reinitiation for others that will come.

(10:00. Once again Jane abruptly stopped speaking, and this was the end of the session, unexpected as it was. This time her eyes opened quickly; looking up, she felt in the air above her head; so real was the pyramid sensation, she said, that she sought to physically touch it. I saw nothing.

(Jane said the pyramid felt like glass above her. Also, that "it was real funny that the pyramid vanished so quickly" at the end of the session. She had no warning of the quick end of the session either.)

SESSION 491
JULY 2, 1969 9:30 PM WEDNESDAY

(On Saturday and Sunday, June 28-29, Jane and I visited Saratoga Springs.

(The material below shows the contents of a discussion Jane and I had before this evening's session, and Seth's answers.)

Good evening.

("Good evening, Seth.")

Now, remember: in one way your reality is a probable system. In some other realities mankind has taken different roads.

In some for example he never was a meat eater. In others the aggressive instincts, as they are called, were almost automatically channeled toward what you would call constructive areas.

The progression in that system incidentally was not swift or certain. Individual development suffered in many ways. The problem of how to handle energy constructively was put in far simpler terms. There was less free will involved. The inhabitants of the system were far more fearful—so fearful that little change was allowed for.

The problem of aggression is simply the problem of using your own energy constructively. When you are forced to use it constructively you learn little. It is true that in this system of which I am speaking, there was a stronger focus upon the arts, and yet there were fewer great artists.

The only way to avoid facing the problem you see was to limit the amount of free energy allotted to the individual, and available en masse. Also safeguards were automatically built into the physical structure so that accumulations of energy could not be repressed—so no buildup could then emerge with violent overtones. Those in this system take further steps very slowly, and it will be more difficult for them to learn to handle large amounts of energy constructively. Those in your own system are more venturesome, more daring. Consciousness is far too varied. No one system could contain it or satisfy it. Generally speaking then, individual entities choose the system which suits their personalities and general leanings. Your system presents a rather abrupt, explosive entrance into largely organized consciousness, but on an individual basis.

Those in your system are relatively impatient, have decided to work with large amounts of energy. Your physical system itself rapidly responds and mirrors the use of this energy. Results are seen quickly. Large groupings and regroupings occur within the mass psyche, huge waves of energy as the race makes important decisions. All of this is done on an unconscious basis, but as a teaching method the results must be seen physically.

Because you respond as physical creatures you respond best of all to tangible physical results. You do not know how far you can go in any given waves of activity until you see it objectified, or nearly so. If you knew how to handle energy effectively, if you fully realized that your thoughts were the motivating factor, were the realities, then you would not need a physical existence, for that is the reason for the physical environment.

It is the clay which you form so that you can see the results of your mental work. You become extremely engrossed in the activity, but you also know in deeper layers of your personality that your existence and the existence of the race will continue.

Quite frankly, your earth is expendable, for it will be created again as often as it is needed. I use the term again, speaking in terms of time again for you. But understand *(smile)* that others are forming their own clay of realities simultaneously. If they do not like what they have created often they throw it away; but always with the idea of learning from their errors, and forming another from the knowledge they have gained.

Not one portion of consciousness is lost in this process, you understand. When you think of a possible destruction of your planet, you imagine perhaps the mutilation of nature as you know it, the species changed. Or you imagine the race of man vanishing, or starting all over again as it were from scratch.

Each epoch that ever existed within your planet in one way you see still does exist, and any consciousness that was involved with it still exists. Each consciousness retains memory of all its experiences, of each gestalt of which it has been part, and of the errors and of the successes in which it has been involved.

In one way all of this happens in the blinking of an eyelid. But in terms of value fulfillment you see, you explore it thoroughly. As you know, there is no destruction, and yet in other terms you must believe for a while that there is, if you are going to work for the good of yourselves and others, as you must.

There are many roads leading to that goal however. Various personalities will find various ways. You help others whether or not you realize that you do, whether or not others realize that you do, whether or not you plan to help. You help others even when your intentions are precisely the opposite.

Many who would seem to set a very poor example for others help others for exactly that reason. Quite simply they are examples of what not to be precisely for this reason. In their avarice and hatred they serve a purpose.

This does not mean that they will not have to progress, that they will not have to learn, but it does mean that they will not be allowed to pass through without helping others regardless of their own intent. In some cases such a situation may be set up by a portion of the personality itself, though this is not usual.

Some automatically soak up the hatred of others like a sponge. They have quite hateful characteristics. In some cases they have chosen these roles, attracting aggressions that others cannot handle. There is so little that you do know that many situations appear meaningless or chaotic.

There is no probable solution, you see, to mankind's difficulties, that is not being tried out in some probable system. There are systems where no violence is allowed, but full energy is given. The teaching process there is different. The system, the body system, short-circuits itself at the contemplation of violent behavior.

Now you must understand that this continues throughout the entire system—animal and plant life. Change is gradual. In many ways it is a sleeping system, change taking place so slowly and nonviolently that the danger is in a constant status quo. The mental associative patterns are completely different from your own. Even abruptness of thought, you see, carries implications of violence, of abrupt change—the breaking of one pattern for another.

Now I will break this pattern and let you take your break. Incidentally, I only know of the existence of such systems—I have had no experience with them.

(10:10-10:26.)

It is not necessary that you know what is going on in these other systems of reality. Some are so alien that you would not recognize them, nor would I, as any indication of conscious life.

There are purposes beyond those that I can tell you. Their meanings unfold as your own development does. Within consciousness all things are incipient, and all creations are lovingly nurtured. You cannot step out of existence or reality even if you try.

It goes without saying that many entities have no experience with your physical reality, and never will. The information gained in each probable system is known, however, and correlated. You must also realize the advantages, challenges and peculiar beauties that your own system provides, and that many of your accomplishments as a race are unique.

These accomplishments are not the ones for which you pat yourselves on the back however. Nature as you know it is also a result of your decision to handle large amounts of energy without strong imposed restraints. The beauties within it are often the result of violent changes, of strong energy, used to change pattern and form, and yet maintain a definite stability. The end products—your foliage, landscapes and skies for example, are of the highest esthetic nature: as esthetic productions they are unequalled.

They are indeed art, though you would never think of them as such. Do you follow me here?

("Yes. I've thought of that." And Jane's childlike paintings show it.)

Now. Accepting the problem of aggression and of the use of strong energy necessitates rather quick reactions, strong unconscious mass communication, quick abilities to transform energy from one kind to another.

Highly unstable explosive energy may lead you to a tragic war. At the last minute however a transformation may occur in which the energy is used instead to form a massive earthquake; the birth of an island or new continent.

It may be used as a thrust to bring forth an invention, literally of earth-shaking proportions. It may be also used to bring forth a gigantic constructive event of equal proportion, according to the inner abilities and intent of the race at the time.

When the race is in deepest stress and faced with great problems, it will call up someone like Christ. It will seek out and indeed from itself produce the very personalities necessary to give it the strength it needs. It makes little difference what circumstances are involved. The myth will grow to a reality, and the reality is far stronger than any purely physical event could be.

There were three men whose lives became confused in history, and merged, and whose composite history became known as the life of Christ, for example. Each of these were highly gifted psychically, knew of their role, and accepted it willingly.

It made no difference to your history. The three men were part of one entity, gaining physical existence in one time. They were not born at the same date however. There are reasons why the entity did not return as one person. For one thing the full consciousness of an entity would be too strong for one physical vehicle. For another the entity wanted a more diversified environment than could otherwise be provided. The entity was born once as John the Baptist, and then he was born in two other forms. One of these is a personality that most stories of Christ refer to.

I will tell you about the other personality at another time. There was constant conscious communication between these three portions of the one entity, though they were born and buried at different dates. Yet the race called up these personalities, so to speak, from its own psychic bank, from the pool of individualized consciousness that was available to it.

You may take your break, ask questions, or end the session as you prefer.

("I guess we'll have to end it."

(10:55. This was the end of the session, rather abruptly. I was tired from writing at such a constant rapid pace, or would have continued the session though it was

getting late. Jane was well-out, etc.; indeed after the session she said she was "still getting stuff.")

SESSION 492
JULY 7, 1969 9:07 MONDAY

Good evening.

("Good evening, Seth.")

Our sessions have many years to run.

In the early days when I first spoke to you, you would not have understood things that I tell you now. In future sessions you will receive answers; answers, for by then you will know the proper questions.

Now I regret that you must be so involved with note-taking that I cannot speak to you in a more conversational tone. Many truths cannot be spoken, so we must search for ways of least distortion. Behind the questions that you are asking there are deeper questions.

Our sessions still will follow many developments, and in some later years when you have also learned more, there will be channels opened of direct experience within the session framework. Behind the symbol of language is essence. Knowledge must be given to you in such a way that it makes sense within your particular framework.

Some knowledge involves concepts that are beyond it. Both of you will have a series of highly vivid and memorable dream experiences, seven in number, and you will remember them. In these you will receive some information that cannot be given verbally. It will come through direct experience. Each dream will mark a point of advance.

There will be no doubt in your mind after the event. You will know the dreams as those I predicted. They represent a necessary stage through which you must pass. They will consist of various illuminations. They will not be close together. They will not be evenly timed. There will be varying intervals between them.

At the end of your seventh dream you will be acquainted with your immediate environment after death. You will indeed then have a glimpse of that next environment. The seven dreams were incipient once your own psychic education began. They will also represent culminating experiences, in that you have been progressing in other levels of reality in the dream state, for some time.

Consciously you have been unaware of this. Each dream however will serve as a breakthrough into your conscious awareness, a graduation drama of a sort of which you will be fully aware. When you are considering the sort of questions of which you spoke earlier this evening, remember not to push too hard for answers on an intellectual basis.

The intellect does not know the answers. The intuitions can deliver within moments knowledge that the intellect struggles *(with)* for years, and may not acquire.

Part of this involves making yourself available intuitively so that the answers may come. The way you phrase any question to some extent colors its answer. Seeking for the questions behind the questions will often give you the initial answer that you wanted. You and Ruburt both will be involved in another period of rather concentrated psychic activity together as a main project, within a short time. After for example his book is done.

Such concentrated periods of activity follow their own patterns and rhythms, and you need rest from them. This period however will answer some of your questions. There are rhythms in your own personalities, quite natural, that flow together, then somewhat apart, and together again. They are ready to come close once more, and these represent the times of your greatest psychic and creative endeavors, of highest accomplishment regardless of time, when both of your abilities reinforce the other's.

The beginning of our sessions represented one such point. The initiation of our other personality represented a second point. Circumstances here however were not of the best. The third such point will find your individual activities heightened; spontaneous visions and occurrences for example on your part; generally better projections on Ruburt's part, and heightened psy-time periods for you both.

You will each devote a half hour daily to this, as you did in the beginning, carried on by the fine results. This period will also see the first of the seven dreams. The next such period will not come for approximately three years. In the meantime you will be assimilating the knowledge and experiences, and Ruburt will be writing about them.

Our sessions will of course continue, with a greater intensity having been gained during the period mentioned. In the sort of work you are doing, both creatively in your arts and in your psychic work, the inner activities and developments run below surface and are unseen. You seem to be on a plateau or level area, and then the work that has been going on beneath springs released to the surface. Results begin to show.

I did not forget the first of my own books, incidentally, but put it off in order that more practical material concerning Ruburt could be given. It will represent a highly concentrated form of activity and focus.

You may take your break and we shall continue.

(9:40—Jane was out of trance easily, but said that Seth was here strongly tonight, even though her voice and delivery were rather average. But Jane said that when Seth is really here she feels a "certain energy" about her that is intensified over ordinary sessions. Yet oddly she remembered some of the material, also.

(Resume at 9:55.)

Now. Answers unfold. And even when they are given to you they must unfold within you or you do not understand them.

You feel your way into them. Much of our material will be far more significant to you after your approaching period of psychic activity. You will not only understand it intellectually, but feel what it means. You will know through experience.

Your doctor friend is still about, due to an extended rest period *(Dr. Pietra)*; once again and for the last time until autumn conditions are good this time, particularly for an apparition. Give us a moment. *(Pause.)*

Tell yourself that you will, while sleeping, be alert to any changed atmosphere within the room; for there will be a change. Tonight and tomorrow night will be best, with a slight possibility on Friday evening, and that will be the last opportunity for a while. Now tell yourself that your conscious mind can be alert while you sleep and dream, alert enough to recognize a changed atmosphere.

It makes no difference you see whether you are awake in your terms or asleep in your terms; if your conscious mind is functioning in either state, you will see him.

Now the suggestion to carry your waking consciousness into the sleep state is of particular value in conscious projections, if you will use it. You would succeed if you use it habitually.

He has found your location, and he will be here. You may instead quite clearly see him in a strong vision within a dream. If so he will announce himself. It is highly important however for any such work that you begin to train yourself to take your waking consciousness with you in sleep. It is the reason why you do not remember quite legitimate projections you have made.

You must train yourself in that respect. The impetus of seeing your doctor friend can be enough however to bypass the lack of training in this instance. If you see him physically and think you are awake, then speak to him mentally. He may appear as a pyramid form of lights, according to various conditions.

You must impress upon yourself before sleep, your desire to meet him consciously. The second group of his experiments should find you in the heightened period of psychic activity that I mentioned this autumn, and then circumstances should be excellent. Do not attempt to approach him simply because there will be unstable elements and a fine balance to be maintained, his visual appearance being dependent upon many conditions.

Any change or abnormality in the room will serve to gain your attention, if you give the proper suggestions. You should also probably make extra note*(s)* to recall your dreams in case the meeting is not as conscious and deliberate as you would like.

Do you have any questions on that particular subject?

("Could Jane see him?")

Ruburt may be able to. The strong impetus however is on the part of your probable self and yourself. Ruburt is more used to working from the dream state and possibly could make connection. In that probable reality however your doctor friend did not meet a probable Jane.

Give me a moment. *(Long pause, eyes closed.)* If you meet him in your own astral body you will have more freedom of expression and communication, for you can speak normally, if you follow me. It would be a good idea therefore to have a general mental outline of any particular questions you would like to ask him.

It would be best if you were sleeping on your right side if possible *(this I seldom do)*, for projection purposes. A foggy white light will initiate an apparition, and possibly a slight lowering of room temperature. An overheated room incidentally, just generally, is poor for such activities. A clear flow of air is good, allowing for more negative ions.

You may take a break and I will continue.

(10:20. During break I described for Jane a very vivid dream I had on Sunday evening, July 6, 1969. It was almost a nightmare—in fact Jane woke me out of it to prevent this seeming reaction on my part, I was fairly sure the dream concerned my father's approaching death, but certain elements in it were similar enough to Seth's suggestions about contacting Dr. Pietra, above, to make me tell Jane about it—on the off chance the dream had been more than it seemed.

(The dream is recorded in my dream book in the usual way. Resume at 10:36.)

Now. Your dream. It did not involve your doctor.

It was a legitimate experience in which you did attempt to find out where your father was going. The barrier was of your own construction, representing two things: the subconscious feeling that a definite barrier exists between one plane and another; and secondly the barrier you felt separated you and your father throughout his life.

Give us a moment. The thrashing around was something else again, and it represented your knowledge that your father would be born again. You experienced his thrashing around in the womb which he shall later enter.

You wanted to help him, to make sure that the birth was accomplished. There were other elements that you have forgotten; a young man who was your younger brother, seen at the age of 12. He was urging you to help your father also. The barrier was not death, but life on the other side of it.

You wanted to help him through the birth and into the next existence. He is now in a period of rest after an exhausting lifetime situation. His mother and Ella *(his sister)* are with him. He has not died in the past because he was still tied to your mother. He will not die at least until he sees her again.

If it had not been for her vitality and the force of her will, he would have died years ago. He wanted out from an early age, and yet there were karmic influences that were not finished, between the two of them.

His mother is helping him now. She was the only one who could ever help him find his way. I told you that the main elements of the personality withdrew a long time ago. Those elements have had considerable experience in another level of existence already.

Do you have questions?

("No, I guess not." Several years ago Seth gave an excellent reading regarding my father, going into more detail on some of the data given here in summary fashion.)

Insert the month of March here, and let it go at that for now. Be assured that his essence is elsewhere. I will continue or you may end the session and begin your suggestions.

("Yes, I'd like to do that.")

My heartiest wishes for a successful endeavor. Now, some evening use your recorder and we can have an informal session.

("Okay.")

One session for the week, that week, for the added work involved on your part. Or get our friend Ruburt to type for you. *(Humorously.)*

("I thought I would.")

A fond good evening.

("Good night, Seth."

(10:55. This session was held on Monday, July 7, 1969. It is Thursday, July 10 as I finish typing the session. I have had no success in contacting Dr. Pietra, or at least in retaining a conscious memory of doing this. I have tried each day and each night, using suggestion, etc.

(On the evening this session was held, for instance, I went to bed early, alone, and used the suggestions mentioned above by Seth re Dr. Pietra, without success.)

SESSION 493
JULY 14, 1969 9:15 PM MONDAY

(The session began with Jane giving impressions on her own while in a light trance state. Seth spoke later.

(Jane has her own records of the preliminary data. Shortly after 8 PM, as she was writing poetry after supper, she began to get impressions that made her quite uneasy eventually. They were difficult to put into words, but involved an accident, she thought, and a hospital emergency room.

(She also had impressions of Bill Gallagher, and a man named Tom whom she could not pinpoint further. She finally became so uneasy that she called the Gallagher residence. There was no answer nor was there any answer when she called again shortly before 9 PM.

(Since session time was near, Jane asked aloud that Seth interpret the subjective data she had been receiving. She wanted a clear and concise interpretation devoid of emotion, feeling there was little use in acting whatever the impressions said; she thought more objective data could be obtained through Seth. Therefore we sat for the regularly scheduled session at 9 PM as usual.

(However, Jane began to give impressions on her own rather than through Seth. These came as she wished however, quite calmly and objectively, and it was easy for me to make notes.

(The whole time she gave impressions on her own, Jane sat quietly in her rocker, hands folded in her lap, eyes closed, voice quiet. She used many pauses, few of them long however.

(For the most part my notes are verbatim. Jane's data is in quotes.

(At 9:05: "I get a small explosion, whatever that means.

(At 9:15: "I hear the tune of One is the Loneliest Number, *a currently popular song.*

("...and a connection with a country store—a madcap driver. An accident near a crossroads. A one-syllable name, man's, beginning with J. Joe. And a fairly long last name starting with M, of foreign extract, involved. And Peggy and Bill."

("It seems 8:15 PM ... a time... I don't know.

("But a Tuesday seems to be involved. I know tonight's Wednesday."

(I explained her error to Jane after the data given on her own was finished; if anything this added to her feeling of urgency, as will be explained.

("Or the other guy is travelling in twos, like say two cycles... Now I get Bill hurt in this, his right arm, or hand or shoulder." [Pause.] "Rather badly. Peg thrown clear.

("Maybe a phone call made at this general store, or whatever it is. I get the

numbers 8051J ... a license or what, I don't know. This could be part of a license or serial number on a motorcycle, I don't know.

("But they do have to call for help.

("I think there are two other people involved. Two other guys. Before, I said one or two. One between 16 and 18, the other between 18 and 24.

("I feel like I'm rocking back and forth like mad. Am I?"

(I said no. Jane was sitting as quietly as ever. In fact, much more quietly than she usually does during sessions.

("Poppa Joe. Maybe one of the kid's relatives, or one of the kids." Pause. "Something about a ring, and Bill. I don't recall if he wears rings; but if not then the ring finger would be hurt, particularly. But I have a picture of a ring, something like the one you wear. Maybe it's the other guy's."

(Jane referred to my old high-school ring, which I still wear.

("And Bill hurt badly enough to end up at the Emergency Room. And somebody else without a leg to stand on, and I hope that's just symbolic.

("The kid—the two boys or young men, seemed to be headed in the direction of Bob Kinner's old coffeehouse that we went to ...a farmhouse on the left, and a curve, the road curves to the right.

("There are two roads that run parallel," [pause at 9:29] "for a little way, then one crosses the other. This is where it seems to happen.

("I also get the word minibike, but I don't know what that refers to.

("Peggy bruised but not hurt, really. One of the kids may not have a license. I don't know ... 1701 Gardner Road."

(Break now from 9:31 to 9:37. Jane was easily out of trance, then back in. We had heard of Gardner Road before, though couldn't recall any connections, or its exact location, etc.

("Some dim connection now with Tom Page, as if he's writing the story. This doesn't happen in bright sunlight. I think the time I gave is approximately correct. It could be foggy and misty."

(Jane had mentioned the fog and lack of brightness earlier, while making her own notes before the session.

("The impression that Bill just has a shirt on, and Peg a jacket or outer garment."

(Pause at 9:40. This was rather lengthy. Then: "I don't get anything else now."

(I explained to Jane now about her error re what day it was. Since this was Monday, and any possible event was predicted for a Tuesday, Jane decided to try again to reach the Gallaghers. This time Peg answered the phone, at 9:45 PM.

(Peggy told Jane that Gardner Road was in Horseheads, and that she would check the address there that Jane had given in trance. Peg also agreed that she and

Bill would be very careful riding their bikes. Jane was much relieved after talking to Peg, saying that before the call she had been "very uptight" over any probabilities involving accidents and the Gallaghers.

(My thought, based on data Seth has given, was that already the probabilities of any such accident had been considerably lessened, merely because the four of us now knew about it consciously. Jane and I hoped that Seth would come through with more information, since the evening was still young.

(At 10:01 Jane said she felt Seth would speak. The session began at 10:03.)

Good evening.

("Good evening, Seth." Seth affectionately calls Bill the Jesuit.)

Now. The accident probability is more closely allied with our Jesuit than with our cat lover, and he has been driving himself too hard.

Such an accident would occur in a period of exuberance, rather than for example when he was driving in connection with his duties at work. In letting down, there is the danger that he would let down too far, forgetting caution.

He should generally watch himself in activities not connected with work, using tools or so forth, for a period of approximately 10 days. There is no need avoiding the one accident and having another of a different kind.

It is the hands, particularly the right one, that would come under such attack.

"Infinite intelligence guides and protects me in my activities." He should say this several times to himself, slowly and meaningfully, morning, noon and evening during the time given. It will automatically allow the inner portion of his personality to protect him from such probable harm.

Now, the information given automatically changes the nature of the probability that was foreseen, for in that probability no forewarning had occurred. Do you follow me?

("Yes.")

Therefore the probability is <u>already</u> altered. Whether or not our Jesuit even knew of Ruburt's impressions, that probability was altered. Knowing the impressions alters the probability further, and taking the steps that I have given still further changes the probabilities. So the information should in no way be treated as negative suggestion.

Other elements have also changed. Our cat lover's knowledge of the impressions has the same effect as the Jesuit's knowledge.

The two lads involved may very well cause an accident in any case, unless actions of their own alter their reactions. There is no connection between them and your friends however, a priori, and there are other elements that could interfere, preventing even an accident to them. They would have been the aggressors, you see.

I suggest you give this information to your friends, so that they do not worry.

("Was Tuesday night the most likely time for the accident?")

I did not hear you.

(Traffic noise was loud. I repeated the question and Jane nodded yes.)

It goes without saying that such an accident would be the result of psychic and psychological forces operating within those involved, and by altering the set as has been done, the previous "results", in quotes, need not occur.

Our Jesuit would want to hurt himself, and become therefore the victim in such an accident, or be the victim of some kind of one-man affair. The boys would want to hurt others. Unnumbered elements can still intrude to change <u>their</u> probability, even now, however; but the probabilities when Ruburt perceived the impressions were that the event would occur. For the reasons given this is now far less a probable event.

Giving this information to your friends will make it still less a probable event. Do you follow me?

("Yes.")

I will then let you do so. The knowledge prickles the balloon of emotions that were building up within our friend. Otherwise they would emerge in an overexuberance when relieved from work pressure, resulting in carelessness. Beneath this of course the psychological need to be hurt, to punish himself, because he cannot strike out against a superior in the work situation.

Ruburt's impressions were therefore correct.

("Good night, Seth."

(10:34.

(See Jane's notes below.)

JANE'S NOTES
JULY 18, 1969

(On Friday, July 18, Bill Gallagher tells us he had a cluster of fairly close near-accident situations since Monday—one involving two boys on bicycles—he stopped about 20 yards from them—but he was going 55 at the foot of Mount Zoar Hill on Holden Road.

(But July 17, Thursday, he was with an associate who did have an accident. He and his boss, Cove Hoover, were driving home from a yearly outing for newspaper staff on Seneca Lake; Bill driving. They were worried about Art Kendall who

was in no shape to drive, so they followed Kendall's car out of Watkins Glen. Kendall leaves main road and takes a country road that parallels Route 14 from Watkins Glen to Horseheads—he guns car. Bill is afraid to drive too fast—as road is full of curves, so Kendall's car speeds out of sight. On a hunch Bill turns off on Chambers Road, Horseheads. There is a heavy low fog. They find Kendall's car finally in a ditch. It had swirled around in road and landed there. Bill said that he probably would have been involved if he continued speeding after Kendall's car to catch him. Kendall wasn't hurt though. [Rob: Please see a NY-state road map.]

(Points of Similarity:

1. The accident issue itself.

2. A one-syllable man's name—<u>Art</u> Kendall. [Though not beginning with J and not of foreign extract.]

3. A mad-cap driver definitely.

4. Two roads that run parallel. Yes. See above

5. Gardner Road mentioned—no, incident on Chambers Road, however, this is in same area: both in Horseheads [?] [Rob: Watkins Glen north, Elmira south.]

6. Fog—definitely.

7. 2 boys on cycles—[See above. Other incident involving 2 boys on bikes.]

8. My impressions said incident would occur with a farmhouse on one side of the road with a curve on the other side; the house on the left. Incident did occur with a farmhouse on the right. A curve on the left.

(Note: Jane's trance data mentioned another newspaperman besides Bill G. —i.e. Tom Page. Page not involved in the Watkins episode, but Kendall, another newspaperman, was. Also Cove Hoover, riding with Bill as they followed Kendall. In fact, Bill drove Hoover's Mercury.)

ESP CLASS
JULY 15, 1969 11:30 PM TUESDAY

(Seth:) You have tales, but tonight is not the night of telling. Now. I have been here and I have not intruded, because you are learning to collect and use energy on your own. I did, indeed, however stand in front of each one of you and looked into your faces and you did not see me. It is some experience to stand before another and see no comprehension in his face ... but I am used to it. Now. You *(JB and SW)* used your energy like a ball that a child plays with, both you and Ruburt. And you tossed it back and forth, but you did not collect and direct it properly, and we shall have to give you lessons. But <u>you</u> shall do the

work.

(To WL) Now I am sitting here for my portrait. You may indeed get only our friend Ruburt. But then you may get more than your friend Ruburt. The camera may be comprehending, or it may not be comprehending.

I do not like to interrupt you in the beginning of your summer...(?)... however. Far be it from me to interrupt when you are not working, when you are not looking within yourselves. The summer season within yourselves is far more enjoyable than the summer streets down which you walk. But far be it from me to mention that you have not been working.

And when I do ask the questions, and I shall ask them, I shall expect some ready answers. When you immerse yourselves completely in physical reality, then you have no time for the inner voice.

([TM:] "That is what I'm doing.")

It is your loss. Now, there is a way—when you are involved in physical activity, and even intense mental work—to change the inner focus so that you are aware of two realities at once and can manipulate quite easily in the physical reality as you must. Now, you ask your Bega, for I have told him the message, and I have told him to tell you. We shall see how good he is. And I want to know what he tells you for I want to see how he is delivering my suggestions.

([TM:] "Is that Bega on the wall?")

Now I ask you, what would Bega be doing on the wall?

([TM:] "You are on the wall.")

I am painted on the wall. *(Referring to Rob's Seth protrait.)*

Now. Your friend has been here this evening as a student, but not exactly the same kind of a student as you are...He is a practice teacher.

You *(SW)* lost some good bets this evening. And you *(CW)* lost many good bets this evening. Now. There is a difference between passivity and alert passivity. And you need to learn the difference. Here you need to learn the difference. Again, I welcome our new member *(LD).*

([LD:] "Did you give me the bump on the head?")

Far be it from me to bump fair ladies on the head! The bump, for this has been a very active evening, was from your playful poltergeist AA. I have better things to do than to bump maidens or madams on the head.

Now. You must realize that within this room, and within any room, at any time there are other personalities that you do not perceive. There are ways of perceiving them if they choose to be perceived. Possibly, with some help from certain directions, we shall see what we can do in other classes. And our friend Ruburt is quite correct, you *(WL)* learn the nature of the inner self first....and then we shall help you in the development of your own abilities. And before too long, we will have a message for you to take to heart.

I have come through simply to let you know that I have been here, and to let you know that I know that you are sliding through the summer.

(To SW and CW) I do have one point to make. The child was a girl... 1432... France... and at one time your sister... Strong literary abilities... some interest in music... Should not be pampered for the personality is already given to indulgence. There may be an allergy to wheat... early in life... Was also known to this one here in Spain, the country now called Spain... in 801 as an uncle then a warrior-type personality, but again given to indulgence.

An entity on a par with the parents. A mole or mark on one of the feet... a possible weak point in the right elbow... Given to high exuberance, quick moods... but not forgiving. The personality should not be indulged, but it should not be shown dissonance... and discipline should be fair, for it will hold grudges otherwise.

I had meant to mention earlier that your daughter and sister were brothers in a previous life... in Afghanistan. You *(SB)*, I believe, 1541-1583, a rug maker, their father... That is, you were their father. There was also another child... and that child will be G's husband in this life. There will be a close connection, then, between the two of you... but also a sense of rivalry. Your mother was a very heavy-handed father to you in that existence. Your father has now strong feminine traits because in Boston in an immediately past life there was a woman... give us a moment... The first name was also Lydia. The last name... your Vice-President to the contrary... was Agnew. There are records of this particular existence twenty-five miles, approximately, west of Boston... at that time... a small town... *(a few missing sentences)*...Three children who died before the age of three, and records, I believe, attesting to this fact... couched in one of the historical societies... or in land-grant information.

Now. We will try to have a session for you *(WL)*, our friend William the Bull, shortly... and clear up some of your difficulties... for some of them <u>are</u> because you are <u>bull-headed</u>. You will not let the inner self speak clearly enough to you... so we will give it the voice that you can hear... And, you will know when we have the session, you will intuitively realize that what we say is true... And there is no need to fight what you are fighting... And the secret that you try so hard to hide from your conscious mind is <u>not</u> that terrible a secret. There is some past life that operated in your case that has caused a block, and we hope that we can help you remove it. Bulls can rip down fences.

Now, I will let my friend... *(laugh from CW)*... you, as Ruburt would say you are looking for it! And those who look for it in this room, get it. The portrait is a portrait of Ruburt as a woman in one of the past lives mentioned... and in that particular instance, as a grandmother of twelve children. Strongly gifted psychically... given to hovering in dark forests... and a midwife. Now, he does not know this, so I will give you the honor of telling him. I will now let our friend take a rest. And you may rest if you are up to it.

Now, I will tell you *(TM)* something. Bega is there and I will let you tell me which portrait is his. You may ask Bega or tell me. But you did not pick the correct portrait. *(TM commented that one was "too much Hebrew.")*

Bega has had many lives...Do not limit yourself in your thinking... do not limit yourself in your feelings... and do not retreat in the summertime from your inner self.

Now. There has been energy present in this room, and strong energy, this evening. But you have not been serious enough about using it, nor have you been playful enough to use it without serious note. You may use it in two ways, you see. You may play with it and use it marvelously... or you may use it seriously... But in between you will not use it at all, for you cannot harness it. And in your own daily activities, in your playful moments, serious moments, you can almost achieve the freedom that the inner self knows. But in your mundane moments, you will not achieve it. And when you half try, you will not achieve it.

(TM holding up a portrait) That is not Bega! I want you to seriously consider each one of the paintings and tell me which one is Bega.

Now. I do not want to see another painting. I do not want an attitude that says, "Is this it?" I want an intuitive feeling on your part and a recognition. Do you intuitively feel that that is a portrait of Bega?

([TM:] "The one I thought was Bega was actually Ruburt.")

We are sorry about that! I never liked wine... I always liked brandy... and no one brings it to me... and Ruburt does not drink it.

([WL:] "I will bring you some next week.")

But how will you get Ruburt to drink it? I always liked a warm brandy even on a summer's night.

Now. What is your *(TM)* intuitive feeling? Now I want you to look at the portrait. Close your eyes. How much reality does the portrait have for you? Can you see it in your mind's eye?

([TM:] "Yes, I can see it with the feeling of a friend.")

That is because it is the portrait of Bega. But you did not pick it out as your first choice. Now, Bega has been here as I have been here and he was calling you to look toward the corner of the room... and you were too intellectually smug to do so as Ruburt is often too intellectually smug to do what I ask him to do. And your own intellectual ideas prevented you from first picking out your intuitive choice, as far as the portraits were concerned.

Now. There is someone else who has been here and who is connected with our new student. But our new student does not know this person... It is no one with whom she has previously communicated. Because she was not ready. This personality is also a student of mine and a practice teacher.

Now, you see what you are willing to see, and it is stupidity to consider suggestion as the result or the cause of what you see. It is stupidity in class to worry that suggestion would cause a given result... for suggestion causes whatever you see. You form your physical reality through suggestion and expectation. You experience what you expect to experience at a subconscious and a conscious level. And therefore as Ruburt is very careful that suggestion is not involved, so he has also had you be overly cautious, and there have been many opportunities in class that you have missed for this reason... and these are the bets that I have spoken about earlier this evening. You have the ability to see more than you saw, and you have the ability. You enjoyed your passivity *(to CW)* to the point of a joyous giving-up; and instead, you see, there is a point within passivity where you are passively alert. And you went beyond the point and lost what you might have seen. As our friend here went beyond the point *(referring to TM)*, looked at the portraits and consciously... for you did not make an original intuitive judgment...but consciously looked at those portraits in terms of nationality, age, and all the requirements that you thought of.

Now again let me tell you, though the hour be late *(quite loudly)* and though Ruburt thinks that such demonstrations as these are hardly worth the effort *(quite softly)* and childish endeavors at best, I still want you to know, as I always want you to know, that my vitality is your own and that the energy that swings through this small frame is but an echo of the energy that swings through your own personality.

I have said before that you have lived many lives and that you can know these existences within yourself. I am not afraid that we shall be kicked out of our apartment. And I also am quite sure that as you grow to know Ruburt and as you grow to know me you will realize that there is a difference in our personalities and that indeed... when I tell you that my vitality spans both space and time, then you will know that I know whereof I am speaking... and that this vitality is your own... Then feel it within yourselves... Now it is being used simply to let you know of its existence... but realize that it is within you for you to use as you will... for your own good... and you *(WL)* are not powerless. I have no body... and I am not powerless... How, therefore, can you feel helpless... or you... or any of you?

My vitality is no more... no more than your own. I come to you from a long way. But the essence of yourself is not of this place nor of this time. Now. I could keep up a demonstration such as this for hours... if only to let you realize that this is your own energy... that the energy that I show is your own... You have this energy and this vitality

Now, in your terms, I am dead! *(Very loud.)* How can you then be less lively? Why is it that I must tell you what vitality is... when, in your terms, I am a gray ghost that flits through the darkness of the night... a face that peers through second-story windows *(in reference to SW's being frightened by a face that appeared at her window recently)* and meets with no response but a sigh of horror. I visit my friends and they nearly faint. *(SW apologized.)*

Apologies always come later.

I said: In your terms I was dead; in my terms, I am forever lively. *(This to clarify a point being discussed by the class.*

(Seth tried to break through again. Jane said, "Wait a minute."

([CW:] "One at a time in the body.")

Now. Ruburt's abilities were so strong since childhood that he feared using them, and so I am quite used to that development. On the other hand, I wanted someone with a strong-enough ego structure to contain what will amount to... 40 years of mediumistic experience. I needed a personality who would be able to maintain psychological stability.

Now, I have maintained psychological stability for centuries so I find it not too much to ask that our friend Ruburt maintain it for a mere 40 years. And we expect you to maintain it. We expect you *(CW)* to maintain it ... and before you get the idea, again, of leaving physical reality before your chores are done, I will give you the boot from the other end.

([CW:] "Was that you that she saw in the window the other night?")

I use many forms, and if you do not like them, I am sorry. Next time I shall be a willowy spiritual young woman, treading very softly, and I shall sing the Ave Maria as the glorious sun sinks in the west...and I shall tippy-toe to your window. And then from this light and spiritual form I will bellow.

Now, there are two simple requests that I have made. One: I have been asking Ruburt to stop smoking cigarettes, a dirty habit, and smoke cigars... and he will not do so.

([WL:] "What brand would you like?")

A fat one.

What I want you to know is this: I come here, I hope, as an endearing personality with characteristics that you can understand. Now these characteristics have been mine, and they are mine, and I am who I say I am. And yet, the Seth that you know, and that you find so endearing and understandable is but a small portion of my reality... the portion that can relate with you most easily.

It is a portion that has been physical. It is a portion that can understand your *(TM)* being overwhelmed with work; it is a portion that can understand your being full with child *(SW)*; it is a portion that can understand the times when you wanted to leave physical reality *(CW)*; it is a portion that can understand the part of you *(SB)* that wanted to be a star; it is a portion that can understand the part of you that wanted to conquer, and is afraid to conquer *(WL)*; it is a portion that can understand the guilt you *(RC)* feel for no reason; it is a portion that can understand the aspirations that you *(LD)* were unable to fulfill... and if you had fulfilled them, you would not be looking into the subjects that you are looking into now. You would not feel the need to look for answers. It is a part that can understand why you *(VM)* have so related to this man; it is a part that can understand why the five, and seven, and eight-year-old girl that you were has related to this man, and not independently gone on. It is the part that can understand why you let your aspirations go *(TM)*.

And this part that you see and that appears in this room... and that can show joy, and show its existence and reality, that can call to you beyond space and time, that shows such energy, that shows you what energy can blow through such a small and slight frame... that self is a small part of my reality. For some time yet, you will need its familiarity. And you will need the human characteristics that you know ... and that were mine...and they are still mine, for this self of mine that I show to you does still exist and grow. But beyond that self, there is another self, and still another self... of which I am fully aware. And that self can see through physical reality. And to that self, physical reality is like a breath of smoke in air ... and that self does not need the characteristics that you know and find so endearing. And yet it is not an unemotional self; it is a self that has condensed emotions; and, it is not distant.

(Jane later said there was but a short break here, while Seth's entity prepared to come through. Gave a hand signal. Jane didn't get any pyramid feeling, though.)

SETH II

(All of the following is by Seth's entity.)

And that self tells you that there is a reality beyond human reality, beyond human characteristics that you know... And within that reality even I am dwarfed and there is knowledge that can never be verbal. And there is experience that cannot be translated in human terms. Although this type of existence seems cold to you, it is a clear and crystal-like existence in which things are known that are beyond your comprehension... in which no time is needed in your terms for experience... in which the inner self condenses all human knowledge that has been received by you through your various existences and reincarnations... has been coded and exists indelibly.

You exist, therefore, now within this reality as present and immediate as you are now... although in my terms, more than fifty centuries of your time has elapsed since your seemingly present existence.

Yet what you are is now, and what your friend Seth is is now. And it exists as light and as the impetus for other dimensions and consciousness.

Know that within your physical atoms now the origins of all consciousness still sings and that all the human characteristics by which you know yourselves still exist within the eye of all our consciousness never diminished but always present; your individualities never diminished... not only never diminished but gaining in experience.

So I am the Seth that is beyond the Seth that you know. And in me the knowledge and vitality of that Seth still rings. In your terms I am a future Seth. But the terms are meaningless to me, for he is what I was in your terms.

We form the reality that you know. We have spoken to you since the beginning of your time. We have inspired and helped those of your prophets who have looked to us.

There is no need to worry about your friend *(Ruburt)*. We want you to realize that there is more than your human reality. We want you to realize that there is consciousness without form, that there is consciousness with will and vitality that comes to you from beyond even those places that your Seth knows. We want you to realize that though it is hard for us to communicate, we spoke with your race before your race learned language. We gave you mental images and upon these images you learned to form the world that you knew.

We gave you the pattern by which your physical selves are formed. We gave you the pattern by which you learned to form your physical reality. We gave you the patterns intricate, involved, and blessed from which you form the reality of each physical thing you know. The most minute cell within your brain has been made from the patterns of consciousness, which we have given you. We gave you the pattern upon which you formed your entire physical universe... and the comprehension that exists within each cell, the knowledge that each cell has, the desire for organization was given by us. The entire webwork was initiated by us. We taught you to form the reality that you know.

NOTES BY RFB

(Note: Some of Seth's voice effects were very loud—I heard Seth rather clearly through two closed doors—after I had retired. The session began late—about 11:30 PM, & lasted well over an hour.

(The session is included in the regular series because of the voice effects; the fact that both Seth & his entity spoke; some new ideas from both entities; and because no regular session was held the next day, Wednesday, July 16.

(The data re the paintings—Bega—Tom M, was interesting, etc. On July 17 Tom M. purchased the painting of Bega as designated by Seth. [On July 16 Carl & Sue Watkins bought the oils of Charlie Painter, the dream hands, & Moses.]

(Very late in the evening, Carl Watkins woke me to express concern because of the length of the session tonight—at perhaps 1 AM or later. Jane then was speaking for Seth's entity. Carl & others were concerned that Jane couldn't exert enough control to come out herself.

(Jane called back to me that she was alright during a break, and this & my waking up served to end the session. Jane said she felt it was a good session, an unusual occasion to get some new ideas, so she went along with Seth & his entity. She also knew the whole session was being recorded.)

NOTES BY RFB
JULY 20, 1969 11:30 AM SUNDAY

(As is obvious from history—nothing developed from the material below! To my relief. RFB—August 14, 1969.

(After retiring at about 1 AM on July 20, 1969, on Sunday morning, after Jane & I had been to the Steak Shop for a few drinks...

(I was lying in bed in a sleepy drowsy state, waiting for Jane to come to bed. In a brief time I seemed to be concerned about the landing of the astronauts Armstrong and Aldrin on the moon this afternoon.

(Actually my concern was over some kind of accident to Armstrong after he & Aldrin had left the lunar module or landing craft—this I believe is scheduled for 2:17 AM Monday, according to [this morning's] Sunday paper.

(I seemed to briefly hover just above the two men after they had left the spindly ladder of the landing craft, & stepped onto the moon surface. Briefly, I saw them quite clearly. Somehow, I knew the one I was concerned about was Armstrong.

(I saw him fall to, or lying, on the moon surface, in some kind of trouble. Aldrin was standing close by—a few feet away, & approaching and/or bending over

Armstrong. Also a few feet away—5 or 6—was the ladder the 2 men had used to descend from the module.

(I believe a death was involved here, though I don't know how or why.

(I fell asleep within seconds after this inner experience. It's possible Jane interrupted it, or brought it to an end as she came to bed. Still, I felt no concern over my experience.

(I do remember that I briefly wondered, as I fell asleep, if the experience reflected a quite natural concern over the moon-landing's potential hazards.

(I do not think that in my experience I ever "stood" on the moon surface. I seemed instead to hover or be suspended just at the head-height of the astronaut, Aldrin—perhaps six feet. —RFB.

(I read this statement at 11:40 AM, Sunday, July 20th, though Rob told me about his experience earlier this morning. —Jane Butts.

(Session 494 is a lost or missing session.)

SESSION 495
AUGUST 13, 1969 9:14 PM WEDNESDAY

(This is our first regularly scheduled session since July 14. We have been on vacation in Florida from July 26 to August 3.)

Now, good evening.

("Good evening, Seth.")

Do you have any questions you would like to ask me?

("No.")

(Humorously:) Is this because you know the answers, or cannot think of the questions?

("Well, I don't know the answers." Nor was I very swift in thinking of questions.)

I will tell you one thing. You have a deep distrust of the marketplace. A distrust so that you do not want to entrust your best works to it. You are not afraid to entrust lesser work to it in terms of commercial art. Portions of this feeling are hangovers from your father's experience, and if you are aware of this you can combat it.

(Long pause... This material stemmed from a discussion Jane and I had had the other day, re selling paintings and how best to go about it. I had forgotten the conversation, as had Jane, and we hadn't asked that Seth discuss it this evening.)

You feel the work is safe while you have it. You put in time and effort in the past to sell your commercial work, but have refused to do the same to sell your paintings. You are aware of this, I know.

There are opportunities however waiting for you, needing only the initiative on your part. There are two men in particular in New York who would be more than willing to show and handle your work—both connected with galleries.

An M W C in particular.

("Got an address?")

There is a connection with a 1200 block on 6th avenue, I believe. I keep getting 61 also however. *(Long pause.)*

A building where they have jam sessions is next door, or nearby. Bill's *(spelled)*, or run by a man named Bill. You must make the effort however, for making the effort itself would show that your attitude has changed. Give us a moment. *(Pause.)*

In order to sell your paintings in any important way, or to achieve a reputation, you must want to achieve a reputation, and want to sell the paintings. Not because you should, or feel you should, but because you want to. And if you want to, you will take them to the best-known marketplace. This in itself will bring into activation positive elements.

The man to whom I have referred is approximately 62, but filled with energy, and would have intuitive understanding of your work. He also needs something new in his own life, and your work would give him new purpose. You could trust him.

("Does his gallery advertise in The New York Times*?")*

(Humorously:) I have not read *The New York Times* lately. *(Pause.)* Give us a moment. *(Long pause, leaning forward, eyes closed.)*

The month of October, and possibly November, this would be the best. If nothing is done then you should wait until March.

There are 3 other galleries who would handle your work. The name Jerry *(spelled)*, the second name beginning with a G... Something like Geraldi *(spelled)*.

What you do not seem to understand is that the search, to show and sell your paintings, will in itself provide fuel for future work. The search in itself will make you feel that you are doing your best to place your paintings so that they will be permanently displayed and cared for. You owe them that much.

Now you may take your break and we shall continue.

(9:40. Jane was out of trance quickly. Resume at 9:48.)

Now. Both of you had psychic abilities to use and develop.

Ruburt nicely channeled these so that they could be used with the writing ability. You have only begun to use your own psychic abilities, in line with your painting.

You have had glimpses, but the two abilities will work hand in hand so that ideas for paintings will occur with greater vividness, and your hand itself will know how to get certain effects that you want, before you are consciously aware of how this is done.

Give your hand full freedom therefore, and it will teach you what you want to know, for it is your way of bringing inner information outward. Then you learn from your own creations, and the physical mind learns by what the hand has done <u>without</u> calculation.

(This is very true, and quite acute on Seth's part. I have had awareness of this occurrence a few times, and puzzled over it, seeing effects in finished work that I wanted, without knowing how I had achieved them. Jane certainly didn't know about this consciously, for I have said nothing about it to her.

(All of the data in this session is very good, very accurate, incidentally, summing up nicely feelings, intuitions, hunches, etc., that I have had. Most of it I haven't spoken of to Jane.)

You are so jealous of your own work that you use your psychic abilities most strongly as an aid to your work. I repeat, often your hand, left alone, will give you effects that you want. Then you can study them.

(I have been doing this.)

You can try this even in regard to color. As an experiment, with a complete palette set up, then almost automatically let your hand drift over the palette and choose its own colors in turn. The intuitions of course will have guided the hand.

I am not suggesting that you relinquish conscious concern and control, but you will be amazed at how the intuitive self will use your hands, and to your conscious advantage, in experiments.

(This is very good data, and at times I have experienced this effect. I will try being more aware of it. I have not heard Jane mention ever trying any such experiment. Moreover, I don't believe she thinks this way consciously.)

This is also excellent therapy whenever you feel you are overly concerned consciously, and will open the doors to inspiration.

Various gradations in color will emerge that could otherwise take years to effect. The inner self of course will take advantage of all the conscious knowledge you have at the same time, and serve it up to you in new patterns.

You have begun to appreciate the workings of your psychic self in your paintings, but you are only beginning. And yes, the entire figures of your people will also emerge, both in movement and repose, and you will be surprised, again, at how well the characterization will show itself through the gestures and even folds of the cloth.

You will be giving life and vitality to the stock human figure that is often used, so that the hands are as alive as the face, and the figures seem caught in motion, begun but never completed.

You should take care in noticing the people that appear in your dreams. Some of these can be used as models. You have known a proportion of them from other existences, and have a knowledge, innate, of their characters and temperaments. *(Long pause.)*

When you become involved in the figure work however, make sure that you allow yourself special freedom in the area of the upper thighs.

("Why is that?")

The flexibility and spring, the gait, the appearance of living legs will depend upon a special fluidity in the area of the upper thigh. You will feel, I believe, more comfortable with a torso, hands and feet, and that is why I mentioned specifically that you allow yourself freedom with this other area.

Do you follow me now?

("I think so.")

You want to make your own people.

("Yes, I've become aware of that.")

You will make them, whole and entire, as well as your heads also, you see. And as they emerge full figure so will you emerge in your stature as an artist, and in confidence.

Now you may take a break or end the session as you prefer.

("We'll take the break."

(10:08. Jane was well dissociated; she thought that perhaps ten minutes had passed, where actually 20 minutes had gone by.

(I explained now to Jane that the material tonight was very good, and that I hadn't given her clues to it, etc., especially as regards the color experiments, characterization, the full-figure work, the essentials required for drawing the full figure convincingly, etc. She did know about my plans to do full figures, however.

(Resume at 10:20.)

Now. I will tell you what you want to do in case you do not know.

You want to do your own people. You want to make your own people, and you want to make their environment. The people will come first, but then you will feel that their personality extends also into their environment.

You want to create a whole new world of your own making, in your own art form, and you will not be satisfied with less. In your paintings the people will be in control of the environment. It will not overwhelm them, and yet they will definitely emerge from it, and psychologically this will represent to you a triumphant emergence of individual personality.

It is important for you psychologically that you express this.

In one way you have begun to do so, in the manner that you have chosen to paint clothing—that is, the types of clothing you have chosen to portray. The environment portion will come later, and you will sense the environment something like a mystic arrangement that a given personality throws about the world around him.

Clothing tells much about character, for a person chooses his clothing. Subconsciously he also chooses his environment, and throws his own character about it so the basic mood, the underlying mood of a personality beneath all the shifting moods, will also be expressed in color that is reflected in the entire painting, the environment as well.

As a glaze is added to a glaze, so the color of the glazes represent the moods within moods that make up the entire psychological framework of the personality. The fluidity of lines also tells much about the characterization; a rigidity of line showing a rigidity of character.

This is also reflected in the environment. By environment I mean those portions of the painting called background. They will attain greater vividness for you. You will see them as extensions of your people, rather than as the medium in which your people happen to appear. Do you have any questions on this material?

("Well, I will. I'd like to study this first though.")

Then I will answer any questions that you have. I will then end our session, with my heartiest regards to you both. I have been with you in your travels. A fond good evening.

("Good evening, Seth. Thank you, it was very good."

(10:35. Jane was out of trance quickly. She remarked that she was certain that as Seth she could see better without glasses than she could see without glasses as Jane. Explaining, she said she felt she could see as well, as Seth, without glasses, as she could see as herself with glasses.

(Once again, the material in the last delivery was very good, with much intuitive insight as regards character, background, emotion, etc., in painting. From this data I will formulate some questions for Seth. At the moment however they will center chiefly about New York City galleries, names, etc.)

SESSION 496
AUGUST 18, 1969 9:10 PM MONDAY

Good evening.

("Good evening, Seth.")

Now. Give us a moment. *(Pause.)*

In the area of 6th Avenue and 61st Street, Carter *(spelled).* You had better include N A N. *(Pause.)* Now I do not know if this is Nan Carter, but I do know the two are connected. And with a group show of some note in 1935, in which I believe this person participated, who now owns, or runs, or is connected with this gallery in this neighborhood.

I suggest you turn on your cooler. I will speak above it. We want Ruburt's temperature lowered.

(Jane sat quietly in trance while I left my seat to turn on the air cooler set into one of our living-room windows. It was a very hot and sticky night. The cooler didn't make so much noise that Seth had any trouble speaking above it.

(Before the session I had asked Jane if Seth could give me some more data on the art and gallery material begun in the last session. I was going to try to put it to practical use, I told Jane not to try too hard, though, to get more data. She said that the impetus would be strong to help me on these subjects. I was a little surprised to hear Seth start right in on the gallery data.)

The man has been himself an artist, therefore. He may be the uncle of the man who runs the gallery, per se, but he has a strong voice in the gallery. At one time connected with the school of ashcan art. Do you follow me?

("Yes."

(Later Jane confirmed that she'd heard of the ashcan school of art.)

His ideas have changed through the years. *(Pause.)* Give us time. There will be a man called Art, as Arthur, but called Art, also connected with this establishment.

A ten-hundred block referring to one of the locations given. *(In the last session.)* This may refer to 72nd Street, and Fifth Avenue.

The Bill's mentioned refer to a delicatessen that is also used as a drinking bar, with some entertainment at times. "The Occasions." They are I believe a group. We will give you what we have. Some will need to be clarified.

The Jerry leads to Lewis, and there is a connection here, but not the one you would suppose. There is an Italian connection. This place is not the 6th Avenue, 61st Street mentioned earlier. You follow here. This is the second occasion.

You may let your pussycat out, and I will see what I can find in the meantime.

(I wasn't too happy about the interruption, but agreed to it. Rooney, our black cat, had been injured somehow in the left front leg, so that for the past four days he had been moving about on three legs. He was now scratching at the door to go out.

(Rooney moved a few feet into the hall, then sat down to rest. In the living room Jane sat still in trance. To use the time I let our other cat, Willy, in the back hall door. After Willy went into the apartment, with my help, Rooney finally ambled out the back way. All of this took several minutes, which I endured impatiently.

(Yet Jane sat quite at ease, still in trance, waiting until I resumed my place and picked up the notebook.)

Three doors down, an establishment having to do with shoes, or a shoeshine establishment with a black grating.

Sevens strongly in the numbers of the address, and zero. At first you will not think this is a place for you. They will not seem to show your kind of work, but this is precisely why they will want to do so. They do not have anyone in their stable who can do good work with figures, or of an objective nature.

Now listen: do not take it for granted that those who do not show your type of art are against it, or will not want it. In New York now, and across the country, it is difficult to find objective work that is not highly stylized or sentimentalized.

Many galleries therefore do not carry objective work because the defects are so clearly seen. They take instead planned distortions, which can cover up such inadequacies, or frankly abstract works.

So at first this gallery will seem to you unsuitable. If I had not told you this you would pass it by, thinking they wanted only abstracts, or your, is it—pop art?

("Yes." This material refers to some remarks I had made earlier, about trying to list galleries in New York City that I thought might be interested in my type of art, judging from their advertisements.)

They will be particularly interested in your people, far more than in landscapes, and in certain of your fruits. You will be doing I believe more work with fruit, of a different nature. I believe that this will involve a magnification of the work you have done with fruit. An apple for example as it might be seen by a fly. A peach as it might be seen, or a pear, by a squirrel.

I do not mean that you will have this in mind particularly, but that you will be looking at fruit in a new way, and from different viewpoints. When you do this, this gallery will be interested.

(At least consciously, I hadn't been considering any such ideas involving fruit, although the ideas here are interesting ones.)

Give us a moment. *(Pause. Then quickly:)*

Jerry A. Fox. The gallery is commercial. From the outside it does not look like a gallery, but is well-enough known. It has foreign outlets as well.

There is something elevated here. Now I do not know. This could refer to lofts. It is more fashionable than the other gallery, or more "in." It deals in larger works than you are now producing, as a rule.

It moved twice in the past two years however, for added space. This is the third location, and in the first location it was run by a different man. There is a woman connected with it who will remind Ruburt of her Lydia *(Nesbitt)*, and a connection with Charlotte.

There is also a connection with postcards. Underneath the establishment there is a connected concern—perhaps framing, I do not know. A basement enterprise.

You should try also for a foundation grant. Save now all of your people *(portraits)*, and do not sell them locally.

You may take your break, and we shall continue.

(9:44. Jane was slow coming out of trance. She said traffic noise had bothered her at the session's start, until Seth had me turn on the cooler. Then her trance had been deep, though she remembered the cat episode.

(Then Jane surprised me by saying that <u>*Fox*</u> *was not the name she had spoken, re Jerry A. She was very definite—that Fox wasn't correct, saying I had misunderstood her. She thought the name was Foss, instead, although she was not as positive here. We speculated about Foch or Foche; Jane said the name was one syllable with a softer sound than Fox—hence Foss. We thought Seth would clear the matter.*

(I told Jane however that we should get some material on a matter broached to her by letter last week by Reverend Crosson, re a speaking engagement in New York City later this year. The gallery data could be continued later.

(9:58.)

Now. Several points.

Ruburt's book should include, as it will, a photograph of Ruburt. It should also include a reproduction of your painting of me, in a prominent place.

It should also include some other reproductions of your paintings as they apply to your psychic personalities. This will also help publicize your own work. It will also add interest to the book. I told you that your portrait of an old woman was yourself as a mother, and that should be included, as should the portraits of Ruburt and Joseph done together.

Now if you follow my advice, when you have guests or when you are at work, whenever you see people, you will then try to get an inner impression of the selves that they have been, or of the entity of which they are part.

You can do this, and well, and it will allow you to work with people who are independent of this place and time. I mentioned this once earlier. Give us a moment. *(Pause. Then humorously:)* Your painting of me can become famous, in time. Do not sell it.

("Okay.")

It can be used also in connection with speeches that Ruburt may give. Just wait. *(Pause, long.)*

There are two things operating. Crosson, not admitting it to himself, is afraid that he cannot hold an audience sufficiently and he wants help. He has been saying the same things over and over. He wants to be the one to introduce someone new, someone who will be known in the field, and added to his crown.

There is nothing wrong in this, beside the vanity, which is natural enough. He also wants to make the path easier for Ruburt. He is pushing on purpose, for he thinks you are not businesslike-enough for your own good, on your own. *(Long pause.)*

Basically, it makes no great difference what you do.

(Whether or not we visit Reverend Crosson this summer at his camp in the Berkshires, in Massachusetts; and whether later in the year Jane speaks in New York City at a meeting of the Spiritual Frontiers Fellowship, with Reverend Crosson.)

There will be no complications resulting from such a meeting of an adverse nature, if you feared this. Some good contacts would be made. They will be made in any case. Ruburt should not plan to do trance work. *(As suggested by Reverend C., on stage.)* His main energies remain with the material. He is an excellent teacher however, and a good speaker.

I am not going to tell you to go or not to go. You must make your own decision. Give us a moment. *(Pause.)* The woman mentioned very shortly <u>may lose or give up her position</u>. There is illness for her in the fairly near future, but if you meet her, it will be of help nevertheless. Through various circumstances she may not even call. <u>Another speaker, thought not available, may change his mind</u>.

(Seth refers to Betty Taylor, one of the editors at Harper's. She told Reverend C. that she would call Jane this week, but as of August 20, Wednesday, has not done so.

(Humorously:) A weekend with the Crossons seem more or less inevitable, and will be of benefit to all four of you.

(Our cat, Willy, now jumped up in Jane's lap. Without coming out of trance Jane put him down and resumed.)

He will ultimately be of help to you in ways you do not now foresee. He is bungling and frightened but he waves brave banners. *(Pause.)* Ruburt is one of his discoveries. He has not fulfilled his potentials, and he knows it, and so he tries to be self-important. But he means well. His wife is his support. He has not always been treated kindly by the psychics that he knows. In many ways he was shoved aside because he did not have the courage of his convictions earlier. *(Long pause at 10:25.)*

At times he can show malice, but in small ways, not harmful ones. Now you may end the session or take a break as you prefer.

We'll take the break.

(10:26, 10:35.)

Now. The repressed nature of Ruburt's fears was responsible for the symptoms at your first encounter with the Crossons. This has been largely cleared.

There is some unresolved relationship between the four of you however. You cannot so easily dismiss him. I do not believe he will be active beyond two years or so, unless he changes and pierces his own overly jaunty exterior.

(Again Willy jumped up into Jane's lap, and again she put him down without leaving trance.)

He needs inner initiation, new stirrings of his own (underlined) creativity. He also needs kindness. If you give him a hand he will be grateful and do his best to repay you. He is no longer precise.

Now do you have any further questions?

("Can you do anything about the mix-up on the name—

(Before I could finish the question about the name, James A Fox, or Foss, Seth spoke out quickly and forcefully.)

The name is Foss. Do you have me loud and clear?

("Yes. F-o-s-s." I spelled it out, my version.)

I was not trying to be foxy. The name is Foss. I do not know the spelling.

Your attitude in any case toward the meeting should be a relaxed one, whether you go or not.

("Okay." Re Crosson, etc.)

Do you have other questions?

("No.")

We will then end our session. *(Leaning forward, amused:)* I trust it meets with your approval, and with Ruburt's.

("Why not ?")

My heartiest regards to you both, and a fond good evening.

("Good evening, Seth, and thank you. 10:45.)

SESSION 497
AUGUST 20, 1969 9:10 PM WEDNESDAY

Good evening.

("Good evening, Seth.")

Now. Ruburt attempted too much last evening for one night's work.

(Seth refers to last night's ESP class, in which Jane and some of her students obtained some unusual effects and experiences. One ESP class member, Sue Watkins, saw Seth in the room, etc.)

The experiences were legitimate enough. In two cases he was using his own energy to sustain and direct the group, and to transport them, so to speak. He had some help from others in the group, but not enough for such sustained effort.

(Jane had remarked several times today that she felt unusually "dragged out," etc.)

Give us a moment. *(Long pause, eyes closed.)*

I would like you to seriously embark upon the hobby of out-of-body travel. There is no reason why you cannot become proficient at it if you are strongly enough motivated. You will find all kinds of people that can serve as models for you. The alteration of consciousness involved will also enable you to make several distinct and advantageous changes of focus, in line with your own work.

This is difficult to put into words. There is no reason, again, why you can't achieve out-of-body proficiency, and when you do, you will be able to experiment with thought creations, trying out, forming, using or discarding, thought paintings. In an out-of-body state you can reach rather easily those environments which thoughts become a sort of plastic pseudo material, almost instantaneously.

Now within this framework you could test out many ideas for paintings, various techniques, and see them or their results immediately. This would be a conscious, alert experience. Do you follow me here?

("Yes.")

The alterations of consciousness would give you a rather unique freedom that I cannot put into words, a perspective and a viewpoint above reality, that would show in your work. We have offered you suggestions to follow before.

For your particular purposes you might imagine that you are walking through, or traveling through, one of your own paintings. Try to throw your consciousness into the environment you have painted. Observe particularly the colors that would be observable to you in many out-of-body states. There are gradations with which you are not familiar. They will inspire changes in your own palette.

There will be all kinds of different spatial relationships for you to explore, and then to attempt to reproduce in your work if you prefer. The disciplines involved in these alterations of consciousness will help you in all other areas, will acquaint you quite personally with other realities, and be a preparation for the time when you will not have a physical body in which to manipulate.

There is personal evidence to be obtained here that can be obtained in no other way. Ruburt has talked of some renewed work, and I heartily suggest that you concentrate strongly at doing joint out-of-body explorations.

In the beginning it will be up to Ruburt to aid you, and with concentration and application he can do so. I do not want this suggestion to go by the board, as it will if you simply file the session and ignore it. I would like this work to begin, and to continue throughout your lives as a joint effort.

I make this as a strong recommendation, for if you are to obtain full benefits from your developments, then you simply must become proficient along these lines. You must implement the sessions and your knowledge with such personal experience. This should not be a haphazard affair, left to chance.

Two evenings a week specific suggestions should be used and attempts made. Now you may take your break and I will give you some pointers. I hope you will follow them. I will, incidentally, comment in sessions concerning your experiences.

(9:35-9:40.)

Now. Initially these will be nighttime experiences, conducted during sleep. Your physical bodies will be well-relaxed at the time.

For that matter you will be giving them additional energy and refreshment because of the experiments. The ideal will be to travel together. Ruburt already knows how to leave the body, using several methods from the sleep state and immediately before it.

These methods will suffice. He must also remind himself however to assist you, and to contact your astral self. If he finds himself astrally awake and sees only your physical body, then you are either on an unconscious astral trip already, or your astral body has not left your physical one.

If he only sees your physical body then he should address you, announce his own out-of-body state and invite you to join him. If you are still in your body and if conditions are good, you will then leave your body and join him. If there is no response then you are on an unconscious projection of your own. When astral contact is made, some manipulations may be necessary in order to maintain them, but there is nothing to worry about if you go your separate ways.

This method simplifies things for you, since on those two nights you need only tell yourself that you will listen for Ruburt's call. You will both learn added control by traveling together. You can also travel further in a cooperative effort.

Now if you make a habit of doing this, of giving these suggestions two evenings a week, you will ultimately be highly successful. I suggest that the two nights be together. Ruburt should try on these nights one of his methods as he falls asleep, and if that does not succeed, tell him to use the other methods that he knows from the dream state.

He can explain these to you again so that you know what to expect. I will give you additional data on those environments that you visit, so that your experiences are paralleled by session discussions throughout the years. To fully develop yourselves psychically, such experiences are necessary. They will also serve as themes in your work and in Ruburt's if they are carried through.

They will give you, again, valuable insights into realities that are not physical, and the period immediately following physical death will hold no shocks for you. You will be in familiar territory.

Do you want a break?

("No." Seth's pace had been good, with few pauses.)

Now then. You will not need too many experiences before your own confidence will allow you to leave your body without Ruburt's assistance, but the joint traveling is still important. You can help and guide each other as you do in physical life.

I will help you if a need arises, but beyond that I will give you some instructions while you are in a projected state. I cannot do this until you achieve a certain proficiency. When you are ready, and after perhaps a year's work on your own, I will outline a general program for you to follow.

There are various kinds of environments that you should visit. You may be more naturally attracted to some over others, and we will deal with a fairly broad spectrum of experiences. Some of these will involve you in those planes of reality in which personalities more or less recently dead now survive.

You may visit your Miss Callahan, for example, as Ruburt has done. You may visit others now dead in those terms, with whom you were once acquainted. Generally speaking, such visits will involve you however with one main environment, so you could do that indefinitely, and we will want you to have more experience than that. *(In Book 1, see Session 28 re Miss Callahan.)*

I am not going to let the matter rest here, I assure you. I will keep at you. Now give us a moment. *(Pause.)*

These sessions have their own logic, and their own continuity. They are leading in certain directions that may not be apparent to you as yet, and they do undergo cycles, which are necessary and natural.

Some of this has to do with my intentions, some with my relative availability. If you recall what I told you, I am always here to some extent. Do you follow me?

("Yes.")

During some cycles I am more strongly focused with you than others, but

I am always close enough to see that the material is being properly delivered and that the necessary structures are being maintained. It goes without saying that your own mental attitudes are important. Without certain attitudes the sessions would have been impossible to begin with.

Your faith in your own work is highly important. Your own out-of-body experiences, if followed through, will even reinforce the sessions, for you will be experiencing circumstances of which I have already told you. You will think of questions, therefore, matters that I take for granted. Do you follow me here?

("Yes.")

The more work you do the better I can help you. There will be seasonal and other variations in your own out-of-body work. Over a period of years however this sort of thing will iron out. There are many factors that operate to help or impede our communications, on both your side and mine.

The structure of the sessions was set up because I felt that in the long run the structure itself would be permanent, able to withstand any natural strains, and also strong enough and flexible enough to permit maximum fulfillment. Many kinds of experience are possible within it, for example.

It is a psychological structure, as I have explained, and you and Ruburt are both a part of it. Now you may take your break or end the session as you prefer.

("We'll take the break."

(10:17. Jane was well dissociated; she didn't remember the material except for the last few words. Resume at 10:28.)

Now. I will not keep you.

("That's all right.")

I suggest that on the two evenings, Ruburt take a warm shower—not a hot one—before retiring. I also suggest contrary to Muldoon that you have a light (underlined) snack. Not a heavy one, but enough so the body is comfortable.

You should be comfortably warm, but not overburdened with blankets. *(Long pause.)* A note to Ruburt: he should keep a robe handy. Use one book for dreams, and leave it on his desk overnight. As a preliminary to the instructions I have given you, for 7 days he should give himself dream suggestions, and on several occasions, though not every night, tell himself that he will awaken after a dream and record it.

As he knows, this facilitates out-of-body states on his part. This should be done a week before you begin your joint experiments.

Now you should begin the same week with new suggestions to recall your dreams, but do it this way, as follows:

(To me:) Before you sleep, simply imagine your open dreambook in the morning, with the dreams recorded. Imagine that you see so many lines of written words. You understand—

("Yes.")

—visualize it, and feel yourself pleased that you have succeeded. The pleasure at your success is important. You have been too intellectual. Do you follow me?

("Yes.")

I will now end the session. I suggest the first week begin this evening, of preliminary exercise. A hearty good evening to you both, and my fondest wishes.

("Good night, Seth."

(10:38. Once again, Jane's trance was a good one. Following Seth's instructions, I recorded several dreams over the next couple of nights after this session; the first I have been able to recall in many weeks. RFB.)

SESSION 498
AUGUST 25, 1969 9:33 PM MONDAY

(This afternoon Jane's editor at Prentice-Hall, Tam Mossman, called her re the Seth book Jane is completing for P/H. Tam also had a couple of questions, which Seth begins to answer in this session.

(Before the session this evening I spent some time blowing off steam about a variety of large issues that we see reflected in our daily news media—such things as corruption, pollution, inflation, the destiny of the race if it persists in its present ways, etc. Actually I feel deeply about these things and become quite furious over actions that seem blatantly destructive to us in the long run. A rather innocent remark made by Jane shortly before 9 PM got me started, hence the session's late beginning.

(Jane also wanted to know about a rather startling experience of her own last Friday afternoon, involving an elderly friend.)

Good evening.

("Good evening, Seth.")

Now. I have several things to say, and we will try to answer questions that you have in mind.

First of all, *(to me)* do not lose your sense of perspective, that larger perspective, that our work should give you. You are also involved in other realities and other experiments. There is more, and there are trends now in your own reality that you do not see.

Not only this, but even if the race as you know it distorts itself beyond belief, or even destroys itself, the many will not forget. The knowledge, hard won, would be as instinct when the race began again. The losers then would become stern teachers, having learned through experience.

Each experiment is a success, regardless of whether it succeeds or fails in your terms, and each experiment also brings with it new elements of creativity, new innovations having appeared. These are retained.

There are various levels all operating, various levels of consciousness and identity. They cannot be forcibly restrained, for they would learn nothing. What they do learn however is always retained. This does not mean that each succeeding earth experiment will be made up of selves who have been through these cycles.

They may be personalities new to the system, new for that matter *(humorously)* to any ideas, completely unused to conceptual thought or vision, beings only now emerging into strong individuality. Consciousness at your level is at a crisis point for many reasons.

Within your system, for the "first time", in quotes, individualized consciousness is strongly-enough organized to do, in quotes, "good or evil." Before that it was protected, somewhat coddled, with instinctual behavior holding it in bounds. It is not able to utilize enough energy to maintain a system of its own, but operates as an adjunct to other stronger systems.

Now some of those within your reality are having their first experience with an ego as you think of it. Others are returning to it, the system, in an effort to learn more. There are guardians, so to speak, within your system, reincarnated for the last time to help keep it in some kind of order while the others mature. There are also some, not physical, who keep an eye out over the whole proceedings.

The training is necessary. The results at any given stage may not appear very hopeful, and in your terms there is indeed what seems to be a cumulative effect. There is a system of checks and balances that do operate. These exist within the inner selves. The system of checks and balances will operate up to a point, and maintain some stability.

There are alarm signals that trigger warnings through the entire physical reality. Disaster indeed shows itself within the dream state before it appears as physical fact.

Your ego is now focused within this reality. You have other egos focused in other realities. The inner self is aware of what is being done in all of these realities. There is some compensation, and the race knows this. Ruburt wrote that there were clumps of consciousness, and of course he is correct. You are a part of many such clumps of consciousness. The abilities and potentials are not only being developed in this system but in others.

The race also realizes well the advantages and disadvantages of the physical reality it has adopted. It knows for example that there is a tendency to go to extremes. I mentioned earlier that the rewards, the challenges and the dangers exist precisely because so much freedom is allowed.

Now. Those within the system know this. Regardless of what you may think of their present performance at any given "time" in quotes, it is from this system that the greatest potentials emerge; for having dealt with it, consciousness undergoes one of the severest tests in learning to handle its own energy.

The horror and the results of mismanagement, and the vulnerability, are the teaching methods that each consciousness has accepted before entering your system. There is no way out but to learn or to ruin the entire system. In no other field of reality are the terms so drastic. For this reason the inner self withholds much of its knowledge. There must be no leaning upon the very basic fact that behind and within the system there is relief. You must believe in the physical reality and accept the vulnerability.

Now, from your system spring some of the most advanced of all identities. They go on and learn from other realities, granted, but yours is the hardest to manage, and those who accept it go off into a certain line of development where the potentials are beyond anything of which you can presently conceive.

Now I am telling you this evening not only because of your own earlier discussion, but also because this material will fit in with other sessions that I have in mind. You are not only ready for them but you are demanding them, and until you are ready you would not understand them.

First, quite simply, there are many who do not see those failings and shortcomings and trends of which you spoke earlier. They cannot be told; they learn. Now alone they would not be permitted to destroy an entire reality. The mixture of consciousness within your system gives some control. The child must mature, and your system is a maturing ground, a very primary one. A beginning school for those who are trying out for particular kinds of experience. Some simply will not succeed. They will continue instead along other lines of development.

Now, you have quite literally put in your time, for centuries. *(Humorously.)* This is one of the reasons that you find yourself very impatient with the development of your fellows, who have not had that advantage as yet. You have learned. You cannot understand why they have not.

There are cycles of entry into your system. Now the first, quote "mass" entries do not give you war. Those entering are at first too bewildered.

Manipulation within the physical universe is strange. They do not realize the potential of their own energy, and it is not until they begin to realize it that they are, quote, "led into temptation."

They have to learn to handle it constructively. Now cooperation is an innate feature to these entering selves. Without it they could not survive long enough to learn anything. The warlike periods do not begin until this group achieves some ability at manipulation. Now while it seems to you that there has been little advance, there has indeed in the overall. Larger masses of individuals than ever before in this cycle realize that killing is wrong.

Now this cycle that I am speaking of goes back to the beginning of history as it is generally known, to your cavemen. You may take your break and we will continue.

(10:20-10:35.)

Now. We will get on with some other subjects. But remember you must consider the race and its inhabitants in the entire context of existence if you are to be realistic.

Give us a moment. *(Pause.)* This earlier material however will be continued at our next session. Now. *(Pause.)*

Both Ruburt's new experiments in class, and his affair with the hands represent growing receptivity and willingness on his part. In many ways the hand episode was the result of class work. Some of the experiments in class gave him confidence, and I gave him confidence and a challenge. The challenge was important. I appeared in class and he did not see me, and his friend did. And he knows why.

Therefore he made the inner decision. Before, he was afraid to see psychic events. Now this was no coincidence. He has poor eyes, because he did not want to see physical events. He did not use vision strongly as an aid, not strongly, say, comparatively speaking. He was poor in forming clear mental images, even as he was poor at seeing physical events.

Therefore with the development of the psychic experience he carried through in the same manner. It was a habit of perception. He did not want to see his mother clearly. He was frightened, hence the pattern developed. He suddenly realized that there was an advantage to be gained here, and he wanted to see immediately after his friend saw my image.

Now. *(Pause.)* The hand experience was legitimate. The visual impression objectified it for him. Before, he would not have allowed this. The difficulty will be one of circulation in the limbs and hands, and are already—the symptoms are already—felt by the woman in question.

Give us a moment. *(Pause.)* I believe the woman knows, and wants to see her husband settled in a good physical environment before she leaves. There is an S M connected here—a relative or friend, who has been dead for some time, who is looking after her.

Give us a moment. *(Pause.)* I will speak to our Aerofranz when he comes to visit. For now there are simply some errors he has made, both in expecting too much on the one hand, and not expecting enough on the other. You know about the psychological bridge that is necessary for communications. He and his Adam are beginning to build it. Work is needed on both of their parts in that he is himself pushing for predictions, —whether he realizes this or not, and trying to bring more "across" in quotes, than the bridge can carry. On the other hand there is not enough regular (underlined) application on his part, but spasmodic activity.

The emotional need of others can be of a help—later. If the foundations are to be properly built there must be some regular application, not overly sober nor over demanding. There are abilities here that can definitely be developed.

There can be an overstimulation on Aerofranz's part however, when he attempts to use Adam to help others at this point. Do you follow there?

("Yes.")

Adam can and will contribute too and strengthen Aerofranz's own personality and characteristics. He can help Aerofranz develop himself. He is no threat to Aerofranz's own personality but Aerofranz should not call upon him to help others until the psychological bridge of which I have spoken has a stronger foundation. In his desire to help others Aerofranz then can demand too much of Adam under present circumstances.

This overstimulates Aerofranz so that he tries to use his nervous energy, it is not that Adam cannot help. It is that the communicating bridge between them must be completed. Then firm results will appear.

Now in the second half of our next session I will go into the other material that our good friend requests. You may take a break or end the session now, as you prefer.

("I guess we'll have to end it, then.")

One note: you also feel at times *(to me)* that you have not done enough through your reincarnations to help the race, or it would be in better condition.

I will elaborate Wednesday.

("Good night, Seth, and thank you."

(11:00. Jane had been "far-out," she said. Seth could have continued indefinitely. "He's got all kinds of energy." But Jane was tired; the session ended rather abruptly. She remembered little of the material.)

SESSIO 499
AUGUST 27, 1969 9:30 PM WEDNESDAY

(Carl and Sue Watkins, both members of Jane's ESP class, were witnesses to the session. Seth's first humorous remarks refer to them as the session opens.)

Good evening.

("Good evening, Seth.")

And good evening to you: you did not get very far... Now give us a moment. *(Pause.)*

This is to your friend Aerofranz's wife-to-be.

Aerofranz wanted a word from me, and the word is: hold out a while. There may be a definite change to another department on her *(Eve's)* part, and this would represent a slight advancement—a half step, but a good one.

There will also be changes in any case in her department, if probabilities continue as I see them now. In any case two men in particular will be involved.

I seem to have A R.

Now. The new department or her position would build upon her present knowledge and duties; that is, the knowledge would be of definite value to her, but the main emphasis of her duties would lie elsewhere. There is a future for her in that company, if (underlined) she chooses to pursue it and is not impatient.

There will be several major breakthroughs in that department. The first beginning to show within a 6-month period. I will have more to say to both of them when I see them. *(Humorously:)* It will be my wedding present.

(Pause.) Now give me a moment. *(This is all Seth gave for Tam and Eve in this session.*

(Humorously again:) You do not consider a dream as a success or a failure. If the dream ends in a moment of destruction you do not consider the dream a failure. In the overall then, when I told you that the planet was dispensable, I meant it somewhat in those terms, for while in your reality you are vulnerable, and agony is real, still it is not the whole reality, and success and failure have no meaning in those (underlined) terms.

The consciousnesses that have made up your race gain valuable experience. You must not forget that the analogy between your physical reality and the dream state does have a basic truth.

Even the physical planet, having vanished, basically would continue to exist. Those responsible for such a destruction would have destroyed only reality as they knew it, in the probable system. Other probable earths and other probable races of mankind coexist, and you are apart of these also. You would be dispensing with an experiment you were not able to handle.

At the same time, again, the experiences would be used. From a larger viewpoint you would know that nothing had been destroyed. Now you should underline the last sentence. Think about it, and then I will answer questions that I believe you will have.

We have been speaking of projections and experiments in them, and if you want to, know what other experiments are being conducted by yourself and others this is one way that you can at least briefly glimpse them.

Any event that you would consider disastrous to your race, brought about by the race itself, would be used in another probable system to avoid the same sort of error. There are disasters and dead end roads that your race has avoided completely, because in other systems of reality the lessons were learned and learned well.

Your own instinct for survival, so-called, is the result, so to speak, of experience in other systems. The original problem was far different. A way was needed to teach these personalities to focus long enough, in your terms, intensely enough, within any given reality.

When the lessons are learned there is no need for physical reality. The survival instinct, strongly connected with the physical self, keeps it anchored in focus within your system. Without it consciousness would tend to float free. It is your anchor.

Now. In conscious projections you allow yourself some freedom. In many cases you do consciously what you do unconsciously in any case. You are able with practice to journey through other systems. You are able to see for yourself not only the experiments that are being tried, but often to come into contact with other portions of yourself, who are involved in those experiments. As for example your Doctor Pietra.

("I was just going to ask you about him.")

I told you that after the prime points the autumn would be the next time of contact. There are two peak periods of activity there, between the 20th and 22nd of September, and October 5 to 17, and then his experiments will be over for now.

If you begin with the experiments I have suggested, then you can hopefully try to contact him in his own reality.

Now, Ruburt has had the first of the seven dreams. *(See the 497th session, for July 7, 1969.)* It is the dream of the sands, and I mentioned the series of dreams earlier. I want to give you an explanation of that dream.

("I don't think Ruburt thought of the dream that way.")

(Jane had the dream in question on August 22, 1969, a Friday night, and has

it recorded in her dream notebook. She described it to me at breakfast Saturday morning, mentioning the impression it had made upon her, but without connecting it to Seth's series of seven dreams.)

Subconsciously Ruburt knew that the dream was important. He did not know it was the first of the seven.

Now. I will have a few comments for our friends here, and I want to continue with the material that I have been giving you. In the meantime take your break. Your own first dream should come shortly.

(9:55-10:02.)

Now. Give us a moment here.

First, the dream. Ruburt saw you and he standing in the middle of an infinite plain of sand. The sands were marked with names and messages. To the left and to the right there were mountains of sand. To the left he saw people approaching the sands upon which he stood. To the right people were leaving the plains of sand, yet the plain itself was empty, filled only with the messages that were written there.

All was silence. You and he were about to step out upon the plain, and he held back because he did not want to disturb the messages.

Now. You and he had both come from another direction. The messages represent *(pause)* philosophies and ideas *(pause)* that the Seth material and his work will change. The dream is personal and yet more than this, these messages and philosophies will be buried not only by the material but by psychic awareness on the part of many individuals like yourselves.

Two things in the dream held him back: a gigantic nostalgia for the writings in the sand that had remained for so long, the jottings of children—and for a moment he did not want to be part of anything that would wipe them out. He wondered aloud in the dream whether or not you and he should really be there: what credentials you had that would give you the right to make new footprints.

There was no empty space, no <u>new</u> road, only the way before you both, that would necessitate your treading upon these jottings and transposing your footsteps <u>over</u> those that were there.

Now the plain was empty. The people coming in from the left represented later generations, in your terms, who had not yet arrived at the plain. The people to the right were those who had already passed beyond it. The plain was empty because it was the repository of ideas. The ideas had been put there by those who had already left.

The old ideas had not been wiped out. The new ideas had not yet taken hold. Part of your responsibility will be to tread upon the old ideas, to clear the distortions; and Ruburt, realizing this, hesitated, but he recognized in the dream exactly what was involved.

When he begins to walk across the sand, and you with him, new messages will appear there. They will be a signal for those people on the left. In your terms those people will be drastically different than those who have gone before. They will not walk upon the old ideas nor dwell within their reality.

You are clearing the sands for them, and giving them new guideposts and in Ruburt's dream he felt them waiting.

Now. There is also a symbolism here with the parting of the waters, a silence and abeyance, a hush. He sees you standing in the middle. See now the empty plain, as a scooped-out and hollow place from which the water has fled. The sand mountains to the left and right.

(Jane was gesturing quite emphatically in here, arms and hands echoing her words, eyes open and very dark, etc.) Now the crest. This represents the concept that these ideas will be so given that they become the springs which will bring new nourishment to an arid world psyche.

There are others behind you that Ruburt never saw, for you are not alone, nor the only ones involved. The dream was a statement of the situation and of his position. The next one will begin as he is bold enough to walk out upon the plain with you.

Now give us a moment. *(Long pause at 10:28.)* You are to a large extent outside of the context. You did not come from the direction that the others came, nor will you continue. You were at right angles you see between the two groups of people.

The people represent those who still have past and future lives in your terms. Your development now will be different. Your challenge and responsibility is also different. For you must go across that plain of ideas, you see, transposing others, and you must go together. And while there are others, you will not be aware of them. You will not have them, in your time, for comfort, and so it will seem to you that you are alone, and that you are set apart from those both coming and going.

So also Ruburt felt. *(Jane learned forward, quite intent.)* It was safer where he was, and he hesitated to take that first step. And the step is the publication of the book, and the ideas that it entails.

Now you may take your break and we shall continue.

(10:33. Jane said she had been far out in trance. As she spoke she was back in the dream location; she saw the sand and the water; amusingly, she also worried about the water "coming back in," she said. Her pace had been fairly rapid.

(During break we also discussed some topics Sue and Carl were interested in,

expecting that Seth would discuss these after break. Sue also wrote out a copy of her dream of Tuesday night, August 26, and gave it to me for these notes:

("I find myself in a room with Carl and Jane, as Jane. She gestures at me and I step out of my dream self—I remember giving my "body" good health suggestions. A strange man [or is it a conscious projection of one of us?] forms a tiny Colonial-type house in the air, and it enlarges until it's regular size. Then Jane, as Seth, pushes us at the house. Suddenly we are in a car, plummeting through moonscape-like scenery. Awake."

(That same night Carl also had a dream involving a large white house, but upon awakening could not recall it clearly.

(Resume at 10:50.)

Now. In other terms and on another level Ruburt felt that symbolically at least he was between birth and death, that egotistically speaking the way of darkness had been parted; and in these terms the mountain to the left represented death, from which he had come, <u>and</u> birth, for he emerged through birth from death; and the mountain to the right represented the death that in your terms has not yet come.

And within that context he knew it was now the time for him to walk out upon those messages that had gone before, and change the distortions, for he knew there would be no other birth and death for him, the time of reincarnations being finished.

(To me.) You will experience your own version in your own way, and your own statement of your situation, Joseph. The whole sand of the plain also represented then a page that must be entirely rewritten.

(Pause at 10:57. Then to Sue:) Now. The house to you now represented a new dimension that you were to explore. You made it familiar.

(Below her dream account Sue had written: "Consciously, I know that Colonial-type houses represent great comfort to me. Whenever I see one, the house sort of <u>radiates</u> comfort at me.")

It was not for example odd in its construction, for you will enter the new dimension through doors that appear familiar, as Ruburt is a friend and not a stranger.

Symbolically the both of you were to follow me into this house, for its rooms contain various realities. The realities merge so walls inside the house did not serve as divisions, and had you followed me you would have seen that passing through one wall would not lead you to a room on the other side, but to numberless rooms within the wall.

Now the walls within the rooms could be compared to your physical time, each wall a moment as you think of it. But each moment can be used as a threshold into experiences that have no time, and I explained this to you, though you do not remember.

You turned the house symbolically into a normal-sized house so that you could enter it, but you did not do so. Its proportions would have changed of course the moment you set your feet inside the door. You learned through the experience, and there will be others.

Give us a moment, Joseph. *(Long pause.)* I told you to take a week to prepare yourself through dream recall for your experiments. For several evenings, see yourself in the environment of Ruburt's dream as given. As you fall asleep give yourself the suggestion that you and he begin to walk upon the sand. See the both of you together, <u>and</u> hand in hand. Now Ruburt should do the same exercise.

Do you have any questions of the material as given this evening?

("How about that mass transfer of consciousness?"

(This question refers to a discussion the four of us had at first break, after Seth had given us data on any possible destruction of our earth, the various probable systems involving other earths, etc. We had wondered what course the entities would take who had manifested on our particular probability-earth, in the event of its literal destruction.)

Now. I told you that the knowledge gained would be retained. Not only this, but it is retained not only by the individual selves as you think of them. It becomes part of the knowledge of all the probable selves in other realities also.

There would indeed be a mass transference of consciousness, but not necessarily at all to one particular reality. The individual consciousnesses involved would not for example necessarily choose to start anew, in the same kind of reality, agreeing to form more or less identical conditions.

They would however definitely go where their experience could be best utilized, and where their intimate knowledge of destruction be best used as a tool. To some degree such a destruction would be felt in all realities. Some probable selves would have shattering dreams of disaster. Other worlds would quake with the psychic reflections.

Give us a moment here. *(Jane paused. As she did so our cat Willy jumped up in her lap; he has done this several times lately. But as before Jane's trance wasn't broken. I put Willy down.)*

I am speaking theoretically, but those in the probable system, according to their own knowledge and capabilities, could also help your own system to avert disaster under certain conditions. This is rather an involved subject; and it would also be highly dependent upon your willingness to be helped. The race has called out before for help, and received it.

It can only accept certain kinds of help, and the help in one way or another must be initiated at least from its own pool of energy, and its own bank of personality gestalts.

I have answered your question simply enough. There will be more to come. You may now end the session or take a break as you prefer.

("I have one question. How is the entity that is about to manifest part of itself through Sue [who is due to give birth in a few weeks], preparing for the event and experience?")

(Jane leaned forward. As Seth her eyes were wide open and very dark; her manner was amused and hearty.)

How many sessions do you want me to take to answer your question?

("I don't care.")

I suggest that you take a break, and I will begin to give you the answer.

(11:15-11:28.)

Now. *(Pause.)* You are intensely focused within physical reality.

As you know, other portions of the self are intensely focused elsewhere. Before physical birth, you have already made the decision to choose this probable reality, and to probe its potentials. The entity is therefore learning to realign its methods of perception.

It is learning the methods of physical perception, as within you it experiences your reactions and becomes familiar with the ways in which you use physical senses to obtain information. It is forming its body in more or less faithful replica to what is required. *(Pause.)* It is using many of your own expectations as a model, and many of its father's.

(This is the type of data my question had intended Seth to give—information of a more general application to many. Seth has also given Sue and Carl some reincarnational personal data in an ESP-class session.)

It is in other words forming a spacesuit according to the information that you have both given it. It has data from its own past lives that will also have a part in its psychic structure, and that is entirely independent of any information you have given it as parents.

It is meant therefore to go its own way. You have simply formed a bridge that helps it make the transition from one reality to another. It is bound to carry within it only those memories however of which even you are unaware *(pointing to Sue and Carl)*, that belong to your species and to your kind.

It will manipulate those memories in its own way, and alter them, and add to the pool of energy from which it has emerged. It is quite familiar with me, now, through your experience. At this moment, in your terms, its view of reality is more pure than your own.

It is aware of you both as psychic entities, and retains strong and unclouded perceptions of your past relationship. These connections must pass from its memory as it matures. The memories can be retained, but the primary focus of activity and the intensity must deal with this personality, and with this existence as you think of it.

The entity is putting its atoms together, busily constructing the necessary equipment, and you both aid it. It weaves into the physical structure all the knowledge it knows it will need. Truths that it has learned will be built-in, so to speak. Anything that the personality knows will be written into the chromosomal structure that you have formed for it.

(Pause.) It hears my voice, but it understands what I am saying mentally. It has come so far into physical reality *(Sue is eight months pregnant)*, that it can perceive telepathically, but it will be some time, as you know, before it will be able to interpret speech as such. It will rely upon inner communication.

To you, your body is solid. The entity can perceive the room in which you sit as if your belly were a window, but it sees with inner sight, and forms the images through the inner senses.

It reacts strongly to your ideas and to its father's telepathically, and so its inner perception of this room, say, is highly colored by your ideas of it. It then mentally perceives the room, right now, more or less as a combination of those ideas you have individually of it. *(Pause.)*

It is strongly aware of your feelings toward it. At times the personality traits that it had earlier color this perception. It pushes these aside impatiently. It has mental images of its own probable future, and parts of it do become frightened at times, to relinquish old adult powers for an infant's helplessness.

It is often bathed in dreams, and it drifts back to other lives and places as a release and a relief from the struggle that is involved in the new formation. This is the dilemma of creation. The inner self does all of this spontaneously, as both of your parts spontaneously—each of your selves spontaneously play their own role.

You may take your break if you prefer. I have hardly begun; or you may continue at another session. The implications of the question, Joseph, are such that it takes a while to even begin with this material.

("That's very good, Seth. I imagine this will be the end of the session. If so, thank you very much—it's been interesting indeed."

(11:50. This was the end of the session. Jane had delivered the above material almost without pause. Her trance had been good, and she remembered little of the material.

(Sue Watkins told us that before Seth began answering my question, her

unborn child had been very active—kicking, etc, within her. When Seth started to consider the question, the fetus became very quiet, Sue said, almost as though listening ...)

SESSION 500
SEPTEMBER 8, 1969 9 :10 PM MONDAY

(On Friday evening, September 5, we had as visitors Dick and Carol Crossed; Edward Gassner, 3664 Culver Road [14622], and Bernard Houlihan, 25 Ewer Avenue [14622]—all of Rochester, New York. No session was held. Ed Gassner offered to do work with Jane and Seth; he is a biologist, Ph.D.

(Jane exchanged phone calls with Betty Taylor [of Harcourt Brace, among other publishers] on September 8 & 9. Betty Taylor called Jane first. During the call she verified several of Seth's points made during the 497th session. Briefly these will be listed here.

(1: See page 362. She verified Seth's statements about Jim Crosson's worries about holding an audience, etc. 2: See page 362. Betty Taylor may soon change her position, moving to Washington DC from New York City to do reporting coverage for various magazines. 3: page 362. Betty Taylor nearly did not call Jane, as Seth mentioned. It develops that another speaker, thought not available, may, or has, change[d] his mind.

(In this session. held on Monday, Seth gave some data re Betty Taylor also. Jane called B.T. the next day and was given verification of some points by B.T. over the phone. Betty would like a copy of the data to study some of the other points. The results of this study will be included with a later session, which may be named here by number at least.)

Good evening.

("Good evening, Seth.")

Now. Ruburt is obviously afraid that he will have not only his own negative tendencies to contend with, but yours as well.

I can tell you this will not be the case for either of you.

Give me a moment. *(Pause.)* Your own tendencies *(to me)* are general ones, against personal encounters, <u>before</u> such encounters are made. They are initial defenses, and oftentimes they are highly negative. However, once a personal encounter has been made, then you accept it for what it is, and respond positively. Do you follow me?

("Yes.")

This applies to both of you, although Ruburt would be more open about initial encounters if he had your support. In this you do identify to some degree with your father's attitude. I am sure you know this.

Your subsequent behavior however does not follow his pattern at all. You are quite free for example in your relationship with our friend Aerofranz *(Tam Mossman)*, and you were with *(Gene)* Bernard, and more than fair with Instream. So this pattern should not be applied in your minds and projected.

You have a tendency to project this upon each other. It will be quite natural, beginning shortly and through the years, that you become acquainted with others who are interested, generally speaking, in psychic phenomena, and with others who will become interested through you.

Now do not look down upon the importance of personal encounters, or the effect of personality. Ruburt's personality shows in his writings and his individual interpretations; your personalities should always be considered as assets. To some extent they have also been affected by the material, and to that extent they are testaments of it.

Now. You will be making contacts with the world at large. These will be part of your work, and they will add depth to your work, not detract from it, as long as they are kept in their proper perspective. Overemphasized, they could be detrimental, but if you fear them you are also giving them undue importance. They will also serve you as supportive, particularly in later years.

There will be developments and friendships that will emerge that will directly concern our work in general, and help spread the material. Over a long period of time such contact will serve you well. One man in particular whom you have not yet met, will give Ruburt an idea for a book, through his questions, that will be most remarkable.

You are not to hide your heads in the sands. You will be asked to go out among men at times. This will also benefit your own personalities, which left alone could be far too solitary for your own overall stability and development.

Your own personality, Joseph, has a beneficial effect upon others. You speak well for the material. You are not afraid of meeting people. You are afraid of the idea of meeting people. Now give us a moment.

Despite all your own tendencies to avoid such contact, you are bringing it about through our sessions, and the importance of the material—the inner self placing you in a position where such contact will come about. This is for your own good, and the same is true of Ruburt.

You know very well what you are doing, in other words. The material is to be a force in your world. *(Pause.)* You are not to avoid contact, and to do us full justice this would be impossible. Now give us a moment.

This does not mean that either of you need travel about in a constant flurry of lectures. It does mean that the psychic activity within the sessions carries its own psychic reality. It reaches out and draws others to you. *(Pause.)*

Some of your best sales, so to speak, will be made as a result of contacts that have been built up in other ways. There will be several men you will meet in this same manner. Two men, *(pause)*, each of whom will serve as a basis for a rather unique kind of portrait work. You will see both of them very clearly as they appeared in several lives.

You will do a series of portraits of one man, each one depicting a different materialization of his personality in various existences. This will be true portrait work—the personality as seen in more than three-dimensional terms. You will meet both men at parties in New York, and one man directly through the Miss Taylor who called this evening.

You may take a break and we will continue.

(9:37. Jane's trance was very good, she said. She told me that as she gave the above data, concerning the individual of whom I will do reincarnational portraits, that she could "almost see this guy." But she couldn't elaborate on any physical characteristics.

(Resume at 9:45.)

Now. Give us a moment. As mentioned earlier, Ruburt must come to his own decision. I have a suggestion, however.

I suggest that under the circumstances, this time Ruburt step aside and let Jim Crosson have his day. He needs it badly, and I have a note for Miss Taylor: it will hurt Jim Crosson badly if he does not have a part in the program. He needs to feel, particularly after retirement, that he is looked up to and needed, and can hold his own and attract an audience.

(The group referred to is the Spiritual Frontiers Fellowship, New York City chapter; the discussed meeting is set for October 20.

(A note: for Seth to offer such advice to Jane, or to us, is quite rare. Almost always it is "make your own decisions," etc., and quite rightly so.)

Ruburt will address the group in any case *(pause)*, and many times in the future. Jim Crosson does not have that much time. *(Pause.)* Ruburt should make no future hard decisions as to what he will and will not do, but give the intuitive self freedom in such cases.

(It had been suggested that Jane do stage trance work when addressing the SFF meeting. Jane had decided she wasn't interested in this type of stage presentation.)

He will not make a practice of contacting the departed for their relatives. It is not his forte. Otherwise he should leave himself open. If probabilities continue as they are now, there will be some considerable relationship with the group Miss Taylor represents through the years. It will work to Ruburt's benefit as he meets other psychics with excellent abilities. He can also learn from the experience.

Ruburt will do much better on his own in a program, but should definitely not shunt Jim Crosson aside, for he is very vulnerable to slights. He will also do very well, lecturing on that occasion of the 20th. Better in fact than usual, and he, at least, will consider it one of the high points of his career.

I suggest, if I may then, that Miss Taylor so inform him.

(As stated, Jane has already called Betty Taylor; a copy of this data is being sent to her also.)

Miss Taylor and I will meet in any case. You will find her a welcome member among your friends. I suggest that again Ruburt invite her here, for she will come, and we will have a session.

(Apropos of the two phone calls involving Betty Taylor, Miss Taylor has expressed an interest in coming to attend a session.

(Pause.) The entire future involvement with that group was incipient on the day that Jim Crosson read Ruburt's first book.

Give us a moment. *(Long pause, eyes closed, at 9:58.)*

Sally May.

("That's M A Y?")

M A Y or M A E. I do not know if the names go together or are separate. Perhaps an aunt. These apply to Miss Taylor, and are impressions.

Of Robert: I believe G: Robert G. *(Pause.)*

With a Gray in the middle of a last name, or a color. Do you follow me?

("Yes.")

An appendicitis operation of perhaps 1936.

(Over the phone BT told Jane she had an operation for appendicitis, but quite a few years later than 1936. Other points in this data either checked out or were close, according to BT, but aren't listed here separately. A closer check by BT later may be added however.)

A relative, a very close friend, an older man *(her father?)* connected with the university. An initial engagement that was broken. *(Checked, etc.)* A grandmother with something wrong with a right leg.

A name with a <u>sound</u> like Gary here or G A or G E R R Y. *(This may apply to BT's married name: Gerrigan or: Gerrighan, etc.)*

A legal document having to do with a house or estate, within the last three months, or to come within three months, that may have to do with family.

A torn ligament. A man with a mustache and rather large ears, fairly close to her; dark mustache *(pause),* with a Harvard or like background. A brother and two sisters.

Separate now. Mana or Marta *(spelled)*, a name.

Ed. This could have been her husband, or a man close. *(Ed was the name of BT's first husband, she told Jane over the phone.)* A middle name beginning with B, or his nickname with a B who worked in a building that from the outside looks like a large *(pause)*, building almost entirely of unbroken plate glass windows on the ground floor, such as those that cars might be displayed in. A corner building, I presume, since I see one side of the building, where the other side is flush to others.

In connection with the building, you see, we have the impression of cars or car insurance, but I do not feel this is correct.

(Over the phone BT told Jane the building description reminded her of a new building that had just gone up across the street from her home address, in the city. It is a corner building.)

Did she perhaps know Miss Carr, for example.

(Pause.) I believe that Sybil Leek is the connection between those two women here.

Ruburt should make it clear that he will accept another engagement however. You may take your break and we will continue.

(10:10. Jane was out of trance quickly. She knew in a general way that impressions were involved. She didn't remember any of the data before the impressions. Also, we might add that we hadn't asked for impressions this evening, and so didn't expect them, etc.

(Resume at 10:25.)

Now. Ruburt will meet *(Arthur)* Ford, and they will have much to say to each other. *(AF being very well-known for his psychic abilities.)*

Crosson <u>will</u> outdo himself. He is using the invitation to prove to himself that he is sought after as a lecturer. *(Long pause.)* There are some family problems on his mind. His wife is anxious for him, and the engagement will give him new impetus that would carry him for several years. Without it he will deflate like a balloon; but he is up to the challenge. He will do a good job.

(Long pause at 10:30.) There is another man who could share the program with him, the one mentioned in our earlier session *(the 496th)*, that was thought not available. Ruburt would take the program away from Crosson quite without meaning to do so. Do you follow me?

("Yes.")

Again: Ruburt will address the group many times throughout the years, and so may I. *(Humorously.)* Ruburt and I together would need a full program.

("I know it." Our cat Willy jumped up into Jane's lap as she spoke.)

Now, do you have any questions or remarks?

("I'll try to change my attitude.")

I will remove your beloved monster.

("Okay." I was about to get up to deposit Willy on the floor.)

I do not mind the cat, but I do not like fleas ... The two of you will serve as bridges to the material. You will impress others through encounters, and by your very presence lead them to read it.

The group may also be instrumental in the future in providing session-to-session transcripts of past sessions.

Now. The material itself will progress, with your assistance, along several lines. The out-of-body experiences will be a portion of your subjective training. My comments in sessions about these experiences will add up in their own manner.

The material has several layers, as you should see by now. There is not just one line of development, but many—all under one direction however, and for one purpose.

From the beginning we have been dealing with the nature of reality, beneath its many guises. The intellectual concepts will be enlarged in all areas—the scientific, metaphysical, psychological and psychic. These are the areas in which you and Ruburt are so personally intrigued.

There will also be, and there is, practical information to be used in daily living, and concepts put in somewhat simpler terms for those who will find them valuable and effective. There will be other instructions for you for your own development. These can also be used by others.

I want you to take a break, but I want also to comment on the dream that has been bothering Ruburt, so take your break and we will continue briefly. At your next session I hope to get back to our material, but this is also legitimate and of benefit.

(10:42. Jane went over her dream for me during break. It was a long dream. She had it three nights ago; when she got up during the night to write it down, she found the task took an hour. It has been on her mind since then.

(Resume at 10:50.)

Now. I will merely clear up a few of the most important points.

The divorce was a distortion *(pause)*, not of memory but of interpretation, representing a psychic separation that occurred between you, not in 1964 but later, when Ruburt became ill—and to some extent (underlined) you did hold him back, as you know from the work with the pendulum that you did. You were for that time divorced from each other in attitude, and lacked communication.

This was the knowledge that the woman had of Ruburt's past life. Ruburt interpreted it in literal terms as a divorce. Now give me a moment. *(Pause.)* This obviously was the second dream.

(This would be the second of seven revelatory dreams Jane is to have, according to Seth in the 492nd session. See the 499th session for material dealing with the first such dream. I am also to have a series of seven such dreams.)

Ruburt did see the Buffalin man. The wife in astral form was also here. Ruburt followed Buff to another layer of existence, *(pause)*, with many who had died that evening. Ruburt formed the prosaic background himself however.

I was the guide he was searching for, and they were looking for me, though they did not know my name. This was a clearing place for personalities leaving the physical plane. In their astral forms they adopted their normal dress, hence the varying costumes. They realized that Ruburt was still physical. This is why he was told he could travel no further. He was afraid momentarily there would be no physical world to return to—simply his personal reaction.

You therefore appeared with the newspapers to reassure him that tomorrow in your terms did exist. The people in the offices did of course have information concerning your lives. The affair with the screen was distorted but legitimate—the screen was his mind—objectified outward, so to speak.

The colors, brilliant and mobile, represented the overall healthy state of his psyche. The image of the woman was indeed himself in future years, signifying to the others that he was a wanderer and should go back. This is why they laughed, since he did not recognize himself. He was therefore sent back to the woman in the first office.

The dream was significant because for the first time he was actively seeking me as a guide, and met with those who were leaving physical reality in a group. In the next such dream he will find me of course, or I will find him.

The last episode merely represented his return to physical reality. He saw the two of you as Italian because this was the most earthy type he could think of. *(Humorously.)* Your image however was as you will be at one time in your future. The beard was legitimate—you were simply older.

("Why the beard?" I can say that I have given no thought to cultivating a beard.

(Humorously again:) I do not know why you will grow a beard. It was not a long one. This is why he had you pretending to be Italian. Do you follow me?

("Yes.")

The new and important development therefore was that he went out to seek me. He asked the woman if she knew me, but she did not. They were sending someone to find me. *(Pause.)* Their state is not one where they can instantaneously communicate with me, or I with them.

Now that I know that Ruburt is actively ready, I will be more close by. Your first dream will come when you are ready, as Ruburt's did. Do you have questions?

("I dreamed about my father last night." September 7, 1969.)

Does that mean you want me to comment on the dream?

("Yes." It wasn't until this moment that I realized I hadn't described the dream to Jane. It was a long one also.)

Give us a moment. Your own interpretation is not quite correct. Your father is waiting, but not for you. The images were somewhat distorted. He will wake up in another bed in another room, where he will be led to understand his true condition.

The dream was symbolic. Your brother Dick was invisible in one episode, and he is psychically very aware of your father's condition. He fears, your father, far more than your brother or you, and he will be free, or feel free, of many issues with your father's death.

(This last sentence as I recorded it is obviously distorted. As Jane spoke I had the odd feeling that she, Seth, and I were all thinking about different events. By this time I was quite weary. I could see that Jane was also.)

Do you have any more questions? About this dream or any matter discussed this evening?

("No, I guess not.")

We will then end our session. My heartiest regards to you both. There was an inverted quality about the dream, because you were looking at things from a different viewpoint.

("Good night, Seth."

(11:15. I explained my dream to Jane so she would have a basis for discussion, since we planned now to ask Seth to explain his above data in relation to the dream. Some of it could apply; I did not understand the reference to bed and bedroom however. I didn't recall my brother Dick in the dream. Jane said she was too tired to clear the matter up this evening, so we'll take it up next session.)

SESSION 501
SEPTEMBER 17, 1969 9:25 PM WEDNESDAY

(Tam and Eve Mossman were witnesses to the session. Tam, the editor at Prentice-Hall who is in charge of the book Jane is writing on the Seth material, has been reading the book in manuscript today.

(We began the session with my taking notes, as usual. Seth's pace was rapid.)

Now, good evening—

([Tam and I:] "Good evening, Seth.")

—and my congratulations.

([Tam:] "Thank you." Tam and Eve were married Saturday, September 13.)

We will be involved in other books, and I have been listening to your conversations. I am pleased with Ruburt's progress, and I am pleased with your reactions to the book.

Now. There are several points in particular that I want to discuss with you. Not my book, but points concerning your own relationship with Adam. Give me a moment.

Now. You may continue at the same level of communication with your friend Adam, or you may go beyond that level into a still greater reality. You have created your version of Adam... The version that you have created knows that you have created him. Do you follow me?

([Tam:] "Yes.")

...but you have not created the personality behind Adam...

(Seth's pace had been increasing, and my notes began to fall behind. Our recorder was set up in case we had to rely upon it, so I laid these notes aside and started up the recorder. While doing this of course I lost some material from Seth, but Tam and I agreed that Seth recapitulated any lost data during the rest of the session.

(Therefore, beginning at the next paragraph, the rest of the session is a verbatim transcript from tape. The session is much longer than usual, since Seth didn't have to go slow for my note-taking, but could plunge ahead. RFB.)

...There is more for your personality to handle if you continue along those lines. However, the very attempt to handle more data in itself enlarges your own consciousness and does not detract from it.

Now: You have the psychological bridge of which I have spoken in our session... I have never seen such an infernal machine *(Humorously, referring to my attempts to get the recorder properly adjusted.*

("Be patient. You'll see some more." RFB.)

You are beginning to form this psychological bridge. Now when you form it you do so with the inner realization that it reaches from you outward and you expect something to be on the other side, or the bridge would be useless. Do not, however, identify the bridge with what waits on the other side. The bridge is a living psychological bridge because in this type of communication feelings and emotions are involved. A steel bridge would get you nowhere. You are weaving threads of psychic energy, insights, and realizations, and also certain personality characteristics to form this bridge outward. Now you are beginning at your end and in doing so you form the initial version of your Adam. As this, Adam is highly legitimate and an aid.

However, at the other end there is something else, and there is no point in continuing to construct the bridge unless you intend to get on the other side. When you begin to get to the other side, continuing our analogy, and with good luck and perseverance there will be someone else on the other side constructing their own bridge to meet yours. This personality will form a bridge in the same way that you do. However the two will meet and merge. You will have a strong structure; you then can communicate. But the structure is not the other personality.

Now taking our analogy of a long bridge, you are now here. *(Seth-Jane gestures indicating Tam's end of the imaginary bridge.)* So with your Adam you must either take him and form the rest of your bridge, with the joy of adventure, not always knowing who may be at the other end, forming their own structure; or play around with the Adam version in which case you will get no further than you are. I am not telling you to do one thing or the other. I am merely pointing out the possibilities.

Now: the personality on the other end of the bridge will be the reality behind Adam.

([Tam:] "Well, is the same one you mentioned as being on the waters in our previous exercise?")

Correct.

([Tam:] "Then Adam was one step in that direction as a result of that exercise?")

And also you see, because you are forming this version of Adam from your end, he does not understand his reality.

([Tam:] "He is a dream of a reality? A mutual dream?")

You are correct. And it began with you and in response to inner legitimate information and perception.

([Tam:] "As a child? As you know, Adam claims that he was born in my infancy.")

A certain portion of Adam was: the version was... you had a body consciousness of a protective nature, but this was only one portion of an entire personality who has yet to appear. Now there is a reason for the bridge framework. The bridge framework takes exercise, understanding, and knowledge on both of your parts, therefore there would be no communication of a strong valid nature until your personality is able to maintain it, for the bridge will not be strong enough to hold. Otherwise there would be too many implications and personality difficulties that could arise.

There are sessions dealing with these psychological bridge communications and it would be helpful if you read them. I want you to realize, however, the validity of the personality behind Adam, and the validity of Adam in relationship to you and to that personality.

Now: In your dreams the other personality can communicate and without the psychological bridge framework, but only in dream reality. When you are ready, you will be able to remember these encounters. I suggest therefore that you write them down in the morning. Over a period of time, you see, these will collect. You will be able to recall various messages and relate these to your own experience. Do you follow me?

([Tam:] "Yes.")

Now: For these reasons I have not wanted you to put too much strain upon Adam, to expect him to be this other personality, or to berate him by comparing him to such another personality. For again, he is your version of this, and he is a way. He will lead you there, if that is where you want to go.

To a large extent, as he is now he has arisen out of you. Now he can indeed disappear back into you at this point, and with little care on your part. He would not disappear as an inner awareness. He would exist within your psyche as a small but definite organization of characteristics that would continue within themselves to retain a sense of identity. He would also for continue his protective devices for your own physical body. You would not overly miss him if he did this at this time.

If, however, you expect too much of him without giving time for this structure to form, you drain him of energy and not the other way around. For you have created him with a certain amount of energy and you cannot demand more than you have given him. At the same time, the psychological structure has not reached far enough outward so that he is gathering enough energy from our symbolistic other side: and at times you are asking him to make the leap. And then you are upset if instead he falls down.

Again: You can follow this process through... Several possibilities show themselves. If you follow this process say two-thirds of the way across, then you are more or less committed to go the other third of the way; committed in terms of your own good. It would be highly difficult then to pull in your bridge and scramble back to the other shore.

But also Adam will have changed, at this point. He will be drawing energy from this other personality. He will be able to do more. But he will still be your version. Later if the process is continued, you will make valid contact with the personality for whom Adam now stands. This personality will then speak, communicate through Adam. Adam will then take on the characteristics of that other personality. He will still not <u>be</u> that personality. He will indeed be the psychological bridge, the psychological framework, structure and image through which that personality can communicate. Do you follow me?

([Tam:] "Very well.")

Good. I could not say this to you in a letter. Now, I do not like the term ascending selves. You follow me?

([Tam:] "Not quite." or "I'm afraid not.")

I do not like the term... one self higher or more developed than....

([Tam:] "Aha, I see.")

Selves that ascend like stairs... yet in order to speak to you intelligently I must use this image at times. Therefore when I tell you that this other personality behind Adam may be a future self of your own, I am in no way telling you that this personality is a part of your personality structure as you think of it, or as your psychologists think of it.

([Tam:] "I see.")

You, as you know yourself, will not grow into this quote "higher" self. This higher self and you exist simultaneously. And yet the abilities and knowledge of this "higher" self can become part of your own conscious knowledge through the psychological bridge of which I have spoken.

Now, I am glad you are giving the notes the boot. *(Humorously, to RFB.)* I will do anything but write the notes for you.

([RFB:] "I enjoy the notes, Seth.")

I would send you an extra set of fingers if I could manage.

([RFB:] "That's all right.")

I wanted to clear some of these issues for you. *(Directed to Tam again.)* I believe you have been brooding about some of them. I also feel you have used Adam as a whipping boy and that is not a very kindly thing to do. *(Smile.*

([Tam:] "On the other hand I wouldn't want any psychic development to come between me and my wife... to get between any feelings for my wife who is at this moment even more important to me than any of my other selves.")

There is no reason why any such development should come between the two of you. In the first place it would only develop when you were ready and entirely prepared, and such a state of readiness and preparation would not occur if you are in a frame of mind where you fear the development for the reasons you have just given.

We will have you dancing over the bridge. *(To Eve:)* Your emotional comfort is and should be important to our Aerofranz. No development would occur, or should, unless the emotional climate that involves both of you were ready for such a development. In the material that I have just given you I mentioned that there were several possibilities. This does not mean that you must make any conscious decision today or tomorrow.

It means that these are latent, they are possibilities that you may pursue. You will not pursue any such possibilities, you will not complete the bridge unless your own emotional feelings are calm. Otherwise you would have a very wavy bridge indeed. *(Smile.)* There are emotional components, sometimes at balance, often not at balance, in any personality as you think of personality. When the two of you live together you have many more elements to integrate: new balances. This shifts and changes the emotional reality of you both. It brings possibilities of various kinds of creations, and other developments.

Sometime we will have a group of sessions or a chapter in a book dealing with the emotional levels of these two people *(indicates RFB and Jane)* and the relationship with psychic activity, the balances that are maintained and changed.

Your full emotional viewpoint has changed—

([Tam:] "You mean in this life, or from a previous relationship?")

Now: In your marriage and relationship your whole emotional climate has turned direction. Hers has changed direction, so that now you have the two together. So that in any psychic development or work that you do, you do not only have your own emotional strength or current, but another with you. As a result you have more potential, more leeway. Also, as a result anything that one of you do will have an effect on the other, and you will notice this in psychic work. When you are highly involved you will feel additional strength from your relationship. If there is any strong aversion, you will be doubly pulled away. Do you follow me?

([Tam:] "Oh yes.")

In any case, there is no need to rush ahead where young ladies may fear to tread. All in good time.

(Tam: Was it correct, the information I got from Adam where we were related in past lives?")

Give me a moment. I believe that the information was correct as far as Adam knows of it. I will have to check. There is a thirty-year difference in birth dates. I will let you know and Ruburt can give us the information... I believe I am with the wrong side of the family *(pause)*. I am not sure here but we do seem to have an uncle. Now this is supplementing the material given by Adam. We have an uncle who deals with vestments...if the term is vestments, having to do with the making of garments of a ceremonial nature.

The uncle seems to be of a distant branch of a well-known family, the last name seems to be made up of two names, beginning with a D, perhaps E. Then a second portion of that name beginning with an M. We will come back to this. I will let you take your break. Perhaps I will see what I can get on it while you chat...

(Break.)

I have several suggestions as always. Our new bride here is not so worried about psychic phenomena. She is only worried about Adam. This will pass in time. She needs a part to play: something in which you can participate, and develop yourself *(directly to Eve)*. You would do well to try experiments in the out-of-body state. You have your own abilities to develop. You do not have to be an Eve to Adam.

You can also find many connections between psychic activity and color and painting in which you are interested. Now I will tell you, you have never seen the colors of a rainbow unless you have seen them from an out-of-body state. If you want to see the colors of a flower, or my dear friends, of an apple, you must get out of your body to do so. Now you do not need to feel that his psychic abilities close you out, or that you do not have your own: or that his abilities will draw him away from you, for they would only bring him closer. Your own abilities are here to be used also, and in your own unique fashion.

You have never seen what design is until you see a spider's web when you are out of the body. You have never seen what design is until you see a spider's web from the spider's viewpoint. Now you can learn to do this. You can use your psychic abilities, to throw your consciousness into the spider. Your body is a very handy mechanism and I do not suggest that you step out of it too long. However, as the earth's atmosphere hides the conditions in the universe from your scientists, so also do the conditions of the body blind you to true color and design. Now you can develop in this way.

You can also develop along the same line in the dream state if you give yourself the suggestion that when you are dreaming you will see color truly and remember the colors that you have seen. You will remember them, and you can try to reproduce them. Now these colors are like nothing in this world. *(Humorously.)*

So do not feel that these abilities are his only or that you do not have a part, for you have your own abilities and you can use them for your own purposes. You can be partners in these endeavors, as you are partners in other endeavors. You need not lag behind. Give us a moment.

Now you have some latent inclinations of a musical nature as I mentioned earlier having to do with past-life experiences. Now simply in a spirit of fun, you see, you can use your abilities, and I will give you hints if you request them. You can use your abilities to hear the kind of music with which you were one time acquainted. This music is part of your experience though you have forgotten. Now: when you hear this music, in your mind try to translate it into color and design. And when you think of color, then, sense its motion.

Motion does have a sound though you may not hear it. Motion does have music though you may not hear it. The very motion of atoms and molecules has music. When you think of color, then, try to hear it, you try to sense the motion, then you can use such experiences in your art work. You can also suggest dreams in which you will hear the sort of music, with which you were acquainted.

Now the sound of the music will suggest colors to you and the colors themselves may appear in your mind as designs. Now all of this involves use of the inner senses, it involves an examination of the inner world. You must look inward with as much wonder as you look outward, and then the two worlds merge. Do you follow me?

([Eve:] "Yes.")

Now since this new venture is a partnership then also remember that in these psychic endeavors there must be a partnership and there will be no difficulty. Also the energy involved in your particular field *(Tam's)* and her particular activities will benefit you both. You will each add to the experience of the other.

Now *(to RFB),* I hope you are taking some of this to heart.

([RFB:] "Yes.")

I go rummaging through my own acquaintanceship with artists for his benefit, and I pass some of this on to you. There is a native spontaneity here, in our lady, that deals well with transparent color, that relates clearly and simply. And I believe she has been worried about what she may consider in the back of her mind as Adam's murky quality. I hope we are clearing that up in this session. She has also picked up your thoughts toward Adam *(to Tam)* and to some extent been influenced by them. If you have ever felt threatened by Adam then she would feel this threat doubly. Do you follow me?

([Tam:] "Yes.")

Now, he would remain the individual that he is, as much as anyone ever remains the individual that he is. He would not turn into Adam. I would make a comment here, but I would not.

(Laughs and comments hard to decipher.)

I would see nothing wrong, myself, with the transformation. Now: to some degree you see you are intuitively aware of Adam's true nature *(to Eve here),* and on an intuitive basis you even relate to the Adam you sense within Aerofranz, but you do not realize when you are doing this. Adam in this respect would be the superior qualities that you sometimes sense in him, the Aerofranz that you know... This does not mean that Aerofranz on his own does not have superior qualities. *(Humorously.)*

I am not trying to rob him of his own sterling nature. but beyond those qualities which you recognize, you intuitively sense other qualities and it is these of which I am speaking.

You can also yourself participate in another way. *(To Eve.)* You would do very well—I can see now, however, that this will not appeal to you and it is to some degree an unusual knack—but you would do very well in finding lost animals. You would have a knack... particularly in finding dogs. You would do very well also in dealing with animals where you cared for them and picked homes for them. On one level I can see this does not appeal to you. On another level, however, you would do very well. It is a knack from previous experiences, a knack you may never use. You may add it to your list of accomplishments. *(Humorously.)*

On our young bride's part... a spontaneity in passivity. Allowed to be passive you feel free to be spontaneous. Passivity, however, should be balanced on your part by more assertive action as far as habitual reactions are concerned. Some of this assertiveness can be met through artwork but it must be a going-out from self: a self-assertion, an expression of self—but directed then outward.

I mentioned some conditions existing in your work environment. *(Eve.)* Give us a moment. There seems to be a shifting on three different layers: the first shift as mentioned earlier beginning in approximately three months, followed by two more shifts, this both of policy and some personnel. If you ride along with it you will be all right. Now we are speaking here of probabilities. At the time of the second shift you could decide to leave, misinterpreting what is going on. There seems to be an older woman connected with the second shift. She is approximately middle-aged, far older than you. I am not sure here, the name of Catherine comes to mind.

When the process is finally over you will be two steps ahead of where you are now, and two steps along this way. You will not directly be connected with the same department, but someway two steps away from it, but you will also be two steps higher. Now one of these shifts may also concern a young man, he will either suddenly leave or it will be a young man suddenly arriving on the scene. I get a T initial here. And in the background the name of Tom, or a last name, Thomas.

I do not see you often. I am trying to keep track of what I want to say to you both. The most important point I want to make, I have made. I did not want you to go dashing across the bridge until it was completed.

([RFB:] "May we take a break now to rewind the tape?")

You may indeed.

(Break.)

This will be a very short session for you have had a week of it. You will have your trip ahead of you, and other trips that I have in store for you. There is one small point I want to mention. Ruburt visited your room one night. *(To Eve.)*

Now: it is quite possible for you at this point now to visit this room. Give yourself the suggestion.

([Tam:] "Oh, great.")

Place your emphasis upon being in this room, and the trip will take care of itself. You will be able I believe to do it now. *(To Tam.)* And you *(to Eve)* may be able to do it now. If you choose the proper circumstances and get the idea when the conditions are good, then you can do it now.

I simply want you to know that all kinds of energy and vitality are possible, that there are all kinds of possibilities for your own development, that there is energy available to you and you can tap it; and knowledge available that you can use. Such knowledge can be highly practical and in many instances, the dreamer is the most practical individual. You do not have to fear that this sort of experience will take you away from reality. It will show you a greater reality than you imagine.

(Voice getting pretty strong in here.)

It will enlarge your concepts, change your ideas of what is real and what is not real and what can be and what cannot be; and what you are and what you can be. You can both discover the greater identity that is your own, and step out of your own shadow image. For you identify yourself with a very small portion of your true identity. And when you use the word, I, you do not realize the I of which you speak.

There are other portions of your personality that have knowledge that you can use. There are advantages and they are these: as you become acquainted with these other portions of your own identity, your own capacities for understanding and learning expand. In one lifetime's work you can learn what it might otherwise take three reincarnations to learn. You are all involved basically with one thing. You are learning to use energy creatively. You are trying to discover how much energy you can direct, what you can create. You can discover these answers for yourselves. You cannot discover them through reading, you must look within yourselves and open your own doors. This is a joyful endeavor.

You should begin it as a child wakes up in the morning. It should not be sober. You make your own reality as I have said, even more times than I wish to remember. This also applies to your inner senses. The more you use your inner senses, the more data you have at your command.

Now I speak through Ruburt. Looking at him you cannot see me and yet you know that I am here. *(Voice very loud. Voice continues quite loud through the following passage.*

(Loud:) The energy that sweeps down through this frame is but a small shadow of the energy that is at my command and at your command. This energy can be translated into knowledge, and when it is translated into knowledge it must also be translated into behavior, then it becomes a psychic adventure. Then you begin to use your consciousness as you should use it.

You are a you who has a consciousness and you can use this consciousness as you will. You can send it out, use it like a flashlight. You can light a universe with it. You are not your consciousness. You are a self who is conscious and has a consciousness. Now I want all of you, including my friend here *(Rob)* to contemplate the part of you who has this consciousness to use. There will seem that there is no place to go beyond that point. And there will appear an apparent dilemma. And yet the dilemma will lead to a further discovery. And by the time you know enough to throw that question back at me, that I have just asked you, then I will have more to tell you concerning the initial creative dilemma of which I have spoken.

And I want you both to know if you do not already know that the creativity and the joy and the wonder that is inherent in each consciousness is present not only in your minds and in your consciousness as you think of it, but also in the smallest cell within your fingertips.

And I want you all to know that this is no recording and I have not prepared my lesson ahead of time. I have indeed come for a personal encounter, and to greet our guests and you must admit that for a gentleman as old as I there is some vitality left in me yet. *(Very loud in here.)*

You have no idea of how Ruburt could use this vitality if only he knew how to do so. Our friend has seen how this vitality can be translated into a hearty roar, or to fuel other furnaces and to make other connections, how it can be used as a fuel. There are always translations of energy. I am not saying good evening, but you may take your break.

(Break.)

I give you whatever blessings I have to give and I will keep track of you both. A fond good evening.

([Tam:] "Good night Seth and thanks so ever so—"

([Rob:] "Good night Seth.")

SESSION 502
SEPTEMBER 22, 1969 9:02 PM MONDAY

(John Bradley was a witness to the session. John had two questions for Seth—one concerning himself, and one about a pet dog that had recently been killed. Seth deals with the questions in the session.)

Now, good evening—

([John and I:] "Good Evening, Seth.")

—and give us a moment with this, for there are several issues involved. We will save the matter of the animal until later. Let us work along with this, and then I will tell you, and you may ask questions. Now.

(To John:) You do not feel free to move. Symbolically you do not feel that you have freedom of motion, and you are expressing this through the body mechanism. You did indeed shake yourself up when you decided to put your smoking aside, but this was simply because you felt subconsciously a loss. The smoking to some extent had been used by you as a method of giving yourself comfort, a way of giving yourself pleasure.

When you turned from the habit, and would have turned to food for comfort, you denied yourself this out of fear of gaining weight. Subconsciously you felt cheated. Now the comfort was needed to begin with so that you could make up for other things that you felt you did not have, and to help you cope with problems, as you are aware.

There are reasons why you chose the particular symptoms that you have, and reasons why they emerged at this particular time. Now. There was the feeling, the inner fear that you do not have freedom of motion in the economic or professional sphere—the fear, quite simply, that you were not going to make it. Some of this has to do with the symbolism you have attached subconsciously to the age of 40, and you see yourself coming closer to it. Some has to do with your assessment of your position within the firm, with your assessment of what you would get outside the firm should you leave it.

(To me:) Slow me down when you want to.

("Okay.")

Some of it has to do with your assessment of your own abilities, and with the growing impatience to use them more fully—and to be well paid for using them. *(Humorously.)*

For some time you had consciously considered various roads that you could take, but subconsciously you became more and more alarmed, and felt severely hampered in your progress.

You have not expressed your bitterness in anything like an adequate fashion. In a large manner, you hide it from your wife for fear she would consider you less manly or less in charge, and would therefore feel less secure and threatened herself.

You have taken it, subconsciously now, as a personal failure that you are not farther ahead, not only financially but in terms of the amount of power you would like to hold. You would like to kick out, but you feel you have lost your footing, hence the symptoms in the feet.

Now what happens is this. You began by wanting to express withheld bitterness, often explosively. At the same time you did not do so. One group of muscles therefore were tensed for action, and the other group of muscles tried to stop the action. You wanted to go ahead but felt you could not, so that this was reflected in your posture long before you felt a symptom.

All feelings are reflected in the body. It showed in your gestures and in the way you walked. Some muscles were habitually tensed, and the balance thrown off. Not until this had gone on for some time did the symptoms become severe enough to get your attention. They are trying to tell you something.

This was reflected in other portions of the body as well. As you noted, you felt off balance subjectively, and unsure. Now. You had grown used to smoking as a way of comforting yourself. You removed the comfort. You refused to add another, and at the same time you did not face the inner problem that was bothering you, that made the comfort so necessary to begin with. We will go into this more deeply, for you can indeed rid yourself of the symptoms, but I would like to make one point here first. When you bought the dog, subconsciously you felt that the dog was almost a symbol of your failure.

([John:] "Why?")

You had not wanted such a dog until you had room and a larger place, and in the past you had not gotten the dog because subconsciously you hoped you would have more land within a brief, foreseeable future. When you bought the dog, and particularly since your wife was so for the idea, you feared that she also took this as a sign that you had made your mind up to the fact, or faced the fact, that you would be where you are for some time.

She knew subconsciously that you would consider that a failure. We will have much more to say. In the meantime take your break, but *(smiling)* keep yourself together.

(9:30-9:40.)

Now. *(To John:)* I have told you that you formed your own physical body and your own image.

You harbored thoughts of immobility. You feared you could not get ahead. You did not know what steps to take. You set up limitations in your mind. You used your imagination, a very valuable tool, against yourself. You saw yourself in the future worse off. You felt your freedom threatened until little by little these ideas began to predominate.

While you tried to deal with them on a conscious level, you became more and more frightened of them, and more and more you began to try to dissociate yourself from them. They were a part of you however, and sought expression.

Now when anything is wrong with your body, it is trying to tell you something. And when you understand what it is trying to say, and if you make an effort to do what is needed, the symptoms are no longer needed as a method of communication.

The body is trying to tell you that you have a problem, and because you did not cope with it, and denied it mentally, it is physically materialized in symbolic body language. Now give us a moment. *(Pause.)*

The family all knew, subconsciously again, that the dog had to go. Everyone was overly nice to the dog, so no one would know consciously, what they knew subconsciously—that you considered the dog the symbol of failure. It was a closely guarded secret by all, hidden, but not entirely, from the conscious minds of those involved. No one wanted the dog killed, but it was not coincidence that you yourself loosened the dog's collar, or that your wife was the one who left the dog; for symbolically the two of you were connected here. Now give us a moment. The act itself was symbolic, and the dog picked up all of your attitudes through its own sense of communication.

([John:] "For what purpose? What was accomplished?")

In the first place none of you would have found it comfortable in the long run, to live with an animal that you considered the symbol for failure. Now I will give you time for questions. Let us follow this through.

The failure was being rejected, you see. Now the dog was a hunting dog. Symbolically you have always equated hunting with a man's work in modern society. That was one connection. You would not feel free to hunt successfully with the animal, for he was, you felt, the symbol of an unsuccessful hunt in the work world.

Each member of the family picked this up. The dog had to be loved. It was a face-saving gesture. No one wanted you to know, and all of this now on a subconscious basis. <u>Under the conditions that were then in operation</u>, and underline that, for you all to have accepted the dog for any length of time would have been an admission and acceptance of failure.

The dog had to go, but it had to appear accidental. And this is exactly what happened. Now we will take up the dog's death later, but give us a moment. The threads of activity are so enmeshed, and I see them as a whole, and must unravel them for you. As Joseph said earlier this is not to say you cannot have a dog, and enjoy him, with a different attitude.

You were particularly frightened during vacation because of the inactivity. Old fears were aroused that you have never faced consciously. You never faced them honestly. You are terrified of inactivity, for many reasons: bodily inactivity, mental inactivity, some of this based upon fear of your mother's disease. You must go, go, go, to prove that you can do so, and any threat to your mobility is not only strongly felt but negatively exaggerated.

This also applies symbolically, and during your vacation, and before it, was one fear that you had not come to terms with. You would consider it beneath you, and unmanly to entertain, and consciously improbable, if you left your job and did not get another—could not get another, of comparable merit indeed.

Supposing you left your job and simply could not find another, what would you do? You could not bear to sit at home. This fear subconsciously nagged at you, and it has for this reason, among other, that the symptoms were with you before vacation. This year you felt the vacation almost as a threat because of the fears that had built up during the year.

You have been concentrating emotionally, and at a certain level, upon failure. Now you translate activity into many areas. You have been frightened of your mother's disease, and you have also translated a fear of inactivity into other than physical realms.

To protect yourself from her disease you had to move quickly physically. You also had to move quickly in the area of work. You were sensitized because of your mother's problem to fear inactivity. Any threat to your motion or advance, even in the business area, becomes highly charged for this reason. Earlier you felt that you could strike out. There was plenty of time. Then you became frightened after the age of 35, and you began to soften up your blows. *(Jane gestured widely, with a fist.)* You began to hold back, become more cautious, and then slowly began to entertain thoughts of the possibility of failure.

Now I am speaking of failure as it would apply to you, in your estimation. All of these attitudes were reflected in the body.

In a moment I will give you a break and then continue. One point: the drug you are now taking over a period of time would not be recommended by me—

(Our cat Willy jumped up in Jane's lap, but she continued to speak as Seth while Willy sought to make himself comfortable.)

—and we will give you recommendations so that you can rid yourself of

the symptoms. To do so will take some effort on your part, but you can remove them completely.

Now you may take your break. And you save your questions *(smile),* after I give you the prescription, when we will have our doctor-to-patient chat.

(10:11-10:32.)

Now. The problem is not in the exterior circumstances but in your own mental attitude toward them, and in the habitual patterns of thought that you have subjectively accepted.

You do have full freedom to move, both physically and in the economic world. You allowed negative patterns of thought to take an upper hand, and fears to predominate. These fears were then symbolically acted out by the body. You do have freedom in your joints, for example. I will try to put this simply.

You do not want to accept the basic fear of immobility and lack of motion. You are too afraid of the fear itself. You recognize it but you do not know what to do about it, and this frightens you further. You act this out subconsciously then, hampering the free motion of the joints, which then become stiffened through the inactivity. The stiffness then convinces you that the joints are indeed at fault; this adds to the problem, which then gives more fuel to the basic fear.

If you allowed this to continue and did not check it, then gradually the inactive joints would be accepted as a basic problem. You would think: "If I could move freely, then I could solve all problems," when the true point is: when you feel free to solve the problems, there will be no physical symptoms to worry about.

Now. The cortisone can be of some intermediate value, but over an extended period of time it will only introduce another element into the system, to which the system will then have to adjust, and it can lead to an extension of the symptoms when the reasons for them are gone.

I do not suggest that this be kept up for any length of time, <u>at a steady rate</u>. The cortisone itself to some extent becomes habitual. Now not habit forming, but habitual. You can prevent this if you cease taking it now and then for several days. It can hold you over but at the same time the body is getting used to a more or less artificial element; element not in terms of chemical. The cortisone is somewhat, say, like a crutch. Do not become addicted to that.

Now you can reverse this process. Negative habits of thought, and <u>withheld</u> feelings and emotions got you into this, and the same, backwards, can get you out.

Now I can tell you what to do, and I can assure you that this works. It is up to you to follow through however. Now in your mind you now have the image of yourself with hampered motion, stiff joints. You have the fears that this image can evoke, and you must be very on guard against projecting this idea or image into the future.

Now. In your spare moments, see yourself in your mind's eye easily performing normal physical pursuits as you did before. Remember the feelings that you had, but see this in your mind's eye as present. Do not compare your present state with your state before you were ill. See yourself in your mind as clearly as possible square dancing, and enjoying yourself.

You must use mental images of mobility and action. At the same time tell yourself often that you are free to move. Do not command yourself to move, or demand it. Simply remind yourself that you are the one who has been projecting these ideas onto your joints and you can remove the ideas. *(Pause.)* Give us a moment.

Now I want you to mentally talk to the portions of your body that hurt you. You do this whether you now it or not, but you have been saying the wrong things. Tell your feet that you free them. They can step forward.

Tell yourself that you are free to move ahead. Do not tell yourself you are feeling fine when you hurt; I do not mean this. You must however realize fully that your ideas are responsible. Give us a moment here. *(Long pause.)* You must face the fact fully that you are and have been frightened, and that fear is a natural reaction, and that there are ways of responding to it that are healthy and constructive. You can face your problems and deal with them. You are free to do so, and you should remind yourself of this fequently, for you doubted your ability to handle the problems. *(Long pause.)*

You must either accept your situation as it is, change it, or at least feel that you have the ability to change it. You feared that you did not have the ability as things stand. *(Long pause.)* You thought that you would not advance. You feared,and do,that changing your job would deny your family.

Now. In the long run your present situation would deny them far more. I am speaking of the physical situation—the illness itself.You have every good chance of ridding yourself of the symptoms now, but you must immediately begin to use your imagination, so that it works for you and not against you.

Now there is something else. You want comfort of a certain kind, and you will not ask it of your wife.You feel, again,that you should not need comfort, that she will interpret such a need either as weakness or that she will become frightened. You have been denying yourself comfort of this kind, and it would help prevent the periods of depression, and the mood of depression that has gradually come over you and robbed you of your resistance.

Give us a moment. *(Pause.)* She is quite able to give it to you. It is to some extent her idea of her place and part, to offer comfort to her man when necessary. You usually prevent her from this role. You have been overdepriving yourself on several points, and the stiffness deprives you even further, you see.

We have some further recommendations. It is difficult in one evening to give you all the important data. You have been denying your own feelings for some time, or only giving lip service to them, and we will have to set you straight and free.

(11:02-11:20.)

Now, I want to give you some practical suggestions before the session is through, so I will speak of the most important ones. Several things are necessary.

Do not force this, but again, for at least five minutes in the overall during the day, imagine as vividly as possible that you are moving normally and easily anyway you choose. Do this almost as a game, not with a heavy hand.

Tell yourself several times a day that you can deal with whatever problems you have. Do not keep thinking of the job situation so that you are hammering yourself over the head with it constantly. Whenever you find yourself projecting failure in any sense into the future, even into tomorrow, stop yourself, remind yourself that your thoughts form reality.

I suggest however that you freely express both bitterness and discontent when you feel them, whenever possible. Do not put it off in other words unless you must. If you are in a position where this is difficult now then imagine the bitterness or discontent is a football, and you are kicking it with all your might. This in itself will activate the legs and feet and prevent you from further stiffening those areas.

Give us a moment. *(Pause.)* The illness has not been thrust upon you, and this is your freedom. Since you have done this to your body, you can stop doing it. Try to become more alert to your own stream of consciousness. Notice when you are giving yourself negative suggestions.

If you catch yourself thinking when something hurts, "I am sore," then ask yourself what you are sore about. You do have freedom, several choices as far as your professional life is concerned. You are overemphasizing the negative aspects of that situation, and the overemphasis makes you feel trapped and powerless.

Now you are also underestimating your own worth, and you have done so consistently for some time. You would be the last to say that that is so, and the reasons are too deep-seated to go into this evening. This underestimation of your own worth leads you to place an overemphasis upon your financial worth to your family. It is in this personal area that a basic fear exists also. This is a high simplification, but you feel that your value as a person and as a man in the family situation is determined not only by your ability to provide, but increases in proportion to your financial status.

There is obviously much more to be said here. Do you have some questions—on the matters at hand?

([John:] "How are things progressing with regards to the company, in light of what you have said in the past?")

Give us a moment. Probabilities always operate, and yet within that framework the large proportion and the points I have made will come to pass. Now you must deduct some points here and there for distortion, but the overall still applies. The time elements as you probably see are not as dependable, even when the event itself is correct. This simply has to do with translations difficult to assess from my standpoint.

([John:] "You said you would say something about the dog's death.")

Give us a moment. Now. *(Pause.)* There is no simple way to put this. On the one hand the accident was an accident. On the other hand you had an individual aggressively attuned that day with withheld violence, who was going to kill one animal or another. On the other hand you had an animal who went searching for friends, knowing quite well that in one way of speaking the friendship was over.

He sensed the rejection sometime earlier, through various cues given, and the animal knew that the rejection would take place, if not on that occasion then another. Now the driver wanted to strike out violently but could never admit this to himself, hence an accidental affair. The dog was disconsolate, and as distracted as a human being might be. The affair involved many people, and was a reality constructed by many people.

Now you may take a break or end the session as your prefer.

([John:] "One further question, that's all I have.")

All right.

([John:] "The report I sent in last week [to Searle.] What will be the effect of that?")

Now. There will be an effect—not one I believe that you have foreseen, and not immediate. You worried them. You are a problem to them, as they are to you, even while you both receive services from the other, and your report may help take all of you off the hook. It may take all of you off the hook—they do not know what to do with you either.

A new position would save face both for you and for them. This will be considered. The effects would be beneficial. There are no ill effects from the event. A long time ago I mentioned that your progress might not necessarily involve the second step, the next obvious one. They might very well surprise you with such a position, a new one, but it would not be entirely what you had in mind; as comprehensive.

(11:50.

(This was, abruptly, the end of the session. Jane's trances had been good. John said the data tonight made good intuitive sense to him, and that he couldn't disagree with it.)

SESSION 503
SEPTEMBER 24, 1969 9:32 PM WEDNESDAY

(At 9:30 Jane said: "I feel real odd. I've got a lot of energy. I feel it all around me. I feel Seth around too but he hasn't come through yet. I was very tired a few minutes ago, doing that filing..."

(Jane added that "If I opened my mouth, I feel like my voice would really fly out real loud, as though I've got all this energy and don't know what to do with it." When the session began however she used her usual Seth voice and speed of delivery.)

Good evening.

("Good evening, Seth.")

Now. I have several opening remarks. Ruburt is more relieved than he realizes, because he realizes that the book meets with Aerofranz's *(Tam Mossman's)* approval; but more, because he knows he has done a good job. He was not sure until lately. You follow the reasons why.

("Yes.")

It was extremely important to him that he relate this whole experience to others, and make a good beginning in transmitting the material. His nature is such that the experience had to be given outward to others, and he knew that in order to do this he had to come to terms with it himself.

There have been changes in the past month, extremely important in his mental and spiritual condition, and along with this the release of mental and psychic energies, and healthy concentration in all areas of his work, with reasonable and optimistic plans for the future.

His change in attitude and performance in your personal areas, is a sign of this. You have also been of great help. Now I suggest that you playfully encourage him to increased motion. He is now aware for the first time clearly, of certain areas of rigidity, and realizes the fear behind them. Some of this is simply that he is afraid of pain if a muscle is suddenly let go. He knows this, but with your encouragement, active but playful, you can accomplish very much here. The body is quite ready to comply now, and he is mentally ready. It is a matter of taking advantage of the opportunity and good conditions.

Give us a moment here. *(Pause.)* Now we are able to speak much more clearly than we could in the past on these matters. The thing is to encourage playful and spontaneous motion while making sure there is no concentration (underlined), upon motions that are still somewhat hampered. Do you follow?

("Yes.")

Some of this has already taken place on its own in the past month *(as Jane has noticed)*, but I thought it better not to mention this, and I believe I was correct. Barriers are broken down you see without any conscious direction applied. Now it is quite all right.

The relaxation exercises that he spoke of are good, if they are done in a playful manner. He knows better now than to tell his body what to do. Now it is a matter of allowing it its freedom.

Also, as you have been, but even more actively, gently encourage him to express his feelings. He had begun to do this, but your encouragement means much to him along this line, as he still looks to see whether you approve or disapprove. In any given case let him for example know if you disagree with what he is saying, while still encouraging him to say it.

I am mentioning these matters this evening because the time is ripe, and proper handling now is important. His body is ready to be released, even areas such as the elbows, and dispersion has taken place here. Therefore the mobility should be encouraged.

Give us a moment. Tell him to think lovingly of his hands, as he has been doing with other areas of his body. He has been still somewhat angry with them, and must realize that they are now ready to work properly. Tell him he is handling his affairs well now.

As the probabilities exist, both of you will be well into the out-of-body work between now and early winter. *(To me:)* You have been operating far more than in the past, and you should shortly now gain conscious awareness. You will probably come to, realizing you have projected, several times, before becoming conscious of the mechanism of getting out.

You have indeed allowed yourself to meet with your friend Sue, and to operate within the apartment in a projected state. The change for the better in your personal, physical and psychic relationship with Ruburt was a necessity for your joint out of body partnership.

Now Ruburt's energies are being released, and once this process begins, as it has, then all the inner improvement will seem to appear at once, though they are the results of several months. The psychic work will pick up, and indeed already has. The desire shown in your personal life on Ruburt's part is very important. Ruburt should tell himself now that all other tensions can leave through his fingertips, not back up there you see but go completely outward. It will help if he imagines tension streaming outward through the fingertips. His idea to have long hair *(smile)* at this particular point is beneficial, for it means to him the luxury of both sexuality and sense, sensual extravagance. These qualities directly in opposition to the overly restrictive, puritan rigidities that he was in the past heir to.

The flowing hair suggests motion to him also. I wanted to give you this material for it will be of help. Now I suggest you take a break and we will turn to other matters. I presume you are ready for one.

("Yes.")

(10:01. Jane left trance as usual, though she said she still had the feeling that the voice could really blare. She was quite relaxed. Resume at 10:15.)

One other small point: Ruburt should continue the psychic and sensual contact with his body, listening to the messages that it gives him. This is most vital.

Now we shall discuss some other material, or if you prefer I will discuss the foot episode. You have your choice.

("Well, can we have a little on the foot bit?")

(While Jane and I were on vacation in Florida in July, I rather severely sunburned my feet; I had trouble walking for several days, but was able to drive home on schedule. The episode took place while we were staying with Jane's father and his wife in Daytona Beach. I thought it most peculiar that only my feet burned when the rest of my body was equally exposed. I also gave suggestion on my part credit for saving, in the nick of time, what could have been a much more stringent situation, possibly averting disablement.)

Give us a moment. You felt that the situation was too hot to handle. You were afraid of getting burned. You were even frightened enough lest you lose your own footing in the psychic atmosphere. You wanted to leave but felt it best that you stay, since Ruburt sees his father so infrequently.

Therefore the burned feet kept you there, yet the burn itself you accepted as a symbol of your fear that you would get burned if you did stay. You made the feet more susceptible to the rays of the sun, rubbing salt into the wound, so to speak, by wading in the ocean.

You also wanted to have an excuse, and a good one, so that you would not have to go out with the couple, lest they become unmanageable. The feet neatly took care of these issues. This was also the reason that neither of you used your abilities in fighting the malady. Both of you subconsciously knew its purpose. You used suggestion to control it, so that it was severe enough to suit your purposes, and yet not so severe that you could not make it home when you wanted to.

(It wasn't until we were back in Elmira that I realized Jane and I had missed a great chance to use our abilities. I talked about how I should have had Jane hypnotize me, for instance, in Florida as soon as we realized how bad the feet were—giving me suggestions for an extra quick recovery, etc. Yet this simple fact occurred to neither of us while in Daytona Beach.)

You preferred spending most of the time in the house, even bored or disgusted, rather than put yourself in a situation that you felt, literally, had possibilities of disaster. I can tell you quite frankly that those possibilities did exist.

The visit however was for the best in the overall. It was quite necessary that you see the situation as it was, and be able to judge any future events. Otherwise Ruburt would have been overwhelmed with pity at calls that would have been received by Midge.

("By Midge?")

Would have been received from Midge, made by Midge. They began before the visit, you remember. Your visit served as a check to Midge, for though you were friendly she saw that she could only go so far. You were burned up, you see.

Now give me a moment. Do you have questions on that material?

("No, that's fine.")

The energy Ruburt felt, and feels, is his own. He is now literally raring to go, to operate at full capacity again, which is why I gave you this evening's earlier material, so you would know best how to help.

He will help you in your out of body episodes. And show you what he knows. Then you will have your own methods, and will be able to return the help as you share your experience. You have also been sending thought forms out—and this is different, than an astral image.

Some of the models for your paintings have been of thought forms sent out by others. Some, of personalities between reincarnations.

I did want to mention that your prayer periods, as you call them, have paid dividends. While retaining your schedules, <u>do</u> allow for spontaneity in your other activities. Now this is something—

(About two pages of personal material are deleted here.

(To resume: Sue Watkins, one of Jane's ESP class members, left three questions last night for Seth to answer when possible. Here is question 1: When I project while I am pregnant, is my astral body pregnant; i.e., does the astral body carry the astral counterpart of the fetus, or does the astral fetus remain in my physical body, within the physical fetus? Does astral projection remove any necessary energy sustenance from

the fetus?

(Jane had read the questions. I now asked Seth:

("Can you say a little bit about Sue's first question, about the astral body of the fetus?" Jane didn't know I was going to ask this question.)

Give us a moment.

The fetus does have its own astral form. Now, this astral form belongs to the individual, the personality as it will be in this life. It is not the astral form that existed in a previous reincarnation, for example.

There are many complicated issues here. I will try to put them simply. *(Long pause.)* There is great energy connected with the fetus. At no time in physical life is so much energy utilized so purposefully, so well directed. It is this charge of energy, of truly cosmic proportion, that allows for this initial breakthrough into matter.

The personality is busy transforming literally infinite data. Much of this work has already been done by the third month of pregnancy. As quickly as the new data forms the fetus and the physical structure, the self from the previous reincarnation must begin to withdraw its hold. It enters briefly then into this process. It does not become the new individual however.

It helps form the new individual, and then it must withdraw. The new self unit must be free and not hampered by the demands that could otherwise be put upon it. The new individual has a deeply buried memory of its past lives, but the personal consciousness of the last reincarnated self must not be superimposed upon this new identity. The new personality, in its small astral body, does visit with other portions of the entire identity. It is even given lessons of a kind, but it is very much its own self.

("Does it project when Sue does, for instance?")

It may or it may not. It does not have to. It may project to other areas entirely, while Sue is somewhere else in her astral form. There is at this time however a very strong connection between the two. On a deeper level they are aware of their locations. The mother knows where the child is, even though she is not conscious of this. The mother may even go out after the child in a projection, and bring it home.

Many abortions, natural ones, are caused when the new personality is having difficulty constructing the new form, projects to others for advice, and is advised not to return. Now you had better take your break.

("Well, I guess we'd better end it.")

I wish you then a fond good evening.

("It's been very interesting.")

The question you asked cannot be answered easily. The answer will lead you into other matters that can be pursued if you wish.

("Thank you Seth, and good evening.")

(11:03. Jane left trance rather quickly. She said Seth still had lots of energy; he could have gone on for hours, etc.)

SESSION 504
SEPTEMBER 29, 1969 9:17 PM MONDAY

Good evening.

("Good evening, Seth.")

Now. This will be a brief session. You need some relaxation, and I will tell you why.

You used up an unwarranted amount of energy at your mother's. Symbolically you did not like to put on the storm windows, feeling that perhaps it would be the last time that you did so, and that you were sealing up the house. The symbolism in your mind was connected with your visit. You did not want to be reminded particularly of your father's condition, and subconsciously you transposed the image of a casket upon the house, so that in sealing up the windows you were sealing up a casket.

(Sunday, September 28, Jane and I and my mother visited Father at the county home. Upon returning the same day I took down the screens and put up the storm windows on the family home in Sayre, PA. I hurried to get the job done and felt quite done in when it was finished. I didn't tell Jane this.)

This was merely your own subconscious symbolism, but you were unaware of it and therefore of its effect upon you, and so I mention it.

(Here is a copy of my dream of September 28, taken from my dream notebook: Color, much forgotten. Father and myself and the whole family—I don't believe Jane was in the dream—had all decided to leave physical reality together. We were all in agreement. We had gathered in the garage out back of the house. I had no regrets except that I wouldn't get to do any more paintings. We were all our present ages, except that Father was there and very active, on his feet, etc.)

In your dream you nicely placed the family in the garage, outside of the closed house, you see. The garage was also a symbol, the place where a vehicle is kept; and your family's car being used no longer, being a symbol of your father's body, that he will soon discard.

The father's body was also a vehicle in bringing you and your brothers into physical existence, and the dream represented several things. On the one hand it represented a quite natural subconscious fear that when the father-creator

(hyphenated) vanished, his issue would go along with him. On another level it stated indeed that the psychic reality of the family in a large manner would disappear from physical reality. Your parents at their death will take the strongest burden of that identity, the family identity, with them. Do you have questions?

("What was Jane's dream about Father?"

(Jane told me she had a dream involving Father on the same evening, Sunday, September 28. She has it recorded.)

This was not a dream, but the first clear recognition on your father's part that he was ready to leave the physical plane entirely. You also picked up this information, and it was the impetus for your dream. He had not fully made the decision earlier. The paper *(which Jane, in her dream, saw my father throw down)* represented the notes your father wrote to himself. The paper was empty. There was nothing else he would do here. He discarded the paper. Earlier he had held it even though it was empty.

Now I would like to add some to the discussion we began in our last session.

The fetus sees the physical environment. The cellular structure at that point responds to light, and activates latent abilities in the cellular structure of the mother's body. Quite literally he sees through her body, and with the aid of her body.

These are not sharp images, but he already begins to build up ideas of shape and form. It goes without saying that the eyelids are also thus equipped. He can see through closed eyelids in other words. He is aware of light and shadow, of shape and form, though he must learn to distinguish those portions of the available field of reality that you accept as objects, from the available field that you do not accept as objects.

He sees more than you do, or more than his mother does, because he does not yet realize that you only accept certain patterns and reject others. By the time he is born he has already learned to accept his parents' idea of what reality is. In a large sense he begins to train himself to focus only upon what you would call physical reality, though he still partially perceives other fields that you do not accept.

He is only recognized and his wants satisfied when he focuses in one particular reality. He learns quickly then to discard the others, for they do not meet his physical ends.

Now the fetus also hears, and the same thing applies here. He hears while within the womb, sounds from the, physical environment, but also sounds within the available range of reality that are not accepted as such. When the infant is born he still hears these sounds and voices, but again they do not meet his physical needs nor bring him milk when he cries, and gradually he discards them, focusing upon that data which best serves his physical purposes.

For sometime he literally perceives many levels of reality at once, and part of what seems to be disorientation is simply the result of early confusion with so much data. According to the situation and the individual, the fetus may still be receiving messages from those he has known in the past. This adds to the confusion, and it is a matter of physical survival that he largely ignores these messages while he learns to focus in physical reality.

He is quite aware of temperature changes for example, and the weather. He is telepathically in communication with animals and other people, and on a different level he is in a kind of communication with plants and other such consciousnesses.

Plants will react quite sharply to an abortion. The fetus however will also react to the death of an animal in the family, and will already be acquainted with the unconscious psychic relationships within the family, long before it reaches the sixth month.

Now you may take your break, then I will continue briefly.

The plants in a room, or in a house, are quite aware of the growing fetus; the plants will also pick up the fact that a member of a family is ill, often in advance of physical symptoms. They are that sensitive to the consciousness within cellular structure. Plants will know whether a fetus is male or female, even if the mother does not.

(9:47-10:00.)

Now. Give us a moment. *(Pause.)* There is a woman who will be waiting for your father, beside Ella. *(Father's deceased sister.)* A woman that he knew before he met your mother, but was also acquainted with her afterward.

She was a strong reality to him afterward, in any case, and he wondered if he should have married her instead. She was either a cousin, or someone he met who was closely connected with his family in the area from which he came. The name Anna is strong here.

(The name doesn't help me identify any such person. I know very little about my father's early life; he never discussed it.)

Give us a moment. Ella was the one strong enough to give love to another, you see, in her relationship to her husband. The only one able to express a close relationship. She never forgot her brothers, and will be waiting for your father.

Otis *(my father's father)* was a woman, born in India two years after Otis's death, and dying at a young age in her early teens. *(Long pause.)* He will have other reincarnations, and will eventually in your terms become a strong entity on his own. He will indeed greet your father. They had been brothers, and your father somewhat resented the change in relationship even while he chose it.

(At last break I asked Jane if Seth could discuss two points: Who would be waiting for Father at his death?; and the situation surrounding a letter Jane recently received from a professor at Cornell, who works in remote sensing and asked Jane to deliver an ESP presentation to his graduate class.)

Otis's personality attains developments by its nature in great spurts and starts; intuitions; and then he must learn to handle them. At times they overburden him. It was like him to leap from one life into another, with a change of sex.

("Why did Jane and I find his photograph so striking?" Sunday at the family home in Sayre, I found a copy my father had made of a very old picture of Otis. It was in a cigar box on a back shelf, along with other odds and ends. Otis was elderly even then; my father was born in 1890. The physical resemblance between my father and grandfather is striking. Otis's photograph exerted a most peculiar fascination for Jane and me. I would like to do a painting from it.)

You recognized the entity that he will become, and so did your father, unconsciously, when he took the picture. He also contacted you once through the *(Ouija)* board. You recognized his intuitive quality. He gobbles great insights, and they bring him sorrow until he learns what they mean. So the sorrow and the knowledge were both there.

(We had forgotten that several years ago we had contacted Otis through the Ouija board.)

Give us a moment. *(Long pause.)* He was afraid your father was not manly. *(Long pause.)*How much of this information do you want? We can go into the family relationship or not, as you choose.

("Let's move on to the other question then, about the doctor from Cornell.")

It is not significant enough, unless you want to go into the deeper material that you mentioned earlier, in connection with perception and the electromagnetic basis for <u>all</u> perception.

("Well, I've always wanted to ask about that. Can you give us a little on it?"

("Earlier this evening I had mentioned to Jane my long-standing interest in Seth's statement, years ago, that all ESP perceptions had an electromagnetic basis. I was curious about this because we have read that no investigation has ever turned up any electromagnetic relationship with ESP. I wondered about building the right kind of instruments, or whether there were still discoveries to be made, etc.)

Give us a moment. *(Pause.)* I would rather tie it in to our information on the fetus—

("Okay.")

—and in that way we can carry on both discussions.

("All right.")

Now. There are electromagnetic structures, so to speak, that are presently beyond your instruments. *(Pause.)* Units that are the basic carriers of perception. They have a very brief life in your terms. Their size varies. Several units may combine for example, many units may combine. To put this as simply as possible, it is not so much that they move through space, as that they use space to move through. There is a difference.

In a manner of speaking, thermal qualities are involved, laws also of attraction and repulsion. The units charge the air through which they pass, and draw to them other units. The units are not stationary in the way that a cell say, is stationary within the body, generally speaking.

Even a cell, for example, only appears stationary.

These units have no home. They are built up in response to emotional intensity. They are one form that emotional intensity takes. They follow their own rules of attraction and repulsion. As a magnet, you see, will attract with its filaments, so these units attract their own kind, and form patterns, which then appear to you as perception.

Now the fetus utilizes these units. So does any consciousness, including that of a plant. Cells are not just responsive to light because this is the order of things, but because an emotional desire to perceive light is present.

The desire appears on this other level in the form of these electromagnetic units, which then cause a light sensitivity. These units are free-wheeling. They can be used in normal perception, or in what you call extrasensory perception.

I will discuss more about their basic nature either this evening or at another session, and I would like to tie this in with the fetus, since the fetus of course is highly involved with perceptive mechanisms.

("Next time, I guess, though this is very interesting."

(I wanted very much to continue, but was almost overwhelmingly tired.)

It is not that you cannot devise instruments to perceive these. Your scientists are simply asking the wrong questions, and do not think in terms of such free-wheeling structures. I bid you a good evening, then. Do you have questions?

("I was wishing we'd get some more information on this tonight.")

Do you want to have a break and continue?

("Okay."

(Amused:) It is your convenience I am thinking of.

("Thank you very much."

(10:30. Jane left trance quickly. After a few minutes I told her I'd have to quit

after all; I was too tired to continue. Then Seth returned.)

Someone has bitten off more than they can chew this evening. The information is available. We will continue it at our next session.

("It's very interesting.")

I wish you then a hearty good evening.

("It's too bad I have to quit.")

I knew it would be a short rather than a long session.

("Good night, Seth."

(10:33. Jane said Seth "was full of energy. You can really feel it when he's going good." Seth could have gone on for hours.)

SESSION 505
OCTOBER 13, 1969 9:34 PM MONDAY

(Jane has been so busy finishing up the manuscript of her book on the Seth material, for Prentice-Hall, that we haven't had a session since September 29.

(Before the session tonight I said I was curious about Seth's interpretation of my dream of October 9. This will be given in the appropriate place in the text. Jane said that Seth was going to talk about the electromagnetic units discussed in the last session—she could "feel him buzzing around.")

Good evening.

("Good evening, Seth")

Now. These units of which we spoke earlier are basically animations rising from consciousness.

I am speaking now of the consciousness within each physical particle regardless of its size; of molecular consciousness, cellular consciousness, as well as the larger gestalts of consciousness with which you are usually more familiar.

Because of Ruburt's limited scientific vocabulary, this is somewhat difficult to explain. Also some of the theories I will present in this discussion will be quite unfamiliar to you.

Now these emanations arise as naturally as breath, and there are other comparisons that can be made, in that there is a coming in and a going out, and transformation within the unit, as what is taken into the lungs for, example is not the same thing that leaves the lung on the exhale stroke.

You could compare these units, simply for an analogy, to the invisible breath of consciousness. This analogy will not carry us far, but it will be enough initially to get the idea across. Breath is of course also a pulsation, and these units operate in a pulsating manner. They are emitted by the cells, for example, in plants, animals, rocks, and so forth.

They would have color if you were able to perceive them physically.

They are electromagnetic, in your terms, following their own patterns of positive and negative charge, and following also certain laws of magnetism. In this instance, like definitely attracts like. *(Pace animated and emphatic; yet with pauses.)*

The emanations are actually emotional tones. *(Pause.)* The variety of tones, for all intents and purposes, are infinite.

These units are just beneath the range of physical matter. None of them are identical. However, there is a structure to them. *(Pause.)* The structure is beyond the range of elecromagnetic qualities as your scientists think of them.

Consciousness automatically produces these emanations, and they are the basis for any kind of perception, both sensory in usual terms, and extrasensory.

I am beginning this material. Later you will see I am making it simple for you, but you will not understand it unless we begin in this manner. I do intend to explain their structure to you; now give us a moment.

These emanations can also appear as sounds, and you will be able to translate them into sounds long before your scientists discover their basic meaning. One of the reasons why they have not been discovered is precisely because they are so cleverly camouflaged within all structures.

Being just beyond the range of matter, having a structure, but a nonphysical structure, and being of a pulsating nature, they can expand or contract. They can completely envelop, for example, a small cell, or retreat to the nucleus within. They combine qualities of a unit and a field, in other words.

This is another reason why they remain a secret from Western scientists. Intensity governs their activity, and their size, since we must use that term. *(Pause.)* Give us a moment with this.

Intensity not only governs their activity and size, but the relative strength of their magnetic nature. They will draw other such units to them, for example, according to the intensity of the emotional tone of the particular consciousness at any given, quote, "point."

These units then obviously change constantly. If you must speak in terms of size, then they change in size constantly, as they contract and expand. Theoretically there is no limit, you see, to their rate of contraction or expansion. They are also absorbent. They do give off thermal qualities, and these are the only hint that your scientists have received of them so far.

Their characteristics draw them toward constant interchange. Clumps of them—*(Jane gestured; her delivery was quite emphatic and animated,)* will be drawn together, literally sealed, only to drop away and disperse once more.

Now. They form, their nature is behind, what is commonly known as air, and they use this to move through. The air in other words *(pause)* can be said to be formed by the animations of these units.

I will try to clear this later, but the air is the result of these units' existence, formed by the interrelationship of the units in their positions and relative distance one from the other, and in what you could call the relative velocity of their motion. Air is what happens when these units are in motion *(pause)*, and it is in terms of weather that their electromagnetic effects appear most clearly to scientists, for example.

These units—let us discuss them as they are related, for example, to a rock. The rock is composed of atoms and molecules each with their own consciousness. This forms a gestalt-rock-consciousness.

These units are sent out indiscriminately by the various atoms and molecules, but portions of them are also directed by the overall rock consciousness. The units are sent out then from the rock, informing the rock as to the nature of its changing environment, the angle of the sun, and temperature changes for example as night falls; and even in the case of a rock, they change as the rock's loosely called emotional tone changes. As the units change they alter the air about them, which is the result of their own activity.

They constantly emanate out from the rock and return to it, in a motion so swift it would seem simultaneous. The units meet with, and to some extent merge with, other units sent out, say, from foliage and all other objects. There is a constant blending, and also attraction and repulsion.

You may take your break and we will continue.

(10:10. Jane's delivery throughout was quite emphatic and animated, even though with many pauses. Her trance had been very good.

(Here is my dream of October 9, that I asked Seth interpret: "Color. I dreamed that I had a cancerous wart or nodule right at the tip of my right thumb, where it bothered me to hold a brush or pencil. Had been there a long time. I believe a doctor told me it was cancer—not very dangerous, could be removed in his office. I had to climb up a long ladder set against a building wall to get to the doctor and even as I talked to him I had to stand below him and look up. He was dominant, round-faced with thick glasses. Wore a white coat, I believe, and peered down at me like an owl."

("Then the thumb was clear. I examined it, and didn't need an operation."

(Resume at 10:25.)

Now, this session also will not be a long one. Ruburt has been using his energy in his book, and I do not begrudge it.

("What do you think of the book?" Jane sent the first 13 chapters of The Seth

Material *to the publisher Monday, October 13.)*

I did want to give you some more material this evening however along these lines... I am pleased with the book. It is a good beginning, and I will have more to say along these lines on another evening. Your dream is largely explained by Ruburt's interpretation.

(Shortly after I had the dream, Jane gave me her own interpretation of what the dream meant. I thought she did well, and agreed with her version since it appeared to be spontaneous. Since Seth's own interpretation agrees with Jane's—though more detailed—it isn't necessary to give Jane's version here, beyond saying the dream concerned my own artwork and related affairs.)

The fear was of an <u>over</u>reliance upon structure. This occurred to you one afternoon, three days before the dream, as you were working.

("Do you know which painting I was working on?")

I would appreciate it, dear friend, if you let me continue for now, though I understand why you want to know. This is not a rebuke. *(Smiling.)* I simply did not want to be interrupted. Give us a moment. *(Pause.)* I do not know the specific painting, although a round object was involved. It was I believe one of the pieces of fruit. The idea flitted through your mind and you did not grab hold of it, but it worried you.

I believe the feeling had to do with the fear there was an overreliance upon structure, in this case, that could impede the sense of motion; that a particular piece of fruit *(pause)*, seemed so perfect in structure that it somehow seemed to be frozen within it, and could not roll.

You ignored the feeling, and there may have been a slight physical symptom at the same time for this reason. This may have involved a plum—I believe it did, and this was somewhat connected in leading you to <u>thumb</u> in your dream.

There is an old nursery rhyme *(pause)*, that you heard as a child. I cannot get it clearly, something like Tom Tucker with his thumb, and the next line had to do with a plum. *(Pause.)* This was part of the association leading to the dream. As mentioned, Ruburt's interpretation was correct. The climbing up was also connected with fruit, as you might climb a tree to pluck it. *(Pause.)* There were no health connotations to the dream, it did not have that kind of meaning. You recognized your fear when you saw it in the dream as objectified on your thumb, and then you allowed it to disappear.

(I asked about which painting was involved because I wanted to be clear about the two most recent I've been working on. Seth verified that the little still life of fruit is the one concerned. The October 9 date would be, I believe, either the day I began this painting, or shortly after I started it. The data is very good, and is presented in

a way in which Jane does not consciously—at least—think. I was concerned about form in this painting, and this concern, linked up with composition, gave me quite a little tussle in this painting. Form and composition usually are easy for me.

(This time I had to work hard before resolving the problem after a couple of days. The painting is almost done now and appears to be successful. It is something of a new departure for me, and embodies a lot of the things I've learned doing my portraits for the past year or so. I hadn't said anything to Jane about my concern with this painting; in fact, everyone who saw it in progress, even at the beginning, seemed to like it, remarking especially upon the form and composition.

(Note that the dream came after I had resolved some of the above-mentioned problems. I was still somewhat uneasy about the decisions I had reached by October 9, but decided to go ahead anyhow, that I was belaboring what were probably rather innocuous points by that time.)

The doctor, the figure, represented your artistic intuitional creative self, your potential self in those terms, to whom you looked for advice and help. You had to climb up, symbolically, but the ladder you see was one-directional rather than crooked, and this shows that the road is clear.

Also, there was someone at the top of the ladder, indicating both the source and the potential of your abilities, also their uplifting tendencies. Had no one been there, you would have been in trouble. You were also making your own way up the ladder, this indicating your knowledge that your own efforts are involved.

You were alone, on your own ladder, indicating the unique quality of the achievements for which you are striving. That is, you are not imitating, and more than this, you will be making your own way into a niche that no one else has taken.

Had it been an elevator, this would have signaled quicker success, but there were no obstacles in the way either, and the rungs, regularly placed, showed a steady progression. You did not backtrack or make false starts.

The dream also shows that you are achieving good contact with your creative self, and that you were able to utilize the help available. Now do you have questions?

("Just briefly: What do you think of that little painting of the trees I did?" This is why, earlier, I asked Seth which painting the dream referred to; I was just finishing up this painting while beginning the fruit still life, on October 9.)

It is a fluid *(pause)*, mobile expression of the vitality that you sensed. It will have healing qualities. It absorbs, and yet gives. It shows spontaneity, in an easily-moving manner rather than in an explosive way.

(I got the idea for this little landscape while driving through the country in

Pennsylvania a few weeks ago, on one of the regular trips Jane, my mother, and I take to see my father.

(I asked because I wasn't sure what *I thought of it.)*

You will know at a later time. You could perhaps at some time paint a portrait of a man who would like to sit within that landscape. You have painted a mind or a spirit as it appears in landscape form. Give us a moment.

(Pause.) These are simply a few suggestions. You can paint landscapes as if they were portraits, and portraits as if they were landscapes. Just thinking of this idea and its implications can lead you to some unique ideas, and there is a possibility that you could hit upon something quite new.

I do not mean a big issue, but a very unique contribution. If a particular person's face was a landscape, what kind of a landscape would it be, for example? Even the planes of the face themselves can suggest mountains or valleys. But beyond this in deeper terms, how would that face be translated if it were not a face but a landscape? What time of day would it suggest? What kind (underlined) of landscape, desert or mountainous, and so forth?

Your treescape, for example: the other way around—what kind of face does it evoke? You see already to some extent that it evokes a portrait. Do you follow me?

("Yes."

(This above data is excellent on Seth's part, full of evocative ideas and intuitive good sense. I have at various times entertained related ideas, but never put them in as concrete form. Because of this I know I haven't discussed them with Jane, as such. The idea of thinking of a person's face as a landscape is very good. I am already thinking of ways to put the suggestions to work on a conscious basis.)

When you have personal questions, and they are quite legitimate, I will try to make a habit of dividing the session between theoretical material and your inquiries. That way continuity will still be maintained, and your personal matters answered to boot.

Now before you boot me, for tiring your hand, you may take a break or end the session as you prefer.

("Well, I'm afraid we'll have to end it then.")

My heartiest wishes to you both.

("It's been very interesting.")

Ruburt will do well on the rest of his book. I told him he was more relieved than he knew, and good evening.

("Good evening, Seth, and thank you."

(10:55. Jane's trance had been good, her pace good, eyes open often, etc. See the 503rd session for September 24 for Seth's comments re Jane's relief at Prentice-Hall's

approval, through Tam Mossman, of Jane's book on the Seth material. And Jane has been doing very well on the balance of the book.

(I thought the data on emotional tones very evocative. See page 418.)

SESSION 506
OCTOBER 27, 1969 9:40 PM MONDAY

(Sometime after 9 PM Jane and I sat to see if Seth would come through. I told Jane she needn't have a session, but she was willing enough if Seth decided to. She has been working long hours on her book for Prentice-Hall, The Seth Material, *and has but a couple of chapters to rewrite.*

(Jane has had two recent, excellent and long sessions for her ESP class however, featuring both Seth and Seth II, and including new material.)

Good evening.

("Good evening, Seth.")

Now. *(Pause, one of many.)* Ruburt need not worry that he has missed a few regular sessions. He has been exercising spontaneity, and paradoxically enough it is upon spontaneity that the regularity of our sessions depends. Do you follow me?

("Yes."

(Pause.) He is doing well with the book. Give us a moment.

The units *(electromagnetic)* about which I have been speaking do not have any specific, regular, preordained "life," in quotes. They will not seem to follow many scientific principles. Since they are the intuitive force just beyond the reach of matter, upon which matter is formed, they will not follow the laws of matter, although at times they will mimic the laws of matter.

It is almost impossible to detect an individual unit, for in its dance of activity it constantly becomes a part of other such units, expanding and contracting, pulsating and changing in intensity, in force, and changing polarity. This last is extremely important.

(Pause, one of many.) With Ruburt's limited vocabulary, this is rather difficult to explain, but it would be as if the positions of your north and south poles changed constantly while maintaining the same relative distance from each other, and by their change in polarity upsetting the stability *(pause)* of the planet—except that because of the greater comparative strength *(pause)* at the poles of the units *(gestures, attempts to draw diagrams in the air)*, a newer stability is almost immediately achieved after each shifting. Is that much clear?

("Yes.")

The shifting of polarity occurs in rhythm with changing emotional intensities, or emotional energies, if you prefer. *(Pause.)* You may use EE. *(Leaning forward, speaking humorously.)*

The "initial," in quotes, originating emotional energy that sets any given unit into motion, and forms it, then causes the unit to become a highly charged electromagnetic field, with those characteristics of changing polarities just mentioned.

The changing polarities are also caused by attraction and repulsion from other like units, which may be attached or detached. There is a rhythm that underlies all of this changing polarity and changing intensities that occur constantly. But the rhythms have to do with the nature of emotional energy itself, and not with the laws of physical matter.

Without an understanding of these rhythms the activity of the units would appear haphazard, chaotic, and there would seem to be nothing to hold the units together. Indeed, they seem to be flying apart at tremendous speeds. *(Gestures.)* The "nucleus," in quotes—now using a cell analogy—if these units were cells, which they are not, then it would be as if the nucleus were constantly changing position, flying off in all directions, dragging the rest of the cell along with it. Do you follow the analogy?

("Yes.")

The units obviously are within the reality of all cells. Now. *(Pause.)* The initiation point is the basic part of the unit, as the nucleus is the important part of the cell. The initiating point is the originating, unique, individual and specific emotional energy, or EE *(pause)*, that forms any given unit. It becomes the entryway into physical matter.

It is the initial three-sided enclosure, from which all matter must spring. The initial point forms the three sides about it; *(gestures; pause.)* There is an explosive nature as the emotional energy is born.

The three-sided effect, instantly formed, leads to an effect that is something like friction, but the effect causes *(gestures)* the three sides to change position, so that you end up with a triangular effect, closed, with the initial point inside the triangle. Now, you understand this is not a physical form.

("Yes."

(Pause.) The energy point, the EE point, from here on, constantly changes the form of the unit, but the procedure I have just mentioned must first occur. The unit may become circular, for example. Now these intensities of EE, forming the units, end up by transforming all available space into what they are. Certain intensities and certain positions of polarity between and among the units, and great groupings of the units, compress energy into solid form.

The emotional energy within the units is obviously the motivating factor, and you can see then why emotional energy can indeed shatter a physical object. You may take your break.

(10:10. Jane was out of trance quickly enough, although it had been a good one. At times her delivery had become quite fast. She said she could feel Seth pushing at her to get her to let the material through as clearly as possible, "without distorting it out of all recognition."

(Jane also had images while giving some of this material, usually where it is indicated she used gestures; but she found this very difficult to put into words.

(Usually, Jane said, she "forgets" as soon as the session is over, whether or not she had images while holding it; unless I ask specifically. Jane said that when she has images they seem so natural to her during the session that she doesn't think of mentioning them later—they are on the way out as soon as the session is over.

(Sometimes, she said, the same images will return to her when she rereads a particular session; she then recognizes them.

(Jane made it a point to mention that in regard to the switch in polarities of the ELM units: "This isn't only with north and south switching, but opposites anywhere on the rim of the circle I used as illustration—such as east and west reversed, etc."

(10:26.)

Now. The intensity of the original emotional energy controls the activity, the strength, the stability, and the relative size of the unit; the rate of its pulsation, and its power to attract and repel other units, and its ability to combine with other units. Now the behavior of these units changes in the following manner. *(Pause.)* When a unit is in the act of combining with another unit, it aligns its components in a characteristic way. When it is separating itself from other units it will align its components in a different way. The polarities change in each case within the unit itself.

It will alter it polarities within itself, adopting the polarity-design of the unit to which it is being attracted, and will change its polarity away from that design upon breaking contact.

Take for example five thousand such units, aligned together, formed together. They would still of course be invisible. But if you could view them each individual unit would have its poles lined up in the same manner. It would look like one single unit—say it is of circular form—so it would appear like a small globe, with the poles lined up as in your earth.

If this large unit were then attracted to another larger unit, circular, with the poles running east and west in your terms, then the first unit would change its own, and all of the units within it would do the same. *(Pause.)*

Now the energy point would be halfway between these poles regardless of their position, and it forms the poles . They revolve therefore about the energy point. *(Gesture.)* The energy point is indestructible basically.

Its intensity however can vary to amazing degrees, so that it could, relatively speaking, be too weak, or fall back *(pause),* not strong enough to form the basis for matter; but to project into another system perhaps where less intensity is required for "materialization," in quotes.

Now these units may also gain so in intensity and strength that they form relatively (underlined) permanent structures within your system, because of the astonishing energy behind them. Your Stockridge...

(Seth paused; Jane frowned, as though groping for a word.

("Oak Ridge?")

No. *(Gesture.)* The remains of temples...

("Oh. Baalbek?")

... These were places for studies concerning the stars.

("Observatories?")

Observatories.

("Yes?" I thought I probably knew the word Seth/Jane was looking for, but I didn't have time to think and write.)

The units so charged with intensive emotional energy, formed patterns for matter that retained their strength. Now these units, while appearing within your system, may also have another reality outside of it, propelling the emotional energy units through the world of matter entirely.

(Pause.) The energy units, as I told you, are relatively indestructible. They can however lose or gain power, fall back into intensities beneath matter, or go through matter, appearing as matter as they do so, and projecting through your system. We will deal with that portion of their activity separately. In such cases however they are in a point of transition obviously, and in a state of becoming. Now you may take a break or end the session as you prefer.

(The house lights flickered momentarily, but didn't go out.

("I guess we'll end it.")

I wanted to give you this material.

("It's very interesting.")

It is only a beginning. I would disregard the analogies if you did not need them. A fond good evening.

("Good evening, Seth."

(10:45. Jane recalled the house lights flickering briefly, saying that at that moment she was "on the way out" of trance.

(After we had talked a bit I deduced that Seth/Jane had been trying for the

word Stonehenge—meaning the ancient Druidic stone monoliths, arranged in a circle in England, etc. Jane then said this was the word Seth had been trying to get her to say. She didn't know why she couldn't say it while in trance, since she knows the word and what it stands for, etc.)

SESSION 507
NOVEMBER 10, 1969 9:07 PM MONDAY

(This session was held to obtains answers to two questions we had for Seth. Both pertained to Jane's book on the Seth material, which she is just finishing. One question had to do with the oil showing two male heads which I painted in 1965. The other concerned the envelope test held in the 300th session. Jane is dealing with both of these points in Chapter Eight of her book.

(Jane said she didn't feel much like having a session. It had been a hectic day for both of us. Since last night we had been discussing the illustrations for the book, and both of the above questions concerned illustrations.)

Good evening.

("Good evening, Seth.")

Now. Let us give you some information concerning the envelope test.

(The 76th, in the 300th session, on November 7, 1966.)

A portion is always connected to the whole of which it is part. From the torn section, then, to me the whole was present, the entire page; and from portions of the whole, the whole can be read or understood. And with enough freedom on the one hand, and training on the other, Ruburt, speaking for me, could give you the entire copy of *The New York Times* from a torn corner.

(This, then, was the question. The envelope object for the test in question was a piece torn from a hidden page of The New York Times. *The piece was small in relation to the page, which I did not see. [Hiding it in the studio while my eyes were closed, etc.] Yet when Seth, through Jane, gave the test results, much accurate data was given concerning the full page that lay in the back room, as well as the actual small envelope object in Jane's hand during the session. We wanted to know how such a thing was possible.)*

This does not involve projection. *(Which we had wondered about this afternoon.)* There were other issues, having to do with Ruburt's own mental characteristics. Now it is true that generally speaking, material of an emotional nature actually has a stronger vitality, and is easier to perceive. Beyond this however Ruburt has <u>no</u> *(smile)* love for detail, and will always use detail as a clue to see where it will lead him. He would not be content simply to give the details on the snatches of paper as you gave them. This is fairly automatic, this tendency, and the nature of his mental life. We use this, I hope to advantage, in our sessions in other ways, and I will have more to say concerning this.

In the tests however we also tried to utilize this characteristic. We tried to use it, since we could not deny it, nor did I go against it, since Ruburt's abilities are what I have to work with and through, beside of course my own. So we used this in that test to enlarge the picture, and bring in further details that did give you a rather complete picture, respectable data, in a way that was fairly natural to Ruburt.

No projection was needed.

The page was whole to me, regardless of the portion of it used as an item. Ruburt did fairly poorly on those test items that were without meaning, comparatively speaking, as far as your results were concerned. He did however leap out from the meaningless data for quite valid information connected to it, though often you could not check this out.

(Pause, one of many short ones, etc.) Now I was teaching him, and I went along with his natural interests and inclinations. The antagonism he had for testing came not from the idea itself so much as from the idea of focusing upon detail for detail's sake.

Only at such times, during that kind of a test, did he become antagonistic. Do you have questions on this material?

("No. that seems to cover it very well.")

(There were questions, but it seemed the above data would give Jane what information she needed for her book, etc.

(Smile.) You might tell him that although he does not know it, he has a fine subconscious understanding of detail, which he then puts together and synthesizes. *(Pause.)* If he understands the creative uses of detail, then he will not be so consciously antagonistic to it. Now. Have you any questions on this?

("No.")

Give us a moment. *(Pause at 9:29.)*

The portrait is of Joseph and Ruburt. These are not portraits of yourselves as past personalities in your terms, or of particular reincarnational selves. They are pictorial representatives of the whole selves that you are. In your terms the selves that are the sum of your reincarnational personalities. These whole selves then are a part of your entity. Your probable selves are also a part of your entity, however. If you want to think in terms of guides, in quotes "angels," then you have the reality behind those terms. Ruburt and Joseph are the names I use for you, for these names themselves imply your greater goals. These personalities are aware of your present existence, and give you advice when you are in the sleep state. They are a source of strength. You can draw upon their knowledge, and you can also draw upon the knowledge of your own reincarnational selves, "past," in quotes, and "future."

("Yes.")

As that newspaper portion was a whole of the entire paper, and there to be read, so is the whole self present in the portions of your personality that you know. Does this give you the information that you requested?

("Yes. One question: as I look at the painting, which of the two heads represents my whole self, for instance?"

Now. Ruburt is the blond one. *(Both are male.*

("Are you going to say something for the appendix for the book?"

(By this I meant to ask Seth if he planned to dictate a chapter, or at least a few pages, for Jane's book on the material. Jane and I have talked about this before. But it can be seen that Seth doesn't directly answer the question.)

There will be more material on the *(ELM)* units of which we have been speaking. *(Jane may use this material in the appendix.)* I wanted to tell <u>you</u> that when Ruburt sends off his book we will try to give you more information on the art gallery material.

("No hurry.")

Now we will have a break. I suggest that at a later time Ruburt study the entire test series again, for there are lessons to be learned there that have still escaped you.

(9:42. Jane's trance had been good. It is true that we can still learn from the envelope test series, which covered a year. In reviewing test results on two items for Jane's chapter on tests in her new book, we are pleasantly surprised to unearth several more excellent bits of information that we had overlooked earlier, etc...

(We found Seth's data tonight on Jane's reaction to tests very interesting. I talked about cases we had read about, where hypnosis was used to get the subject to focus only upon the test item, ignoring any other data even if relevant. The discussion veered around to our wondering how Jane would do under such conditions, when Seth abruptly resumed at 9:50.)

That course would not give the results you might think with Ruburt, or anyone else. When that course works it is because knowingly or unknowingly the suggestions given follow the natural inclinations. In extrasensory perceptions, so to speak, as in so-called normal perception, the natural inclinations of the personality dictate the kind of information that will be sought from any available field of data. The basic <u>inclinations</u> can be extended, for example, but not completely redirected, <u>unless there is an extraordinary impetus.</u> *(Long pause.)*

There are many areas of knowledge in which any given individual is uninterested. He will not bother to use normal perception to obtain it. Much of the material dealing with perception that I have given makes this point quite clear. *(Pause.)* Ruburt is correct. I give him access to large fields of focus, I help him change the energy that he uses in perception into <u>other</u> directions, to turn it inward. I made information available to him. Then according to his basic characteristics, he used that information accordingly. I gave him nudges to lead him in the proper direction. Do you have questions?

(I put the question poorly: "Would hypnosis reach that level of your perception?"

(Pause.) Are you asking whether or not I would be reached if Ruburt were hypnotized?

("Not exactly. I was wondering whether the hypnosis would influence the way Ruburt let the information come out.")

I would not suggest that it be used.

("No. I wouldn't want to use it either."

(A long time ago, Jane and I discussed this method of obtaining trance data, and decided not to use it for various reasons. We now are sure it was a good decision.)

I believe that the answer is implied in an earlier statement I made this evening.

("Yes." [Pause.] "I see.")

You may end the session or take a break, as you prefer.

("We'll take the break and see what happens."

(10:01. Jane's trance had been good but she came out quickly. She didn't remember the data.

(At 10:17 Jane sat to see if the session would resume. It did not. While waiting she told me she felt "real light, as if I could float up some place."

(Jane said she didn't really want to speak for Seth's entity tonight, if that's what she was trying to do, so I suggested she break it off. Jane said "things were significant in the room," a phrase she has used before when preparing to speak for Seth's entity, or Seth II as we sometimes call "him.")

SESSION 508
NOVEMBER 20, 1969 9 PM THURSDAY

(The session is incomplete as far as notes go. It was held primarily so that Rich Conz, of The Elmira Star-Gazette, *could photograph Jane in trance. We wanted the photos for Jane's book on the Seth material, which is now practically finished. Rich*

also brought with him contact proofs of photos he took of Jane and me yesterday afternoon.

(The session was also witnessed by Diane Sorino, a friend of Rich's. Jane and I sat for the session by 8:45, to see if one would be held, etc. Rich had not seen a session before, although he was somewhat cognizant of what would take place.

(Rich took forty shots, most of which turned out well, as we saw later. Some of them are excellent. Most of them are of Jane in trance, from a variety of angles; I appear in a few to show our procedure in note-taking, etc. We are highly pleased with them.

(The session began ordinarily enough, but before long an interaction between Rich and Seth began to show. Seth's pace also speeded up considerably, and I began to fall behind. But more than this, words cannot really record the very humorous exchange that developed between Rich and Seth. I saw Jane, as Seth, laugh herself far more than ever before in trance. Seth did most of the talking as usual; and more and more his attention became riveted upon Rich as the latter buzzed around, taking photo after photo, with flash. The interaction between the two finally became so funny and fast paced that I laid the notes aside and surrendered to laughter.

(Rich was half embarrassed and half serious; at the height of the exchange between the two, Seth's addresses to Rich were so fast I couldn't hope to record them. After pictures were over, Seth also returned several times to answer some of Rich's questions. The session itself, between parries at Rich, Seth addressed to Rich and to Diane, answering questions they had asked before its beginning.

(Rich asked some good questions. Seth told us that he had been a Catholic in two past lives. In another past life, Seth said he had been a member of a religion that no longer existed in our terms; that he would tell Jane and me about it some time, and that we would find it very interesting.

(The notes that follow are verbatim, or nearly so unless otherwise indicated. They are given because there are several points in them of interest to Jane. Rich began taking pictures about five minutes after the session began.)

Good evening.

("Good evening, Seth.")

Now. If it makes Ruburt nervous to have his picture taken, it does not bother me, and I welcome you *(Rich and Diane)* to our session. I have a few remarks to make to our friend Ruburt in opening the session. It seems to me that by now he could learn to trust his impulses. He did not feel that he wanted to lecture or to be connected with the group as yet, and indeed the time has not yet come. He will be involved with that organization. Tell him that I told him not to intellectualize in such instances, but to follow his original impulses.

(This passage grows out of a very recent call from Betty Taylor, of the Spiritual

Frontiers Fellowship group, to Jane, concerning a weekend visit to Pawling, New York in early December, and a possible lecture tour of the Northeast. Betty offered to book Jane on this tour, etc.)

Now. Give us a moment. I want to clear up some points regarding your portrait of the old woman, that you are using in the book. It is a past life portrait, though the clothing is interpretive on your part. This was an existence in which you were the mother of five, as I have told you. The existence however was some time ago, BC, hence you see the clothing itself does not apply. Now this was a Near East life. There are also other portraits that you will do involving your family at that time. Give us a moment, for some other data...

Now. You lived to an old age, and this was fairly unusual. One of your children was a leader of a tribe. One became an important member of a Mongoloid tribe. You have had several dreams involving in this particular episode. If you give yourself the proper suggestions, you can remember some details from that existence; and also suggest dream information.

(I have no dream recall of the above life. My dream recall has been very poor recently, etc.)

Now. I am pleased with the book, and I told Ruburt's class *(last week)* that I will shortly begin to write my own. *(Smile.)*

("Good.")

Now. When I begin my book—

(Seth now broke off and began speaking to Rich as he moved around Jane. Now Seth was just beginning to pay some attention to the activity about him. Humorously, Jane wagged a finger at Rich.)

—You can take pictures of me for my book cover—and I will put in a word for you... Just do not tell me to look at the birdie.

You can tell, Joseph, our Aerofranz *(Tam Mossman)* that if he needs an outline, I will see that he gets a unique outline.

("He'll probably want one.")

This will in no way hamper Ruburt's own book.

(Jane and Tam have been discussing her second book for P/Hall; the subject possibly to be on dreams, Seth, and astral projection.

("You'll have both of the books going at once?")

We can do both of them together. *(Humorously:)* He *(Jane)* need not type my own book up unless he learns to spell better, however. Tell him to give himself proper suggestions concerning my project. He has put me off on it to some extent.

("I thought so.")

I would like the book, mine, to run approximately the same length as the one which he has just finished. There will be 20 chapters, and I will write the headings for them. I will also see that all the proper information is given in time, and I will try to see to it that Ruburt has the experiences that he should have in order to write his own next book.

("He'll certainly be pleased to hear that.")

I certainly hope that he will be. Tell him that he is as stubborn out of his body as he is when he is in it.

Now. I will take a break, and let our suffering photographer rest his weary hands.

(9:15. Jane left trance quickly, although it had been a good one, she said. She did not remember being bothered by the picture-taking, or the flashgun, etc.; in trance she gave no sign, for instance, that the flashgun interfered in any way, etc.

(During break both Rich and Diane asked questions that Seth undertook to answer to some extent. However the pace soon became too fast for my notes; because of this and the funny goings-on between Rich and Seth, I soon gave up note-taking. The session itself lasted perhaps until 10:15. But with Seth returning several times to speak to Rich and Diane, it was close to midnight before the affair was wound up.

(There follow a few excerpts from Seth's comments after the session resumed at 9:27.)

Now. Ruburt is a teacher in this level of reality, as I am a teacher in another level of reality... *(To Diane:)* so if you come to his classes there will be more than pretty tales of reincarnation for you, for you must learn to work and develop your own abilities.

Human personality entails more than three dimensions. There are abilities that you do not use, so you must learn what they are. This is a portion of your personality that speaks to you in your dreams. This is the inner part of you...

... You have a whole self, a multidimensional self of which your present personality is a small part. It is your responsibility to expand your awareness, to utilize these abilities...

This is not the hope of the individual.... But it represents the hope of the race at this time—that you need to use these abilities...

Then you can reach out, you can feel the reality of other personalities. Then you can communicate with them... You cannot communicate with your fellows unless you know who and what you are, and unless you can make a bridge from yourself to others.

—Now there are no limitations to the self. There is no top nor bottom to the self... I will say at least that you are limited as a self only by what you perceive. Even physically you are more than you know, for the chemicals that are your body, and the atoms and molecules and the breath that leaves your lungs... becomes part of your atmosphere in this room...

... But your thoughts also have a reality that you do not know. They have a reality that you do not perceive. Now I am going to give you a quickie course. The atoms and the molecules in this chair, you see, and in our friend's camera, all have a consciousness...

(Much missed in here.) ... Now if you come to class you must begin to think deeply about such matters ... You must travel through your own consciousness, for then you will find you are making your own journey through a different space. You must navigate...

(To Rich, after a break at 9:36-9:45:) Better rich than poor... Now. You think this kind of affair strange, because you do not realize that you yourselves exist independently of your physical bodies... *(etc.)*

SESSION 509
NOVEMBER 24, 1969 9:10 PM MONDAY

(Today Jane had been reading Experimental Psychology, *by C.G. Jung, first American edition, published by Jung's heirs in 1968, etc.)*

Good evening.

("Good evening, Seth.")

Now. There is one large point, underestimated by all of your psychologists, when they list the characteristics or attributes of consciousness. I am going to tie in this material with our discussion on what you call our EE units *(electromagnetic)*, as there is a very close connection.

Now let us start with Jung for a bit. He presumes that consciousness must be organized about an ego structure. And what he calls the unconscious, not so egotistically organized, he therefore considers without consciousness, without consciousness of a self.

He makes a good point, saying that the ego cannot know unconscious material directly. He does not realize however, nor do your other psychologists, what I have told you often—that there is an inner ego; and it is this inner ego that organizes what Jung would call unconscious material.

Again, when you are in a state that is not the normal waking one, when you have forsaken this daily self, you are nevertheless conscious and alert. You merely block out the memory from the normal waking ego. So when the attributes of consciousness are given, creativity is largely ignored. It is assigned instead primarily to the unconscious. My point is that the unconscious is conscious.

Creativity is one of the most important attributes and aspects of consciousness. We will differentiate between normal ego consciousness then, and consciousness that only appears unconscious to that ego.

Now the inner ego is the organizer of experience that Jung would call unconscious. The inner ego is another term for what we call the inner self. As the outer ego manipulates within the environment and physical reality, so the inner ego or self organizes and manipulates within an inner reality. The inner ego creates that physical reality with which the outer ego then deals.

Now all the richly creative, original work that is done by this inner self is not unconscious. It is purposeful, highly (underlined) discriminating, performed by the inner conscious ego, of which the exterior ego is but a shadow, and not you see the other way around.

Jung's dark side of the self is the ego, not the unconscious. The complicated, infinitely varied, unbelievably rich tapestry of Jung's, in quotes "unconscious," could hardly be unconscious. It is the product of an inner consciousness with far more sense of identity and purpose than the daily ego. It is the daily ego's ignorance and limited focus that makes it view so-called unconscious activity as chaotic.

The conscious ego rises indeed out of quote "the unconscious," but the unconscious being the creator of the ego, is necessarily far more conscious than its offspring. The ego is simply not conscious enough to be able to contain the vast knowledge that belongs to the inner conscious self from which it springs.

It is this inner self, out of the massive knowledge and unlimited scope of its consciousness, that forms the physical world, that provides stimuli to keep the ego constantly at the job of awareness. It is the inner self, termed here the inner ego, that organizes, initiates, projects, controls the EE units of which we have been speaking lately, transforming energy into objects, into matter.

The energy of this inner self is directed and used by it to richly form from itself, from components and inner experience, a material counterpart in which the outer ego then can act out its role. The outer ego is most in the role, acting out a play that the inner self has written.

This is not to say that the outer ego is a puppet. It is to say that the outer ego is far less conscious than the inner ego or the inner self, that its perception is less, that it is far less stable, though it makes great pretense at stability; that it springs from the inner self, and is less rather than more, aware. *(Pause.)*

Now. The ego is spoon-fed, being given only those feelings and emotions, only that data, that it can handle. This data is then presented to it in a highly specialized manner, usually in terms of information picked up by the physical senses. The inner self is obviously not only conscious, but conscious of itself, both as an individuality apart from others, and as an individuality that is a part of all other consciousness.

In your terms it is continually aware, both of this apartness and unity-with. The outer ego is not continuously, in your terms, aware of anything. It frequently forgets itself. When it becomes swept up in a strong emotion it seems to lose itself. There is unity then but no sense of apartness. When it most vigorously maintains its sense of individuality it is no longer aware of unity-with.

The inner ego however is always aware of both aspects of its reality. In the deepest sense *(pause)*, this inner self is organized about its primary aspect, which is creativity. It constantly translates the components of its gestalt into reality, either physical reality through the EE units I have mentioned, or into other realities equally as valid.

Now you may take your break and we shall continue.

(9:47.) One small point, not in the discussion:

At this party affair, mentioned before session, there are two men who will give you fine ideas for portraits. They will be together, I believe, and you should add them to your people series; for one you have known before, and the other influenced your life at one time, though you did not know him personally. In their faces you should see aspects of their past personalities.

Write down here D A R... That is all that came spontaneously to connect them. I do have the reincarnational backgrounds, but would prefer to continue with our present discussion.

(9:50. Jane's trance had been good, she said, but she was out of it quickly at break.

(At about 8:50 PM Jane received a phone call from Tom Hartley, a newspaper friend of ours, inviting us to a party next Saturday, November 29. In view of Seth's data above, it will be interesting to see what develops. We didn't expect any such data, nor had we asked Seth to comment on Tom's call.

(As soon as she received the invitation from Tom, Jane now reminded me, she accepted it without consulting with me, even though I sat almost beside her as she spoke on the phone. This in itself is very unusual, since neither of us as a rule would commit the other without first asking. I thought it odd at the time; but since we usually go out on Saturday evening anyhow, the thought of dropping in at the projected party did not unduly disturb.

(Jane now told me that just before Seth mentioned the phone call in the session, she had an image of a man in the distance, in a kind of milky fog or atmosphere. She was aware only of the shape of the head, as it began to move closer toward her. She felt, but did not see, the other male companion, yet knew the two were together, as mentioned by Seth.

(Jane said my asking questions helped her a good deal in recalling details, whereas she thought she had no memory of any detail. Her impression was of a face with "no hair at the sides, or perhaps bald." Yet not necessarily bald, she said, not necessarily old. No glasses. Face seemed to be quite small and round rather than square or rectangular. "Sort of a naked kind of a face." Ears must have been close to the head. "I didn't see the features, except that nothing stuck out."

(Jane could offer nothing about the second male. I do not know whether I have met the two men mentioned by Seth or not; I am inclined to think I haven't. On the other hand Tom Hartley told Jane the party was primarily for newspaper people, and I have met some of this local group... I didn't press Seth with questions since it seemed he preferred to continue with the Jung reply.

(In reference to this, I asked a question at break: Since Jung was "dead," how had his published ideas now changed, etc.

(10:05.)

Now. The EE units are the forms basic experience takes when directed by this inner self.

These then form physical objects, physical matter. Matter is the shape that basic experience takes when it intrudes into three dimensional systems. Matter is the shape of your dreams. Your dreams, emotions, feelings, thoughts, are (underlined) transformed into physical matter purposefully by this inner self.

An individual inner self, then, through constant massive effort of great creative intensity, cooperates with all other inner selves to form and maintain the physical reality that you know, so that physical reality is an offshoot or by-product of *(pause)*, the highly conscious creative inner self.

(Long pause.)

Buildings appear to be made of rock or wood or steel. They appear fairly permanent to the physical senses. They are actually oscillating, ever-moving, highly charged gestalts of EE units *(pause)*, organized and maintained by collective efforts on the part of inner selves. They are solidified emotions, solidified subjective states, given physical materialization.

The powers of consciousness are clearly not understood then, nor its multidimensional aspects. As I have told you, the self is literally unlimited. Each individual has his part to play in projecting these EE units into physical actuality. Therefore physical matter can be legitimately described as an extension of the self, as much as the physical body is a projection of the inner self.

Now it is obvious that the body grows up about the inner self, and that trees grow out of the ground, whereas buildings do not ordinarily spring up like flowers of their own accord; so the inner self has various methods of creation, and uses the EE units in different ways, as you shall see as we continue with this discussion.

Having determined upon physical reality as a dimension in which it will project itself, the inner self therefore first of all takes care to form and maintain the physical basis upon which all else must depend—those physical properties of earth that can be called natural ones.

We have to a very brief extent begun to explain that phenomena in a recent session. The inner self has a vast and infinite reservoir from which to draw knowledge and gain experience. *(Pause.)* All kinds of choices are available, and the diversity of physical matter is a reflection of this deep source of variety.

With the natural structures formed and maintained, other physical secondary properties, secondary constructions, are projected. The deepest, most basic and abiding subjective experience is translated however into those natural elements; the ample landscape that sustains physical life.

Now we will continue with this discussion at our next session. Jung enlarged on some of his concepts shortly before he died. *(Leaning forward, humorously emphatic:)* He has changed a good many of them since then. Now you may take a break or end the session as you prefer.

("We'll take the break."

(10:30. Jane's trance was deep. She said she thought the delivery had lasted perhaps ten minutes, instead of the 25 it had actually taken. Resume at 10:43.)

We will shortly end the session.

Suffice it to say however that in the future what I am telling you will be more generally known. Men will become familiar to some extent with their own inner identity, with other forms of their own consciousness. *(Pause.)*

Throughout the ages some have recognized the fact that there is self-consciousness and purpose in certain dream and sleep states, and have maintained, even in waking life, the sense of continuity of this inner self. To such people it is no longer possible to identify completely with the ego consciousness. They are too obviously aware of themselves as more. When such knowledge is gained, the ego can accept it, for it finds to its surprise that it is not less conscious, but more conscious, that its limitations are dissipated; now it is not true, and I emphasize this strongly, that so-called unconscious material, given any freedom, will draw energy away from the egotistically organized self in a normal personality.

Quite the contrary, the ego is replenished, and rather directly. *(Pause.)* It is the fear that the unconscious, so-called, is chaotic, that causes psychologists to make such statements, and there *(pause)* is also something in the nature of those who practice psychology, a fascination, in many cases, already predisposed to fear the so-called unconscious in direct proportion to its attraction for them.

(Pause.) The ego maintains its stability, its seeming stability, and its health,

from the constant subconscious and unconscious nourishment that it receives. Too much nourishment will not kill it. *(Emphatic.)* Do you follow me here?

("Yes.")

Only when such nourishment is for some reason cut off to a considerable degree, is the ego threatened by starvation... We will have more to say concerning the ego's relationship with the so-called unconscious. In a healthy personality the inner self easily projects all experience into EE units, where they are translated into actuality. Physical matter therefore acts as a feedback. Now we will end our session unless you have questions.

("I guess not. It's been very interesting.")

My heartiest regards, and a fond good evening to you both.

("Did you like your pictures?" The photos taken by Rich Conz.)

I did indeed, and the young man who took them.

(10:56.)

SESSION 510
JANUARY 19 1970 9 PM MONDAY

(This is the first regular session held since November 24, 1969, although Seth has spoken in ESP class occasionally since then.

(Within the last two weeks Jane delivered the final version of her book, The Seth Material, *to Prentice-Hall. They have asked her to do a book on Seth, dreams, and reincarnation.*

(Here are some corroborative notes re pages 436-37 of the last session, dealing with our invitation to a party given by Tom Hartley on Saturday, November 29. Seth's predictions, and Jane's own data, given at break, were borne out very well. Seth talked about two men connected with me in the past in various ways; I would meet these men at the party. I did meet two such men, and they were together, also as Seth predicted. They are Don Simmons and Pete Tomoski, high school classmates of mine from Sayre, PA; I had not seen them for 33 years [1937]. They are friends, it developed, of Tom Hartley, a fact totally unknown and unexpected by me.

(Both men approached me at the party, at separate times, and introduced themselves; both recognized and called me by name; I did not recognize either of them. Seth could develop this material, since I do not know how one of these men "influenced my life at one time," etc. Nor was I able to make any connection with the initials or letters given, D A R..

(Pete and Don drove to Elmira from Sayre in one car; "together", as mentioned by Seth.

(Jane's own data, given at break, was also very good. See the description of her inner images during session. Don Simmons fit very well her description of a round, rather small face, with ears close to the head, no glasses, a naked kind of face. At the party however, I do not recall Jane leaping with recognition when she met Don Simmons...

(Bill Gallagher, who was at the party also, wondered if Pete Tomoski. a barber by trade, wore a toupee. This was highly interesting for Jane's data speculated about the inner image with "no hair at the sides, or perhaps bald." Yet not necessarily bald, Jane added, to me at the time. Checking with Tom Hartley's wife after the party, Jane learned for sure that Pete Tomoski does wear a toupee, being self-conscious of his baldness because he is a barber...

(Note: Jane's own data mentioned an image of but one person, while she felt that two were involved, or "there." She gave a physical description of her inner image, which Don Simmons fit well. However, the hair portion of the data applies to Don's friend Pete; whom, presumably, "Jane could offer nothing about."

(Jane began speaking for Seth in an average voice, with pauses, with her eyes open and very dark much of the time; many and varied gestures, etc.)

Now *(smile)*—Welcome after your long vacation.

("Good evening, Seth.")

Now I have several preliminary remarks to make, before the main part of our session.

When there is close rapport between the two of you, then this helps on both of your parts in several important ways. You both automatically then add to the health and well-being of the other. There is more energy generated, positive energy, than the two of you separately could generate. Do you follow me here?

("Yes.")

Your food is more nourishing. *(Pause.)* When Ruburt thinks of you in a loving manner as he prepares food, certain alterations are affected in the food so that it is actually brought to a greater states of relative perfection. Your own bodies also then use it more effectively.

Now if there are arguments at the table this real benefit is lessened. You should not become upset about the news, particularly during a meal. This will affect your digestion, but more importantly it will cut down on the nourishment that you receive.

When the two of you are in rapport, you do more good for each other than you do, say, during prayer periods when less rapport exists in the entire situation. The prayer periods or their equivalent become much more effective when you are in good rapport otherwise.

(To me.) Your gumboil had already begun in incipient form before you visited your mother *(yesterday, Sunday, January 18)*, but is specifically caused by the meal there. The meal brought it out, so to speak. Suggestion will remove it. Three glasses of milk, whole, not skimmed milk, will also help, taken within one day. This has a healing effect on particular tissues, and a soothing effect on the acids that are connected.

Now. I have been helping Ruburt. The energy that I would put into sessions has gone into some private talks to him while he slept. These have resulted in necessary insights on his part that will themselves cause the release of energy from the inner self.

(For the last several days Jane has been telling me about a string of insights and realizations she has been experiencing, both asleep and awake. She feels these are very beneficial and has begun putting them to immediate use. She feels she has lately realized a group of truths that she hadn't understood before, etc.)

I am working on some other material just now that you will be given *(pause)*, and so you must bear with me for a few moments. *(Pause.)*

For example, I would like to give you some idea of the contents of my own book. Many issues will be involved. The book will include a description of the way in which it is being written; the procedures necessary so that my own ideas can be spoken by Ruburt, or for that matter translated at all, in vocal terms. *(Long pause.)*

I do not have a physical body, and yet I will be writing a book. The first chapter will explain how and why.

(By now Jane's pace had slowed considerably, and her eyes were often closed. She took many pauses, some of them long.)

The next chapter will describe what you may call my present environment; my present in quote "characteristics," my associates—and you may tell your Aerofranz *(Tam Mossman)* that I smiled as I used the word. By it I mean those others with whom I come in contact.

The next chapter will describe my work, and those dimensions of reality into which it takes me, for as I travel into your reality I also travel into others, to fulfill that purpose which is mine to fill.

The next chapter will deal with my past in your terms, and some of those personalities that I have been and have known. At the same time I will make it clear that there is no past, present or future, and explain that there is no contradiction even though I may speak in terms of past existences. This may possibly run two chapters.

The next chapter will give the story of our meeting, you *(to me)*, Ruburt and I, from my viewpoint of course, and the ways in which I contacted Ruburt's inner awareness long before either of you knew anything about psychic phenomena, or my existence.

(Pause.) The next chapter will deal with the experience of any personality at the point of death, and with the many variations on this basic experience. I will use some of my own deaths as examples.

The next chapter will deal with existence after death, with its many variations. Both of these chapters will bear on reincarnation as it applies to death, and some emphasis will also be given to death <u>at the end of</u> the last reincarnation.

The next chapter will deal with the emotional realities of love, and kinship between personalities; what happens to these during succeeding reincarnations *(pause),* for some fall by the wayside and some are retained.

The next chapter will deal with your physical reality as it appears to me and others like me. This chapter will contain some rather fascinating points, for not only do you form the physical reality that you know, you are also forming other quite valid environments in other realities by your present thoughts, desires and emotions.

The next chapter will deal with the eternal validity of dreams as gateways into these other realities, and as open areas through which the inner self glimpses the many facets of its experience, and communicates with other levels of its reality.

The next chapter will deal further with this subject, as I relate the various ways that I have entered the dreams of others, both as an instructor and as a guide.

The next chapter will deal with the basic methods of communication that are used by any consciousness, according to its degree, whether or not it is physical. This will lead up to the basic communication used by human personalities as you understand them, and point out these inner communications as existing independently of the physical senses *(pause),* which are merely physical extensions of inner perception.

I will tell the reader how he sees what he sees, or hears what he hears, and why. I hope to show through the entire book that the reader himself is independent of his physical image; and I hope, myself, to give him some methods that will prove my thesis to him.

The next chapter will relate what experience I have had in all my existences, with those pyramid gestalts of which I speak in the material, and with my own and about my own relationship with the personality you call Seth Two, and with multidimensional consciousnesses far more evolved than I.

My message to the reader will be: "basically, you are no more of a physical personality than I am, and in telling you of my reality I tell you of your own."

Now you may take a break.

(9:50. Jane left trance easily, although it had been a good one. She said she knew from the beginning of the session that Seth was "putting me out deeper." She knew Seth was talking about his own projected book, and avoided blocking, etc. She hadn't been using suggestion in an effort to get this material tonight.

(As we talked Jane recalled that yesterday she "had a small glimmer" that she might be ready for Seth's material on his own book; Jane linked this information up with the recent insights she has been attaining.

(10:05.)

Now. There will be a chapter on the religions of the world, on the distortions and truths within them; the <u>three</u> Christs; and some data concerning a lost religion *(pause; one of many)*, belonging to a people of which you have no information. These people lived on a planet in the same space that your planet now occupies, in quotes "before" your planet existed. They destroyed it through their own error, and here reincarnated when your planet was prepared. Their memories *(long pause)*, became the basis for the birth of religion as you now think of it. *(Long pause at 10:15.)*

There will be a chapter on probable gods, and probable systems.

There will be a question-and-answer chapter.

There will be a final chapter in which I will ask the reader to close his eyes and become aware of the reality in which I exist, and of his own inner reality. I will give the methods. In this chapter I will invite the reader to use his inner senses, to see me in his own way. *(Long pause.)*

While my communications will come exclusively through Ruburt at all times, to protect the integrity of the material, I will invite the reader to become aware of me as a personality, so that he may then realize that communication from other realities is possible, and that he himself is therefore open to perception that is not physical.

Now this is my outline for the book, and contains merely a sketch of my intentions. I am not giving a fuller outline, for I do not want Ruburt to anticipate me. The difficulties involved in such communications will be given thoroughly. It will be made clear that so-called paranormal communications come from various levels of reality, and that those communications describe the reality in which they exist. So I will describe mine, and others of which I have knowledge.

This is not to say that other dimensions do not exist of which I am ignorant. I will dictate the book during our sessions. *(Long pause.)* You may take a break and I will briefly continue.

(10:29. Again Jane's trance had been good. Her last pause had been quite long; when I mentioned this Jane said she thought that Seth had been trying to get the title of his book through; at the same time Jane had been In the process of coming out of trance. Again her pace had been slow, her eyes often closed.

(Resume at a faster rate at 10:32.)

Now. I will not keep you.

This is the title for our book *(Smile:) Seth Speaks:* (colon) *the Eternal Validity of the Soul.* I am using the term soul, for it will have instant meaning to most readers. *(Long pause.)* I suggest you equip yourself with some good pens. Ask our friend Ruburt to kindly mail my outline, on my behalf, to our friend Aerofranz. *(Smile.)*

I wish you a hearty good evening. My best wishes to you both. I am pleased with our new venture. Now tell Ruburt that this book will in no way interfere with his own writing, neither with the Seth dream book, his novel, nor the poetry which he shall shortly begin again. Good evening.

("Good evening, Seth.")

Do you have questions?

("No. You've been doing very well."

(10:37. After the trance was over Jane said she hadn't been trying to think of titles for Seth's own book, etc., nor had she been speculating about its contents.)

Books by Jane Roberts from Amber-Allen Publishing

Seth Speaks: The Eternal Validity of the Soul. This essential guide to conscious living clearly and powerfully articulates the furthest reaches of human potential, and the concept that each of us creates our own reality.

The Nature of Personal Reality: Specific, Practical Techniques for Solving Everyday Problems and Enriching the Life You Know.. In this perennial bestseller, Seth challenges our assumptions about the nature of reality and stresses the individual's capacity for conscious action.

The Individual and the Nature of Mass Events. Seth explores the connection between personal beliefs and world events, how our realities merge and combine "to form mass reactions such as the overthrow of governments, the birth of a new religion, wars, epidemics, earthquakes, and new periods of art, architecture, and technology."

The Magical Approach: Seth Speaks About the Art of Creative Living. Seth reveals the true, magical nature of our deepest levels of being, and explains how to live our lives spontaneously, creatively, and according to our own natural rhythms.

The Oversoul Seven Trilogy (The Education of Oversoul Seven, The Further Education of Oversoul Seven, Oversoul Seven and the Museum of Time). Inspired by Jane's own experiences with the Seth Material, the adventures of Oversoul Seven are an intriguing fantasy, a mind-altering exploration of our inner being, and a vibrant celebration of life.

The Nature of the Psyche. Seth reveals a startling new concept of self, answering questions about the inner reality that exists apart from time, the origins and powers of dreams, human sexuality, and how we choose our physical death.

The "Unknown" Reality, Volumes One and Two. Seth reveals the multidimensional nature of the human soul, the dazzling labyrinths of unseen probabilities involved in any decision, and how probable realities combine to create the waking life we know.

Dreams, "Evolution," and Value Fulfillment, Volumes One and Two. Seth discusses the material world as an ongoing self-creation—the product of a conscious, self-aware and thoroughly animate universe, where virtually every possibility not only exists, but is constantly encouraged to achieve its highest potential.

The Way Toward Health. Woven through the poignant story of Jane Roberts' final days are Seth's teachings about self-healing and the mind's effect upon physical health.

Available in bookstores everywhere.